Linear Network Optimization

Linear Network Optimization: Algorithms and Codes

DIMITRI P. BERTSEKAS

The MIT Press
Cambridge, Massachusetts
London, England

This book was printed and bound in the United States of America.

Library of Congress Cataloging-in-Publication Data

Bertsekas, Dimitri P.
    Linear network optimization : algorithms and codes / Dimitri P. Bertsekas.
        p.   cm.
    Includes bibliographical references and index.
    ISBN 0-262-02334-2
    1. Network analysis (Planning). 2. Mathematical optimization. 3. Algorithms. I. Title.
    T57.85.B43   1991
    658.4'032–dc20

91-27588
CIP

To my brother Pamikos

Contents

Preface

Linear network optimization problems, such as shortest path, assignment, max-flow, transportation, and transhipment, are undoubtedly the most common optimization problems in practice. Extremely large problems of this type, involving thousands and even millions of variables, can now be solved routinely, thanks to recent algorithmic and technological advances. On the theoretical side, despite their relative simplicity, linear network problems embody a rich structure with both a continuous and a combinatorial character. Significantly, network ideas have been the starting point for important developments in linear and nonlinear programming, as well as combinatorial optimization.

Up to the late seventies, there were basically two types of algorithms for linear network optimization: the *simplex* method and its variations, and the *primal-dual* method and its close relative, the *out-of-kilter* method. There was some controversy regarding the relative merit of these methods, but thanks to the development of efficient implementation ideas, the simplex method emerged as the fastest of the two for most types of network problems.

A number of algorithmic developments in the eighties have changed significantly the situation. New methods were invented that challenged the old ones, both in terms of practical efficiency and theoretical worst-case performance. Two of these methods, originally proposed by the author, called *relaxation* and *auction*, will receive a lot of attention in this book. The relaxation method is a dual ascent method resembling the coordinate ascent method of unconstrained nonlinear optimization that significantly outperforms in practice both the simplex and the primal-dual methods for many types of problems. Auction is a form of dual coordinate ascent method, based on the notion of ϵ-complementary slackness and scaling ideas. This algorithm, together with its extensions, has excellent computational complexity, which is superior to that of the classical methods for many types of problems. Some auction algorithms have also proved to be very effective in practice, particularly for assignment and max-flow problems.

One of the purposes of the book is to provide a modern and up-to-date synthesis of old and new algorithms for linear network flow problems. The coverage is focused and selective, concentrating on the algorithms that have proved most successful in practice or otherwise embody important methodological ideas. Two fundamental ideas of mathematical programming are emphasized: *duality* and *iterative cost improvement*. Algorithms are grouped in three categories: (a) *primal cost improvement methods, including simplex methods,* which iteratively improve the primal cost by moving flow around simple cycles, (b) *dual ascent methods*, which iteratively improve the dual cost by changing the prices of a subset of nodes by equal amounts, and (c) *auction algorithms*, which try to improve the dual cost approximately along coordinate directions.

The first two classes of methods are dual to each other when viewed in the context of Rockafellar's monotropic programming theory [Roc84]; they are based on cost improvement along elementary directions of the circulation space (in the primal case) or the differential space (in the dual case). Auction algorithms are fundamentally different; they have their origin in nondifferentiable optimization and the ϵ-subgradient method in particular [BeM73].

A separate chapter is devoted to each of the above types of methods. The introductory chapter establishes some basic material and treats a few simple problems such as max-flow and shortest path. A final chapter discusses some of the practical performance aspects of the various methods.

A second purpose of the book is to supply state-of-the-art FORTRAN codes based on some of the algorithms presented. These codes illustrate implementation techniques commonly used in network optimization and should be helpful to practitioners. The listings of the codes appear in appendixes at the end of the book, and are also available on diskette from the author. I am thankful to Giorgio Gallo and Stefano Pallotino who gave me permission to include two of their shortest path codes.

The book can be used for a course on network optimization or for part of a course on introductory optimization; such courses have flourished in engineering, operations research, and applied mathematics curricula. The book contains a large number of examples and exercises, which should enhance its suitability for classroom instruction.

I was fortunate to have several outstanding collaborators in my linear network optimization research, and I would like to mention those with whom I have worked extensively. Eli Gafni programmed for the first time the auction algorithm and the relaxation method for assignment problems in 1979 and assisted with the computational experimentation. The idea of ϵ-scaling arose during my interactions with Eli at that time. Paul Tseng worked with me on network optimization starting in 1982. Together we developed the RELAX codes, we developed several extensions to the basic relaxation method and we collaborated closely and extensively on a broad variety of other subjects. Paul also read a substantial part of the book, and offered several helpful suggestions. Jon Eckstein worked with me on auction and other types of network optimization algorithms starting in 1986. Jon made several contributions to the theory of the ϵ-relaxation method, and coded its first implementation. Jon also proofread parts of the book, and his comments resulted in several substantive improvements. David Castañon has been working with me on auction algorithms for assignment, transportation, and minimum cost flow problems since 1987. Much of our joint work on these subjects appears in Chapter 4, particularly in Sections 4.2 and 4.4. David and I have also collaborated extensively on the implementation of various network flow algorithms. Our interactions have resulted in several improvements in the codes of the appendixes.

Funding for the research relating to this book was provided by the National Science Foundation and by the Army Research Office through the Center for Intelligent Control Systems at MIT. The staff of MIT Press worked with professionalism to produce the book quickly and efficiently.

Linear Network Optimization

1

Introduction

1.1 PROBLEM FORMULATION

This book deals with a single type of network optimization problem with linear cost, known as the *transshipment* or *minimum cost flow* problem. In this section, we formulate this problem together with several special cases. One of the most important special cases is the *assignment problem*, which we will discuss in detail because it is simple and yet captures most of the important algorithmic aspects of the general problem.

Example 1.1. The Assignment Problem

Suppose that there are n persons and n objects that we have to match on a one-to-one basis. There is a benefit or value a_{ij} for matching person i with object j, and we want to assign persons to objects so as to maximize the total benefit. There is also a restriction that person i can be assigned to object j only if (i, j) belongs to a set of given pairs $\mathcal{A}$. Mathematically, we want to find a set of person-object pairs $(1, j_1), \ldots, (n, j_n)$ from $\mathcal{A}$ such that the objects $j_1, \ldots, j_n$ are all distinct, and the total benefit $\sum_{i=1}^{n} a_{ij_i}$ is maximized.

The assignment problem is important in many practical contexts. The most obvious ones are resource allocation problems, such as assigning employees to jobs, machines to tasks, etc. There are also situations where the assignment problem appears as a subproblem in various methods for solving more complex problems.

We may associate any assignment with the set of variables $\{x_{ij} \mid (i,j) \in \mathcal{A}\}$, where $x_{ij} = 1$ if person i is assigned to object j and $x_{ij} = 0$ otherwise. We may then formulate the assignment problem as the linear program

$$\text{maximize} \quad \sum_{(i,j)\in\mathcal{A}} a_{ij}x_{ij}$$

subject to

$$\sum_{\{j\mid(i,j)\in\mathcal{A}\}} x_{ij} = 1, \qquad \forall \; i = 1,\ldots,n, \qquad\qquad (1.1)$$

$$\sum_{\{i\mid(i,j)\in\mathcal{A}\}} x_{ij} = 1, \qquad \forall \; j = 1,\ldots,n,$$

$$0 \leq x_{ij} \leq 1, \qquad \forall \; (i,j) \in \mathcal{A}.$$

Actually we should further restrict x_{ij} to be either 0 or 1; however, as we will show in the next chapter, the above linear program has a remarkable property: if it has a feasible solution at all, then it has an optimal solution where all x_{ij} are either 0 or 1. In fact, the set of its optimal solutions includes all the optimal assignments.

Another important property of the assignment problem is that it can be represented by a graph as shown in Fig. 1.1. Here, there are $2n$ nodes divided into two groups: n corresponding to persons and n corresponding to objects. Also, for every $(i,j) \in \mathcal{A}$, there is an arc connecting person i with object j. In the terminology of network problems, the variable x_{ij} is referred to as the *flow* of arc (i,j). The constraint $\sum_{\{j\mid(i,j)\in\mathcal{A}\}} x_{ij} = 1$ indicates that the total outgoing flow from node i should be equal to 1, which may be viewed as the (exogenous) *supply* of the node. Similarly, the constraint $\sum_{\{i\mid(i,j)\in\mathcal{A}\}} x_{ij} = 1$ indicates that the total incoming flow to node j should be equal to 1, which may be viewed as the (exogenous) *demand* of the node.

Before we can proceed with a formulation of more general network flow problems we must introduce some notation and terminology.

1.1.1   Graphs and Flows

We define a *directed graph*, $\mathcal{G} = (\mathcal{N}, \mathcal{A})$, to be a set $\mathcal{N}$ of *nodes* and a set $\mathcal{A}$ of pairs of distinct nodes from $\mathcal{N}$ called *arcs*. The numbers of nodes and arcs of $\mathcal{G}$ are denoted by N and A, respectively, and we assume throughout that $1 \leq N < \infty$ and $0 \leq A < \infty$. An arc (i,j) is viewed as an ordered pair, and is to be distinguished from the pair (j,i). If (i,j) is an arc, we say that (i,j) is *outgoing* from node i and *incoming* to node j; we also say that j is an *outward neighbor* of i and that i is an *inward neighbor* of j. We say that arc (i,j) is *incident* to i and to j, and that i is the *start* node and j is the

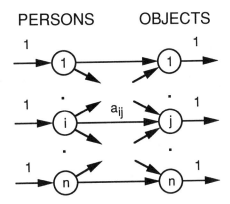

Figure 1.1   The graph representation of an assignment problem.

end node of the arc. The *degree* of a node i is the number of arcs that are incident to i.

A graph is said to be *bipartite* if its nodes can be partitioned into two sets $\mathcal{S}$ and $\mathcal{T}$ such that every arc has its start in $\mathcal{S}$ and its end in $\mathcal{T}$. The assignment graph of Fig. 1.1 is an example of a bipartite graph, with $\mathcal{S}$ and $\mathcal{T}$ being the sets of persons and objects, respectively.

We do not exclude the possibility that there is a separate arc connecting a pair of nodes in each of the two directions. However, we do not allow more than one arc between a pair of nodes in the same direction, so that we can refer unambiguously to the arc with start i and end j as arc (i, j). This was done for notational convenience. Our analysis can be simply extended to handle multiple arcs with start i and end j; the extension is based on modifying the graph by introducing for each such arc, an additional node, call it n, together with the two arcs (i, n) and (n, j). The codes in the appendixes can handle graphs that have multiple arcs between any pair of nodes in the same direction, without the above modification.

Paths and Cycles

A *path* P in a directed graph is a sequence of nodes $(n_1, n_2, \ldots, n_k)$ with $k \geq 2$ and a corresponding sequence of $k - 1$ arcs such that the ith arc in the sequence is either (n_i, n_{i+1}) (in which case it is called a *forward* arc of the path) or (n_{i+1}, n_i) (in which case it is called a *backward* arc of the path). A path is said to be *forward* (or *backward*) if all of its arcs are forward (respectively, backward) arcs. We denote by P^+ and P^- the sets of forward and backward arcs of P, respectively. Nodes n_1 and n_k are called the *start node* (or *origin*) and the *end node* (or *destination*) of P, respectively.

A *cycle* is a path for which the start and end nodes are the same. A path is said to be *simple* if it contains no repeated arcs and no repeated nodes, except that the start and end nodes could be the same (in which case the path is called a *simple cycle*). These definitions are illustrated in Fig. 1.2.

Note that the sequence of nodes $(n_1, n_2, \ldots, n_k)$ is not sufficient to specify a path; the sequence of arcs is also important, as Fig. 1.2(c) shows. The difficulty arises when for two successive nodes n_i and n_{i+1} of the path, both (n_i, n_{i+1}) and (n_{i+1}, n_i) are arcs, so there is ambiguity as to which of the two is the corresponding arc of the path. However, when the path is known to be forward or is known to be backward, it is uniquely specified by the sequence of its nodes. Throughout the book, we will make sure that the intended sequence of arcs is explicitly defined in ambiguous situations.

A graph that contains no simple cycles is said to be *acyclic*. A graph is said to be *connected* if for each pair of nodes i and j, there is a path starting at i and ending at j; it is said to be *strongly connected* if for each pair of nodes i and j, there is a forward path starting at i and ending at j. For example, the assignment graph of Fig. 1.1 may be connected but cannot be strongly connected.

We say that $\mathcal{G}' = (\mathcal{N}', \mathcal{A}')$ is a *subgraph* of $\mathcal{G} = (\mathcal{N}, \mathcal{A})$ if $\mathcal{G}'$ is a graph, $\mathcal{N}' \subset \mathcal{N}$, and $\mathcal{A}' \subset \mathcal{A}$. A *tree* is a connected acyclic graph. A *spanning tree* of a graph $\mathcal{G}$ is a subgraph of $\mathcal{G}$ that is a tree and that includes all the nodes of $\mathcal{G}$.

Flow and Divergence

A *flow vector* x in a graph $(\mathcal{N}, \mathcal{A})$ is a set of scalars $\{x_{ij} \mid (i, j) \in \mathcal{A}\}$. We refer to x_{ij} as the flow of the arc (i, j), and we place no restriction (such as nonnegativity) on its value. The *divergence vector* y associated with a flow vector x is the N-dimensional vector with coordinates

$$y_i = \sum_{\{j \mid (i,j) \in \mathcal{A}\}} x_{ij} - \sum_{\{j \mid (j,i) \in \mathcal{A}\}} x_{ji}, \qquad \forall \, i \in \mathcal{N}. \tag{1.2}$$

Thus, y_i is the total flow departing from node i less the total flow arriving at i; it is referred to as the divergence of i. For example, an assignment corresponds to a flow vector x with $x_{ij} = 1$ if person i is assigned to object j and $x_{ij} = 0$ otherwise (see Fig. 1.1); the assigned pairs involve each person exactly once and each object exactly once, if the divergence of each person node i is $y_i = 1$, and the divergence of each object node j is $y_j = -1$.

We say that node i is a *source* (respectively, *sink*) for the flow vector x if $y_i > 0$ (respectively, $y_i < 0$). If $y_i = 0$ for all $i \in \mathcal{N}$, then x is called a *circulation*. These definitions are illustrated in Fig. 1.3. Note that by adding Eq. (1.2) over all $i \in \mathcal{N}$, we obtain

$$\sum_{i \in \mathcal{N}} y_i = 0$$

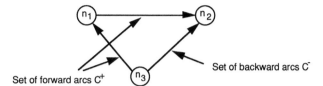

(a) A simple forward path P = (n_1, n_2, n_3, n_4).
    The path P = $(n_1, n_2, n_3, n_4, n_3, n_2, n_3)$ is also legitimate;
    it is not simple, and it is neither forward nor backward.

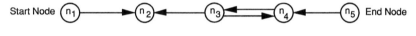

(b) A simple cycle C = (n_1, n_2, n_3, n_1) which is neither forward nor backward.

(c) Path P = $(n_1, n_2, n_3, n_4, n_5)$ with corresponding sequence of arcs
    { $(n_1, n_2), (n_3, n_2), (n_3, n_4), (n_5, n_4)$ }.

Figure 1.2   Illustration of various types of paths. Note that for the path (c) it is necessary to specify the sequence of arcs of the path (rather than just the sequence of nodes) because both (n_3, n_4) and (n_4, n_3) are arcs. For a somewhat degenerate example that illustrates the fine points of the definitions, note that for the graph of (c), the node sequence

$$C = (n_3, n_4, n_3)$$

is associated with four cycles:

(1) The simple forward cycle with

$$C^+ = \{(n_3, n_4), (n_4, n_3)\}, \qquad C^- : \text{empty.}$$

(2) The simple backward cycle with

$$C^- = \{(n_4, n_3), (n_3, n_4)\}, \qquad C^+ : \text{empty.}$$

(3) The (nonsimple) cycle with

$$C^+ = \{(n_3, n_4)\}, \qquad C^- = \{(n_3, n_4)\}.$$

(4) The (nonsimple) cycle with

$$C^+ = \{(n_4, n_3)\}, \qquad C^- = \{(n_4, n_3)\}.$$

Note that the node sequence (n_3, n_4, n_3) determines the cycle uniquely if it is specified that the cycle is either forward or is backward.

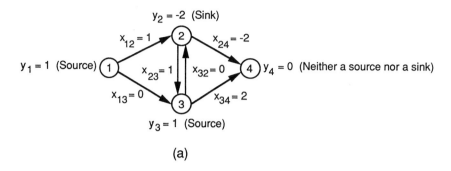

$y_2 = -2$ (Sink)

$x_{12} = 1$ ② $x_{24} = -2$

$y_1 = 1$ (Source) ① $x_{23} = 1$ $x_{32} = 0$ ④ $y_4 = 0$ (Neither a source nor a sink)

$x_{13} = 0$ ③ $x_{34} = 2$

$y_3 = 1$ (Source)

(a)

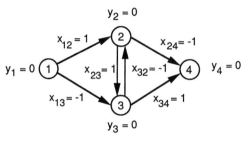

$y_2 = 0$

$x_{12} = 1$ ② $x_{24} = -1$

$y_1 = 0$ ① $x_{23} = 1$ $x_{32} = -1$ ④ $y_4 = 0$

$x_{13} = -1$ ③ $x_{34} = 1$

$y_3 = 0$

(b) A circulation

Figure 1.3 Illustration of various types of flows. The flow in (b) is a circulation because $y_i = 0$ for all i.

for any divergence vector y.

In applications, a negative arc flow indicates that whatever flow represents (material, electric current, etc.), moves in a direction opposite to the direction of the arc. We can always change the sign of the arc flow to positive as long as we change the arc direction, so in many situations we can assume without loss of generality that all arc flows are nonnegative. For the development of a general methodology, however, this device is often cumbersome, which is why we prefer to simply accept the possibility of negative arc flows.

Conformal Decomposition

It is often convenient to break down a flow vector into the sum of simpler components. A particularly useful decomposition arises when the components involve simple paths and cycles with orientation which is consistent to that of the original flow vector. This leads to the notion of a conformal realization, which we proceed to discuss.

We say that a path P *conforms* to a flow vector x if $x_{ij} > 0$ for all forward arcs (i, j) of P and $x_{ij} < 0$ for all backward arcs (i, j) of P, and furthermore either P is a cycle or else the start and end nodes of P are a source and a sink of x, respectively. Roughly, a path conforms to a flow vector if it "carries flow in the forward direction" – that is, in the direction from the start node to the end node. In particular, for a forward cycle to conform to a flow vector, all its arcs must have positive flow; for a forward path which is not a cycle to conform to a flow vector, its arcs must have positive flow, and in addition the start and end nodes must be a source and a sink, respectively.

A *simple path flow* is a flow vector that corresponds to sending a positive amount of flow along a simple path; more precisely, it is a flow vector x of the form

$$x_{ij} = \begin{cases} a & \text{if } (i, j) \in P^+ \\ -a & \text{if } (i, j) \in P^- \\ 0 & \text{otherwise,} \end{cases} \qquad (1.3)$$

where a is a positive scalar, and P^+ and P^- are the sets of forward and backward arcs, respectively, of some simple path P.

We say that a simple path flow x^s *conforms* to a flow vector x if the path P corresponding to x^s via Eq. (1.3) conforms to x. This is equivalent to requiring that

$$0 < x_{ij} \qquad \text{for all arcs } (i, j) \text{ with } 0 < x_{ij}^s,$$

$$x_{ij} < 0 \qquad \text{for all arcs } (i, j) \text{ with } x_{ij}^s < 0,$$

and that either P is a cycle or else the divergence (with respect to x) of the start node of P is positive and the divergence (with respect to x) of the end node of P is negative.

We now show that any flow vector can be decomposed into a set of conforming simple path flows. This result, illustrated in Fig. 1.4, turns out to be fundamental for our purposes. The proof is based on an algorithm that can be used to construct the constituent conforming components one by one. Such constructive proofs are often used in network optimization.

Proposition 1.1:   (*Conformal Realization Theorem*) A nonzero flow vector x can be decomposed into the sum of t simple path flow vectors $x^1, x^2, \ldots, x^t$ that conform to x, with t being at most equal to the sum of the numbers of arcs and nodes $A + N$. If x is integer, then $x^1, x^2, \ldots, x^t$ can also be chosen to be integer. If x is a circulation, then $x^1, x^2, \ldots, x^t$ can be chosen to be simple circulations, and $t \leq A$.

Proof: We first assume that x is a circulation. Our proof consists of showing how to obtain from x a simple circulation x' conforming to x and such that

$$0 \leq x_{ij}' \leq x_{ij} \qquad \text{for all arcs } (i, j) \text{ with } 0 \leq x_{ij}, \qquad (1.4a)$$

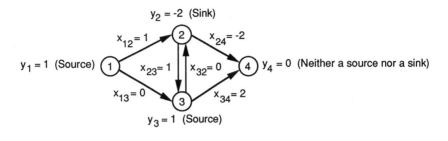

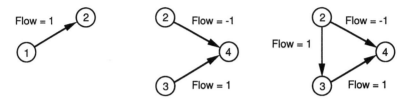

Figure 1.4   Decomposition of a flow vector x into three simple path flows conforming to x. The corresponding simple paths are $(1, 2)$, $(3, 4, 2)$, and $(2, 3, 4, 2)$. The first two are not cycles; they start at a source and end at a sink. Consistent with the definition of conformance of a path flow, each arc (i, j) of these paths carries positive (or negative) flow only if $x_{ij} > 0$ (or $x_{ij} < 0$, respectively). Arcs $(1, 3)$ and $(3, 2)$ do not belong to any of these paths because they carry zero flow. In this example, the decomposition is unique, but in general this need not be the case.

$$x_{ij} \leq x'_{ij} \leq 0 \qquad \text{for all arcs } (i, j) \text{ with } x_{ij} \leq 0, \tag{1.4b}$$

$$x_{ij} = x'_{ij} \qquad \text{for at least one arc } (i, j) \text{ with } x_{ij} \neq 0. \tag{1.4c}$$

Once this is done, we subtract x' from x. We have $x_{ij} - x'_{ij} > 0$ only for arcs (i, j) with $x_{ij} > 0$, $x_{ij} - x'_{ij} < 0$ only for arcs (i, j) with $x_{ij} < 0$, and $x_{ij} - x'_{ij} = 0$ for at least one arc (i, j) with $x_{ij} \neq 0$. If x is integer, then x' and $x - x'$ will also be integer. We then repeat the process (for at most A times) with the circulation x replaced by the circulation $x - x'$ and so on, until the zero flow is obtained. This is guaranteed to happen eventually because $x - x'$ has at least one more arc with zero flow than x.

We now describe the procedure by which x' with the properties (1.4) is obtained; see Fig. 1.5. Choose an arc (i, j) with $x_{ij} \neq 0$. Assume that $x_{ij} > 0$. (A similar procedure can be used when $x_{ij} < 0$.) Construct a sequence of node subsets $T_0, T_1, \ldots$, as follows: Take $T_0 = \{j\}$. For $k = 0, 1, \ldots$, given T_k, let

$$T_{k+1} = \big\{ n \notin \cup_{p=0}^{k} T_p \mid \text{there is a node } m \in T_k, \text{ and either an arc } (m, n)$$

$$\text{such that } x_{mn} > 0 \text{ or an arc } (n, m) \text{ such that } x_{nm} < 0 \big\},$$

and mark each node $n \in T_{k+1}$ with the label "(m,n)" or "(n,m)," where m is a node of T_k such that $x_{mn} > 0$ or $x_{nm} < 0$, respectively. The procedure terminates when T_{k+1} is empty. We may view T_k as the set of nodes n that can be reached from j with a path of k arcs carrying "positive flow" in the direction from j to n.

We claim that one of the sets T_k contains node i. To see this, consider the set $\cup_k T_k$ of all nodes that belong to one of the sets T_k. By construction, there is no outgoing arc from $\cup_k T_k$ with positive flow and no incoming arc into $\cup_k T_k$ with negative flow. If i did not belong to $\cup_k T_k$, there would exist at least one incoming arc into $\cup_k T_k$ with positive flow, namely the arc (i,j). Thus, the total flow of arcs incoming to $\cup_k T_k$ must be positive, while the total flow of arcs outgoing from $\cup_k T_k$ is negative or zero. On the other hand, these two flows must be equal, since x is a circulation; this can be seen by adding the equation

$$\sum_{\{n|(m,n)\in\mathcal{A}\}} x_{mn} = \sum_{\{n|(n,m)\in\mathcal{A}\}} x_{nm}$$

over all nodes $m \in \cup_k T_k$. Therefore, we obtain a contradiction, and it follows that one of the sets T_k contains node i.

We now trace labels backward from i until node j is reached. [This will happen eventually because if "(m,n)" or "(n,m)" is the label of node n and $n \in T_{k+1}$, then $m \in T_k$, so a "cycle" of labels cannot be formed before reaching j.] In particular, let "(i_1,i)" or "(i,i_1)" be the label of i, let "(i_2,i_1)" or "(i_1,i_2)" be the label of i_1, etc., until a node i_k with label "(i_k,j)" or "(j,i_k)" is found. The cycle $C = (j, i_k, i_{k-1}, \ldots, i_1, i, j)$ is simple, it contains (i,j) as a forward arc, and is such that all its forward arcs have positive flow and all its backward arcs have negative flow (see Fig. 1.2). Let $a = \min_{(m,n)\in C} |x_{mn}| > 0$. Then the circulation x', where

$$x'_{ij} = \begin{cases} a & \text{if } (i,j) \in C^+ \\ -a, & \text{if } (i,j) \in C^- \\ 0 & \text{otherwise,} \end{cases}$$

has the required properties (1.4).

Consider now the case where x is not a circulation. We form an enlarged graph by introducing a new node s and by introducing for each node $i \in \mathcal{N}$ an arc (s,i) with flow x_{si} equal to the divergence y_i of Eq. (1.2). Then (by using also the fact $\sum_{i\in\mathcal{N}} y_i = 0$) the resulting flow vector is seen to be a circulation in the enlarged graph. This circulation, by the result just shown, can be decomposed into at most $A + N$ simple circulations of the enlarged graph, conforming to the flow vector. Out of these circulations, we consider those containing node s, and we remove s and its two incident arcs while leaving the other circulations unchanged. As a result we obtain a set of at most $A + N$ path flows of the original graph, which add up to x. These path flows also conform to x, as is required in order to prove the proposition.   **Q.E.D.**

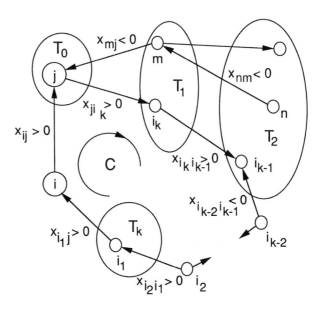

Figure 1.5   Construction of a cycle of nonzero flow arcs used in the proof of the Conformal Realization Theorem.

1.1.2   The Minimum Cost Flow Problem

The minimum cost flow problem is to find a set of arc flows that minimize a linear cost function subject to the constraints that they produce a given divergence vector and lie within some bounds; that is,

$$\text{minimize} \quad \sum_{(i,j)\in\mathcal{A}} a_{ij}x_{ij} \qquad\qquad\qquad \text{(MCF)}$$

subject to

$$\sum_{\{j|(i,j)\in\mathcal{A}\}} x_{ij} - \sum_{\{j|(j,i)\in\mathcal{A}\}} x_{ji} = s_i, \qquad \forall\, i \in \mathcal{N}, \qquad (1.5)$$

$$b_{ij} \le x_{ij} \le c_{ij}, \qquad \forall\, (i,j) \in \mathcal{A}, \qquad\qquad (1.6)$$

where a_{ij}, b_{ij}, c_{ij}, and s_i are given scalars.

We use the following terminology.

a_{ij}: the *cost coefficient* (or simply *cost*) of (i,j).

b_{ij} and c_{ij}: the *flow bounds* of (i,j).

$[b_{ij}, c_{ij}]$: the *feasible flow range* of (i,j).

s_i: the *supply* of node i.

We also refer to the constraints (1.5) and (1.6) as the *conservation of flow constraints*, and the *capacity constraints*, respectively. A flow vector satisfying both of these constraints is called *feasible*, and if it satisfies just the capacity constraints, it is called *capacity-feasible*. If there exists at least one feasible flow vector, problem (MCF) is called *feasible*; otherwise it is called *infeasible*. Note that for feasibility we must have

$$\sum_{i \in \mathcal{N}} s_i = 0, \tag{1.7}$$

since by Eq. (1.2), for any flow vector, the sum of all the corresponding node divergences must be zero.

For a typical application of the minimum cost flow problem, think of the nodes as locations (cities, warehouses, or factories) where a certain product is produced or consumed. Think of the arcs as transportation links between the locations, each with transportation cost a_{ij} per unit transported. The problem then is to move the product from the production points to the consumption points at minimum cost while observing the capacity constraints of the transportation links.

On occasion, we will consider the variation of the minimum cost flow problem where the lower or the upper flow bound of some of the arcs is either $-\infty$ or ∞, respectively. In these cases, we will explicitly state so; thus, *in the absence of a contrary statement, we implicitly assume that every arc has real lower and upper flow bounds.*

The minimum cost flow problem is a special case of a linear programming problem, but it has a much more favorable structure than a general linear program. It has certain special properties that strongly affect the performance of algorithms. For example, the minimum cost flow problem with integer data can be solved using integer calculations exclusively. Furthermore, some methods (relaxation, auction) are very efficient for some minimum cost flow problems but are less efficient or inapplicable for general linear programs. In practice, minimum cost flow problems can often be solved hundreds and even thousands of times faster than general linear programs of comparable dimension.

The assignment problem is a special case of the minimum cost flow problem [see Eq. (1.1); by reversing the sign of the cost function, maximization can be turned into minimization]. Two other important special cases are described below.

Example 1.2. The Max-Flow Problem

In the max-flow problem there are two special nodes: the *source* (s) and the *sink* (t). Roughly, the objective is to push as much flow as possible from s into t while observing the capacity constraints. More precisely, we want to make the divergence of all nodes other than s and t equal to zero while maximizing the divergence of s (or, equivalently, minimizing the divergence of t).

The max-flow problem arises in many practical contexts, such as calculating the throughput of a highway system or a communication network. It also arises often as a subproblem in more complicated problems or algorithms.

We formulate this problem as a special case of the minimum cost flow problem by assigning cost zero to all arcs and by introducing an arc (t, s) with cost -1 and with an appropriately large upper flow bound and small lower flow bound, as shown in Fig. 1.6. Mathematically, the problem is as follows:

$$\text{maximize} \quad x_{ts}$$

$$\text{subject to}$$

$$\sum_{\{j|(i,j)\in\mathcal{A}\}} x_{ij} - \sum_{\{j|(j,i)\in\mathcal{A}\}} x_{ji} = 0, \qquad \forall\ i \in \mathcal{N} \text{ with } i \neq s \text{ and } i \neq t,$$

$$\sum_{\{j|(s,j)\in\mathcal{A}\}} x_{sj} = \sum_{\{i|(i,t)\in\mathcal{A}\}} x_{it} = x_{ts}, \qquad (1.8)$$

$$b_{ij} \leq x_{ij} \leq c_{ij}, \qquad \forall\ (i,j) \in \mathcal{A} \text{ with } (i,j) \neq (t,s),$$

$$\sum_{\{i|(i,t)\in\mathcal{A}\}} b_{it} \leq x_{ts} \leq \sum_{\{i|(i,t)\in\mathcal{A}\}} c_{it}.$$

The upper and lower bounds on x_{ts} are introduced in order to place the problem in the minimum cost flow format; they are actually redundant since they are implied by the upper and lower bounds on the flows of the arcs of $\mathcal{A}$. Also, viewing the problem as a maximization is consistent with its intuitive interpretation. Alternatively, we could write the problem as a minimization of $-x_{ts}$ subject to the same constraints.

In an alternative formulation the flow bounds on x_{ts} could be discarded, since they are implied by other bounds, namely $b_{it} \leq x_{it} \leq c_{it}$ for all $(i,t) \in \mathcal{A}$. We would then be dealing with a special case of the version of the minimum cost flow problem in which some of the flow bounds are $-\infty$ and/or ∞.

Example 1.3. The Transportation Problem

This problem is the same as the assignment problem except that the node supplies need not be 1 or -1 and maximization is replaced by minimization.

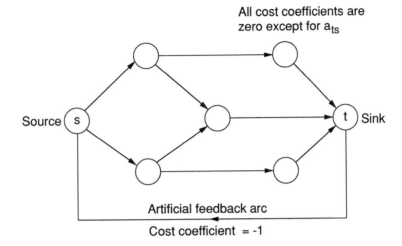

Figure 1.6 The minimum cost flow representation of a max-flow problem. At the optimum, the flow x_{ts} equals the maximum flow that can be sent from s to t through the subgraph obtained by deleting arc (t, s).

It has the form

$$\text{minimize} \quad \sum_{(i,j)\in\mathcal{A}} a_{ij}x_{ij}$$

$$\text{subject to}$$

$$\sum_{\{j|(i,j)\in\mathcal{A}\}} x_{ij} = \alpha_i, \qquad \forall\, i = 1, \ldots, m, \tag{1.9}$$

$$\sum_{\{i|(i,j)\in\mathcal{A}\}} x_{ij} = \beta_j, \qquad \forall\, j = 1, \ldots, n,$$

$$0 \leq x_{ij} \leq \min\{\alpha_i, \beta_j\}, \qquad \forall\, (i,j) \in \mathcal{A}.$$

Here α_i and β_j are positive scalars, which for feasibility must satisfy

$$\sum_{i=1}^{m} \alpha_i = \sum_{j=1}^{n} \beta_j,$$

[see Eq. (1.7)]. In an alternative formulation, the upper bound constraint $x_{ij} \leq \min\{\alpha_i, \beta_j\}$ could be discarded, since it is implied by the conservation of flow and the nonnegativity constraints.

1.1.3   Transformations and Equivalences

The minimum cost flow problem can be represented in several equivalent forms, which we describe below.

Setting the Lower Flow Bounds to Zero

The lower flow bounds b_{ij} can be changed to zero by a translation of variables, that is, by replacing x_{ij} by $x_{ij} - b_{ij}$ and by adjusting the upper flow bounds and the supplies according to

$$c_{ij} := c_{ij} - b_{ij},$$

$$s_i := s_i - \sum_{\{j|(i,j)\in\mathcal{A}\}} b_{ij} + \sum_{\{j|(j,i)\in\mathcal{A}\}} b_{ji}.$$

Optimal flows and the optimal value of the original problem are obtained by adding b_{ij} to the optimal flow of each arc (i,j) and adding $\sum_{(i,j)\in\mathcal{A}} a_{ij}b_{ij}$ to the optimal value of the transformed problem, respectively. Working with the transformed problem saves computation time and storage, and for this reason most network flow codes assume that all lower flow bounds are zero.

Eliminating the Upper Flow Bounds

Once the lower flow bounds have been changed to zero, it is possible to eliminate the upper flow bounds, obtaining a problem with just a nonnegativity constraint on all the flows. This can be done by introducing an additional nonnegative variable z_{ij} that must satisfy the constraint

$$x_{ij} + z_{ij} = c_{ij}.$$

(In linear programming terminology, z_{ij} is known as a *slack variable*.) The resulting problem is a minimum cost flow problem involving for each arc (i,j), an extra node with supply c_{ij}, and two outgoing arcs, corresponding to the flows x_{ij} and z_{ij}; see Fig. 1.7.

Reduction to a Circulation Format

The problem can be put into *circulation format*, in which all node supplies are zero. One way of doing this is to introduce a new node t and an arc (t,i) for each node i with nonzero supply s_i. We may then introduce the constraint $s_i \leq x_{ti} \leq s_i$ and an arbitrary cost for the flow x_{ti}. Alternatively, we may introduce an arc (t,i) and a constraint $0 \leq x_{ti} \leq s_i$ for all i with $s_i > 0$, and an arc (i,t) and a constraint $0 \leq x_{it} \leq -s_i$ for all i with $s_i < 0$. The cost of these arcs should be very small (i.e., large negative) to force the corresponding flows to be at their upper bound at the optimum; see Fig. 1.8.

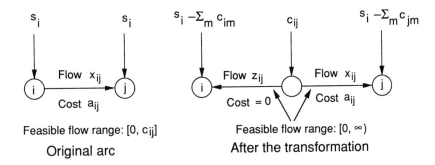

Figure 1.7   Eliminating the upper capacity bound by replacing each arc with a node and two outgoing arcs. Since for feasibility we must have $z_{ij} = c_{ij} - x_{ij}$, the upper bound constraint $x_{ij} \leq c_{ij}$ is equivalent to the lower bound constraint $0 \leq z_{ij}$. Furthermore, in view again of the equation $x_{ij} = c_{ij} - z_{ij}$, the conservation of flow equation

$$-\sum_j z_{ij} - \sum_j x_{ji} = s_i - \sum_j c_{ij}$$

for the modified problem is equivalent to the conservation of flow equation

$$\sum_j x_{ij} - \sum_j x_{ji} = s_i$$

for the original problem. Using these facts, it can be seen that the feasible flow vectors (x, z) of the modified problem can be paired on a one-to-one basis with the feasible flow vectors x of the original problem, and that the corresponding costs are equal. Thus, the modified problem is equivalent to the original problem.

Reduction to a Transportation or an Assignment Problem

Finally, the minimum cost flow problem may be transformed into a transportation problem of the form (1.9); see Fig. 1.9. The transportation problem (1.9) can itself be converted into an assignment problem by creating α_i unit supply sources (β_j unit demand sinks) for each transportation problem source i (sink j, respectively). For this reason, any algorithm that solves the assignment problem can be extended into an algorithm for the minimum cost flow problem. This motivates a useful way to develop and analyze new algorithmic ideas; apply them to the simpler assignment problem and generalize them using the construction just given to the minimum cost flow problem.

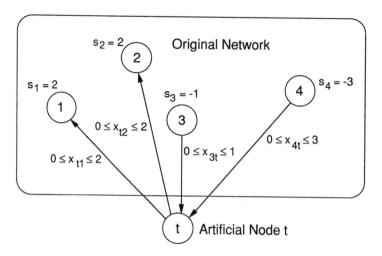

Figure 1.8   A transformation of the minimum cost flow problem into a circulation format. All artificial arcs have very large negative cost, to force the corresponding flows to their upper bounds at the optimum.

EXERCISES

Exercise 1.1

Use the algorithm of the proof of the Conformal Realization Theorem to decompose the flow vector of Fig. 1.10 into simple path flows.

Exercise 1.2

Convert the minimum cost flow problem of Fig. 1.11 into a linear network flow problem involving only nonnegativity constraints on the variables.

Exercise 1.3

Consider the minimum cost flow problem and let p_i be a scalar for each node i. Change the cost of each arc (i, j) from a_{ij} to $a_{ij} + p_j - p_i$. Show that the optimal flow vectors are unaffected. *Note:* This transformation is often useful; for example to make all arc costs nonnegative – see Section 1.3.5.

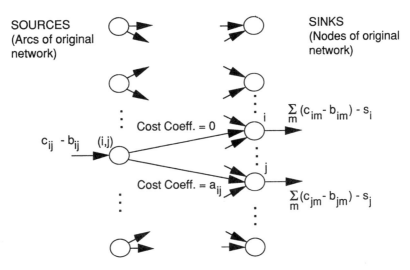

Figure 1.9 Transformation of a minimum cost flow problem into a transportation problem of the form (1.9). The idea is to introduce a new node for each arc and introduce a slack variable for every arc flow; see Fig. 1.7. This not only eliminates the upper bound constraint on the arc flows, as in Fig. 1.7, but also creates a bipartite graph structure. In particular, we take as sources of the transportation problem the arcs of the original network, and as sinks of the transportation problem the nodes of the original network. Each transportation problem source has two outgoing arcs with cost coefficients as shown. The supply of each transportation problem source is the feasible flow range length of the corresponding original network arc. The demand of each transportation problem sink is the sum of the feasible flow range lengths of the outgoing arcs from the corresponding original network node minus the supply of that node, as shown. An arc flow x_{ij} in (MCF) corresponds to flows equal to x_{ij} and $c_{ij} - b_{ij} - x_{ij}$ on the transportation problem arcs $\big((i,j),j\big)$ and $\big((i,j),i\big)$, respectively.

Exercise 1.4 (Breadth-First Search)

Let i and j be two nodes of a directed graph $(\mathcal{N}, \mathcal{A})$.

(a) Consider the following algorithm, known as *breadth-first search*, for finding a path from i to j. Let $T_0 = \{i\}$. For $k = 0, 1, \ldots$, let

$$T_{k+1} = \{n \notin \cup_{p=0}^{k} T_p \mid \text{for some node } m \in T_k, \ (m,n) \text{ or } (n,m) \text{ is an arc}\},$$

and mark each node $n \in T_{k+1}$ with the label "(m,n)" or "(n,m)," where m is a node of T_k such that (m,n) or (n,m) is an arc, respectively. The algorithm terminates if either (1) T_{k+1} is empty or (2) $j \in T_{k+1}$. Show

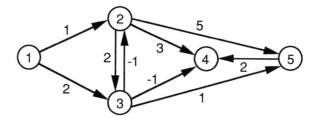

Figure 1.10   Flow vector for Exercise 1.1. The arc flows are the numbers shown next to the arcs.

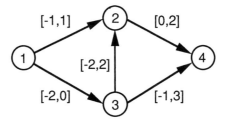

Figure 1.11   Minimum cost flow problem for Exercise 1.2. All arc costs are equal to 1, and all node supplies are equal to zero. The feasible flow ranges of the arcs are shown next to the arcs.

that case (1) occurs if and only if there is no path from i to j. If case (2) occurs, how would you use the labels to construct a path from i to j?

(b) Show that a path found by breadth-first search has a minimum number of arcs over all paths from i to j.

(c) Modify the algorithm of part (a) so that it finds a *forward* path from i to j.

Exercise 1.5 (Path Decomposition Theorem)

Use the Conformal Realization Theorem to show that a forward path P can be decomposed into a (possibly empty) collection of simple forward cycles, together with a simple forward path that has the same start node and end node as P. (Here "decomposition" means that the union of the arcs of the component paths is equal to the set of arcs of P with the multiplicity of repeated arcs properly accounted for.)

Exercise 1.6 (Inequality Constrained Minimum Cost Flows)

Consider the following variation of the minimum cost flow problem:

$$\text{minimize} \quad \sum_{(i,j)\in\mathcal{A}} a_{ij}x_{ij}$$

subject to

$$\underline{s}_i \leq \sum_{\{j|(i,j)\in\mathcal{A}\}} x_{ij} - \sum_{\{j|(j,i)\in\mathcal{A}\}} x_{ji} \leq \overline{s}_i, \qquad \forall\, i \in \mathcal{N},$$

$$b_{ij} \leq x_{ij} \leq c_{ij}, \qquad \forall\, (i,j) \in \mathcal{A},$$

where the bounds $\underline{s}_i$ and $\overline{s}_i$ on the divergence of node i are given. Convert this problem into the standard form of the minimum cost flow problem by adding an extra node and an arc from this node to every other node.

Exercise 1.7 (Node Throughput Constraints)

Consider the minimum cost flow problem with the additional constraints that the total flow of the outgoing arcs from each node i must lie within a given range $[\underline{t}_i, \overline{t}_i]$, that is,

$$\underline{t}_i \leq \sum_{\{j|(i,j)\in\mathcal{A}\}} x_{ij} \leq \overline{t}_i.$$

Convert this problem into the standard form of the minimum cost flow problem by adding an extra node and an extra arc for each existing node.

Exercise 1.8 (Piecewise Linear Arc Costs)

Consider the minimum cost flow problem with the difference that, instead of the linear form $a_{ij}x_{ij}$, each arc's cost function has the piecewise linear form

$$f_{ij}(x_{ij}) = \begin{cases} a_{ij}^1 x_{ij} & \text{if } b_{ij} \leq x_{ij} \leq m_{ij} \\ a_{ij}^1 m_{ij} + a_{ij}^2(x_{ij} - m_{ij}) & \text{if } m_{ij} \leq x_{ij} \leq c_{ij}, \end{cases}$$

where m_{ij}, a_{ij}^1, and a_{ij}^2 are given scalars satisfying $b_{ij} \leq m_{ij} \leq c_{ij}$ and $a_{ij}^1 \leq a_{ij}^2$.

(a) Show that the problem can be converted to a linear minimum cost flow problem where each arc (i,j) is replaced by two arcs with arc cost coefficients a_{ij}^1 and a_{ij}^2, and arc flow ranges $[b_{ij}, m_{ij}]$ and $[0, c_{ij} - m_{ij}]$, respectively.

(b) Generalize to the case of piecewise linear cost functions with more than two pieces.

1.2   THREE BASIC ALGORITHMIC IDEAS

In this section we will explain three main ideas underlying minimum cost flow algorithms:

(a) Primal cost improvement. Here we try to iteratively improve the cost to its optimal value by constructing a corresponding sequence of feasible flows.

(b) Dual cost improvement. Here we define a problem related to the minimum cost flow problem, called *dual problem*, whose variables are called *prices*. We then try to iteratively improve the dual cost to its optimal value by constructing a corresponding sequence of prices. Dual cost improvement algorithms also iterate on flows, which are related to the prices through a property called *complementary slackness*.

(c) Auction. This is a process that generates a sequence of prices in a way that is reminiscent of real-life auctions. Strictly speaking, there is no primal or dual cost improvement here, although one may view the auction process as trying to iteratively improve the dual cost in an approximate sense. In addition to prices, auction algorithms also iterate on flows, which are related to prices through a property called *ϵ-complementary slackness*; this is an approximate form of the complementary slackness property mentioned above.

For simplicity, in this chapter we will explain these ideas primarily through the assignment problem and the max-flow problem, deferring a more detailed development to subsequent chapters. Our illustrations, however, are relevant to the general minimum cost flow problem, since this problem can be reduced to the assignment problem (as was shown in the preceding section). Except for the max-flow analysis and the duality theory, the explanations in this section are somewhat informal. Precise statements of algorithms and results will be given in subsequent chapters.

1.2.1   Primal Cost Improvement

An important algorithmic idea for the minimum cost flow problem is to start from an initial feasible flow vector and then generate a sequence of feasible flow vectors, each having a better cost than the preceding one. The difference of any two successive flow vectors must be a circulation (since both are feasible), and for many interesting algorithms, including the simplex method, this circulation involves only a simple cycle. This idea will be first illustrated in terms of the assignment problem.

Multi-Person Swaps in the Assignment Problem

Consider the $n \times n$ assignment problem and suppose that we have a feasible assignment, that is, a set of n pairs (i, j) involving each person i exactly once and each object j exactly once. Consider now what happens if we do a *two-person swap*, that is, we replace two pairs (i_1, j_1) and (i_2, j_2) from the assignment with the pairs (i_1, j_2) and (i_2, j_1). The resulting assignment will still be feasible, and it will have a higher value if and only if

$$a_{i_1 j_2} + a_{i_2 j_1} > a_{i_1 j_1} + a_{i_2 j_2}.$$

Unfortunately, it may be impossible to improve the current assignment by a two-person swap, even if the assignment is not optimal; see Fig. 2.1. It turns out, however, that an improvement is possible by means of a *k-person swap*, for some $k \geq 2$, where a set of pairs $(i_1, j_1), \ldots, (i_k, j_k)$ from the current assignment is replaced by the pairs $(i_1, j_2), \ldots, (i_{k-1}, j_k), (i_k, j_1)$. This can be shown in the context of the minimum cost flow representation of the assignment problem:

$$\text{maximize} \quad \sum_{(i,j) \in \mathcal{A}} a_{ij} x_{ij}$$

$$\text{subject to}$$

$$\sum_{\{j \mid (i,j) \in \mathcal{A}\}} x_{ij} = 1, \qquad \forall \ i = 1, \ldots, n, \tag{2.1}$$

$$\sum_{\{i \mid (i,j) \in \mathcal{A}\}} x_{ij} = 1, \qquad \forall \ j = 1, \ldots, n,$$

$$0 \leq x_{ij} \leq 1, \qquad \forall \ (i, j) \in \mathcal{A}.$$

Feasible assignments correspond to feasible flow vectors $\{x_{ij} \mid (i, j) \in \mathcal{A}\}$ such that x_{ij} is either 0 or 1, and a k-person swap corresponds to a simple cycle with k forward arcs (corresponding to the new assignment pairs) and k backward arcs (corresponding to the current assignment pairs that are being replaced); see Fig. 2.2. Thus, *performing a k-person swap is equivalent to pushing one unit of flow along the corresponding simple cycle*. The k-person swap improves the assignment if and only if the *value* of the k-person swap, defined by

$$a_{i_k j_1} + \sum_{m=1}^{k-1} a_{i_m j_{m+1}} - \sum_{m=1}^{k} a_{i_m j_m}, \tag{2.2}$$

is positive.

By associating k-person swaps with simple cycle flows, we can show that a value-improving k-person swap exists if the current assignment is not optimal. For a detailed proof, see the subsequent Prop. 2.1. The main argument is

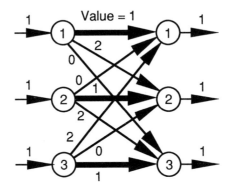

Figure 2.1   An example of a nonoptimal feasible assignment that cannot be improved by a two-person swap. The value of each pair is shown next to the corresponding arc. Here, the value of the assignment $\{(1,1),(2,2),(3,3)\}$ is left unchanged at 3 by any two-person swap. Through a three-person swap, however, we obtain the optimal assignment, $\{(1,2),(2,3),(3,1)\}$, which has value 6.

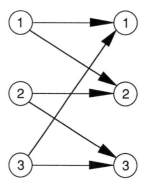

Figure 2.2   Correspondence of a k-person swap to a simple cycle. This is the same example as in the preceding figure. The backward arcs of the cycle are $(1,1)$, $(2,2)$, and $(3,3)$, and correspond to the current assignment pairs. The forward arcs of the cycle are $(1,2)$, $(2,3)$, and $(3,1)$, and correspond to the new assignment pairs. The k-person swap is value-improving because the sum of the values of the forward arcs $(2+2+2)$ is greater than the sum of the values of the backward arcs $(1+1+1)$.

based on the Conformal Realization Theorem (Prop. 1.1). Briefly, the difference between the flow vector corresponding to an optimal assignment and the vector corresponding to the current assignment is a circulation with arc flows equal to 0, 1, or -1, which can be decomposed into several conforming simple cycles (that is, k-person swaps). Thus, the value of the optimal assignment is equal to the value of the current assignment plus the sum of the values of the k-person swaps. It follows that if the current assignment is not optimal, then the value of at least one of the k-person swaps must be positive.

Primal cost improvement algorithms for the assignment problem are based on successive k-person swaps, each having positive or at least non-negative value. There are several different algorithms of this type, including various forms of the simplex method, which will be discussed in detail in the next chapter.

Extension to the Minimum Cost Flow Problem

The algorithmic ideas just described for the assignment problem can be extended to the minimum cost flow problem

$$\text{minimize} \quad \sum_{(i,j)\in\mathcal{A}} a_{ij}x_{ij} \tag{MCF}$$

subject to

$$\sum_{\{j|(i,j)\in\mathcal{A}\}} x_{ij} - \sum_{\{j|(j,i)\in\mathcal{A}\}} x_{ji} = s_i, \qquad \forall\, i \in \mathcal{N},$$

$$b_{ij} \leq x_{ij} \leq c_{ij}, \qquad \forall\, (i,j) \in \mathcal{A}.$$

The role of k-person swaps is played by simple cycles with special properties. In particular, let x be a nonoptimal feasible flow vector, and let x^* be another feasible flow vector with smaller cost than x (for example, x^* could be an optimal flow vector). The difference $w = x^* - x$ is a circulation satisfying, for all arcs (i,j),

$$b_{ij} \leq x^*_{ij} < x_{ij} \qquad \text{for all arcs } (i,j) \text{ with } w_{ij} < 0, \tag{2.3a}$$

$$x_{ij} < x^*_{ij} \leq c_{ij} \qquad \text{for all arcs } (i,j) \text{ with } 0 < w_{ij}. \tag{2.3b}$$

According to the Conformal Realization Theorem (Prop. 1.1), w can be decomposed into the sum of several simple cycle flows x^s, $s = 1,\ldots,t$, which are conforming in the sense that, for all arcs (i,j),

$$w_{ij} < 0 \qquad \text{for all arcs } (i,j) \text{ with } x^s_{ij} < 0, \tag{2.4a}$$

$$0 < w_{ij} \qquad \text{for all arcs } (i,j) \text{ with } 0 < x^s_{ij}. \tag{2.4b}$$

Let us define a path P to be *unblocked with respect to* x if $x_{ij} < c_{ij}$ for all forward arcs $(i,j) \in P^+$ and $b_{ij} < x_{ij}$ for all backward arcs $(i,j) \in P^-$. From Eqs. (2.3) and (2.4), we see that each of the simple cycle flows x^s involves a cycle that is unblocked with respect to x. Let us define also the *cost of a simple cycle* C as the sum of the costs of the forward arcs minus the sum of the costs of the backward arcs of C, that is,

$$\sum_{(i,j)\in C^+} a_{ij} - \sum_{(i,j)\in C^-} a_{ij}.$$

Since $w = x^* - x$, the cost of w (that is, $\sum_{(i,j)\in\mathcal{A}} a_{ij}w_{ij}$) is equal to the cost of x^* minus the cost of x, so the cost of w must be negative. On the other hand, w is the sum of the simple cycle flows x^s, so the cost of w is equal to the sum of the costs of the corresponding simple cycles multiplied by positive constants (the flow values of the corresponding simple cycle flows). Therefore, the cost of at least one of these simple cycles must be negative. We have thus proved the following proposition.

Proposition 2.1:   Consider the minimum cost flow problem and let x be a feasible flow vector which is not optimal. Then there exists a simple cycle flow that when added to x, produces a feasible flow vector with smaller cost that x; the corresponding cycle is unblocked with respect to x and has negative cost.

The major primal cost improvement algorithm for the minimum cost flow problem, the simplex method, uses simple cycle flows to produce improved feasible flow vectors, as will be discussed in the next chapter.

1.2.2   Application to the Max-Flow Problem – The Max-Flow/Min-Cut Theorem

We will now illustrate the preceding primal cost improvement approach in terms of the max-flow problem. In the process we will derive one of the most celebrated theorems of network optimization. To get a sense of the main ideas, consider the minimum cost flow formulation of the max-flow problem, given in Example 1.2, which involves the artificial feedback arc (t, s). Then, a negative cost cycle must necessarily include the arc (t, s), since this is the only arc with nonzero cost. By Prop. 2.1, if a feasible flow vector x is not optimal, there must exist a simple cycle with negative cost that is unblocked with respect to x; this cycle must consist of the arc (t, s) and a path from s to t, which is unblocked with respect to x. Thus, by adding to x the corresponding path flow, we obtain an improved flow vector. By similar reasoning, it follows that if there is no path from s to t that is unblocked with respect to a given flow vector x, then x must be optimal.

The max-flow/min-cut theorem and the Ford-Fulkerson algorithm, to be described shortly, are based on the above ideas. However, in view of the simplicity of the max-flow problem, the subsequent analysis will be couched in first principles; it will also develop some concepts that will be useful later. First some definitions are needed.

Cuts in a Graph

A *cut* Q in a graph $(\mathcal{N}, \mathcal{A})$ is a partition of the node set $\mathcal{N}$ into two nonempty subsets, a set $\mathcal{S}$ and its complement $\mathcal{N} - \mathcal{S}$; we will use the notation $Q = [\mathcal{S}, \mathcal{N} - \mathcal{S}]$. Note that the partition is ordered in the sense that the cut $[\mathcal{S}, \mathcal{N} - \mathcal{S}]$ is distinct from the cut $[\mathcal{N} - \mathcal{S}, \mathcal{S}]$. For a cut $Q = [\mathcal{S}, \mathcal{N} - \mathcal{S}]$, we will use the notation

$$Q^+ = \{(i,j) \in \mathcal{A} \mid i \in \mathcal{S}, j \notin \mathcal{S}\},$$

$$Q^- = \{(i,j) \in \mathcal{A} \mid i \notin \mathcal{S}, j \in \mathcal{S}\},$$

and we will say that Q^+ and Q^- are the *sets of forward and backward arcs of the cut*, respectively. We will say that the cut Q is *nonempty* if $Q^+ \cup Q^- \neq \emptyset$; otherwise we will say that Q is *empty*. We will say that the cut $[\mathcal{S}, \mathcal{N} - \mathcal{S}]$ *separates node s from node t* if $s \in \mathcal{S}$ and $t \notin \mathcal{S}$. These definitions are illustrated in Fig. 2.3.

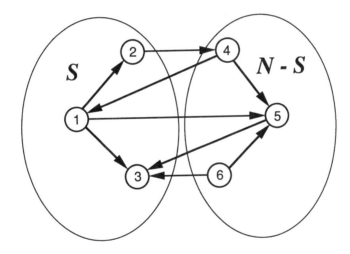

Figure 2.3   Illustration of a cut $Q = [\mathcal{S}, \mathcal{N} - \mathcal{S}]$, where $\mathcal{S} = \{1, 2, 3\}$. We have

$$Q^+ = \{(2,4), (1,5)\}, \qquad Q^- = \{(4,1), (5,3), (6,3)\}.$$

Given a flow vector x, the *flux across a nonempty cut* $Q = [\mathcal{S}, \mathcal{N} - \mathcal{S}]$ is defined to be the total net flow coming out of $\mathcal{S}$, that is, the scalar

$$F(Q) = \sum_{(i,j) \in Q^+} x_{ij} - \sum_{(i,j) \in Q^-} x_{ij}.$$

Using the definition of the divergence of a node [see Eq. (1.2)] and the following calculation, it can be seen that $F(Q)$ is also equal to the sum of the divergences y_i of the nodes in $\mathcal{S}$:

$$F(Q) = \sum_{\{(i,j)\in\mathcal{A}|i\in\mathcal{S},j\notin\mathcal{S}\}} x_{ij} - \sum_{\{(i,j)\in\mathcal{A}|i\notin\mathcal{S},j\in\mathcal{S}\}} x_{ij}$$

$$= \sum_{i\in\mathcal{S}} \left(\sum_{\{j|(i,j)\in\mathcal{A}\}} x_{ij} - \sum_{\{j|(j,i)\in\mathcal{A}\}} x_{ji} \right) = \sum_{i\in\mathcal{S}} y_i. \tag{2.5}$$

(The second equality holds because the flow of an arc with both end nodes in $\mathcal{S}$ cancels out within the parentheses; it appears twice, once with a positive and once with a negative sign.)

Given flow bounds b_{ij} and c_{ij} for each arc (i,j), the *capacity of a nonempty cut* Q is

$$C(Q) = \sum_{(i,j)\in Q^+} c_{ij} - \sum_{(i,j)\in Q^-} b_{ij}. \tag{2.6}$$

Clearly, for any capacity-feasible flow vector x, the flux $F(Q)$ across Q is no larger than the cut capacity $C(Q)$. If $F(Q) = C(Q)$, then Q is said to be a *saturated cut with respect to* x; the flow of each forward (backward) arc of such a cut must be at its upper (lower) bound. By convention, every empty cut is also said to be saturated. The following is a simple but very useful result.

Proposition 2.2: Let x be a capacity-feasible flow vector, and let s and t be two nodes. Then exactly one of the following two alternatives holds:

(1) There exists a path from s to t that is unblocked with respect to x.

(2) There exists a saturated cut Q that separates s from t.

Proof: The proof is obtained by constructing an algorithm that terminates with either a path as in (1) or a cut as in (2). Consider the following algorithm, which is similar to the breadth-first search algorithm of Exercise 1.4; see Fig. 2.4. It generates a sequence of node sets $\{T_k\}$, starting with $T_0 = \{s\}$; each set T_k represents the set of nodes that can be reached from s with an unblocked path of k arcs.

Unblocked Path Search Algorithm

For $k = 0, 1, \ldots$, given T_k, terminate if either T_k is empty or $t \in T_k$; otherwise, set

$$T_{k+1} = \Big\{n \notin \cup_{i=0}^{k} T_i| \text{ there is a node } m \in T_k, \text{ and either an arc } (m,n)$$

$$\text{such that } x_{mn} < c_{mn}, \text{ or an arc } (n,m) \text{ such that } b_{nm} < x_{nm}\Big\},$$

and mark each node $n \in T_{k+1}$ with the label "(m,n)" or "(n,m)," where m is a node of T_k and (m,n) or (n,m) is an arc with the property stated in the above equation, respectively.

Since the algorithm terminates if T_k is empty, and T_k must consist of nodes not previously included in $\cup_{i=0}^{k-1} T_i$, the algorithm must eventually terminate. Let $\mathcal{S}$ be the union of the sets T_i upon termination. There are two possibilities:

(a) The final set T_k contains t, in which case, by tracing labels backward from t, an unblocked path P from s to t can be constructed. The forward arcs of P are of the form (m,n) with $x_{mn} < c_{mn}$ and the label of n being "(m,n)"; the backward arcs of P are of the form (n,m) with $b_{nm} < x_{nm}$ and the label of n being "(n,m)." Any cut separating s from t must contain a forward arc (m,n) of P with $x_{mn} < c_{mn}$ or a backward arc (n,m) of P with $b_{nm} < x_{nm}$, and therefore cannot be saturated. Thus, the result is proved in this case.

(b) The final set T_k is empty, in which case from the equation defining T_k, it can be seen that the cut $Q = [\mathcal{S}, \mathcal{N} - \mathcal{S}]$ is saturated and separates s from t. To show that there is no unblocked path from s to t, note that for any such path, we must have either an arc $(m,n) \in Q^+$ with $x_{mn} < c_{mn}$ or an arc $(n,m) \in Q^-$ with $b_{nm} < x_{nm}$, which is impossible, since Q is saturated.

Q.E.D.

A generalization of Prop. 2.2 that involves two disjoint subsets of nodes $\mathcal{N}^+$ and $\mathcal{N}^-$ in place of s and t is given in Exercise 2.14.

The Max-Flow/Min-Cut Theorem

Consider now the max-flow problem. We have a graph $(\mathcal{N}, \mathcal{A})$ with flow bounds b_{ij} and c_{ij} for the arcs, and two special nodes s and t. We want to maximize the divergence out of s over all capacity-feasible flow vectors having zero divergence for all nodes other than s and t. Given any such flow vector and any cut Q separating s from t, the divergence out of s is equal to the flux across Q [cf. Eq. (2.5)], which in turn is no larger than the capacity of Q. Thus, if the max-flow problem is feasible, we have

$$\text{Maximum Flow} \leq \text{Capacity of } Q. \qquad (2.7)$$

The following theorem asserts that equality is attained for some Q. Part (a) of the theorem will assume the existence of an optimal solution to the max-flow problem. This assumption need not be satisfied; indeed it is possible that the max-flow problem has no feasible solution at all (consider a graph consisting

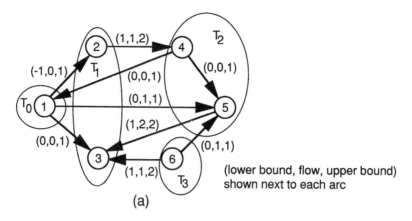

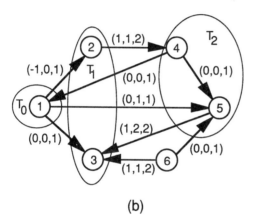

Figure 2.4 Illustration of the unblocked path search algorithm for finding an unblocked path from node 1 to node 6, or a saturated cut separating 1 from 6. The triplet (lower bound, flow, upper bound) is shown next to each arc. The figure shows the successive sets T_k generated by the algorithm. In case (a) there exists a unblocked path from 1 to 6, namely the path $(1, 3, 5, 6)$. In case (b), where the flow of arc $(6, 5)$ is at the lower bound rather than the upper bound, there is a saturated cut $[\mathcal{S}, \mathcal{N} - \mathcal{S}]$ separating 1 from 6, where $\mathcal{S} = \{1, 2, 3, 4, 5\}$ is the union of the sets T_k.

of a path from s to t the arcs of which have disjoint feasible flow ranges). In Chapter 2, however, we will show using the theory of the simplex method (see Prop. 3.1 in Section 2.3), that the max-flow problem (and indeed every minimum cost flow problem) has an optimal solution if it has at least one feasible solution. [This can also be easily shown using a fundamental result of mathematical analysis, the Weierstrass Theorem (see e.g. [Lue69], [Rud76]), which states that a continuous function attains a maximum over a nonempty and compact set.] If the lower flow bound is zero for every arc, the max-flow problem has at least one feasible solution, namely the zero flow vector. Thus the theory of Chapter 2 (or the Weierstrass Theorem) guarantees that the max-flow problem has an optimal solution in this case. This is stated as part (b) of the following theorem, even though its complete proof must await the developments of Chapter 2.

Proposition 2.3: (Max-Flow/Min-Cut Theorem)

   (a) If x^* is an optimal solution of the max-flow problem, then the divergence out of s corresponding to x^* is equal to the minimum cut capacity over all cuts separating s from t.

   (b) If all lower arc flow bounds are zero, the max-flow problem has an optimal solution, and the maximal divergence out of s is equal to the minimum cut capacity over all cuts separating s from t.

Proof: (a) Let F^* be the value of the maximum flow, that is, the divergence out of s corresponding to x^*. There cannot exist an unblocked path P from s to t with respect to x^*, since by increasing the flow of the forward arcs of P and by decreasing the flow of the backward arcs of P by a common positive increment, we would obtain a flow vector with divergence out of s larger than F^*. Therefore, by Prop. 2.2, there must exist a cut Q, that is saturated with respect to x^* and separates s from t. The flux across Q is equal to F^* and is also equal to the capacity of Q [since Q is saturated; see Eqs. (2.5) and (2.6)]. Since we know that F^* is less or equal to the minimum cut capacity [cf. Eq. (2.7)], the result follows.

(b) See the discussion preceding the proposition.   **Q.E.D.**

The Ford-Fulkerson Algorithm

We now turn to an algorithm for solving the max-flow problem. This algorithm is of the primal cost improvement type, because it improves the primal cost (the divergence out of s) at every iteration. The idea is that, given a feasible flow vector x (i.e., one that is capacity-feasible and has zero divergence out of every node other than s and t), and a path P from s to t, which is unblocked with respect to x, we can increase the flow of all forward arcs $(i, j) \in P^+$ and decrease the flow of all backward arcs $(i, j) \in P^-$ by the positive amount

$$\delta = \min\big\{\{c_{ij} - x_{ij} \mid (i,j) \in P^+\}, \{x_{ij} - b_{ij} \mid (i,j) \in P^-\}\big\}.$$

The resulting flow vector $\bar{x}$, given by

$$\bar{x}_{ij} = \begin{cases} x_{ij} + \delta & \text{if } (i,j) \in P^+ \\ x_{ij} - \delta & \text{if } (i,j) \in P^- \\ x_{ij} & \text{otherwise,} \end{cases}$$

is feasible, and it has a divergence out of s that is larger by δ than the divergence out of s corresponding to x. We refer to P as an *augmenting path*, and we refer to the operation of replacing x by $\bar{x}$ as a *flow augmentation* along P. Such an operation may also be viewed as a modification of x along the negative cost cycle consisting of P and an artificial arc (t,s) that has cost -1; see the formulation of the max-flow problem as a minimum cost flow problem in Example 1.2 and Fig. 1.6, and the discussion at the beginning of the present subsection.

The algorithm starts with a feasible flow vector x. If the lower flow bound is zero for all arcs, the zero flow vector can be used as a starting vector; otherwise, a feasible starting flow vector can be obtained by solving an auxiliary max-flow problem with zero lower flow bounds – see Exercise 2.5. At each iteration the algorithm has a feasible flow vector x and uses the unblocked path search method, given in the proof of Prop. 2.2, to either generate a new feasible flow vector with larger divergence out of s or terminate with a maximum flow and a minimum capacity cut.

Typical Iteration of Ford-Fulkerson Algorithm

> Use the unblocked path search method to either (1) find a saturated cut separating s from t or (2) find an unblocked path P with respect to x starting from s and ending at t. In case (1), terminate the algorithm; the current flow vector solves the max-flow problem. In case (2), perform an augmentation along P and go to the next iteration.

Figure 2.5 illustrates the Ford-Fulkerson algorithm.

Based on the preceding discussion, we see that with each augmentation the Ford-Fulkerson algorithm will improve the primal cost (the divergence out of s) by the augmentation increment δ. Thus, if δ is bounded below by some positive number, the algorithm can execute only a finite number of iterations and must terminate with an optimal solution. In particular, if the arc flow bounds are integer and the initial flow vector is also integer, δ will be a positive integer at each iteration, and the algorithm will terminate. The same is true even if the arc flow bounds and the initial flow vector are rational; by multiplication with a suitably large integer, one can scale these numbers up to integer while leaving the problem essentially unaffected.

On the other hand, if the problem data are irrational, proving termination of the Ford-Fulkerson algorithm is nontrivial. The proof (outlined in Exercise 2.10) depends on the use of the specific unblocked path search

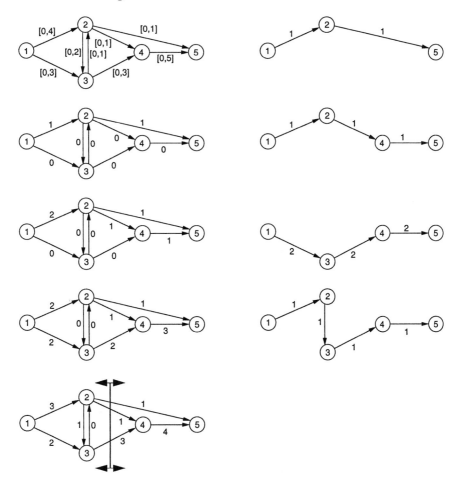

Figure 2.5 Illustration of the Ford-Fulkerson algorithm for finding a maximum flow from node $s = 1$ to node $t = 5$. The arc flow bounds are shown next to the arcs in the top left figure, and the starting flow is zero. The sequence of successive flow vectors is shown on the left, and the corresponding sequence of augmentations is shown on the right. The saturated cut obtained is $[\{1, 2, 3\}, \{4, 5\}]$. The capacity of this cut as well as the maximum flow is 5.

method of Prop. 2.2; this method yields augmenting paths with as few arcs as possible (Exercise 2.10). If unblocked paths are constructed using a different method, then, surprisingly, the Ford-Fulkerson algorithm need not terminate, and the generated sequence of divergences out of s may converge to a value strictly smaller than the maximum flow (for an example, see Exercise 2.9, and for a different example, see [FoF62], or [PaS82], p. 126, or [Roc84], p. 92).

Even with integer problem data, if the augmenting paths are constructed using a different unblocked path search method the Ford-Fulkerson algorithm may terminate in a very large number of iterations; see Fig. 2.6.

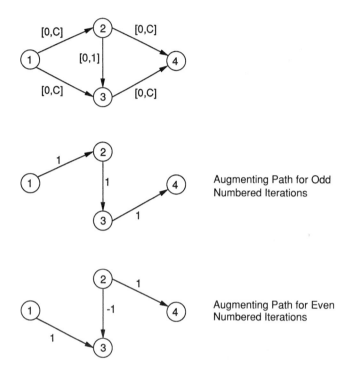

Figure 2.6 An example showing that if the augmenting paths used in the Ford-Fulkerson algorithm do not have a number of arcs that is as small as possible, the number of iterations may be very large. Here, C is a large integer. The maximum flow is $2C$, and can be produced after a sequence of $2C$ augmentations using the three-arc augmenting paths shown in the figure. If on the other hand the two-arc augmenting paths $(1, 2, 4)$ and $(1, 3, 4)$ are used, only two augmentations are needed.

The number of augmentations of the Ford-Fulkerson algorithm, with the unblocked path search method given, can be estimated as $O(NA)$ for an $O(NA^2)$ running time [since each augmentation requires $O(A)$ operations]; see Exercise 2.10. Several max-flow algorithms with more favorable worst case complexity estimates are available; see the references and Chapter 4.

1.2.3   Duality and Dual Cost Improvement

Linear programming duality theory deals with the relation between the original linear program and another linear program called *dual*. To develop an intuitive understanding of duality, we will focus on the assignment problem and consider a closely related economic equilibrium problem. Consider matching the n objects with the n persons through a market mechanism, viewing each person as an economic agent acting in his or her own best interest. Suppose that object j has a price p_j and that the person who receives the object must pay the price p_j. Then the net value of object j for person i is $a_{ij} - p_j$, and each person i will logically want to be assigned to an object j_i with maximal value, that is, with

$$a_{ij_i} - p_{j_i} = \max_{j \in A(i)} \{a_{ij} - p_j\}, \tag{2.8}$$

where

$$A(i) = \{j \mid (i,j) \in \mathcal{A}\}$$

is the set of objects that can be assigned to person i. When this condition holds for all persons i, we say that the assignment and the set of prices satisfy *complementary slackness* (CS for short); the name comes from standard linear programming terminology. The economic system is then at equilibrium, in the sense that no person would have an incentive to unilaterally seek another object. Such equilibrium conditions are naturally of great interest to economists, but there is also a fundamental relation with the assignment problem. We have the following proposition.

Proposition 2.4:   If a feasible assignment and a set of prices satisfy the complementary slackness conditions (2.8) for all persons i, then the assignment is optimal and the prices are an optimal solution of the following problem

$$\min_{\substack{p_j \\ j=1,\dots,n}} \left\{ \sum_{i=1}^{n} \max_{j \in A(i)} \{a_{ij} - p_j\} + \sum_{j=1}^{n} p_j \right\}, \tag{2.9}$$

called the *dual problem*. Furthermore, the benefit of the optimal assignment and the optimal cost of the dual problem are equal.

Proof: The total cost of any feasible assignment $\{(i, k_i) \mid i = 1, \dots, n\}$ satisfies

$$\sum_{i=1}^{n} a_{ik_i} \le \sum_{i=1}^{n} \max_{j \in A(i)} \{a_{ij} - p_j\} + \sum_{j=1}^{n} p_j, \tag{2.10}$$

for any set of prices $\{p_j \mid j = 1, \dots, n\}$, since the first term of the right-hand side is no less than

$$\sum_{i=1}^{n} (a_{ik_i} - p_{k_i}),$$

while the second term is equal to $\sum_{i=1}^{n} p_{k_i}$. On the other hand, the given assignment and set of prices, denoted by $\{(i, j_i) \mid i = 1, \ldots, n\}$ and $\{\bar{p}_j \mid j = 1, \ldots, n\}$, respectively, satisfy the CS conditions, so we have

$$a_{ij_i} - \bar{p}_{j_i} = \max_{j \in A(i)} \{a_{ij} - \bar{p}_j\}, \qquad i = 1, \ldots, n.$$

By adding this relation over all i, we see that

$$\sum_{i=1}^{n} a_{ij_i} = \sum_{i=1}^{n} \left(\max_{j \in A(i)} \{a_{ij} - \bar{p}_j\} + \bar{p}_{j_i} \right).$$

Therefore, the assignment $\{(i, j_i) \mid i = 1, \ldots, n\}$ attains the maximum of the left-hand side of Eq. (2.10) and is optimal for the primal problem, while $\{\bar{p}_j \mid j = 1, \ldots, n\}$ attains the minimum of the right-hand side of Eq. (2.10) and is optimal for the dual problem. Furthermore, the two optimal values are equal.   **Q.E.D.**

Duality for the Minimum Cost Flow Problem

Consider now the minimum cost flow problem, which in a duality context will also be referred to as the *primal problem*. To develop duality theory for this problem, we introduce a price vector $p = \{p_j \mid j \in \mathcal{N}\}$, and we say that a flow-price vector pair (x, p) satisfies *complementary slackness (or CS for short)* if x is capacity-feasible and

$$p_i - p_j \leq a_{ij} \qquad \text{for all } (i, j) \in \mathcal{A} \text{ with } x_{ij} < c_{ij}, \tag{2.11a}$$

$$p_i - p_j \geq a_{ij} \qquad \text{for all } (i, j) \in \mathcal{A} \text{ with } b_{ij} < x_{ij}. \tag{2.11b}$$

The above conditions also imply that we must have

$$p_i = a_{ij} + p_j \qquad \text{for all } (i, j) \in \mathcal{A} \text{ with } b_{ij} < x_{ij} < c_{ij}. \quad .$$

An equivalent way to write the CS conditions is that, for all arcs (i, j), we have $b_{ij} \leq x_{ij} \leq c_{ij}$ and

$$x_{ij} = \begin{cases} c_{ij} & \text{if } p_i > a_{ij} + p_j \\ b_{ij} & \text{if } p_i < a_{ij} + p_j. \end{cases}$$

The above definition of CS and the subsequent proposition are also valid for the variations of the minimum cost flow problem where $b_{ij} = -\infty$ and/or $c_{ij} = \infty$ for some arcs (i, j). In particular, in the case where in place of the capacity constraints $b_{ij} \le x_{ij} \le c_{ij}$ there are only nonnegativity constraints $0 \le x_{ij}$, the CS conditions take the form

$$p_i - p_j \le a_{ij}, \qquad \forall\ (i,j) \in \mathcal{A}, \tag{2.11c}$$

$$p_i - p_j = a_{ij} \qquad \text{for all } (i,j) \in \mathcal{A} \text{ with } 0 < x_{ij}. \tag{2.11d}$$

The dual problem is obtained by a procedure which is standard in duality theory. We view p_i as a Lagrange multiplier associated with the conservation of flow constraint for node i and we form the corresponding Lagrangian function

$$L(x,p) = \sum_{(i,j)\in\mathcal{A}} a_{ij}x_{ij} + \sum_{i\in\mathcal{N}} \left(s_i - \sum_{\{j|(i,j)\in\mathcal{A}\}} x_{ij} + \sum_{\{j|(j,i)\in\mathcal{A}\}} x_{ji} \right) p_i$$

$$= \sum_{(i,j)\in\mathcal{A}} (a_{ij} + p_j - p_i)x_{ij} + \sum_{i\in\mathcal{N}} s_i p_i. \tag{2.12}$$

Then the dual function value $q(p)$ at a vector p is obtained by minimizing $L(x,p)$ over all capacity-feasible flows x,

$$q(p) = \min_x \bigl\{ L(x,p) \mid b_{ij} \le x_{ij} \le c_{ij}, (i,j) \in \mathcal{A} \bigr\}. \tag{2.13}$$

Because the Lagrangian function $L(x,p)$ is separable in the arc flows x_{ij}, its minimization decomposes into A separate minimizations, one for each arc (i,j). Each of these minimizations can be carried out in closed form, yielding

$$q(p) = \sum_{(i,j)\in\mathcal{A}} q_{ij}(p_i - p_j) + \sum_{i\in\mathcal{N}} s_i p_i, \tag{2.14a}$$

where

$$q_{ij}(p_i - p_j) = \min_{x_{ij}} \bigl\{ (a_{ij} + p_j - p_i)x_{ij} \mid b_{ij} \le x_{ij} \le c_{ij} \bigr\}$$

$$= \begin{cases} (a_{ij} + p_j - p_i)b_{ij} & \text{if } p_i \le a_{ij} + p_j \\ (a_{ij} + p_j - p_i)c_{ij} & \text{if } p_i > a_{ij} + p_j. \end{cases} \tag{2.14b}$$

The dual problem is

$$\begin{aligned} &\text{maximize } q(p) \\ &\text{subject to no constraint on } p, \end{aligned} \tag{2.15}$$

with the dual functional q given by Eq. (2.14).

Figure 2.7 illustrates the form of the functions q_{ij}. Since each of these functions is piecewise linear, the dual function q is also piecewise linear. The dual function also has some additional interesting structure. In particular, suppose that all node prices are changed by the same amount. Then the values of the functions q_{ij} do not change, since these functions depend on the price differences $p_i - p_j$. If in addition we have $\sum_{i \in \mathcal{N}} s_i = 0$, as we must if the problem is feasible, we see that the term $\sum_{i \in \mathcal{N}} s_i p_i$ also does not change. Thus, the dual function value does not change when all node prices are changed by the same amount, implying that the equal cost surfaces of the dual cost function are unbounded. Figure 2.8 illustrates the dual function for a simple example.

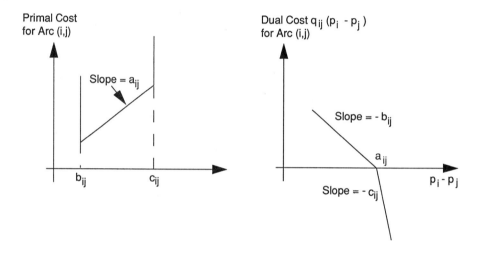

Figure 2.7 Form of the dual cost function q_{ij} for arc (i, j).

The following proposition is basic.

Proposition 2.5: If a feasible flow vector x^* and a price vector p^* satisfy the complementary slackness conditions (2.11a) and (2.11b), then x^* is an optimal primal solution and p^* is an optimal dual solution. Furthermore, the optimal primal cost and the optimal dual cost are equal.

Proof: We first show that for any feasible flow vector x and any price vector p, the primal cost of x is no less than the dual cost of p.

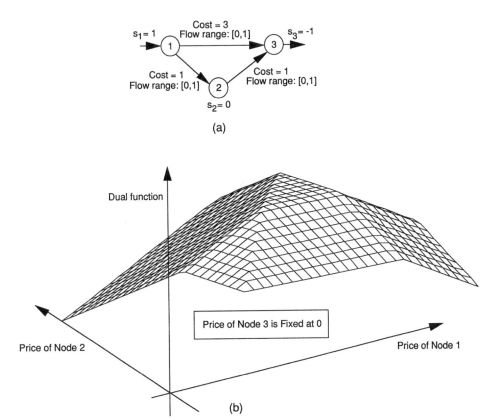

Figure 2.8   Form of the dual cost function q for the 3-node problem in (a). The optimal flow is $x_{12} = 1$, $x_{23} = 1$, $x_{13} = 0$. The dual function is

$$q(p_1, p_2, p_3) = \min\{0, 1 + p_2 - p_1\} + \min\{0, 1 + p_3 - p_2\}$$
$$+ \min\{0, 3 + p_3 - p_1\} + p_1 - p_3.$$

Diagram (b) shows the graph of the dual function in the space of p_1 and p_2, with p_3 fixed at 0. For a different value of p_3, say γ, the graph is "translated" by the vector (γ, γ); that is, we have $q(p_1, p_2, 0) = q(p_1 + \gamma, p_2 + \gamma, \gamma)$ for all (p_1, p_2). The dual function is maximized at the vectors p that satisfy CS together with the optimal x. These are the vectors of the form $(p_1 + \gamma, p_2 + \gamma, \gamma)$, where

$$1 \leq p_1 - p_2, \qquad p_1 \leq 3, \qquad 1 \leq p_2.$$

Indeed, we have

$$q(p) \leq L(x,p)$$

$$= \sum_{(i,j)\in\mathcal{A}} a_{ij}x_{ij} + \sum_{i\in\mathcal{N}} \left(s_i - \sum_{\{j|(i,j)\in\mathcal{A}\}} x_{ij} + \sum_{\{j|(j,i)\in\mathcal{A}\}} x_{ji} \right) p_i \qquad (2.16)$$

$$= \sum_{(i,j)\in\mathcal{A}} a_{ij}x_{ij},$$

where the last equality follows from the feasibility of x. On the other hand, we have by the definition (2.13) of q

$$q(p^*) = \min_x \left\{ L(x,p^*) \mid b_{ij} \leq x_{ij} \leq c_{ij}, (i,j) \in \mathcal{A} \right\} = L(x^*,p^*) = \sum_{(i,j)\in\mathcal{A}} a_{ij}x_{ij}^*,$$

where the second equality is true because

(x^*, p^*) satisfies CS if and only if

$$x_{ij}^* \text{ minimizes } (a_{ij} + p_j^* - p_i^*)x_{ij} \text{ over all } x_{ij} \in [b_{ij}, c_{ij}], \ \forall \ (i,j) \in \mathcal{A},$$

and the last equality follows from the Lagrangian expression (2.12) and the feasibility of x^*. Therefore, x^* attains the minimum of the primal cost on the right-hand side of Eq. (2.16), and p^* attains the maximum of $q(p)$ on the left-hand side of Eq. (2.16), while the optimal primal and dual values are equal. **Q.E.D.**

     There are also several other important duality results. In particular:

(a) The converse of the preceding proposition can be shown. That is, if x^* and p^* are optimal flow and price vectors for the minimum cost flow problem, and its dual problem, respectively, then x^* must be feasible and together with p^* it must satisfy CS.

(b) If the minimum cost flow problem (with upper and lower bounds on the arc flows) is feasible, then it can be shown that optimal primal and dual solutions x^* and p^* with equal cost exist. If the problem data (a_{ij}, b_{ij}, c_{ij}, and s_i) are integer, then these optimal solutions can be taken to be integer. [If some of the arc flows have no upper bound constraints the situation is somewhat more complicated, because it is possible that there exist feasible flow vectors of arbitrarily small (i.e., large negative) cost; such a problem will be called *unbounded* in Chapter 2. Barring this possibility, the existence of primal and dual optimal solutions with equal cost will be shown in Section 2.2.]

We will prove these results constructively in Chapter 2 (see Prop. 2.3 in Section 2.2 and Prop. 3.2 in Section 2.3) by deriving algorithms that obtain primal and dual optimal solutions, which are integer if the problem data are integer.

Interpretation of Complementary Slackness and the Dual Problem

As in the case of the assignment problem, the CS conditions have an economic interpretation. In particular, think of each node i as choosing the flow x_{ij} of each of its outgoing arcs (i, j) from the range $[b_{ij}, c_{ij}]$, on the basis of the following economic considerations: For each unit of the flow x_{ij} that node i sends to node j along arc (i, j), node i must pay a transportation cost a_{ij} plus a storage cost p_j at node j; for each unit of the residual flow $c_{ij} - x_{ij}$ that node i does not send to j, node i must pay a storage cost p_i. Thus, the total cost to node j is

$$(a_{ij} + p_j)x_{ij} + (c_{ij} - x_{ij})p_i.$$

It can be seen that the CS conditions (2.11) are equivalent to requiring that node i act in its own best interest by selecting the flow that minimizes the corresponding costs for each of its outgoing arcs (i, j); that is,

(x, p) satisfies CS if and only if

$$x_{ij} \text{ minimizes } (a_{ij} + p_j - p_i)z_{ij} \text{ over all } z_{ij} \in [b_{ij}, c_{ij}], \ \forall \ (i,j) \in \mathcal{A}.$$

To interpret the dual function $q(p)$, we continue to view a_{ij} and p_i as transportation and storage costs, respectively. Then, for a given price vector p and supply vector s, the dual function

$$q(p) = \min_{\substack{b_{ij} \le x_{ij} \le c_{ij}, \\ (i,j) \in \mathcal{A}}} \left\{ \sum_{(i,j) \in \mathcal{A}} a_{ij}x_{ij} + \sum_{i \in \mathcal{N}} \left(s_i - \sum_{\{j \mid (i,j) \in \mathcal{A}\}} x_{ij} + \sum_{\{j \mid (j,i) \in \mathcal{A}\}} x_{ji} \right) p_i \right\}$$

is the minimum total transportation and storage cost to be incurred by the nodes, by choosing flows that satisfy the capacity constraints.

Suppose now that we introduce an organization that sets the node prices and collects the transportation and storage costs from the nodes. We see that if the organization wants to maximize its total revenue (given that the nodes will act in their own best interest), it must choose prices that solve the dual problem optimally.

Finally, we provide in Fig. 2.9, a geometric view of the relation between the primal and the dual problem. This geometric interpretation is directed toward the advanced reader and will not be needed in what follows. It demonstrates why the cost of any feasible flow vector is no less than the dual cost of any price vector, and why the optimal primal and dual costs are equal.

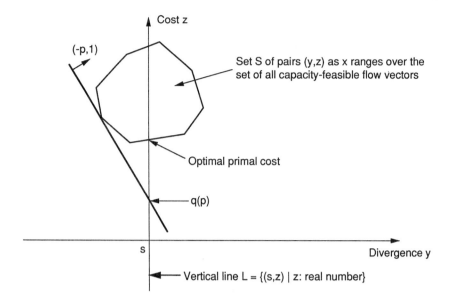

Figure 2.9   Geometric interpretation of duality for the reader who is familiar with the notion and the properties of hyperplanes in a vector space. Consider the (polyhedral) set S consisting of all pairs (y, z), where y is the divergence vector corresponding to x and z is the cost of x, as x ranges over all capacity-feasible flow vectors. Then feasible flow vectors correspond to common points of S and the vertical line

$$L = \{(s, z) \mid z : \text{ real number}\}.$$

The optimal primal cost corresponds to the lowest common point.

On the other hand, for a given price vector p, the dual cost $q(p)$ can be expressed as [cf. Eq. (2.13)]

$$q(p) = \min_{x: \text{ capacity feasible}} L(x, p) = \min_{(y,z) \in S} \left\{ z - \sum_{i \in \mathcal{N}} y_i p_i \right\} + \sum_{i \in \mathcal{N}} s_i p_i.$$

Based on this expression, it can be seen that $q(p)$ corresponds to the intersection point of the vertical line L with the hyperplane

$$\left\{ (y, z) \,\middle|\, z - \sum_{i \in \mathcal{N}} y_i p_i = q(p) - \sum_{i \in \mathcal{N}} s_i p_i \right\},$$

which supports from below the set S, and is normal to the vector $(-p, 1)$. The dual problem is to find a price vector p for which the intersection point is as high as possible. The figure illustrates the equality of the lowest common point of S and L (optimal primal cost), and the highest point of intersection of L by a hyperplane that supports S from below (optimal dual cost).

Dual Cost Improvement Algorithms

In analogy with primal cost improvement algorithms, one may start with a price vector and try to successively obtain new price vectors with improved dual cost. The major algorithms of this type involve price changes along a particular type of directions, known as *elementary*. Such directions are of the form $d = (d_1, \ldots, d_N)$, where

$$d_i = \begin{cases} 1 & \text{if } i \in \mathcal{S} \\ 0 & \text{if } i \notin \mathcal{S}, \end{cases}$$

where $\mathcal{S}$ is a connected subset of nodes. Different algorithms correspond to different methods for determining the node set $\mathcal{S}$. Given an elementary direction of cost improvement and a corresponding set $\mathcal{S}$, the prices are iterated according to

$$p_i := \begin{cases} p_i + \gamma & \text{if } i \in \mathcal{S} \\ p_i & \text{if } i \notin \mathcal{S}, \end{cases}$$

where γ is some positive scalar that is small enough to ensure that the new price vector has an improved dual cost.

The existence of at least one elementary direction of improvement at a nonoptimal price vector will be shown in Chapter 3. This is an important and remarkable result, which may be viewed as a dual version of the result of Prop. 2.1 (at a nonoptimal flow vector, there exists at least one unblocked simple cycle with negative cost). In fact both results are special cases of a more general theorem concerning elementary vectors of subspaces, which is central in the theory of *monotropic programming*; see [Roc70], [Roc84].

Most dual cost improvement methods, simultaneously with changing p along a direction of dual cost improvement, also iterate on a flow vector x satisfying CS together with p. They terminate when x becomes feasible, at which time, by Prop. 2.5, the pair (x, p) must consist of a primal and a dual optimal solution.

In Chapter 3 we will discuss two main methods that select elementary directions of dual cost improvement in different ways:

(a) In the *primal-dual method*, the elementary direction has a *steepest ascent property*, that is, it provides the maximal rate of improvement of the dual cost per unit change in the price vector.

(b) In the *relaxation (or coordinate ascent) method*, the elementary direction is computed so that it has a small number of nonzero elements (i.e., the set $\mathcal{S}$ has few nodes). Such a direction may not be optimal in terms of rate of dual cost improvement, but can typically be computed much faster than the steepest ascent direction. Often the elementary direction has only one nonzero element, in which case only one node price coordinate is changed; this motivates the name "coordinate ascent." Note, however, that coordinate ascent directions cannot be used exclusively to improve the dual cost, as is shown in Fig. 2.10.

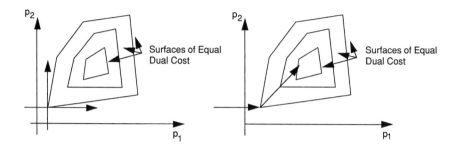

Figure 2.10 (a) The difficulty with using coordinate ascent iterations exclusively. The dual cost is piecewise linear, so at some corner points it may be impossible to improve the dual cost by changing any *single* price coordinate. (b) A dual cost improvement is possible by changing several price coordinates by equal amounts, which corresponds to an elementary direction.

As will be shown in Chapter 3, both the primal-dual method and the relaxation method terminate if the problem data are integer. Furthermore, simultaneously with an optimal price vector, they provide an optimal flow vector.

1.2.4   Auction

Our third type of algorithm represents a significant departure from the cost improvement idea; at any one iteration, it may deteriorate both the primal and the dual cost, although in the end it does find an optimal primal solution. It is based on an approximate version of complementary slackness, called ϵ-*complementary slackness*, and while it implicitly tries to solve a dual problem, it actually attains a dual solution that is not quite optimal. This subsection introduces the main ideas underlying auction algorithms. Chapter 4 provides a more complete discussion.

Naive Auction

Let us return to the assignment problem and consider a natural process for finding an equilibrium assignment and price vector. We will call this process the *naive auction algorithm*, because it has a serious flaw, as will be seen shortly. Nonetheless, this flaw will help motivate a more sophisticated and correct algorithm.

The naive auction algorithm proceeds in iterations and generates a sequence of price vectors and partial assignments. By a *partial assignment* we mean an assignment where only a subset of the persons have been matched with objects. A partial assignment should be contrasted with a feasible or complete assignment where all the persons have been matched with objects on a one-to-one basis. At the beginning of each iteration, the CS condition [cf. Eq. (2.8)]

$$a_{ij_i} - p_{j_i} = \max_{j \in A(i)} \{a_{ij} - p_j\}$$

is satisfied for all pairs (i, j_i) of the partial assignment. If all persons are assigned, the algorithm terminates. Otherwise some person who is unassigned, say i, is selected. This person finds an object j_i which offers maximal value, that is,

$$j_i = \arg \max_{j \in A(i)} \{a_{ij} - p_j\}, \tag{2.17}$$

and then:

(a) Gets assigned to the best object j_i; the person who was assigned to j_i at the beginning of the iteration (if any) becomes unassigned.

(b) Sets the price of j_i to the level at which he or she is indifferent between j_i and the second best object, that is, he or she sets p_{j_i} to

$$p_{j_i} + \gamma_i, \tag{2.18}$$

where

$$\gamma_i = v_i - w_i, \tag{2.19}$$

v_i is the best object value,

$$v_i = \max_{j \in A(i)} \{a_{ij} - p_j\}, \tag{2.20}$$

and w_i is the second best object value,

$$w_i = \max_{j \in A(i), j \neq j_i} \{a_{ij} - p_j\}. \tag{2.21}$$

(Note that as p_{j_i} is increased, the value $a_{ij_i} - p_{j_i}$ offered by object j_i to person i is decreased. γ_i is the largest increment by which p_{j_i} can be increased, while maintaining the property that j_i offers maximal value to i.)

This process is repeated in a sequence of iterations until each person has an assigned object.

We may view this process as an auction where at each iteration the bidder i raises the price of a preferred object by the *bidding increment* γ_i. Note that γ_i cannot be negative, since $v_i \geq w_i$ [compare Eqs. (2.20) and (2.21)], so the object prices tend to increase. The choice γ_i is illustrated in Fig. 2.11. Just as in a real auction, bidding increments and price increases spur competition by making the bidder's own preferred object less attractive to other potential bidders.

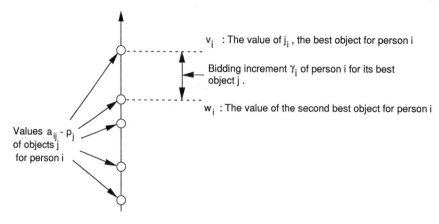

Figure 2.11   In the naive auction algorithm, even after the price of the best object j_i is increased by the bidding increment γ_i, j_i continues to be the best object for the bidder i, so CS is satisfied at the end of the iteration. However, $\gamma_i = 0$ if there is a tie between two or more objects that are most preferred by i.

ϵ-Complementary Slackness

Unfortunately, the naive auction algorithm does not always work (although it is an excellent initialization procedure for other methods, such as primal-dual or relaxation, and it is useful in other specialized contexts; see Section 4.3). The difficulty is that the bidding increment γ_i is zero when two or more objects offer maximum value for the bidder i. As a result, a situation may be created where several persons contest a smaller number of equally desirable objects without raising their prices, thereby creating a never ending cycle; see Fig. 2.12.

To break such cycles, we introduce a perturbation mechanism, motivated by real auctions where each bid for an object must raise its price by a minimum positive increment, and bidders must on occasion take risks to win their preferred objects. In particular, let us fix a positive scalar ϵ, and say that a partial assignment and a price vector p satisfy ϵ-*complementary slackness (ϵ-CS for short)* if

$$a_{ij} - p_j \geq \max_{k \in A(i)} \{a_{ik} - p_k\} - \epsilon \qquad (2.22)$$

for all assigned pairs (i, j). In words, to satisfy ϵ-CS, all assigned persons of the partial assignment must be assigned to objects that are within ϵ of being best.

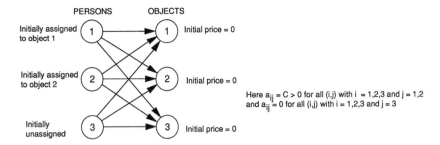

At Start of Iteration #	Object Prices	Assigned Pairs	Bidder	Preferred Object	Bidding Increment
1	0,0,0	(1,1), (2,2)	3	2	0
2	0,0,0	(1,1), (3,2)	2	2	0
3	0,0,0	(1,1), (2,2)	3	2	0

Figure 2.12 Illustration of how the naive auction algorithm may never terminate for a problem involving three persons and three objects. Here objects 1 and 2 offer benefit $C > 0$ to all persons, and object 3 offers benefit 0 to all persons. The algorithm cycles as persons 2 and 3 alternately bid for object 2 without changing its price because they prefer equally object 1 and object 2 ($\gamma_i = 0$; compare Fig. 2.11).

The Auction Algorithm

We now reformulate the previous auction process so that the bidding increment is always at least equal to ϵ. The resulting method, the *auction algorithm*, is the same as the naive auction algorithm, except that the bidding increment γ_i is

$$\gamma_i = v_i - w_i + \epsilon \tag{2.23}$$

rather than $\gamma_i = v_i - w_i$ as in Eq. (2.19). With this choice, the ϵ-CS condition is satisfied, as illustrated in Fig. 2.13. The particular increment $\gamma_i = v_i - w_i + \epsilon$ used in the auction algorithm is the maximum amount with this property. Smaller increments γ_i would also work as long as $\gamma_i \geq \epsilon$, but using the largest possible increment accelerates the algorithm. This is consistent with experience from real auctions, which tend to terminate faster when the bidding is aggressive.

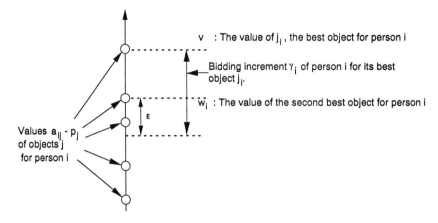

Figure 2.13   In the auction algorithm, even after the price of the preferred object j_i is increased by the bidding increment γ_i , j_i will be within ϵ of being most preferred, so the ϵ-CS condition holds at the end of the iteration.

It can be shown that this reformulated auction process terminates, necessarily with a feasible assignment and a set of prices that satisfy ϵ-CS. To get a sense of this, note that if an object receives a bid at m iterations, its price must exceed its initial price by at least $m\epsilon$. Thus, for sufficiently large m, the object will become "expensive" enough to be judged "inferior" to some object that has not received a bid so far. It follows that only for a limited number of iterations can an object receive a bid while some other object still has not yet received any bid. On the other hand, once every object has received at least one bid, the auction terminates. (This argument assumes that any person can bid for any object, but it can be generalized to the case where the set of feasible person-object pairs is limited, as long as at least one feasible assignment exists; see Prop. 1.2 in Section 4.1.) Figure 2.14 shows how the auction algorithm, based on the bidding increment $\gamma_i = v_i - w_i + \epsilon$ [see Eq. (2.23)], overcomes the cycling problem of the example of Fig. 2.12.

When the auction algorithm terminates, we have an assignment satisfying ϵ-CS, but is this assignment optimal? The answer depends strongly on the size of ϵ. In a real auction, a prudent bidder would not place an excessively high bid for fear of winning the object at an unnecessarily high price. Consistent with this intuition, we can show that if ϵ is small, then the final assignment will be "almost optimal." In particular, we will show that *the total benefit of the final assignment is within $n\epsilon$ of being optimal*. The idea is that a feasible assignment and a set of prices satisfying ϵ-CS may be viewed as satisfying CS for a *slightly different* problem, where all benefits a_{ij} are the same as before except the benefits of the n assigned pairs, which are modified by no more than ϵ.

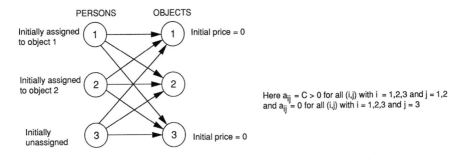

At Start of Iteration #	Object Prices	Assigned Pairs	Bidder	Preferred Object	Bidding Increment
1	0,0,0	(1,1), (2,2)	3	2	ϵ
2	0,ϵ,0	(1,1), (3,2)	2	1	2ϵ
3	2ϵ,ϵ,0	(2,1), (3,2)	1	2	2ϵ
4	2ϵ,3ϵ,0	(1,2), (2,1)	3	1	2ϵ
5	4ϵ,3ϵ,0	(1,2), (3,1)	2	2	2ϵ
6	...	...	...	...	...

Figure 2.14   Illustration of how the auction algorithm overcomes the cycling problem for the example of Fig. 2.12 by making the bidding increment at least ϵ. The table shows one possible sequence of bids and assignments generated by the auction algorithm, starting with all prices equal to 0 and with the partial assignment $\{(1,1),(2,2)\}$. At each iteration except the last, the person assigned to object 3 bids for either object 1 or 2, increasing its price by ϵ in the first iteration and by 2ϵ in each subsequent iteration. In the last iteration, after the prices of 1 and 2 reach or exceed C, object 3 receives a bid and the auction terminates.

Proposition 2.6:   A feasible assignment, which satisfies ϵ-complementary slackness together with some price vector, is within $n\epsilon$ of being optimal. Furthermore, the price vector is within $n\epsilon$ of being an optimal solution of the dual problem.

Proof: Let A^* be the optimal total assignment benefit

$$A^* = \max_{\substack{k_i, i=1,\ldots,n \\ k_i \neq k_m \text{ if } i\neq m}} \sum_{i=1}^{n} a_{ik_i}$$

and let D^* be the optimal dual cost

$$D^* = \min_{\substack{p_j \\ j=1,\ldots,n}} \left\{ \sum_{i=1}^{n} \max_{j\in A(i)} \{a_{ij} - p_j\} + \sum_{j=1}^{n} p_j \right\}.$$

If $\{(i, j_i) \mid i = 1, \ldots, n\}$ is the given assignment satisfying the ϵ-CS condition together with a price vector $\bar{p}$, we have

$$\max_{j\in A(i)} \{a_{ij} - \bar{p}_j\} - \epsilon \leq a_{ij_i} - \bar{p}_{j_i}.$$

By adding this relation over all i, we see that

$$D^* \leq \sum_{i=1}^{n} \left(\max_{j\in A(i)} \{a_{ij} - \bar{p}_j\} + \bar{p}_{j_i} \right) \leq \sum_{i=1}^{n} a_{ij_i} + n\epsilon \leq A^* + n\epsilon.$$

Since we showed in Prop. 2.4 that $A^* = D^*$, it follows that the total assignment benefit $\sum_{i=1}^{n} a_{ij_i}$ is within $n\epsilon$ of the optimal value A^*, while the dual cost of $\bar{p}$ is within $n\epsilon$ of the optimal dual cost.   **Q.E.D.**

Suppose now that the benefits a_{ij} are all integer, which is the typical practical case. (If a_{ij} are rational numbers, they can be scaled up to integer by multiplication with a suitable common number.) Then the total benefit of any assignment is integer, so if $n\epsilon < 1$, any complete assignment that is within $n\epsilon$ of being optimal must be optimal. It follows that *if*

$$\epsilon < \frac{1}{n}$$

and the benefits a_{ij} are all integer, then the assignment obtained upon termination of the auction algorithm is optimal.

Figure 2.15 shows the sequence of generated object prices for the example of Fig. 2.14 in relation to the contours of the dual cost function. It can be seen from this figure that each bid has the effect of setting the price of the object receiving the bid nearly equal (within ϵ) to the price that minimizes the dual cost with respect to that price, with all other prices held fixed (this will be shown rigorously in Secton 4.1). Successive minimization of a cost function along single coordinates is a central feature of coordinate descent and relaxation methods, which are popular for unconstrained minimization of smooth functions and for solving systems of smooth equations. Thus, the auction algorithm can be interpreted as an approximate coordinate descent method; as such, it is related to the relaxation method discussed in the previous subsection.

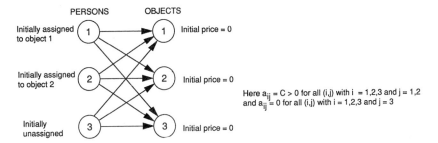

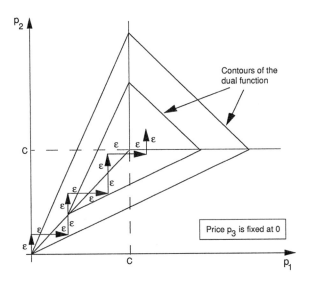

Figure 2.15   A sequence of prices p_1 and p_2 generated by the auction algorithm for the example of Figs. 2.12 and 2.14. The figure shows the equal dual cost surfaces in the space of p_1 and p_2 with p_3 fixed at 0.

Scaling

Figure 2.15 also illustrates a generic feature of auction algorithms. The amount of work needed to solve the problem can depend strongly on the value of ϵ and on the maximum absolute object benefit

$$C = \max_{(i,j)\in\mathcal{A}} |a_{ij}|.$$

Basically, for many types of problems, the number of iterations up to termination tends to be proportional to C/ϵ. This can be seen from the figure, where the total number of iterations is roughly C/ϵ, starting from zero initial prices.

Note also that there is a dependence on the initial prices; if these prices are "near optimal," we expect that the number of iterations needed to solve the problem will be relatively small. This can be seen from the figure; if the initial prices satisfy $p_1 \approx p_3 + C$ and $p_2 \approx p_3 + C$, the number of iterations up to termination is quite small.

The preceding observations suggest the idea of ϵ-*scaling*, which consists of applying the algorithm several times, starting with a large value of ϵ and successively reducing ϵ until it is less than some critical value (for example, $1/n$, when a_{ij} are integer). Each application of the algorithm provides good initial prices for the next application. This is a common idea in nonlinear programming; it is encountered, for example, in barrier and penalty function methods; see e.g. [Ber82a], [Lue84]. An alternative form of scaling, called *cost scaling*, is based on successively representing a_{ij} with an increasing number of bits while keeping ϵ at a constant value.

In practice, scaling is typically beneficial, particularly for sparse assignment problems, that is, problems where the set of feasible assignment pairs is severely restricted.

Extension to the Minimum Cost Flow Problem

The ϵ-CS condition (2.22) can be generalized for the minimum cost flow problem. For a capacity-feasible flow vector x and a price vector p it takes the form

$$p_i - p_j \leq a_{ij} + \epsilon \qquad \text{for all } (i,j) \in \mathcal{A} \text{ with } x_{ij} < c_{ij}, \qquad (2.24a)$$

$$p_i - p_j \geq a_{ij} - \epsilon \qquad \text{for all } (i,j) \in \mathcal{A} \text{ with } b_{ij} < x_{ij}, \qquad (2.24b)$$

[cf. Eq. (2.11)]. It will be shown in Section 4.1 (Prop. 4.1) that if the problem data are integer, if $\epsilon < 1/N$, where N is the number of nodes, and if x is feasible and satisfies the ϵ-CS condition (2.24) together with some p, then x is optimal.

The auction algorithm can also be generalized for the minimum cost flow problem; see Chapter 4. A broad generalization, called *generic auction algorithm*, is given in Section 4.4. It involves price increases and flow changes that preserve ϵ-CS. An interesting special case of the generic algorithm, called ϵ-*relaxation*, is discussed in Section 4.5. This algorithm may also be obtained by using the transformation of Section 1.1.3 to convert the minimum cost flow problem into an assignment problem and by applying the auction algorithm to this problem. We may view ϵ-relaxation as an approximate coordinate ascent method for maximizing the piecewise linear dual cost function (2.14) introduced in the preceding subsection; see Section 4.5.

1.2.5   Good, Bad, and Polynomial Algorithms

We have already discussed several types of methods, so the natural question arises: is there a best method and what criterion should we use to rank methods?

A practitioner who has a specific type of problem to solve, perhaps repeatedly, with the data and size of the problem within some limited range, will usually be interested in one or more of the following:

(a) Fast solution time.

(b) Flexibility to use good starting solutions (which the practitioner can usually provide, on the basis of his or her knowledge of the problem).

(c) The ability to perform sensitivity analysis (resolve the problem with slightly different problem data) quickly.

(d) The ability to take advantage of parallel computing hardware.

(e) Small memory requirements (this seems to be a diminishing concern nowadays).

Given the diversity of these considerations, it is not surprising that there is no algorithm that will dominate the others in all or even most practical situations. Otherwise expressed, every type of algorithm that we will discuss is best given the right type of practical problem. Thus, to make intelligent choices, the practitioner needs to understand the properties of different algorithms relating to speed of convergence, flexibility, parallelization, and suitability for specific problem structures. For challenging problems, the choice of algorithm is usually settled by experimentation with several candidates.

A theoretical analyst may also have difficulty ranking different algorithms for specific types of problems. The most common approach for this purpose is worst-case computational complexity analysis. Here one tries to bound the number of elementary numerical operations needed by a given algorithm with some measure of the "problem size," that is, with some expression of the form

$$Kf(N, A, C, U, S), \tag{2.25}$$

where

N is the number of nodes.

A is the number of arcs.

C is the arc cost range $\max_{(i,j)\in\mathcal{A}} |a_{ij}|$.

U is the maximum arc flow range $\max_{(i,j)\in\mathcal{A}}(c_{ij} - b_{ij})$.

S is the supply range $\max_{i\in\mathcal{N}} |s_i|$.

f is some known function.

K is a (usually unknown) constant.

If a bound of this form can be found, we say that the *running time* or *operation count of the algorithm is* $O\big(f(N, A, C, U, S)\big)$. If $f(N, A, C, U, S)$ can be written as a polynomial function of the number of bits needed to express the problem data, the algorithm is said to be *polynomial*. Examples of polynomial complexity bounds are $O\big(N^\alpha A^\beta\big)$ and $O\big(N^\alpha A^\beta \log C\big)$, where α and β are positive integers. The bound $O\big(N^\alpha A^\beta\big)$ is sometimes said to be *strongly polynomial* because it involves only the graph size parameters. A bound of the form $O\big(N^\alpha A^\beta C\big)$ is not polynomial because C is not a polynomial expression of $\log C$, the number of bits needed to express a single number of value C. Bounds like $O\big(N^\alpha A^\beta C\big)$, which are polynomial in the problem data rather than in the number of bits needed to express the data, are called *pseudopolynomial*.

A common assumption in theoretical computer science is that polynomial algorithms are "better" than pseudopolynomial, and pseudopolynomial algorithms are "better" than exponential (for example, those with a bound of the form $K2^{g(N,A)}$, where g is a polynomial in N and A). Furthermore, it is thought that two polynomial algorithms can be compared in terms of the degree of the polynomial bound; e.g., an $O(N^2)$ algorithm is "better" than an $O(N^3)$ algorithm. Unfortunately, quite often this assumption is not supported by computational practice in linear programming and network optimization. Pseudopolynomial and even exponential algorithms are often faster in practice than polynomial ones. In fact, the simplex method for general linear programs is an exponential algorithm [KlM72], [Chv83], and yet it is still used widely, because it performs very well in practice.

There are two main reasons why worst-case complexity estimates may fail to predict the practical performance of network flow algorithms. First, the upper bounds they provide may be very pessimistic as they may correspond to possible but highly unlikely problem instances. (Average complexity estimates would be more appropriate for such situations. However, obtaining these is usually hard, and the statistical assumptions underlying them may be inappropriate for many types of practical problems.) Second, worst-case complexity estimates involve the (usually unknown) constant K, which may dominate the estimate for all except for unrealistically large problem sizes. Thus, a comparison between two algorithms that is based on the size-dependent terms of running time estimates, and does not take into account the corresponding constants may be far from the mark.

This book is guided more by insights obtained through computational practice than by insights gained by estimating computational complexity. However, this is not to suggest that worst-case complexity analysis is useless; for all its unreliability, it has repeatedly proved its value by illuminating the computational bottlenecks of many algorithms and by stimulating the use of efficient data structures. For this reason, throughout the book, we will comment on available complexity estimates, and we will try to relate these estimates to computational practice. However, the treatment of complexity bounds is brief, and most of the corresponding proofs are omitted.

E X E R C I S E S

Exercise 2.1

Solve the max-flow problem of Fig. 2.16 using the Ford-Fulkerson method, where $s = 1$ and $t = 5$.

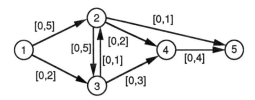

Figure 2.16   Max-flow problem for Exercise 2.1. The arc capacities are shown next to the arcs.

Exercise 2.2

Use ϵ-CS to verify that the assignment of Fig. 2.17 is optimal and obtain a bound on how far from optimal the given price vector is. State the dual problem and verify the correctness of the bound by comparing the dual value of the price vector with the optimal dual value.

Exercise 2.3

Consider the assignment problem.

(a) Show that every k-person swap can be accomplished with a sequence of $k - 1$ successive two-person swaps.

(b) In light of the result of part (a), how do you explain that a nonoptimal assignment may not be improvable by any two-person swap?

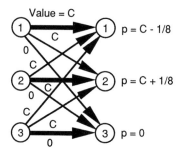

Figure 2.17 Assignment problem for Exercise 2.2. Objects 1 and 2 have value C for all persons. Object 3 has value 0 for all persons. Object prices are as shown. The thick lines indicate the given assignment.

Exercise 2.4 (Feasible Distribution Theorem)

Show that the minimum cost flow problem has a feasible solution if and only if $\sum_{i \in \mathcal{N}} s_i = 0$ and for every cut $Q = [\mathcal{S}, \mathcal{N} - \mathcal{S}]$ we have

$$\text{Capacity of } Q \ \geq \sum_{i \in \mathcal{S}} s_i.$$

Show also that feasibility of the problem can be determined by solving a max-flow problem with zero lower flow bounds. *Hint:* Assume first that all lower flow bounds b_{ij} are zero. Introduce two nodes s and t. For each node $i \in \mathcal{N}$ with $s_i > 0$ introduce an arc (s, i) with feasible flow range $[0, s_i]$, and for each node $i \in \mathcal{N}$ with $s_i < 0$ introduce an arc (i, t) with feasible flow range $[0, -s_i]$. Apply the max-flow/min-cut theorem. In the general case, transform the problem to one with zero lower flow bounds.

Exercise 2.5 (Finding a Feasible Flow Vector)

Show that one may find a feasible solution of a feasible minimum cost flow problem by solving a max-flow problem with zero lower flow bounds. Furthermore, if the supplies s_i and the arc flow bounds b_{ij} and c_{ij} are integer, show that the feasible solution found will be integer. *Hint:* Use the hint of Exercise 2.4.

Exercise 2.6 (Integer Approximations of Feasible Solutions)

Given a graph $(\mathcal{N}, \mathcal{A})$ and a flow vector x, show that there exists an integer flow vector $\bar{x}$ having the same divergence vector as x and satisfying

$$|x_{ij} - \bar{x}_{ij}| < 1, \qquad \forall \ (i, j) \in \mathcal{A}.$$

Hint: For each arc (i, j), define the integer flow bounds

$$b_{ij} = \lfloor x_{ij} \rfloor, \qquad c_{ij} = \lceil x_{ij} \rceil.$$

Use the result of Exercise 2.5.

Exercise 2.7 (Maximal Matching/Minimal Cover Theorem)

Consider a bipartite graph consisting of two sets of nodes $\mathcal{S}$ and $\mathcal{T}$ such that every arc has its start node in $\mathcal{S}$ and its end node in $\mathcal{T}$. A *matching* is a subset of arcs such that all the start nodes of the arcs are distinct and all the end nodes of the arcs are distinct. A maximal matching is a matching with a maximal number of arcs.

(a) Show that the problem of finding a maximal matching can be formulated as a max-flow problem.

(b) Define a *cover* $\mathcal{C}$ to be a subset of $\mathcal{S} \cup \mathcal{T}$ such that for each arc (i, j), either $i \in \mathcal{C}$ or $j \in \mathcal{C}$ (or both). A minimal cover is a cover with a minimal number of nodes. Show that the number of arcs in a maximal matching and the number of nodes in a minimal cover are equal. *Hint:* Use the max-flow/min-cut theorem.

Exercise 2.8 (Feasibility of an Assignment Problem)

Show that an assignment problem is infeasible if and only if there exists a subset of person nodes I and a subset of object nodes J such that I has more nodes than J, and every arc with start node in I has an end node in J. *Hint:* Use the maximal matching/minimal cover theorem of the preceding exercise.

Exercise 2.9 (Ford-Fulkerson Method – Counterexample [Chv83])

This exercise illustrates how the version of the Ford-Fulkerson method where augmenting paths need not have as few arcs as possible may not terminate for a problem with irrational arc flow bounds. Consider the max-flow problem shown in Fig. 2.18.

(a) Verify that an infinite sequence of augmenting paths is characterized by the table of Fig. 2.18; each augmentation increases the divergence out of the source s but the sequence of divergences converges to a value which can be arbitrarily smaller than the maximum flow.

(b) Solve the problem with the Ford-Fulkerson method as given in Section 1.2.

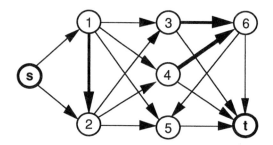

After Iter. #	Augm. Path	x_{12}	x_{36}	x_{46}	x_{65}
$6k + 1$	$(s, 1, 2, 3, 6, t)$	σ	$1 - \sigma^{3k+2}$	$\sigma - \sigma^{3k+1}$	0
$6k + 2$	$(s, 2, 1, 3, 6, 5, t)$	$\sigma - \sigma^{3k+2}$	1	$\sigma - \sigma^{3k+1}$	σ^{3k+2}
$6k + 3$	$(s, 1, 2, 4, 6, t)$	σ	1	$\sigma - \sigma^{3k+3}$	σ^{3k+2}
$6k + 4$	$(s, 2, 1, 4, 6, 3, t)$	$\sigma - \sigma^{3k+3}$	$1 - \sigma^{3k+3}$	σ	σ^{3k+2}
$6k + 5$	$(s, 1, 2, 5, 6, t)$	σ	$1 - \sigma^{3k+3}$	σ	σ^{3k+4}
$6k + 6$	$(s, 2, 1, 5, 6, 4, t)$	$\sigma - \sigma^{3k+4}$	$1 - \sigma^{3k+3}$	$\sigma - \sigma^{3k+4}$	0
$6(k + 1) + 1$	$(s, 1, 2, 3, 6, t)$	σ	$1 - \sigma^{3(k+1)+2}$	$\sigma - \sigma^{3(k+1)+1}$	0

Figure 2.18   Max-flow problem illustrating that if the augmenting paths in the Ford-Fulkerson method do not have a minimum number of arcs, then the method may not terminate. All lower arc flow bounds are zero. The upper flow bounds are larger than one, with the exception of the thick-line arcs; these are arc $(3, 6)$ which has upper flow bound equal to one, and arcs $(1, 2)$ and $(4, 6)$ which have upper flow bound equal to $\sigma = \left(-1 + \sqrt{5} \right)/2$. (Note a crucial property of σ; it satisfies $\sigma^{k+2} = \sigma^k - \sigma^{k+1}$ for all integer $k \geq 0$.) The table gives a sequence of augmentations.

Exercise 2.10 (Termination of the Ford-Fulkerson Algorithm)

Consider the Ford-Fulkerson algorithm as described in Section 1.2.2. This exercice addresses the termination issue when the problem data are noninteger. Let x^0 be the initial feasible flow vector; let x^k, $k = 1, 2, \ldots$, be the flow vector after the kth augmentation; and let P_k be the corresponding augmenting path. An arc (i, j) is said to be a k^+-*bottleneck* if $(i, j) \in P_k^+$ and $x_{ij}^k = c_{ij}$, and it is said to be a k^--*bottleneck* if $(i, j) \in P_k^-$ and $x_{ij}^k = b_{ij}$.

(a) Show that if $k < \bar{k}$ and an arc (i, j) is a k^+-bottleneck and a $\bar{k}^+$-bottleneck, then for some m with $k < m < \bar{k}$ we must have $(i, j) \in P_m^-$.

Similarly, if an arc (i, j) is a k^--bottleneck and a $\overline{k}^-$-bottleneck, then for some m with $k < m < \overline{k}$ we must have $(i, j) \in P_m^+$.

(b) Show that P_k is a path with a minimal number of arcs over all augmenting paths with respect to x^{k-1}. (This property depends on the implementation of the unblocked path search as a breadth-first search.)

(c) For any path P that is unblocked with respect to x^k, let $n_k(P)$ be the number of arcs of P, let $a_k^+(i)$ be the minimum of $n_k(P)$ over all unblocked P from s to i, and let $a_k^-(i)$ be the minimum of $n_k(P)$ over all unblocked P from i to t. Show that for all i and k we have

$$a_k^+(i) \le a_{k+1}^+(i), \qquad a_k^-(i) \le a_{k+1}^-(i).$$

(d) Show that if $k < \overline{k}$ and arc (i, j) is both a k^+-bottleneck and a $\overline{k}^+$-bottleneck, or is both a k^--bottleneck and a $\overline{k}^-$-bottleneck, then $a_k^+(t) < a_{\overline{k}}^+(t)$.

(e) Show that the algorithm terminates after $O(NA)$ augmentations, for an $O(NA^2)$ running time.

Exercise 2.11 (Duality for Nonnegativity Constraints)

Consider the version of the minimum cost flow problem where there are non-negativity constraints

$$\text{minimize} \quad \sum_{(i,j) \in \mathcal{A}} a_{ij} x_{ij}$$

subject to

$$\sum_{\{j \mid (i,j) \in \mathcal{A}\}} x_{ij} - \sum_{\{j \mid (j,i) \in \mathcal{A}\}} x_{ji} = s_i, \qquad \forall \, i \in \mathcal{N},$$

$$0 \le x_{ij}, \qquad \forall \, (i, j) \in \mathcal{A}.$$

Show that if a feasible flow vector x^* and a price vector p^* satisfy the following CS conditions

$$p_i^* - p_j^* \le a_{ij}, \qquad \text{for all } (i, j) \in \mathcal{A},$$

$$p_i^* - p_j^* = a_{ij} \qquad \text{for all } (i, j) \in \mathcal{A} \text{ with } 0 < x_{ij}^*,$$

then x^* is optimal. Furthermore, p^* is an optimal solution of the following dual problem:

$$\text{maximize} \quad \sum_{i \in \mathcal{N}} s_i p_i$$

$$\text{subject to} \quad p_i - p_j \le a_{ij}, \qquad \forall \, (i, j) \in \mathcal{A}.$$

Hint: Complete the details of the following argument. Define

$$q(p) = \begin{cases} \sum_{i \in \mathcal{N}} s_i p_i & \text{if } p_i - p_j \leq a_{ij}, \ \forall \ (i,j) \in \mathcal{A} \\ -\infty & \text{otherwise} \end{cases}$$

and note that

$$q(p) = \sum_{(i,j) \in \mathcal{A}} \min_{0 \leq x_{ij}} \left(a_{ij} + p_j - p_i \right) x_{ij} + \sum_{i \in \mathcal{N}} s_i p_i$$

$$= \min_{0 \leq x} \left\{ \sum_{(i,j) \in \mathcal{A}} a_{ij} x_{ij} + \sum_{i \in \mathcal{N}} \left(s_i - \sum_{\{j | (i,j) \in \mathcal{A}\}} x_{ij} + \sum_{\{j | (j,i) \in \mathcal{A}\}} x_{ji} \right) p_i \right\}.$$

Thus, for any feasible x and any p, we have

$$q(p) \leq \sum_{(i,j) \in \mathcal{A}} a_{ij} x_{ij} + \sum_{i \in \mathcal{N}} \left(s_i - \sum_{\{j | (i,j) \in \mathcal{A}\}} x_{ij} + \sum_{\{j | (j,i) \in \mathcal{A}\}} x_{ji} \right) p_i$$

$$= \sum_{(i,j) \in \mathcal{A}} a_{ij} x_{ij}. \tag{2.26}$$

On the other hand, we have

$$q(p^*) = \sum_{i \in \mathcal{N}} s_i p_i^* = \sum_{(i,j) \in \mathcal{A}} \left(a_{ij} + p_j^* - p_i^* \right) x_{ij}^* + \sum_{i \in \mathcal{N}} s_i p_i^* = \sum_{(i,j) \in \mathcal{A}} a_{ij} x_{ij}^*,$$

where the second equality is true because the CS conditions imply that $(a_{ij} + p_j^* - p_i^*) x_{ij}^* = 0$ for all $(i,j) \in \mathcal{A}$, and the last equality follows from the feasibility of x^*. Therefore, x^* attains the minimum of the primal cost on the right-hand side of Eq. (2.26). Furthermore, p^* attains the maximum of $q(p)$ on the left side of Eq. (2.26), which means that p^* is an optimal solution of the dual problem.

Exercise 2.12 (Node-Disjoint Paths)

Given two nodes i and j in a graph, consider the problem of finding the maximum number of paths starting at i and ending at j that are node-disjoint in the sense that any two of them share no nodes other than i and j. Formulate this problem as a max-flow problem.

Exercise 2.13 (Hall's Theorem of Distinct Representatives)

Given finite sets $S_1, S_2, \ldots, S_k$, we say that the collection $\{s_1, s_2, \ldots, s_k\}$ is a system of distinct representatives if $s_i \in S_i$ for all i and $s_i \neq s_j$ for $i \neq j$. (For example, if $S_1 = \{a, b, c\}$, $S_2 = \{a, b\}$, $S_1 = \{a\}$, then $s_1 = c$, $s_2 = b$, $s_3 = a$ is a system of distinct representatives). Show that there exists no system of distinct representatives if and only if there exists an index set $I \subset \{1, 2, \ldots, k\}$ such that the number of elements in $\cup_{i \in I} S_i$ is less than the number of elements in I. *Hint:* Consider a bipartite graph with each of the right side nodes representing an element of $\cup_{i \in I} S_i$, with each of the left side nodes representing one of the sets $S_1, S_2, \ldots S_k$, and with an arc from a left node S to a right node s if $s \in S$. Use the maximal matching/minimal cover theorem of Exercise 2.7.

Exercise 2.14

Prove the following generalization of Prop. 2.2. Let x be a capacity-feasible flow vector, and let $\mathcal{N}^+$ and $\mathcal{N}^-$ be two disjoint subsets of nodes. Then exactly one of the following two alternatives holds:

(1) There exists a path that starts at some node of $\mathcal{N}^+$, ends at some node of $\mathcal{N}^-$, and is unblocked with respect to x.

(2) There exists a saturated cut $Q = [\mathcal{S}, \mathcal{N} - \mathcal{S}]$ such that $\mathcal{N}^+ \subset \mathcal{S}$ and $\mathcal{N}^- \subset \mathcal{N} - \mathcal{S}$.

Exercise 2.15 (Duality and the Max-Flow/Min-Cut Theorem)

Consider a feasible max-flow problem and let $Q = [\mathcal{S}, \mathcal{N} - \mathcal{S}]$ be a minimum capacity cut separating s and t. Consider also the minimum cost flow problem formulation (1.8) for the max-flow problem (see Example 1.2). Show that the price vector

$$p_i = \begin{cases} 1 & \text{if } i \in \mathcal{S} \\ 0 & \text{if } i \notin \mathcal{S} \end{cases}$$

is an optimal solution of the dual problem. Furthermore, show that the max-flow/min-cut theorem expresses the equality of the primal and the dual optimal values. *Hint:* Relate the capacity of Q with the dual function value corresponding to p.

Exercise 2.16

Consider a feasible max-flow problem. Show that if the upper flow bound of each arc is increased by $\alpha > 0$, then the value of the maximum flow is increased by no more than αA, where A is the number of arcs.

Exercise 2.17 (Dual Cost Improvement Directions)

Consider the assignment problem. Let p_j be the price of object j, let T be a subset of objects, and let

$$S = \Big\{ i \mid \text{the maximum of } a_{ij} - p_j \text{ over } j \in A(i) \text{ is attained}$$
$$\text{by some element of } T \Big\}.$$

Suppose that

(1) For each $i \in S$, the maximum of $a_{ij} - p_j$ over $j \in A(i)$ is attained only by elements of T.

(2) S has more elements than T.

Show that the direction $d = (d_1, \ldots, d_n)$, where $d_j = 1$ if $j \in T$ and $d_j =$ if $j \notin T$, is a direction of dual cost improvement. *Note*: Directions of th type are used by the most common dual cost improvement algorithms for t assignment problem.

THE SHORTEST PATH PROBLEM

The shortest path problem is a classical and important combinatorial probl that arises in many contexts. We are given a directed graph $(\mathcal{N}, \mathcal{A})$ with no numbered $1, \ldots, N$. Each arc $(i, j) \in \mathcal{A}$ has a cost or "length" a_{ij} associat with it. The length of a path $(i_1, i_2, \ldots, i_k)$, which consists exclusively forward arcs, is equal to the length of its arcs

$$\sum_{n=1}^{k-1} a_{i_n i_{n+1}}.$$

This path is said to be *shortest* if it has minimum length over all paths with the same origin and destination nodes. The length of a shortest path is also called the *shortest distance*. The shortest distance from a node to itself is taken to be zero by convention. The shortest path problem deals with finding shortest distances between selected pairs of nodes. [Note that here we are optimizing over forward paths, that is, paths consisting of forward arcs; when we refer to a path (or a cycle) in connection with the shortest path problem, we implicitly assume that the path (or the cycle) is forward.]

All the major shortest path algorithms are based on the following simple proposition.

Proposition 3.1:   Let $d = (d_1, d_2, \ldots, d_N)$ be a vector satisfying

$$d_j \leq d_i + a_{ij}, \qquad \forall \, (i, j) \in \mathcal{A} \tag{3.1}$$

and let P be a path starting at a node i_1 and ending at a node i_k. If

$$d_j = d_i + a_{ij}, \qquad \text{for all arcs } (i,j) \text{ of } P \tag{3.2}$$

then P is a shortest path from i_1 to i_k.

Proof: By adding Eq. (3.2) over the arcs of P, we see that the length of P is $d_{i_k} - d_{i_1}$. By adding Eq. (3.1) over the arcs of any other path P' starting at i_1 and ending at i_k, we see that the length of P' must be at least equal to $d_{i_k} - d_{i_1}$. Therefore, P is a shortest path.   **Q.E.D.**

The conditions (3.1) and (3.2) will be called the *complementary slackness (CS) conditions for the shortest path problem*. This terminology is motivated by the connection of the problem of finding a shortest path from i_1 to i_k with the following minimum cost flow problem

$$\text{minimize} \quad \sum_{(i,j)\in\mathcal{A}} a_{ij}x_{ij} \tag{3.3}$$

subject to

$$\sum_{\{j|(i,j)\in\mathcal{A}\}} x_{ij} - \sum_{\{j|(j,i)\in\mathcal{A}\}} x_{ji} = s_i, \qquad \forall\, i \in \mathcal{N},$$

$$0 \le x_{ij}, \qquad \forall\, (i,j) \in \mathcal{A},$$

where

$$s_{i_1} = 1, \qquad s_{i_k} = -1, \qquad s_i = 0, \qquad \forall\, i \neq i_1, i_k.$$

It can be seen that a path P from i_1 to i_k is shortest if and only if the path flow x defined by

$$x_{ij} = \begin{cases} 1 & \text{if } (i,j) \text{ belongs to } P \\ 0 & \text{otherwise} \end{cases} \tag{3.4}$$

is an optimal solution of the minimum cost flow problem (3.3).

The CS conditions (3.1) and (3.2) of Prop. 3.1 are in effect the CS conditions for the equivalent minimum cost flow problem (3.3), which take the form

$$p_i \le a_{ij} + p_j, \qquad \forall\, (i,j) \in \mathcal{A}, \tag{3.5}$$

$$p_i = a_{ij} + p_j, \qquad \text{for all arcs } (i,j) \text{ with } 0 < x_{ij} \tag{3.6}$$

[cf. Eqs. (2.11c) and (2.11d)]. Indeed, if we associate the given path P in Prop. 3.1 with the flow vector of Eq. (3.4), and we identify p_i with $-d_i$, we see that the conditions (3.1) and (3.2) are identical to the CS conditions (3.5) and (3.6). Thus, the optimality of the path P under the conditions of Prop. 3.1 can also be inferred from the general result of Prop. 2.5, which asserts optimality of feasible pairs (x, p) satisfying CS. It also follows from the same general result that if a vector d satisfies the conditions of Prop. 3.1, then $p = -d$ is an optimal solution of the dual problem corresponding to the minimum cost flow problem (3.3).

Most shortest path algorithms can be viewed as primal cost or dual cost improvement algorithms for an appropriate variation of the minimum cost flow problem (3.3), as we will see later. However, the shortest path problem is simple, so we will discuss it first without much reference to cost improvement. This choice serves a dual purpose. First, it provides an opportunity to illustrate some basic concepts in the context of a simple problem, which is rich in intuition. Second, it allows the early development of some ideas and results that will be used later in a variety of other algorithmic contexts.

1.3.1 A General Single Origin/Many Destinations Shortest Path Method

The shortest path problem can be posed in a number of ways; for example, finding a shortest path from a single origin to a single destination, or finding a shortest path from each of several origins to each of several destinations. We will focus initially on the single origin/many destinations problem. For concreteness, we take the origin node to be node 1.

Let us now describe a prototype shortest path method that contains several interesting algorithms as special cases. In this method, we start with some vector $(d_1, d_2, \ldots, d_N)$, we successively select arcs (i, j) that violate the CS condition (3.1), that is, $d_j > d_i + a_{ij}$, and we set

$$d_j := d_i + a_{ij}.$$

This is continued until the CS condition $d_j \leq d_i + a_{ij}$ is satisfied for all arcs (i, j).

A key idea is that, in the course of the algorithm, d_i can be interpreted for all i as the length of some path P_i from 1 to i. Therefore, if $d_j > d_i + a_{ij}$ for some arc (i, j), the path obtained by extending path P_i by arc (i, j), which has length $d_i + a_{ij}$, is a better path than the current path P_j, which has length d_j. Thus, the algorithm finds successively better paths from the origin to various destinations.

It should be noted that replacing the current path P_j with the shorter path consisting of P_i followed by the arc (i, j), as discussed above, is essentially a *primal cost improvement operation*; in the context of a minimum cost flow formulation of the many destinations shortest path problem [cf. Eq. (3.3)], it can be interpreted as pushing one unit of flow along the cycle that starts at 1, traverses P_i and (i, j) in the forward direction, and then traverses P_j in the backward direction. The cost of this cycle, as defined earlier in Section 1.2.1, is equal to the length of P_i, plus the length of (i, j), minus the length of P_j, and is therefore negative. Thus the general algorithm of this section can be viewed as a primal cost improvement algorithm. It will be seen in Chapter 3 (Exercise 2.3) that an important special case, Dijkstra's method to be discussed shortly, can also be viewed as a dual cost improvement algorithm. Another algorithm, the auction/shortest path algorithm to be presented in Section 4.3, does not fit the framework of the present section (even though it crucially depends on the CS conditions of Prop. 3.1); it will be shown to be a dual cost improvement algorithm.

It is usually most convenient to implement the prototype shortest path method by examining the outgoing arcs of a given node i consecutively. The corresponding algorithm, referred to as *generic*, maintains a list of nodes V, called the *candidate list*, and a vector $d = (d_1, d_2, \ldots, d_N)$, where each d_j, called the *label of node j*, is either a real number or ∞. Initially,

$$V = \{1\}, \tag{3.7}$$

$$d_1 = 0, \qquad d_i = \infty, \qquad \forall\ i \neq 1. \tag{3.8}$$

The algorithm proceeds in iterations and terminates when V is empty. The typical iteration (assuming V is nonempty) is as follows:

Typical Iteration of the Generic Shortest Path Algorithm

> Remove a node i from the candidate list V. For each outgoing arc $(i, j) \in \mathcal{A}$, with $j \neq 1$, if $d_j > d_i + a_{ij}$, set
>
> $$d_j := d_i + a_{ij} \tag{3.9}$$
>
> and add j to V if it does not already belong to V.

It can be seen that, in the course of the algorithm, the labels are monotonically nonincreasing. Furthermore, we have

$d_i < \infty \qquad \Longleftrightarrow \qquad i$ has entered the candidate list V at least once.

Figure 3.1 illustrates the algorithm. The following proposition gives its main properties.

Proposition 3.2:   Consider the generic shortest path algorithm.

(a) At the end of each iteration, the following conditions hold:

   (i) $d_1 = 0$.

   (ii) If $d_j < \infty$ and $j \neq 1$, then d_j is the length of some path that starts at 1, never returns to 1, and ends at j.

   (iii) If $i \notin V$, then either $d_i = \infty$ or else

   $$d_j \leq d_i + a_{ij}, \qquad \forall\ j \text{ such that } (i, j) \in \mathcal{A}.$$

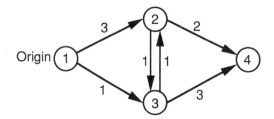

Iteration #	Candidate List V	Node Labels	Node out of V
1	$\{1\}$	$(0, \infty, \infty, \infty)$	1
2	$\{2, 3\}$	$(0, 3, 1, \infty)$	2
3	$\{3, 4\}$	$(0, 3, 1, 5)$	3
4	$\{4, 2\}$	$(0, 2, 1, 4)$	4
5	$\{2\}$	$(0, 2, 1, 4)$	2
	$\emptyset$	$(0, 2, 1, 4)$	

Figure 3.1   Illustration of the generic shortest path algorithm. The numbers next to the arcs are the arc lengths. Note that node 2 enters the candidate list twice. If in iteration 2 node 3 was removed from V instead of node 2, each node would enter V only once. Thus, the order in which nodes are removed from V is significant.

(b) If the algorithm terminates, then upon termination, for all $j \neq 1$ such that $d_j < \infty$, d_j is the shortest distance from 1 to j and

$$d_j = \min_{(i,j) \in \mathcal{A}} \{d_i + a_{ij}\}; \tag{3.10}$$

furthermore, $d_j = \infty$ if and only if there is no path from 1 to j.

(c) If the algorithm does not terminate, then there exist paths of arbitrarily small (i.e., large negative) length that start at 1 and never return to 1.

Proof: (a) Condition (i) holds because initially $d_1 = 0$, and by the rules of the algorithm, d_1 cannot change.

We prove (ii) by induction on the iteration count. Indeed, initially (ii) holds, since node 1 is the only node j with $d_j < \infty$. Suppose that (ii) holds at the start of some iteration at which a node i is removed from V. If $i = 1$, which happens only at the first iteration, then at the end of the iteration we have $d_j = a_{1j}$ for all outward neighbors j of 1, and $d_j = \infty$ for all other $j \neq 1$, so d_j has the required property. If $i \neq 1$, then $d_i < \infty$ (which is true for all nodes of V by the rules of the algorithm), and (by the induction hypothesis) d_i is the length of some path P_i starting at 1, never returning to 1, and ending at i. When a label d_j changes as a result of the iteration, d_j is set to $d_i + a_{ij}$, which is the length of the path P_j consisting of P_i followed by arc (i, j). Since $j \neq 1$, P_j never returns to 1. This completes the induction proof of (ii).

To prove (iii), note that for any i, each time i is removed from V, the condition $d_j \leq d_i + a_{ij}$ is satisfied for all $(i, j) \in \mathcal{A}$ by the rules of the algorithm. Up to the next entrance of i into V, d_i stays constant, while the labels d_j for all j with $(i, j) \in \mathcal{A}$ cannot increase, thereby preserving the condition $d_j \leq d_i + a_{ij}$.

(b) We first introduce the sets

$$I = \{i \mid d_i < \infty \text{ upon termination}\},$$

$$\overline{I} = \{i \mid d_i = \infty \text{ upon termination}\},$$

and we show that we have $d_i \in \overline{I}$ if and only if there is no path from 1 to j. Indeed, if $i \in I$, then, since $i \notin V$ upon termination, it follows from condition (iii) of part (a) that $j \in I$ for all $(i, j) \in \mathcal{A}$. Therefore, if $j \in \overline{I}$, there is no path from any node of I (and in particular, node 1) to node j. Conversely, if there is no path from 1 to j, it follows from condition (ii) of part (a) that we cannot have $d_j < \infty$ upon termination, so $j \in \overline{I}$.

We show now that for all $i \in I$, we have $d_j = \min_{(i,j) \in \mathcal{A}}\{d_i + a_{ij}\}$ upon termination. Indeed, conditions (ii) and (iii) of part (a) imply that upon termination we have, for all $i \in I$,

$$d_j \leq d_i + a_{ij}, \qquad \forall \, j \text{ such that } (i, j) \in \mathcal{A}$$

while d_i is the length of some path P_i from 1 to i. Fix a node $m \in I$. By adding this condition over the arcs (i, j) of any path P from 1 to m, we see that the length of P is no less than d_m. Hence P_m is a shortest path from 1 to m. Furthermore, the equality $d_j = d_i + a_{ij}$ must hold for all arcs (i, j) on the shortest paths P_m, $m \in I$, implying that $d_j = \min_{(i,j) \in \mathcal{A}}\{d_i + a_{ij}\}$.

(c) If the algorithm never terminates, some label d_j must decrease strictly an infinite number of times, generating a corresponding sequence of distinct paths P_j as per condition (ii) of part (b). Each of these paths can be decomposed into a simple path from 1 to j plus a collection of simple cycles, as in Exercise 1.5. Since the number of simple paths from 1 to j is finite, and the length of the path P_j is monotonically decreasing, it follows that P_j eventually must involve a cycle with negative length. By replicating this cycle a sufficiently large number of times, one can obtain paths from 1 to j with arbitrarily small length.   **Q.E.D.**

Termination and the Existence of Negative Length Cycles

So far we have imposed no assumptions on the structure of the graph of the problem or the lengths of the arcs. Thus, Prop. 3.2 does not guarantee that the algorihm will terminate. On the other hand, Prop. 3.2 shows that the generic algorithm will terminate if and only if there is a lower bound on the length of all paths that start at node 1 and never return to node 1. Thus, the algorithm will terminate if and only if there is no path starting at node 1, never returning to 1, and containing a cycle with negative length. One can detect the presence of such a cycle (and stop the algorithm) once some label d_j becomes less than $(N-1)\min_{(i,j)\in\mathcal{A}} a_{ij}$, which is a lower bound to the length of all simple paths.

Bellman's Equation and Shortest Path Construction

When all cycles have nonnegative length and there exists a path from 1 to every node j, then Prop. 3.2 shows that the generic algorithm terminates and that, upon termination, all labels are finite and satisfy

$$d_j = \min_{(i,j)\in\mathcal{A}}\{d_i + a_{ij}\}, \qquad \forall\, j \neq 1, \tag{3.11a}$$

$$d_1 = 0. \tag{3.11b}$$

This equation, which is in effect the CS conditions of Prop. 3.1, is called *Bellman's equation*. It expresses that the shortest distance from 1 to j is the sum of the shortest distance from 1 to the node preceding j on the shortest path, plus the length of the arc connecting that node to j.

From Bellman's equation, we can obtain the shortest paths (as opposed to the shortest path lengths) if all cycles not including node 1 have strictly positive length. To do this, select for each $j \neq 1$ one arc (i,j) that attains the minimum in $d_j = \min_{(i,j)\in\mathcal{A}}\{d_i + a_{ij}\}$ and consider the subgraph consisting of these $N-1$ arcs; see Fig. 3.2. To find the shortest path to any node j, start from j and follow the corresponding arcs of the subgraph backward until node 1 is reached. Note that the same node cannot be reached twice before node 1 is reached, since a cycle would be formed that [on the basis of Eq. (3.11)] would have zero length. [Let $(i_1, i_2, \ldots, i_k, i_1)$ be the cycle and add the equations

$$d_{i_1} = d_{i_2} + a_{i_2 i_1}$$

$$\cdots$$

$$d_{i_{k-1}} = d_{i_k} + a_{i_k i_{k-1}}$$

$$d_{i_k} = d_{i_1} + a_{i_1 i_k},$$

obtaining $a_{i_2 i_1} + \cdots + a_{i_k i_{k-1}} + a_{i_1 i_k} = 0$.] Since the subgraph is connected and has $N - 1$ arcs, it must be a spanning tree. We call this subgraph a *shortest path spanning tree*, and we note that it has the special structure of having a root (node 1), with every arc of the tree directed away from the root. The preceding argument can also be used to show that Bellman's equation has no solution other than the shortest distances; see Exercise 3.12.

A shortest path spanning tree can also be constructed in the process of executing the generic shortest path algorithm by recording the arc (i, j) every time d_j is decreased to $d_i + a_{ij}$; see Exercise 3.3.

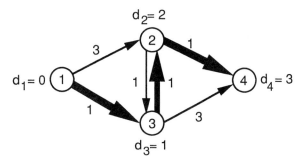

Figure 3.2   Example of construction of shortest path spanning tree. The arc lengths are shown next to the arcs, and the shortest distances are shown next to the nodes. For each $j \neq 1$, we select an arc (i, j) such that

$$d_j = d_i + a_{ij}$$

and we form the shortest path spanning tree. The arcs selected in this example are $(1, 3)$, $(3, 2)$, and $(2, 4)$.

Implementations of the Generic Algorithm

There are many implementations of the generic algorithm; they differ in how they select the node to be removed from the candidate list V. They are broadly divided into two categories:

(a) *Label setting methods.* In these methods, the node i removed from V is a node with minimum label. Under the assumption that *all arc lengths are nonnegative*, these methods have a remarkable property: each node will enter V at most *once*; its label has its permanent or final value the first time it is removed from V. The most time consuming part of these methods is calculating the minimum label node from V at each iteration;

there are several implementations, that use a variety of creative methods to calculate this minimum.

(b) *Label correcting methods.* In these methods the choice of the node i removed from V is less sophisticated than in label setting methods, and requires less calculation. However, a node may enter V multiple times.

Generally in practice, when the arc lengths are nonnegative, the best label setting methods and the best label correcting methods are competitive. There are also several worst case complexity bounds for label setting and label correcting methods. The best bounds correspond to label setting methods. The best practical methods, however, are not necessarily the ones with the best complexity bounds, as will be discussed shortly.

1.3.2   Label Setting (Dijkstra) Methods

The basic label setting method, first published by Dijkstra [Dij59] but also discovered independently by several other researchers, is the special case of the generic algorithm where the node j removed from the candidate list V at each iteration has minimum label, that is,

$$d_j = \min_{i \in V} d_i.$$

For convenient reference, let us state this method explicitly.

Initially, we have

$$V = \{1\}, \tag{3.12}$$

$$d_1 = 0, \qquad d_i = \infty, \qquad \forall\ i \neq 1. \tag{3.13}$$

The method proceeds in iterations and terminates when V is empty. The typical iteration (assuming V is nonempty) is as follows:

Typical Iteration of the Label Setting Method

Remove from the candidate list V a node i such that

$$d_i = \min_{j \in V} d_j.$$

For each outgoing arc $(i, j) \in \mathcal{A}$, with $j \neq 1$, if $d_j > d_i + a_{ij}$, set

$$d_j := d_i + a_{ij} \tag{3.14}$$

and add j to V if it does not already belong to V.

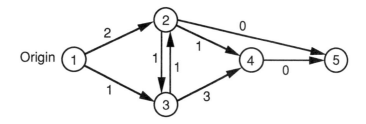

Iteration #	Candidate List V	Node Labels	Node out of V
1	$\{1\}$	$(0, \infty, \infty, \infty, \infty)$	1
2	$\{2, 3\}$	$(0, 2, 1, \infty, \infty)$	3
3	$\{2, 4\}$	$(0, 2, 1, 4, \infty)$	2
4	$\{4, 5\}$	$(0, 2, 1, 3, 2)$	5
5	$\{4\}$	$(0, 2, 1, 3, 2)$	4
	$\emptyset$	$(0, 2, 1, 3, 2)$	

Figure 3.3   Example illustrating the label setting method. At each iteration, the node with the minimum label is removed from V. Each node enters V only once.

Figure 3.3 illustrates the label setting method.

Some insight into the label setting method can be gained by considering the set W of nodes that have already been in V but are not currently in V,

$$W = \{i \mid d_i < \infty, i \notin V\}. \tag{3.15}$$

We will see that as a consequence of the policy of removing from V a minimum label node, W contains nodes with "small" labels throughout the algorithm, in the sense that

$$d_j \leq d_i, \qquad \text{if } j \in W \text{ and } i \notin W. \tag{3.16}$$

On the basis of this property and the assumption $a_{ij} \geq 0$, it can be seen that when a node i is removed from V, we have, for all $j \in W$ for which (i, j) is an arc,

$$d_j \leq d_i + a_{ij}.$$

Hence, once a node enters W, it stays in W and its label does not change further. Thus, W can be viewed as the set of *permanently labeled nodes*, that

is, the nodes that have acquired a final label, which by Prop. 3.2, must be
equal to their shortest distance from the origin.

To understand why the property (3.16) is preserved, consider an iteration
in which node i is removed from V, and assume that Eq. (3.16) holds at the
start of the iteration. Then, any label d_j that changes during the iteration
must correspond to a node $j \notin W$ (as was argued below), and at the end of
the iteration it must satisfy $d_j = d_i + a_{ij} \geq d_i \geq d_k$ for all $k \in W$, thereby
maintaining Eq. (3.16).

The following proposition makes the preceding arguments more precise
and proves some additional facts.

Proposition 3.3:   Assume that all arc lengths are nonnegative and that
there exists at least one path from node 1 to each other node.

(a) For any iteration of the label setting method, the following hold for the
set
$$W = \{i \mid d_i < \infty, i \notin V\}.$$

(i) No node belonging to W at the start of the iteration will enter the
candidate list V during the iteration.

(ii) At the end of the iteration, we have $d_i \leq d_j$ for all $i \in W$ and
$j \notin W$.

(iii) For each node i, consider paths that start at 1, end at i, and have
all their other nodes in W at the end of the iteration. Then the
label d_i at the end of the iteration is equal to the length of the
shortest of these paths ($d_i = \infty$ if no such path exists).

(b) In the label setting method, all nodes will be removed from the candidate
list V exactly once in order of increasing shortest distance from node 1;
that is, i will be removed before j if the final labels satisfy $d_i < d_j$.

Proof: (a) Properties (i) and (ii) will be proved simultaneously by induction
on the iteration count. Clearly (i) and (ii) hold for the initial iteration at which
node 1 exits V and enters W.

Suppose that (i) and (ii) hold for iteration $k-1$, and suppose that during
iteration k, node i satisfies $d_i = \min_{j \in V} d_j$ and exits V. Let W and $\overline{W}$ be the
set of Eq. (3.15) at the start and at the end of iteration k, respectively. Let d_j
and $\overline{d}_j$ be the label of each node j at the start and at the end of iteration k,
respectively. Since by the induction hypothesis we have $d_j \leq d_i$ for all $j \in W$,
and $a_{ij} \geq 0$ for all arcs (i,j), it follows that $d_j \leq d_i + a_{ij}$ for all arcs (i,j) with
$j \in W$. Hence, a node $j \in W$ cannot enter V at iteration k. This completes
the induction proof of property (i), and shows that
$$\overline{W} = W \cup \{i\}.$$

Thus, at iteration k, the only labels that may change are the labels d_j of nodes
$j \notin \overline{W}$ such that (i,j) is an arc; the label $\overline{d}_j$ at the end of the iteration will

be $\min\{d_j, d_i + a_{ij}\}$. Since $a_{ij} \geq 0$, $d_i \leq d_j$ for all $j \notin W$, and $d_i = \overline{d}_i$, we must have $\overline{d}_i \leq \overline{d}_j$ for all $j \notin W$. Since by the induction hypothesis we have $d_m \leq d_i$ and $d_m = \overline{d}_m$ for all $m \in \overline{W}$, it follows that $\overline{d}_m \leq \overline{d}_j$ for all $m \in \overline{W}$ and $j \notin \overline{W}$. This completes the induction proof of property (ii).

To prove property (iii), choose any node i and consider the subgraph consisting of the nodes $W \cup \{i\}$ together with the arcs that have both end nodes in $W \cup \{i\}$. Consider also a modified shortest path problem involving this subgraph and the same origin and arc lengths as in the original shortest path problem. In view of properties (i) and (ii), the label setting method applied to the modified shortest path problem yields the same sequence of nodes exiting V and the same sequence of labels as when applied to the original problem up to the current iteration. By Prop. 3.2, the label setting method for the modified problem terminates with the labels equal to the shortest distances of the modified problem at the current iteration. This means that the labels at the end of the iteration have the property stated in the proposition.

(b) By Prop. 3.2, we see that, under our assumptions, the label setting method will terminate with all labels finite. Therefore, each node will enter V at least once. At each iteration the node removed from V is added to W, and according to property (i) (proved above), no node from W is ever returned to V. Therefore, each node will be removed from V and simultaneously entered in W exactly once, and, by the rules of the algorithm, its label cannot change after its entrance in W. Property (ii) then shows that each new node added to W has a label at least as large as the labels of the nodes already in W. Therefore, the nodes are removed from V in the order stated in the proposition. **Q.E.D.**

Performance and Implementations of the Label Setting Method

In label setting methods, the candidate list V is typically maintained with the help of some data structure that facilitates the removal and the addition of nodes, and also facilitates finding the minimum label node from the list. The choice of data structure is crucial for good practical performance as well as for good theoretical worst case performance.

To gain some insight into this, we first consider a naive implementation that will serve as a yardstick for comparison. By Prop. 3.3, there will be exactly N iterations, and in each of these the candidate list V will be searched for a minimum label node. Suppose this is done by examining all nodes in sequence, checking whether they belong to V, and finding one with minimum label among those who do. Searching V in this way requires $O(N)$ operations per iteration, for a total of $O(N^2)$ operations. Also during the algorithm, we must examine each arc (i, j) exactly once to check whether $j \neq 1$ or whether the condition $d_j > d_i + a_{ij}$ holds, and to set $d_j := d_i + a_{ij}$ if it does. This requires $O(A)$ operations, which is dominated by the preceding $O(N^2)$ estimate.

The $O(A)$ operation count for arc examination is unavoidable and cannot be reduced. However, the $O(N^2)$ operation count for minimum label searching can be reduced considerably by using appropriate data structures. The best estimates of the worst case running time that have been thus obtained are $O(A + N \log N)$ and $O(A + N\sqrt{\log C})$, where C is the arc length range $C = \max_{(i,j)\in\mathcal{A}} a_{ij}$; see [FrT84], [AMO88]. On the basis of present experience, however, the methods that perform best in practice have far worse running time estimates. We will discuss two of these methods.

Binary Heap Method

Here the nodes are organized as a binary heap on the basis of label values and membership in V; see Fig. 3.4. The node at the top of the heap is the node of V that has minimum label, and the label of every node in V is no larger than the labels of all the nodes that are in V and are its descendants in the heap. Nodes that are not in V may be in the heap but may have no descendants that are in V.

At each iteration, the top node of the heap is removed from V. Furthermore, the labels of some nodes already in V may decrease, so these may have to be repositioned in the heap; also, some other nodes may enter V for the first time and have to be inserted in the heap at the right place. It can be seen that each of these removals, repositionings, and insertions can be done in $O(\log N)$ time. Since there is one removal per iteration, and at most one repositioning or node insertion per arc (each arc is examined at most once), the total operation count for maintaining the heap is $O(A \log N)$. This dominates the $O(A)$ operation count to examine all arcs, so the worst case running time of the method is $O(A \log N)$. For sparse graphs, where $A << N^2$, the binary heap method performs very well in practice.

Dial's Algorithm [Dia69]

This algorithm requires that all arc lengths be nonnegative integers. It uses a naive yet often surprisingly effective method for finding the minimum label node in V. We first note that, since every finite label is equal to the length of some path with no cycles [Prop. 3.3(a), part (iii)], the possible label values range from 0 to $(N - 1)C$, where

$$C = \max_{(i,j)\in\mathcal{A}} a_{ij}.$$

Suppose that for each possible label value, we keep a list of the nodes that have this label value. Then we may scan the $(N-1)C+1$ possible label values

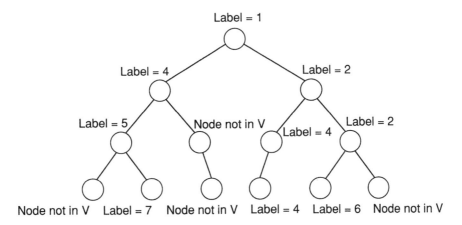

Figure 3.4   A binary heap organized on the basis of node labels is a binary balanced tree such that the label of each node of V is no larger than the labels of all its descendants that are in V. Nodes that are not in V may have no descendants that are in V. The topmost node, called the *root*, has the minimum label. The tree is balanced in that the numbers of arcs in the paths from the root to any nodes with no descendants differ by at most 1. If the label of some node decreases, the node must be moved upward toward the root, requiring $O(\log N)$ operations. [It takes $O(1)$ operations to compare the label of a node i with the label of one of its descendants j, and to interchange the positions of i and j if the label of j is smaller. Since there are $\log N$ levels in the tree, it takes at most $\log N$ such comparisons and interchanges to move a node upward to the appropriate position once its label is decreased.] Similarly, when the topmost node is removed from V, moving the node downward to the appropriate level in the heap requires at most $\log N$ steps and $O(\log N)$ operations. (Each step requires the interchange of the position of the node and the position of one of its descendants. The descendant must be in V for the step to be executed; if both descendants are in V, the one with smaller label is selected.)

(in ascending order) looking for a label value with nonempty list, instead of scanning the candidate list V. As will be seen shortly, this leads to a worst case operation count of $O(NC)$ for minimum label node searching, and to an $O(A + NC)$ operation count overall. The algorithm is pseudopolynomial, but for small values of C (much smaller than N) it performs very well in practice.

To visualize the algorithm, it is useful to think of each integer in the range $[0, (N-1)C]$ as some kind of container, referred to as a *bucket*. Each bucket b holds the nodes with label equal to b. A data structure such as a doubly linked list (see Fig. 3.5) can be used to maintain the set of nodes belonging to a given bucket, so that checking the emptiness of a bucket and

Bucket b	0	1	2	3	4	5	6	7	8
Contents	3	–	1,4,5	2,7	–	6	–	–	–
$FIRST(b)$	3	0	1	2	0	6	0	0	0

Node i	1	2	3	4	5	6	7
Label d_i	2	3	0	2	2	5	3
$NEXT(i)$	4	7	0	5	0	0	0
$PREVIOUS(i)$	0	0	0	1	4	0	2

Figure 3.5   Organization of the candidate list V in buckets using a doubly linked list. For each bucket b we maintain the first node of the bucket in an array element $FIRST(b)$, where $FIRST(b) = 0$ if bucket b is empty. For every node i we maintain two array elements, $NEXT(i)$ and $PREVIOUS(i)$, giving the next node and the preceding node, respectively, of node i in the bucket where i is curently residing [$NEXT(i) = 0$ or $PREVIOUS(i) = 0$ if i is the last node or the first node in its bucket, respectively]. In this example, there are 7 nodes and 8 buckets.

inserting or removing a node from a bucket are easy, requiring $O(1)$ operations.

Figure 3.6 illustrates the method with an example. Tracing steps, we see that the method starts with the origin node 1 in bucket 0 and all other buckets empty. At the first iteration, each node j with $(1, j) \in \mathcal{A}$ enters the candidate list V and is inserted in bucket $d_j = a_{1j}$. If for some j we have $d_j = 0$, then node j is inserted in bucket 0, and is removed next from V. After we are done with bucket 0, we proceed to check bucket 1. If it is nonempty, we repeat the process, removing from V all nodes with label 1 and moving other nodes to smaller numbered buckets as required; if not, we check bucket 2, and so on.

We note that it is sufficient to maintain only $C + 1$ buckets, rather than $(N - 1)C + 1$, thereby significantly saving in memory. The reason is that if we are currently searching bucket b, then all buckets beyond $b + C$ are known to be empty. To see this, note that the label d_j of any node j must be of

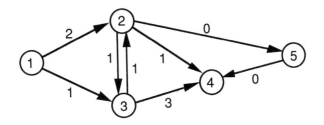

Iter.	Cand.	Node	Buck.	Buck.	Buck.	Buck.	Buck.	Out
#	List V	Labels	0	1	2	3	4	of V
1	$\{1\}$	$(0,\infty,\infty,\infty,\infty)$	1	–	–	–	–	1
2	$\{2,3\}$	$(0,2,1,\infty,\infty)$	1	3	2	–	–	3
3	$\{2,4\}$	$(0,2,1,4,\infty)$	1	3	2	–	4	2
4	$\{4,5\}$	$(0,2,1,3,2)$	1	3	2,5	4	–	5
5	$\{4\}$	$(0,2,1,2,2)$	1	3	2,4,5	–	–	4
	$\emptyset$	$(0,2,1,2,2)$	1	3	2,4,5	–	–	

Figure 3.6   An example illustrating Dial's method.

the form $d_i + a_{ij}$, where i is a node that has already been removed from the candidate list. Since $d_i \leq b$ and $a_{ij} \leq C$, it follows that $d_j \leq b + C$.

The idea of using buckets to maintain the nodes of the candidate list can be generalized considerably. In particular, buckets of width larger than 1 may be used. This results in fewer buckets to search over, thereby alleviating the $O(NC)$ bottleneck of the operation count of the algorithm. There is a price for this, namely the need to search for a minimum label node within the current bucket. This search can be speeded up by using buckets with nonuniform widths, and by breaking down buckets of large width into buckets of smaller width at the right moment. With intelligent strategies of this type, one may obtain label setting methods with very good polynomial complexity bounds; see [Joh77], [DeF79], [AMO88].

1.3.3   Label Correcting Methods

In these methods, the selection of the node to be removed from the candidate list V is faster than in label setting methods, at the expense of multiple entrances of nodes in V.

All of these methods use some type of queue to maintain the candidate list V. They differ in the way the queue is structured, and in the choice of the queue position into which nodes are entered.

The simplest of these methods, operates in cycles of iterations. In each cycle the nodes are scanned in some order; when a node i is found to belong to V, an iteration removing i from V is performed. This is a variant of one of the first methods proposed for the shortest path problem, known as the *Bellman-Ford method*. It is possible to show that if all cycles have nonnegative length this method requires at most N cycles; see Exercise 3.4. Each cycle consists of at most N iterations, requiring a total of $O(A)$ operations (each arc is examined at most once in each cycle). Thus, the total operation count for the method is $O(NA)$.

The best practical implementations of label correcting methods are more sophisticated than the one just described. Their worst case complexity bound is no better than the $O(NA)$ bound for the simple implementation derived above, and in some cases it is far worse. Yet their practical performance is far better.

The D'Esopo-Pape Algorithm

In this method, a node is always removed from the top of the queue used to store the candidate list V. A node, upon entrance in the queue, is placed at the bottom of the queue if it has never been in the queue before; otherwise it is placed at the top. The idea here is that when a node i is removed from the queue, its label affects the labels of a subset B_i of the neighbor nodes j with $(i,j) \in \mathcal{A}$. When the label of i changes again, it is likely that the labels of the nodes in B_i will require updating also. It is thus intuitively sensible to place the node at the top of the queue so that the labels of the nodes in B_i get a chance to be updated as quickly as possible.

The D'Esopo-Pape algorithm is very simple to implement and performs very well in practice for a broad variety of problems. Despite this fact, examples have been constructed [Ker81], [ShW81], where it performs very poorly. In particular, in these examples, the number of times some nodes enter the candidate list V is not polynomial. References [Pal84] and [GaP88] give a polynomial variation of the algorithm, which is the basis for the code of Appendix A.2.

The Threshold Algorithm

The premise of this algorithm is that *it is generally a good policy to remove from the candidate list a node with relatively small label*. When the arc lengths are nonnegative, this policy tends to reduce the number of times a node reenters the candidate list. In particular, when the node with smallest label is removed from the candidate list, as in Dijkstra's algorithm, this node never reenters the list; see also the discussion preceding Prop. 3.3 and Exercise 3.7.

The threshold algorithm attempts to emulate approximately the minimum label selection policy of Dijkstra's algorithm with a much smaller computational effort. The candidate list V is organized into two distinct queues Q' and Q'' using a *threshold* parameter s. The queue Q' contains nodes with "small" labels; that is, it contains only nodes whose labels are no larger than s. At each iteration, a node is removed from Q', and any node j to be added to the candidate list is inserted in Q''. When the queue Q' is exhausted, the entire candidate list is repartitioned. The threshold is adjusted and the queues Q' and Q'' are recalculated, so that Q' consists of the nodes with labels that are no larger than the new threshold.

The performance of this method is quite sensitive to the method used to adjust the thresholds. For example, if s is taken to be equal to the current minimum label, the method is identical to Dijkstra's algorithm; if s is larger than all node labels, Q'' is empty and the algorithm reduces to the generic label correcting method. With an effective choice of threshold, the practical performance of the algorithm is very good. A number of heuristic approaches have been developed for selecting the threshold (see [GKP85a], [GKP85b], and [GaP88]). If all arc lengths are nonnegative, a bound $O(NA)$ on the operation count of the algorithm can be shown; see Exercise 3.7.

1.3.4   Single Origin/Single Destination Methods

Suppose that there is only one destination, call it t, and we want to find the shortest distance from the origin node 1 to t. We could use our earlier single origin/all destinations algorithms, but some improvements are possible.

Label Setting

Suppose first that we use the label setting method. Then we can stop the method when the destination t becomes permanently labeled; further computation will not improve the label d_t. If t is closer to the origin than many other nodes, the saving in computation time will be significant. Note that this approach can also be used when there are several destinations. The method is stopped when all destinations have been permanently labeled.

Another interesting possibility is to use a *two-sided label setting method*; that is, a method that simultaneously proceeds from the origin to the destination *and* from the destination to the origin. In this method, we successively label permanently the closest nodes to the origin (with their shortest distance *from* the origin) and the closest nodes to the destination (with their shortest distance *to* the destination). When some node gets permanently labeled from both sides, the labeling can stop; by combining the forward and backward paths of each labeled node and by comparing the resulting origin-to-destination paths, one can obtain a shortest path (see Exercise 3.8). For many problems, this approach can lead to a dramatic reduction in the total number of iterations. However, this two-sided labeling approach does not work when there are multiple destinations.

Label Correcting

Unfortunately, when label correcting methods are used, it may not be easy to realize the savings just discussed in connection with label setting. The difficulty is that even after we discover several paths to the destination t (each marked by an entrance of t into V), we cannot be sure that better paths will not be discovered later. In the presence of additional problem structure, however, the number of times various nodes will enter V can be reduced considerably.

Suppose that at the start of the algorithm we have, for each node i, an *underestimate* u_i of the shortest distance from i to t (we require $u_t = 0$). For example, if all arc lengths are nonnegative we may take $u_i = 0$ for all i. (We do not exclude the possibility that $u_i = -\infty$ for some i, which corresponds to the case where no underestimate is available for the shortest distance of i.) The following algorithm is a modified version of the generic shortest path algorithm.

Initially

$$V = \{1\},$$

$$d_1 = 0, \qquad d_i = \infty, \qquad \forall \, i \neq 1.$$

The algorithm proceeds in iterations and terminates when V is empty. The typical iteration (if V is assumed nonempty) is as follows.

Typical Iteration of the Generic Single Origin/Single Destination Algorithm

Remove a node i from V. For each outgoing arc $(i, j) \in \mathcal{A}$, with $j \neq 1$, if

$$d_i + a_{ij} < \min\{d_j, d_t - u_j\}$$

set

$$d_j := d_i + a_{ij}$$

and add j to V if it does not already belong to V.

The preceding iteration is the same as that of the generic algorithm, except that the test $d_i + a_{ij} < d_j$ for entering a node j into V is replaced by the more stringent test $d_i + a_{ij} < \min\{d_j, d_t - u_j\}$. (In fact, when the trivial underestimate $u_j = -\infty$ is used for all $j \neq t$ the two iterations coincide.) The idea is as follows: The label d_j corresponds at all times to the best path found thus far from 1 to j (cf. Prop. 3.2). Intuitively, the purpose of entering node j in V when its label is reduced is to generate shorter paths to the destination that pass through node j. If P_j is the path from 1 to j corresponding to $d_i + a_{ij}$, then $d_i + a_{ij} + u_j$ is an underestimate of the shortest path length among the set of paths $\mathcal{P}_j$ that first follow path P_j to node j and then follow some other path from j to t. If

$$d_i + a_{ij} + u_j \geq d_t,$$

then the current best path to t, which corresponds to d_t, is at least as short as any of the paths in $\mathcal{P}_j$, which have P_j as their first component. It is unnecessary to consider such paths, and for this reason node j need not be entered in V. In this way, the number of node entrances in V may be sharply reduced.

Figure 3.7 illustrates the algorithm. The following proposition proves its validity.

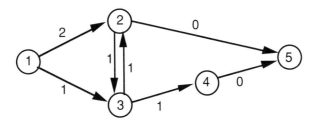

Iter. #	Candidate List V	Node Labels	Node out of V
1	$\{1\}$	$(0, \infty, \infty, \infty, \infty)$	1
2	$\{2, 3\}$	$(0, 2, 1, \infty, \infty)$	2
3	$\{3, 5\}$	$(0, 2, 1, \infty, 2)$	3
4	$\{5\}$	$(0, 2, 1, \infty, 2)$	5
	$\emptyset$	$(0, 2, 1, \infty, 2)$	

Figure 3.7   Illustration of the generic single origin/single destination algorithm. Here the destination is $t = 5$ and the underestimates of shortest distances to t are $u_i = 0$ for all i. Note that at iteration 3, when node 3 is removed from V, the label of node 4 is not improved to $d_4 = 2$ and node 4 is not entered in V. The reason is that $d_3 + a_{34}$ (which is equal to 2) is not smaller than $d_5 - u_4$ (which is also equal to 2). Note also that upon termination the label of a node other than t may not be equal to its shortest distance (e.g. d_4).

Proposition 3.4:   Consider the generic single origin/single destination algorithm.

(a) At the end of each iteration, the following conditions hold:

    (i) $d_1 = 0$.

    (ii) If $d_j < \infty$ and $j \neq 1$, then d_j is the length of some path that starts at 1, never returns to 1, and ends at j.

(b) If the algorithm terminates, then upon termination, either $d_t < \infty$, in which case d_t is the shortest distance from 1 to t, or else there is no path from 1 to t.

(c) If the algorithm does not terminate, there exist paths of arbitrarily small length that start at 1 and never return to 1.

Proof: (a) The proof is identical to the corresponding parts of Prop. 3.2.

(b) If upon termination we have $d_t = \infty$, then the extra test $d_i + a_{ij} + u_j < d_t$ for entering V is always passed, so the algorithm generates the same label sequences as the generic (many destinations) shortest path algorithm. Therefore, Prop. 3.2(b) applies and shows that there is no path from 1 to t.

Let $\bar{d}_j$ be the final values of the labels d_j obtained upon termination and suppose that $\bar{d}_t < \infty$. Assume, to arrive at a contradiction, that there is a path $P_t = (1, j_1, j_2, \ldots, j_k, t)$ that has length L_t with $L_t < \bar{d}_t$. For $m = 1, \ldots, k$, let L_{j_m} be the length of the path $P_m = (1, j_1, j_2, \ldots, j_m)$.

Let us focus on the node j_k preceding t on the path P_t. We claim that $L_{j_k} < \bar{d}_{j_k}$. Indeed, if this were not so, then j_k must have been removed at some iteration from V with a label d_{j_k} satisfying $d_{j_k} \leq L_{j_k}$. If d_t is the label of t at the start of that iteration, we would then have

$$d_{j_k} + a_{j_k t} \leq L_{j_k} + a_{j_k t} = L_t < \bar{d}_t \leq d_t,$$

implying that the label of t would be reduced at that iteration from d_t to $d_{j_k} + a_{j_k t}$, which is less than the final label $\bar{d}_t$ – a contradiction. Next we focus on the node j_{k-1} preceding j_k and t on the path P_t. We use a similar (though not identical) argument to show that $L_{j_{k-1}} < \bar{d}_{j_{k-1}}$. Indeed, if this were not so, then j_{k-1} must have been removed at some iteration from V with a label $d_{j_{k-1}}$ satisfying $d_{j_{k-1}} \leq L_{j_{k-1}}$. If d_{j_k} and d_t are the labels of j_k and t at the start of that iteration, we would then have

$$d_{j_{k-1}} + a_{j_{k-1} j_k} \leq L_{j_{k-1}} + a_{j_{k-1} j_k} = L_{j_k} < \bar{d}_{j_k} \leq d_{j_k}, \tag{3.17}$$

and since $L_{j_k} + u_{j_k} \leq L_t < \bar{d}_t \leq d_t$, we would also have

$$d_{j_{k-1}} + a_{j_{k-1} j_k} < d_t - u_{j_k}. \tag{3.18}$$

From Eqs. (3.17) and (3.18), it follows that the label of j_k would be reduced at that iteration from d_{j_k} to $d_{j_k} + a_{j_k t}$, which is less than the final label $\overline{d}_{j_k}$ – a contradiction.

Proceeding similarly, we obtain $L_{j_m} < \overline{d}_{j_m}$ for all $m = 1, \ldots, k$, and in particular $a_{1j_1} = L_{j_1} < \overline{d}_{j_1}$. Since

$$a_{1j_1} + u_{j_1} \leq L_t < \overline{d}_t,$$

and d_t is monotonically nonincreasing throughout the algorithm, we see that at the first iteration, j_1 will enter V with the label a_{1j_1}, which cannot be less than the final label $\overline{d}_{j_1}$. This is a contradiction; the proof of part (b) is complete.

(c) The proof is identical to the proof of Prop. 3.2(c).   **Q.E.D.**

There are a number of possible implementations of the algorithm of this subsection, which parallel the ones given earlier for the many destinations problem. An interesting possibility to speed up the algorithm arises when an *overestimate* v_j of the shortest distance from j to t is known *a priori*. (We require $v_t = 0$; also $v_j = \infty$ implies that no overestimate is known for j.) The idea is that the method still works if the test $d_i + a_{ij} < d_t - u_j$ is replaced by the possibly sharper test $d_i + a_{ij} < D - u_j$, where D is any overestimate of the shortest distance from 1 to t with $D \leq d_t$ (check the proof of Prop. 3.4). We can obtain estimates D that may be strictly smaller than d_t by using the scalars v_j as follows: each time the label of a node j is reduced, we check whether $d_j + v_j < D$; if this is so, we replace D by $d_j + v_j$. In this way, we make the test for future admissibility into the candidate list V more stringent and save some unnecessary node entrances in V. This idea is used in some versions of the branch-and-bound method for integer programming; see Section 1.4 of [Ber87].

1.3.5   Multiple Origin/Multiple Destination Methods

Consider now the all-pairs shortest path problem where we want to find a shortest path from each node to each other node. The *Floyd-Warshall algorithm* is specifically designed for this problem, and it is not any faster when applied to the single destination problem. It starts with the initial condition

$$D_{ij}^0 = \begin{cases} a_{ij}, & \text{if } (i,j) \in \mathcal{A} \\ \infty, & \text{otherwise} \end{cases}$$

and generates sequentially for all $k = 0, 1, \ldots, N-1$, and all nodes i and j,

$$D_{ij}^{k+1} = \begin{cases} \min\left\{D_{ij}^k, \ D_{i(k+1)}^k + D_{(k+1)j}^k\right\}, & \text{if } j \neq i \\ \infty, & \text{otherwise.} \end{cases}$$

An induction argument shows that D_{ij}^k gives the shortest distance from node i to node j using only nodes from 1 to k as intermediate nodes. Thus, D_{ij}^N gives the shortest distance from i to j (with no restriction on the intermediate nodes). There are N iterations, each requiring $O(N^2)$ operations, for a total of $O(N^3)$ operations.

Unfortunately, the Floyd-Warshall algorithm cannot take advantage of sparsity of the graph. It appears that for sparse problems it is typically better to apply a single origin/all destinations algorithm separately for each origin. If all the arc lengths are nonnegative, a label setting method can be used separately for each origin. If there are negative arc lengths (but no negative length cycles), one can of course apply a label correcting method separately for each origin, but there is another alternative that results in a superior worst-case complexity. It is possible to apply a label correcting method only *once* to a single origin/all destinations problem and obtain an equivalent all-pairs shortest path problem with nonnegative arc lengths; the latter problem can be solved using N separate applications of a label setting method. This alternative is based on the following proposition, which applies to the general minimum cost flow problem.

Proposition 3.5:   Every minimum cost flow problem with arc costs a_{ij} such that all simple forward cycles have nonnegative cost is equivalent to another minimum cost flow problem involving the same graph and nonnegative arc costs $\hat{a}_{ij}$ of the form

$$\hat{a}_{ij} = a_{ij} + d_i - d_j, \qquad \forall \ (i,j) \in \mathcal{A},$$

where the scalars d_i can be found by solving a single origin/all destinations shortest path problem. The two problems are equivalent in the sense that they have the same constraints, and the cost function of one is the same as the cost function of the other plus a constant.

Proof: Let $(\mathcal{N}, \mathcal{A})$ be the graph of the given problem. Introduce a new node 0 and an arc $(0, i)$ for each $i \in \mathcal{N}$, thereby obtaining a new graph $(\mathcal{N}', \mathcal{A}')$. Consider the shortest path problem involving this graph, with arc lengths a_{ij} for the arcs $(i, j) \in \mathcal{A}$ and 0 for the arcs $(0, i)$. Since all incident arcs of node 0 are outgoing, all simple forward cycles of $(\mathcal{N}', \mathcal{A}')$ are also simple forward cycles of $(\mathcal{N}, \mathcal{A})$ and, by assumption, have nonnegative length. Since any forward cycle can be decomposed into a collection of simple forward cycles (cf. Exercise 1.5), all forward cycles (not necessarily simple) of $(\mathcal{N}', \mathcal{A}')$ have nonnegative length. Furthermore, there is at least one path from node 0 to every other node i, namely the path consisting of arc $(0, i)$. Therefore, the shortest distances d_i from node 0 to all other nodes i can be found by a label correcting method, and by Prop. 3.2, we have

$$\hat{a}_{ij} = a_{ij} + d_i - d_j \geq 0, \qquad \forall \ (i,j) \in \mathcal{A}.$$

Let us now view $\sum_{(i,j)\in\mathcal{A}} \hat{a}_{ij}x_{ij}$ as the cost function of a minimum cost flow problem involving the graph $(\mathcal{N}, \mathcal{A})$ and the constraints of the original problem. We have

$$
\sum_{(i,j)\in\mathcal{A}} \hat{a}_{ij}x_{ij} = \sum_{(i,j)\in\mathcal{A}} \left(a_{ij} + d_i - d_j\right)x_{ij}
$$

$$
= \sum_{(i,j)\in\mathcal{A}} a_{ij}x_{ij} + \sum_{i\in\mathcal{N}} d_i \left(\sum_{\{j|(i,j)\in\mathcal{A}\}} x_{ij} - \sum_{\{j|(j,i)\in\mathcal{A}\}} x_{ji} \right)
$$

$$
= \sum_{(i,j)\in\mathcal{A}} a_{ij}x_{ij} + \sum_{i\in\mathcal{N}} d_i s_i,
$$

where s_i is the given supply of node i. Thus, the two cost functions $\sum_{(i,j)\in\mathcal{A}} \hat{a}_{ij}x_{ij}$ and $\sum_{(i,j)\in\mathcal{A}} a_{ij}x_{ij}$ differ by the constant $\sum_{i\in\mathcal{N}} d_i s_i$.   **Q.E.D.**

It can be seen now that the all-pairs shortest path problem can be solved by using a label correcting method to solve the single origin/all destinations problem described in the above proof, thereby obtaining the scalars d_i and $\hat{a}_{ij}$, and by then applying a label setting method N times to solve the all-pairs shortest path problem involving the nonnegative arc lengths $\hat{a}_{ij}$. The shortest distance D_{ij} from i to j is obtained by adding $d_i - d_j$ to the shortest distance from i to j found by the label setting method.

Still another possibility for solving the all-pairs shortest path problem is to solve N separate single origin/all destinations problems but to also use the results of the computation for one origin to start the computation for the next origin. This can be done efficiently in the context of the simplex method presented in the next chapter; see also [GaP86], [GaP88].

EXERCISES

Exercise 3.1

Consider the graph of Fig. 3.8. Find a shortest path from 1 to all nodes using the binary heap method, Dial's algorithm, and the D'Esopo-Pape algorithm.

Exercise 3.2

Consider the graph of Fig. 3.8. Find a shortest path from node 1 to node 6 using the generic single origin/single destination method of Section 1.3.4 with all distance underestimates equal to zero.

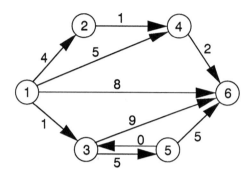

Figure 3.8   Graph for Exercises 3.1 and 3.2. The arc lengths are the numbers shown next to the arcs.

Exercise 3.3 (Shortest Path Tree Construction)

Consider the single origin/all destinations shortest path problem and assume that all cycles have nonnegative length. Consider the generic algorithm of Section 1.3.1, and assume that each time a label d_j is decreased to $d_i + a_{ij}$ the arc (i, j) is recorded in an array $PRED(j)$. Consider the subgraph of the arcs $PRED(j)$, $j \in \mathcal{N}$, $j \neq 1$. Show that after the first iteration this subgraph is a tree rooted at the origin, and that upon termination it is a shortest path tree.

Exercise 3.4 (The Bellman-Ford Algorithm)

Consider the single origin/all destinations shortest path problem. Assume that there is a path from the origin to all destinations, and that all cycles have nonnegative length. The Bellman-Ford algorithm starts with the initial conditions

$$d_1^0 = 0, \qquad d_j^0 = \infty, \qquad \forall\, j \neq 1$$

and generates d_j^k, $k = 1, 2, \ldots$, according to

$$d_1^k = 0, \qquad d_j^k = \min_{(i,j) \in \mathcal{A}} \{ d_i^{k-1} + a_{ij} \}, \qquad \forall\, j \neq 1.$$

(a) Show that for all k, d_j^k is the shortest distance from 1 to j using paths with k arcs or less.

(b) Show that the algorithm terminates after at most N iterations, in the sense that for some $k \leq N$ we have $d_j^k = d_j^{k-1}$ for all j. Conclude that the running time of the algorithm is $O(NA)$.

(c) Consider a label correcting method that operates in cycles of iterations. In each cycle the nodes are scanned in a fixed order, and when a node i is found to belong to V an iteration removing i from V is performed (thus, there are as many as N iterations in a single cycle). Show that if $\overline{d}_j^k$ is the label of node j at the end of the kth cycle then $\overline{d}_j^k \leq d_j^k$, where d_j^k are the iterates of the Bellman-Ford algorithm. Conclude that this label correcting method has an $O(NA)$ running time.

Exercise 3.5 (Min-Path/Max-Tension Theorem)

For a price vector $p = (p_1, \ldots, p_N)$, define the *tension* of arc (i, j) as $t_{ij} = p_i - p_j$ and the tension of a forward path P as $T_P = \sum_{(i,j) \in P^+} t_{ij}$. Show that the shortest distance between two nodes i_1 and i_2 is equal to the maximal tension T_P over all forward paths P starting at i_1 and ending at i_2, and all price vectors p satisfying the constraint $t_{ij} \leq a_{ij}$ for all arcs (i, j). Interpret this as a duality result. *Note*: An intuitive explanation of this result in terms of a mechanical model is given in Section 4.3; see Fig. 3.1 of that section.

Exercise 3.6 (Path Bottleneck Problem)

Consider the framework of the shortest path problem. For any path P, define the *bottleneck arc* of P as an arc that has maximum length over all arcs of P. Consider the problem of finding a path connecting two given nodes and having minimum length of bottleneck arc. Derive an analog of Prop. 3.1 for this problem. Consider also a single origin/all destinations version of this problem. Develop an analog of the generic algorithm of Section 1.3.1, and prove an analog of Prop. 3.2. *Hint:* Replace $d_i + a_{ij}$ with $\max\{d_i, a_{ij}\}$.

Exercise 3.7 (Complexity of the Generic Algorithm)

Consider the generic algorithm, and assume that all arc lengths are nonnegative.

(a) Consider a node j satisfying at some time

$$d_j \leq d_i, \qquad \forall \ i \in V.$$

Show that this relation will be satisfied at all subsequent times and that j will never again enter V. Furthermore, d_j will remain unchanged.

(b) Suppose that the algorithm is structured so that it removes from V a node of minimum label at least once every k iterations (k is some integer). Show that the algorithm will terminate in at most kN iterations.

(c) Show that the running time of the threshold algorithm is $O(NA)$. *Hint:* Define a cycle to be a sequence of iterations between successive repartitionings of the candidate list V. In each cycle, the node of V with minimum label at the start of the cycle will be removed from V during the cycle.

Exercise 3.8 (Two-Sided Label Setting)

Consider the shortest path problem from an origin node 1 to a destination node t, and assume that all arc lengths are nonnegative. This exercise considers an algorithm where label setting is applied simultaneously and independently from the origin and from the destination. In particular, the algorithm maintains a subset of nodes W, which are permanently labeled from the origin, and a subset of nodes V, which are permanently labeled from the destination. When W and V have a node i in common the algorithm terminates. The idea is that a shortest path from 1 to t cannot contain a node $j \notin W \cup V$; any such path must be longer than a shortest path from 1 to i followed by a shortest path from i to t (unless j and i are equally close to both 1 and to t).

Consider two subsets of nodes W and V with the following properties:

(1) $1 \in W$ and $t \in V$.

(2) W and V have nonempty intersection.

(3) If $i \in W$ and $j \notin W$, then the shortest distance from 1 to i is less than or equal to the shortest distance from 1 to j.

(4) If $i \in V$ and $j \notin V$, then the shortest distance from i to t is less than or equal to the shortest distance from j to t.

Let d_i^1 be the shortest distance from 1 to i using paths all the nodes of which, with the possible exception of i, lie in W ($d_i^1 = \infty$ if no such path exists), and let d_i^t be the shortest distance from i to t using paths all the nodes of which, with the possible exception of i, lie in V ($d_i^t = \infty$ if no such path exists).

(a) Show that such W, V, d_i^1, and d_i^t can be found by applying a label setting method simultaneously for the single origin problem with origin node 1 and for the single destination problem with destination node t.

(b) Show that the shortest distance D_{1t} from 1 to t is given by

$$D_{1t} = \min_{i \in W} \left\{ d_i^1 + d_i^t \right\} = \min_{i \in W \cup V} \left\{ d_i^1 + d_i^t \right\} = \min_{i \in V} \left\{ d_i^1 + d_i^t \right\}.$$

(c) Show that the nonempty intersection condition (2) can be replaced by the condition $\min_{i \in W} \left\{ d_i^1 + d_i^t \right\} \leq \max_{i \in W} d_i^1 + \max_{i \in V} d_i^t$.

Exercise 3.9 (k Shortest Node-Disjoint Paths)

Consider a graph with an origin 1, a destination t, and a length for each arc. We want to find k paths from 1 to t which share no node other 1 and t and which are such that the sum of the k path lengths is minimum. Formulate this problem as a minimum cost flow problem. *Hint:* Replace each node i other than 1 and t with two nodes i and i' and a connecting arc (i, i') with flow bounds $0 \leq x_{ii'} \leq 1$.

Exercise 3.10 (The Doubling Algorithm)

The *doubling algorithm* for solving the all-pairs shortest path problem is given by

$$D_{ij}^1 = \begin{cases} a_{ij}, & \text{if } (i,j) \in \mathcal{A} \\ 0, & \text{if } i = j \\ \infty, & \text{otherwise} \end{cases}$$

$$D_{ij}^{2k} = \begin{cases} \min_m \{ D_{im}^k + D_{mj}^k \}, & \text{if } i \neq j, \ k = 1, 2, \ldots, \lfloor \log(N-1) \rfloor \\ 0, & \text{if } i = j, \ k = 1, 2, \ldots, \lfloor \log(N-1) \rfloor. \end{cases}$$

Show that for $i \neq j$, D_{ij}^k gives the shortest distance from i to j using paths with 2^{k-1} arcs or fewer. Show also that the running time is $O(N^3 \log m^*)$, where m^* is the maximum number of arcs in a shortest path.

Exercise 3.11 (Nonstandard Initial Conditions)

It is sometimes useful to start the generic algorithm with initial conditions other than the standard $V = \{1\}$, $d_1 = 0$, $d_j = \infty$ for $j \neq 1$. Such a possibility arises, for example, when shortest paths with respect to slightly different arc lengths are known from an earlier optimization. This exercise characterizes initial conditions under which the algorithm maintains its validity.

(a) Suppose that the initial V and d in the generic algorithm satisfy conditions (i), (ii), and (iii) of part (a) of Prop. 3.2. Show that the algorithm is still valid in the sense that parts (b) and (c) of Prop. 3.2 hold.

(b) Use the result of part (a) to derive "promising" initial conditions for application of the generic algorithm using paths from 1 to all other nodes, which are shortest with respect to slightly different arc lengths.

Exercise 3.12 (Uniqueness of Solution of Bellman's Equation)

Assume that all cycles have positive length. Show that if a vector $d = (d_1, d_2, \ldots, d_N)$ satisfies

$$d_j = \min_{(i,j) \in \mathcal{A}} \{ d_i + a_{ij} \}, \qquad \forall \, j \neq 1,$$

$$d_1 = 0,$$

then for all j, d_j is the shortest distance from 1 to j. Show by example that this need not be true if there is a cycle of length 0. *Hint:* Consider the arcs (i, j) attaining the minimum in the above equation and consider the paths formed by these arcs.

1.4   NOTES AND SOURCES

Network problems are discussed in many books ([BeG62], [Dan63], [BuS65], [Iri69], [Hu69], [FrF70], [Chr75], [Mur76], [Law76], [Zou76], [BaJ78], [Min78], [KeH80], [JeB80], [PaS82], [Chv83], [GoM84], [Lue84], [Roc84], [BJS90]). Several of these books discuss linear programming first and develop linear network optimization as a special case. An alternative approach that relies heavily on duality, is given in [Roc84]. Bibliographies on the subject are provided in [GoM77], [VoR82], and [VoR85].

1.1.   The conformal realization theorem has been developed in different forms in several sources [FoF62], [BuS65]. In our presentation we follow [Roc84].

1.2.   The primal cost improvement approach for network optimization was initiated by Dantzig [Dan51], who specialized the simplex method to the transportation problem. The extensive subsequent work using this approach is surveyed at the end of Chapter 2.

The max flow-min cut theorem was discovered independently in [DaF56], [EFS56], and [FoF56b]. The proof that the Ford-Fulkerson algorithm with breadth-first search has polynomial complexity $O(NA^2)$ (Exercise 2.10) is due to [EdK72]. With proper implementation, this bound was improved to $O(N^2 A)$ in [Din70], and to $O(N^3)$ in [Kar74]. A number of algorithms based on augmentation ideas were subsequently proposed ([Che77], [MKM78], [Gal80], [GaN80]). A different approach, which bears a close connection to the auction and ϵ-relaxation ideas discussed in Chapter 4, was proposed in [Gol85b]; see also [GoT86], [AhO86].

The dual cost improvement approach was initiated by Kuhn [Kuh55] who proposed the *Hungarian method* for the assignment problem. (The name of the algorithm honors its connection with the research of the Hungarian mathematician Egervary [Ege31].) Work using this approach is surveyed in Chapter 3.

The auction approach was initiated by the author in [Ber79] for the assignment problem, and in [Ber86a], [Ber86b] for the minimum cost flow problem. Work using this approach is surveyed at the end of Chapter 4.

The feasible distribution theorem (Exercise 2.5) is due to [Gal57] and [Hof60]. The maximal matching/minimal cover theorem is due to [Kon31] and [Ege31]. The theory of distinct representatives (Exercise 2.13) originated with [Hal56]; see also [HoK56] and [MeD58].

1.3. Work on the shortest path problem is very extensive. Literature surveys are given in [Dre69], [GPR82], and [DeP84]. The generic algorithm was first explicitly suggested as a unifying framework of many of the existing shortest path algorithms in [Pal84] and [GaP86].

The first label setting method was suggested in [Dij59], and also independently in [Dan60] and [WhH60]. The binary heap and related implementations were suggested in [Joh77]. Dial's algorithm was proposed in [Dia69] and received considerable attention after the appearance of [DGK79]; see also [DeF79]. For related algorithms using variable size buckets, see [Joh77], [DeF79], and [AMO88].

Label correcting methods were proposed in [Bel57] and [For56]. The D'Esopo-Pape algorithm appeared in [Pap74] based on an earlier suggestion of D'Esopo. The threshold algorithm is developed in [GKP85a], [GKP85b], and [GGK86a].

Two-sided label setting methods for the single origin/single destination problem (Exercise 3.8) were proposed in [Nic66]; see also [HKS89], which contains extensive computational results.

The Floyd-Warshall algorithm was given in [Flo62] and uses a theorem due to [War62]. Alternative algorithms for the all-pairs problem are given in [Dan67] and [Tab73].

2

Simplex Methods

The main idea of primal cost improvement is to start with a feasible flow vector x and to generate a sequence of other feasible flow vectors, each having a smaller primal cost than its predecessor. The main idea is that if the current flow vector is not optimal, an improved flow vector can be obtained by pushing flow along a simple cycle C with negative cost, that is,

$$\sum_{(i,j)\in C^+} a_{ij} - \sum_{(i,j)\in C^-} a_{ij} < 0,$$

where C^+ and C^- are the sets of forward and backward arcs of C, respectively (see Prop. 2.1 in Section 1.2).

There are several methods for finding negative cost cycles, but the most successful in practice are specialized versions of the simplex method for linear programming. This chapter focuses on methods of this type.

Simplex methods are not only useful for algorithmic solution of the problem; they also provide constructive proofs of some important analytical results. Chief among these are duality theorems asserting the equality of the primal and the dual optimal values, and the existence of optimal primal and dual solutions which are integer if the problem data are integer (see Prop. 2.3 in Section 2.2 and Prop. 3.2 in Section 2.3).

2.1   MAIN IDEAS IN SIMPLEX METHODS

To simplify the presentation, we first consider the version of the minimum cost flow problem with only nonnegativity constraints on the flows:

$$\text{minimize} \quad \sum_{(i,j)\in\mathcal{A}} a_{ij}x_{ij} \qquad\qquad \text{(MCF–N)}$$

subject to

$$\sum_{\{j|(i,j)\in\mathcal{A}\}} x_{ij} - \sum_{\{j|(j,i)\in\mathcal{A}\}} x_{ji} = s_i, \qquad \forall\, i \in \mathcal{N}, \qquad (1.1)$$

$$0 \le x_{ij}, \qquad \forall\, (i,j) \in \mathcal{A}, \qquad (1.2)$$

where a_{ij}, and s_i are given scalars.

We saw in Section 1.1.3 that the general minimum cost flow problem with upper and lower bounds on the arc flows can be converted to one with nonnegativity constraints. Thus, once we develop the main method for the simpler problem above, its extension to the more general problem will be straightforward.

The most important difference between the minimum cost flow problem with nonnegativity constraints and the one with upper and lower bounds is that the former can be *unbounded*. By this we mean that feasible flows may take arbitrarily large values, while the corresponding cost takes arbitrarily small (i.e., large negative) values. In particular, *the problem is unbounded if it is feasible and there exists a simple forward cycle with negative cost*, since then we can reduce the cost to arbitrarily large negative values by adding arbitrarily large flow along the negative cost cycle to any feasible flow vector. [In fact, we have seen an instance of this result in connection with the shortest path problem; cf. the corresponding minimum cost flow problem (3.3) in Section 1.3.] The converse is also true: *if the problem is unbounded, there must exist a simple forward cycle with negative cost*. This follows from Prop. 3.5 in Section 1.3, which implies that if the cost of every simple forward cycle is nonnegative, then the cost function of the problem is bounded from below by some constant.

Spanning Trees and Basic Flow Vectors

The main idea of the simplex method is to generate negative cost cycles by using a *spanning tree* of the given graph. Recall from Section 1.1 that a tree is an acyclic connected graph, and that a spanning tree of a given graph is a subgraph that is a tree and includes all nodes of the given graph. A *leaf node* of a tree is defined to be a node with a single incident arc. Figure 1.1 illustrates a spanning tree and a leaf node. The following lemma proves some important properties.

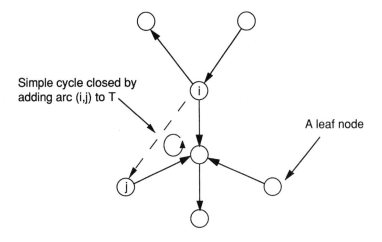

Simple cycle closed by
adding arc (i,j) to T

A leaf node

Figure 1.1   Illustration of a spanning tree T. Note that that there is a unique simple path of T connecting any pair of nodes. Furthermore, the addition of any arc to T [arc (i, j) in the figure] creates a unique simple cycle in which (i, j) is a forward arc.

Lemma 1.1:   Let T be a subgraph of a graph with N nodes.

   (a) If T is acyclic and has at least one arc, then it must have at least one leaf node.

   (b) T is a spanning tree if and only if it is connected and has N nodes and $N - 1$ arcs.

   (c) If T is a tree, for any two nodes i and j of T there is a unique simple path of T starting at i and ending at j. Furthermore, any arc e that is not in T, when added to T, creates a unique simple cycle in which e is a forward arc.

   (d) If T is a tree and an arc (i, j) of T is deleted, the remaining arcs of T form two disjoint trees, one containing i and the other containing j.

Proof: (a) Choose a node n_1 of T with at least one incident arc e_1 and let n_2 be the opposite node of that arc. If n_2 is a leaf node, the result is proved; else choose an arc $e_2 \neq e_1$ that is incident to n_2, and let n_3 be the opposite end node. If n_3 is a leaf node, the result is proved; else continue similarly. Eventually a leaf node will be found, for otherwise some node will be repeated in the sequence, which is impossible since T is acyclic.

(b) Let T be a spanning tree. Then T has N nodes, and since it is connected and acyclic, it must have a leaf node n_1. (We assume without loss of generality that $N \geq 2$.) Delete n_1 and its unique incident arc from T, thereby obtaining a connected graph T_1, which has $N - 1$ nodes and is acyclic. Repeat the process with T_1 in place of T, obtaining T_2, T_3, and so on. After $N - 1$ steps and $N - 1$ arc deletions, we will obtain T_{N-1}, which consists of a single node. This proves that T has $N - 1$ arcs.

Suppose now that T is connected and has N nodes and $N - 1$ arcs. If T had a simple cycle, by deleting any arc of the cycle, we would obtain a graph T_1 that would have $N - 2$ arcs and would still be connected. Continuing similarly if necessary, we obtain for some $k \geq 1$ a graph T_k, which has $N - k - 1$ arcs, and is connected and acyclic (i.e., it is a spanning tree). This is a contradiction, because we proved earlier that a spanning tree has exacly $N - 1$ arcs. Hence, T has no simple cycle and must be a spanning tree.

(c) There is at least one simple path starting at a node i and ending at a node j because T is connected. If there were a second path starting at i and ending at j, by reversing this path so that it starts at j and ends at i, and by concatenating it to the first path, we would form a cycle. It can be seen that this cycle must contain a simple cycle, since otherwise the two paths would be identical. This contradicts the hypothesis that T is a tree.

If arc e is added to T, it will form a simple cycle together with any simple path that lies in T and connects its end nodes. Since there is only one such path, it follows that e, together with the arcs of T, forms a unique simple cycle in which e is a forward arc.

(d) It can be seen that removal of a single arc from any connected graph either leaves the graph connected or else creates exactly two connected components. The unique simple path of T connecting i to j consists of arc (i, j); with the removal of this arc, no path connecting i to j remains, and the graph cannot stay connected. Hence, removal of (i, j) must create exactly two connected components, which must be trees since, being subgraphs of T, they must be acyclic.   **Q.E.D.**

Suppose that we have a feasible problem and we are given a spanning tree T. A key property for our purposes is that there is a flow vector x, satisfying the conservation of flow constraints (1.1), with the property that only arcs of T can have a nonzero flow. Such a flow vector is called *basic* and is uniquely determined by T, as the following proposition shows.

Proposition 1.1:   Assume that $\sum_{i \in \mathcal{N}} s_i = 0$. Then, for any spanning tree T, there exists a unique flow vector x that satisfies the conservation of flow constraints (1.1) and is such that all arcs not in T have zero flow. In particular, if an arc (i, j) of T separates T into two components T_i and T_j, containing i and j respectively, we have

$$x_{ij} = \sum_{n \in T_i} s_n.$$

Proof: To show uniqueness, note that for any flow vector x and arc $(i,j) \in T$ the flux across the cut $[T_i, \mathcal{N} - T_i]$ is equal to the sum of divergences of the nodes of T_i [see Eq. (2.5) in Section 1.2.2]. Thus, if x satisfies the conservation of flow constraints, the flux across the cut must be $\sum_{n \in T_i} s_n$. If in addition all arcs of the cut carry zero flow except for (i,j), this flux is just x_{ij}, so we must have

$$x_{ij} = \begin{cases} \sum_{n \in T_i} s_n & \text{if } (i,j) \in T \\ 0 & \text{if } (i,j) \notin T. \end{cases}$$

Thus, if a flow vector has the required properties, it must be equal to the vector x defined by the preceding formula.

To show existence, i.e. that the flow vector x, defined by the preceding formula, satisfies the conservation of flow constraints, we use a constructive proof based on the algorithm of Fig. 1.2. (An alternative algorithm is outlined in Exercise 1.4.)   **Q.E.D.**

Note that a basic flow vector need not be feasible; some of the arc flows may be negative, violating the lower bound constraints (see the example of Fig. 1.2). If the corresponding basic flow vector is feasible, the spanning tree will be called (with slight abuse of terminology) a *feasible tree*.

Overview of the Simplex Method

The simplex method starts with a feasible tree and proceeds in iterations, generating another feasible tree and a corresponding feasible basic flow vector at each iteration. The cost of each basic flow vector is no worse than the cost of its predecessor. At each iteration (also called a *pivot* in the standard terminology of linear programming), the method operates roughly as follows:

(a) It uses a convenient method to add one arc to the tree so as to generate a simple cycle with negative cost.

(b) It pushes along the cycle as much flow as possible without violating feasibility.

(c) It discards one arc of the cycle, thereby obtaining another feasible tree to be used at the next iteration.

Thus, each tree $\overline{T}$ in the sequence generated by the simplex method differs from its predecessor T by two arcs: the *out-arc* e, which belongs to T but not to $\overline{T}$, and the *in-arc* $\overline{e}$, which belongs to $\overline{T}$ but not to T; see Fig. 1.3. We will use the notation

$$\overline{T} = T + \overline{e} - e$$

to express this relation. The arc $\overline{e}$ when added to T closes a unique simple cycle in which $\overline{e}$ is a forward arc. This is the cycle along which we try to push

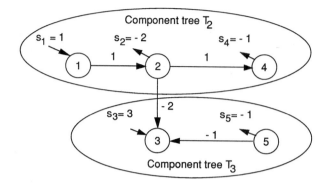

Iteration #	Leaf Node Selected	Arc Flow Computed
1	1	$x_{12} = 1$
2	5	$x_{53} = -1$
3	3	$x_{23} = -2$
4	2	$x_{24} = 1$

Figure 1.2 Method for constructing the flow vector corresponding to T, starting from the arc incident to some leaf node and proceeding "inward." The algorithm maintains a tree R, a flow vector x, and scalars $w_1, \ldots, w_N$. Upon termination, x is the desired flow vector. Initially, $R = T$, $x = 0$, and $w_i = s_i$ for all $i \in \mathcal{N}$.
Step 1: Choose a leaf node $i \in R$. If (i, j) is the unique incident arc of i, set

$$x_{ij} := w_i, \qquad w_j := w_j + w_i;$$

if (j, i) is the unique incident arc of i, set

$$x_{ji} := -w_i, \qquad w_j := w_j - w_i.$$

Step 2: Delete i and its incident arc from R. If R now consists of a single node, terminate; else, go to Step 1.

We now show that if $\sum_{n \in \mathcal{N}} s_n = 0$, the flow vector thus constructed satisfies the conservation of flow equations. Consider the typical iteration where the leaf node i of R is selected in Step 1. Suppose that (i, j) is the unique incident arc of R [the proof is similar if (j, i) is the incident arc]. Then just before this iteration, w_i is equal by construction to $s_i - \sum_{\{k \neq j | (i,k) \in \mathcal{A}\}} x_{ik} + \sum_{\{k | (k,i) \in \mathcal{A}\}} x_{ki}$, so by setting x_{ij} to w_i, the conservation of flow constraint is satisfied at node i. Upon termination, it is seen that for the last node i of R, w_i is equal to both $\sum_{n \in \mathcal{N}} s_n$ and $s_i - \sum_{\{k | (i,k) \in \mathcal{A}\}} x_{ik} + \sum_{\{k | (k,i) \in \mathcal{A}\}} x_{ki}$. Since $\sum_{n \in \mathcal{N}} s_n = 0$, the conservation of flow constraint is satisfied at this last node as well.

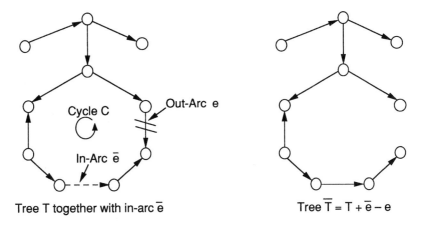

Figure 1.3   Successive trees T and $\overline{T}$ generated by the simplex method.

flow. (By convention, we require that the orientation of the cycle is the same as the orientation of the arc $\overline{e}$.)

Leaving aside for the moment the issue of how to select an initial feasible tree, the main questions now are:

(1) How to select the in-arc so as to close a cycle with negative cost or else detect that the current flow is optimal.

(2) How to select the out-arc so as to obtain a new feasible tree and associated flow vector.

(3) How to ensure that the method makes progress, eventually improving the primal cost. (The problem here is that even if a negative cost cycle is known, it may not be possible to push a positive amount of flow along the cycle because some backward arc on the cycle has zero flow. Thus, the flow vector may not change and the primal cost may not decrease strictly at any one pivot; in linear programming terminology, such a pivot is known as *degenerate*. Having to deal with degeneracy is the price for simplifying the search for a negative cost cycle.)

We take up these questions in sequence.

2.1.1   Using Prices to Obtain the In-Arc

Despite the fact that the simplex method is a primal cost improvement algorithm, it makes essential use of price vectors and duality ideas. In particular, the complementary slackness (CS) conditions

$$p_i - p_j \le a_{ij}, \qquad \forall\ (i,j) \in \mathcal{A}, \tag{1.3a}$$

$$p_i - p_j = a_{ij}, \qquad \text{for all } (i,j) \in \mathcal{A} \text{ with } 0 < x_{ij} \qquad (1.3b)$$

[see Eqs. (2.11c) and (2.11d) in Section 1.2] will play an important role. If x is feasible and together with p satisfies these CS conditions, then x is an optimal solution of the problem (MCF-N) and p is an optimal solution of its dual problem

$$\text{maximize } \sum_{i \in \mathcal{N}} s_i p_i$$

$$\text{subject to } \quad p_i - p_j \leq a_{ij}, \qquad \forall \ (i,j) \in \mathcal{A};$$

the proof of this closely parallels the proof of Prop. 2.4 in Section 1.2 and is outlined in Exercise 2.11 in Section 1.2.

Along with a feasible tree T, the simplex method maintains a *price vector* $p = (p_1, \ldots, p_N)$ such that

$$p_i - p_j = a_{ij}, \qquad \forall \ (i,j) \in T.$$

This is obtained as follows: Fix a node r, called the *root of the tree*, and set p_r to some arbitrary scalar value; for any node i, let P_i be the unique simple path of T starting at the root node r and ending at i, and define p_i by

$$p_i = p_r - \sum_{(m,n) \in P_i^+} a_{mn} + \sum_{(m,n) \in P_i^-} a_{mn}, \qquad (1.4)$$

where P_i^+ and P_i^- are the sets of forward and backward arcs of P_i, respectively. To see that with this definition of p_i we have $p_i - p_j = a_{ij}$ for all $(i,j) \in T$, write Eq. (1.4) for nodes i and j, subtract the two equations, and note that the paths P_i and P_j differ by just the arc (i,j).

For an equivalent construction method, select p_r arbitrarily, set the prices of the outward neighbors j of r with $(r,j) \in T$ to $p_j = p_r - a_{rj}$ and the prices of the inward neighbors j of r with $(j,r) \in T$ to $p_j = p_r + a_{jr}$, and then repeat the process with the neighbors j replacing r. Figure 1.4 gives an example.

It can be seen from Eq. (1.4), that *for each pair of nodes i and j, the price difference $(p_i - p_j)$ is independent of the arbitrarily chosen root node price p_r*; write Eq. (1.4) for node i and for node j, and subtract. Therefore, for each arc (i,j), the scalar

$$r_{ij} = a_{ij} + p_j - p_i, \qquad (1.5)$$

called the *reduced cost* of the arc, is uniquely defined by the spanning tree T. By the definition of p, we have

$$r_{ij} = 0, \qquad \forall \ (i,j) \in T,$$

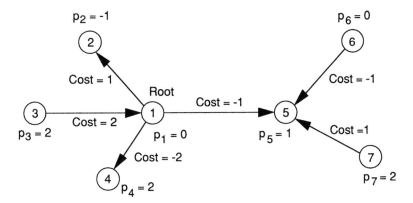

Figure 1.4   Illustration of the prices associated with a spanning tree. The root is chosen to be node 1, and its price is arbitrarily chosen to be 0. The other node prices are then uniquely determined by the requirement $p_i - p_j = a_{ij}$ for all arcs (i,j) of the spanning tree.

so if in addition we have

$$r_{ij} \geq 0, \qquad \forall \ (i,j) \notin T,$$

then the pair (x,p) satisfies the CS conditions (1.3a) and (1.3b). It then follows from Prop. 2.5 of Section 1.2 (more precisely, from the version of that proposition that applies to the problem with only nonnegativity constraints) that x is an optimal primal solution and p is an optimal dual solution.

If on the other hand, we have

$$r_{\bar{i}\bar{j}} < 0 \qquad\qquad\qquad\qquad (1.6)$$

for some arc $\bar{e} = (\bar{i}, \bar{j})$ not in T, then we claim that the unique simple cycle C formed by T and the arc $(\bar{i}, \bar{j})$ has negative cost. Indeed, the cost of C can be written in terms of the reduced costs of its arcs as

$$\sum_{(i,j)\in C^+} a_{ij} - \sum_{(i,j)\in C^-} a_{ij} = \sum_{(i,j)\in C^+} \left(a_{ij} + p_j - p_i\right) - \sum_{(i,j)\in C^-} \left(a_{ij} + p_j - p_i\right)$$
$$= \sum_{(i,j)\in C^+} r_{ij} - \sum_{(i,j)\in C^-} r_{ij}. \qquad\qquad (1.7)$$

Since $r_{ij} = 0$ for all $(i,j) \in T$ [see Eq. (1.5)], and $\bar{e}$ is a forward arc of C by convention, we have

$$\text{Cost of } C \ = r_{\bar{i}\bar{j}},$$

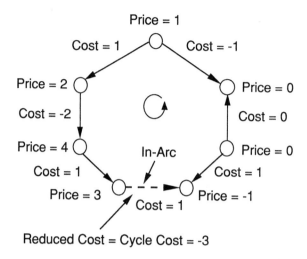

Figure 1.5   Obtaining a negative cost cycle in the simplex method. All arcs of the cycle have zero reduced cost, so the reduced cost of the in-arc is also the cost of the cycle, based on the calculation of Eq. (1.7). Thus, if the in-arc is chosen to have negative reduced cost, the cost of the cycle is also negative.

which is negative by Eq. (1.6); see Fig. 1.5.

The role of the price vector p associated with a feasible tree now becomes clear. By checking the sign of the reduced cost

$$r_{ij} = a_{ij} + p_j - p_i,$$

of all arcs (i, j) not in T, we will either verify optimality if r_{ij} is nonnegative for all (i, j), or else we will obtain a negative cost cycle by discovering an arc (i, j) for which r_{ij} is negative. The latter arc is the in-arc that will enter the tree of the next iteration.

There is a great deal of flexibility for selecting the in-arc. For example, one may search for an in-arc with *most negative* reduced cost; this rule requires a lot of computation – a comparison of r_{ij} for all arcs (i, j) not in the current tree. A simpler alternative is to search the list of arcs not in the tree and to select the *first* arc with negative reduced cost. Most practical simplex codes use an intermediate strategy. They maintain a *candidate list of arcs*, and at each iteration they search through this list for an arc with most negative reduced cost; in the process, arcs with nonnegative reduced cost are deleted from the list. If no arc in the candidate list has a negative reduced cost, a new candidate list is constructed. One way to do this is to scan the full arc list and enter in the candidate list all arcs with negative reduced cost, up to the point where the candidate list reaches a maximum size, which is chosen heuristically. This procedure can also be used to construct the initial candidate list.

2.1.2   Obtaining the Out-Arc

Let T be a feasible tree generated by the simplex method with corresponding flow vector x and price vector p which are nonoptimal. Suppose that we have chosen the in-arc $\bar{e}$ and we have obtained the corresponding negative cost cycle C formed by T and $\bar{e}$. There are two possibilities:

(a) All arcs of C are oriented like $\bar{e}$, that is, C^- is empty. Then C is a forward cycle with negative cost, indicating that the problem is unbounded. Indeed, since C^- is empty, we can increase the flows of the arcs of C by an arbitrarily large common increment, while maintaining feasibility of x. The primal cost function changes by an amount equal to the cost of C for each unit flow change along C. Since C has negative cost, we see that the primal cost can be decreased to arbitrarily small (i.e. large negative) values.

(b) The set C^- of arcs of C with orientation opposite to that of $\bar{e}$ is nonempty. Then

$$\delta = \min_{(i,j)\in C^-} x_{ij} \tag{1.8}$$

is the maximum increment by which the flow of all arcs of C^+ can be increased and the flow of all arcs of C^- can be decreased, while still maintaining feasibility. The simplex method computes δ and changes the flow vector from x to $\bar{x}$, where

$$\bar{x}_{ij} = \begin{cases} x_{ij} & \text{if } (i,j) \notin C \\ x_{ij} + \delta & \text{if } (i,j) \in C^+ \\ x_{ij} - \delta & \text{if } (i,j) \in C^-. \end{cases} \tag{1.9}$$

Any arc $e = (i,j) \in C^-$ that attains the minimum in the equation $\delta = \min_{(i,j)\in C^-} x_{ij}$ satisfies $\bar{x}_{ij} = 0$ and can serve as the out-arc; see Fig. 1.6. (A more specific rule for selecting the out-arc will be given later.) The new tree is

$$\overline{T} = T + \bar{e} - e \tag{1.10}$$

and its associated basic flow vector is $\bar{x}$, given by Eq. (1.9).

Figures 1.7 and 1.8 illustrate the simplex method for some simple examples.

Note that the price vector $\bar{p}$ associated with the new tree $\overline{T}$ can be conveniently obtained from p as follows: Let $\bar{e} = (\bar{i}, \bar{j})$ be the in-arc and let e be the out-arc. If we remove e from T we obtain two trees, $T_{\bar{i}}$ and $T_{\bar{j}}$,

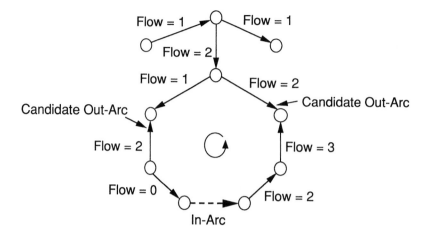

Figure 1.6   Choosing the out-arc in the simplex method. The in-arc $(4,5)$ closes a cycle C. The arcs of C^- are $(3,2)$, $(7,6)$ and $(1,7)$, and define the flow increment $\delta = \min_{(i,j)\in C^-} x_{ij}$. Out of these arcs, the ones attaining the minimum are the candidates for out-arc, as shown.

containing the nodes $\bar{i}$ and $\bar{j}$, respectively; see Fig. 1.9. Then it is seen from the definition (1.4) that a price vector $\bar{p}$ associated with $\overline{T}$ is given by

$$\bar{p}_i = \begin{cases} p_i & \text{if } i \in T_{\bar{i}} \\ p_i - r_{\bar{i}\bar{j}} & \text{if } i \in T_{\bar{j}}, \end{cases} \tag{1.11}$$

where

$$r_{\bar{i}\bar{j}} = a_{\bar{i}\bar{j}} + p_{\bar{j}} - p_{\bar{i}}$$

is the reduced cost cost of the in-arc $(\bar{i},\bar{j})$. Thus, to update the price vector, one needs to increase the prices of the nodes in $T_{\bar{j}}$ by the common increment $(-r_{\bar{i}\bar{j}})$. We may also use any other price vector, obtained by adding the same constant to all the prices $\bar{p}_i$ defined above; it will simply correspond to a different price for the root node. The formula

$$\bar{p}_i = \begin{cases} p_i + r_{\bar{i}\bar{j}} & \text{if } i \in T_{\bar{i}} \\ p_i & \text{if } i \in T_{\bar{j}}, \end{cases} \tag{1.12}$$

involving a decrease of the prices of the nodes in $T_{\bar{i}}$, is useful in some implementations.

Note that if the flow increment $\delta = \min_{(i,j)\in C^-} x_{ij}$ [cf. Eq. (1.8)] is positive, then the cost corresponding to $\bar{x}$ will be strictly smaller than the cost corresponding to x (by δ times the cost of the cycle C). Thus, when $\delta > 0$,

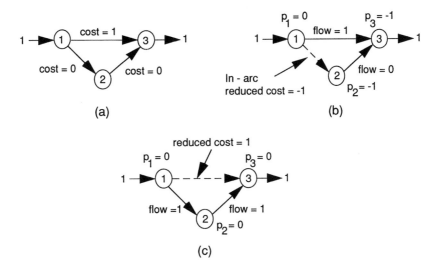

(a)

(b)

(c)

Figure 1.7 Illustration of the simplex method for the problem described in figure (a). The starting tree consists of arcs $(1, 3)$ and $(2, 3)$ and the corresponding flows and prices are as shown in figure (b). Arc $(1, 2)$ has negative reduced cost and is thus eligible to be an in-arc. Arc $(1, 3)$ is the only arc eligible to be the out-arc. The new tree is shown in figure (c). The corresponding flow is optimal because the reduced cost of arc $(1, 3)$ is positive.

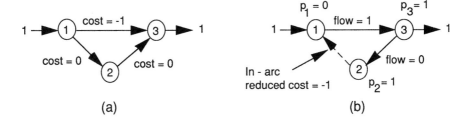

(a)

(b)

Figure 1.8 Illustration of the simplex method for the problem described in figure (a); this is an unbounded problem because the cycle $(1, 3, 2, 1)$ has negative cost. The starting tree consists of arcs $(1, 3)$ and $(2, 3)$ and the corresponding flows and prices are as shown in figure (b). Arc $(1, 2)$ has negative reduced cost and is thus eligible to be an in-arc. However, all the arcs of the corresponding cycle have the same orientation, so the problem is declared to be unbounded.

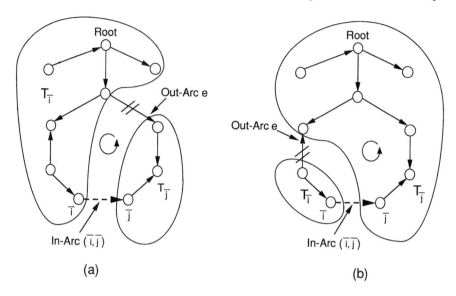

Figure 1.9   Component trees $T_{\bar{i}}$ and $T_{\bar{j}}$, obtained by deleting the out-arc e from T, where $\bar{e} = (\bar{i}, \bar{j})$ is the in-arc; these are the components that contain $\bar{i}$ and $\bar{j}$, respectively. Depending on the position of the out-arc e, the root node may be contained in $T_{\bar{i}}$ as in figure (a), or in $T_{\bar{j}}$ as in figure (b).

the simplex method will never reproduce x and the corresponding tree T in future iterations.

On the other hand, if $\delta = 0$, then $\bar{x} = x$, and the pivot is degenerate. In this case there is no guarantee that the tree T will not be repeated after several degenerate iterations with no interim improvement in the primal cost. We thus need to provide for a mechanism that precludes this from happening.

2.1.3   Dealing with Degeneracy

Suppose that the feasible trees generated by the simplex method are all distinct (which is true in particular when all pivots are nondegenerate). Then, since the number of distinct feasible trees is finite, the method will eventually terminate. Upon termination, there are two possibilities:

(a) The final flow and price vectors are primal and dual optimal, respectively.

(b) The problem is shown to be unbounded because at the final iteration, the cycle closed by the current tree and the in-arc $\bar{e}$ has no arc with orientation opposite to that of $\bar{e}$.

Unfortunately, if the tree sequence is not generated with some care, there is no guarantee that a tree will not be repeated an infinite number of times. To rule out this possibility, thereby ensuring termination of the method, we will use feasible trees with a special property called *strong feasibility*. We will make sure that the initial tree has this property, and we will choose the out-arc in a way that the property is maintained by the algorithm.

Let us fix the root node r used to compute the price vectors associated with feasible trees. Given a feasible tree T, we say that arc $(i, j) \in T$ is *oriented away* from the root if the unique simple path of T from the root to j passes through i. A feasible tree T with corresponding flow vector x is said to be *strongly feasible* if every arc (i, j) of T with $x_{ij} = 0$ is oriented away from the root. Figure 1.10 illustrates strongly feasible trees.

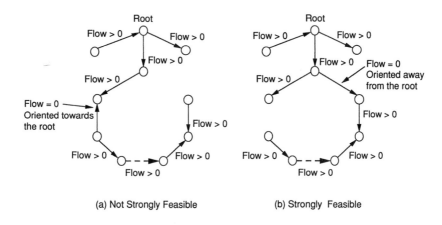

(a) Not Strongly Feasible   (b) Strongly Feasible

Figure 1.10   Illustration of a strongly feasible tree. The tree in (a) is not strongly feasible because the arc with zero flow on the tree is not oriented away from the root. The tree in (b) is strongly feasible. Note that these two trees are obtained from the strongly feasible tree in Fig. 1.6 by choosing a different out-arc.

The following proposition motivates the use of strongly feasible trees.

Proposition 1.2:   If the feasible trees generated by the simplex method are all strongly feasible, then these trees are distinct.

Proof: With each feasible tree T, with corresponding basic feasible vector x and price vector p, we associate the two scalars

$$c(T) = \sum_{(i,j)\in\mathcal{A}} a_{ij}x_{ij} \tag{1.13}$$

$$w(T) = \sum_{i\in\mathcal{N}} (p_r - p_i), \tag{1.14}$$

where r is the root node. [The price differences $p_r - p_i$ are uniquely determined by T according to

$$p_r - p_i = \sum_{(m,n)\in P_i^+} a_{mn} - \sum_{(m,n)\in P_i^-} a_{mn}$$

[see Eq. (1.4)], so $w(T)$ is uniquely determined by T. Note that, $w(T)$ may be viewed as the "aggregate length" of T; it is the sum of the lengths of the paths P_i from the root to the nodes i along the tree T, where the length of an arc (m,n) is a_{mn} or $-a_{mn}$ depending on whether (m,n) is or is not oriented away from the root, respectively.]

We will show that if T and $\overline{T} = T + \overline{e} - e$ are two successive feasible trees generated by the simplex method, then either $c(\overline{T}) < c(T)$ or else $c(\overline{T}) = c(T)$ and $w(\overline{T}) < w(T)$. This proves that no tree can be repeated.

Indeed, if the pivot that generates $\overline{T}$ from T is nondegenerate, we have $c(\overline{T}) < c(T)$, and if it is degenerate we have $c(\overline{T}) = c(T)$. In the former case the result is proved, so assume the latter case holds, and let $\overline{e} = (\overline{i}, \overline{j})$ be the in-arc. Then after the pivot, $\overline{e}$ still has zero flow, and since $\overline{T}$ is strongly feasible, $\overline{e}$ must be oriented away from the root node r. This implies that r belongs to the subtree $T_{\overline{j}}$, and by Eq. (1.11) we have

$$w(\overline{T}) = w(T) + |T_{\overline{j}}| r_{\overline{i}\overline{j}}, \tag{1.15}$$

where $r_{\overline{i}\overline{j}}$ is the reduced cost of $\overline{e}$, and $|T_{\overline{j}}|$ is the number of nodes in the subtree $T_{\overline{j}}$. Since $r_{\overline{i}\overline{j}} < 0$, it follows that $w(\overline{T}) < w(T)$.   **Q.E.D.**

The next proposition shows how to select the out-arc in a simplex iteration so as to maintain strong feasibility of the generated trees.

Proposition 1.3:   Let T be a strongly feasible tree generated by the simplex method, let $\overline{e} = (\overline{i}, \overline{j})$ be the in-arc, let C be the cycle formed by T and $\overline{e}$, suppose that C^- is nonempty, let $\delta = \min_{(i,j)\in C^-} x_{ij}$, and let $\hat{C}$ be the set of candidate out-arcs, that is, the set

$$\hat{C} = \{(i,j) \in C^- \mid x_{ij} = \delta\}.$$

Define the *join of C* as the first node of C that lies on the unique simple path of T that starts from the root and ends at $\overline{i}$ (see Fig. 1.11). Suppose that the out-arc e is chosen to be the arc of $\hat{C}$ encountered first as C is traversed in the forward direction (the direction of $\overline{e}$) starting from the join node. Then the next tree $\overline{T} = T + \overline{e} - e$ generated by the simplex method is strongly feasible.

Proof: Since the arcs of T which are not in C will not change their flow or orientation relative to the root, to check strong feasibility of $\overline{T}$, we need only be concerned with the arcs of $C + \overline{e} - e$ for which $\overline{x}_{ij} = 0$. These will be the arcs of $\hat{C} - e$ and possibly arc $\bar{e}$ (in the case $\delta = 0$). By choosing e to be the first encountered arc of $\hat{C}$, all of the arcs of $\hat{C} - e$ will be encountered after e, and following the pivot, they will be oriented away from the join and therefore also from the root. If $\delta = 0$, the arcs (i, j) of $\hat{C}$ satisfy $x_{ij} = 0$, so by strong feasibility of T, all of them, including e, must be encountered *after* $\bar{e}$ as C is traversed in the direction of $\bar{e}$ starting from the join. Therefore, $\bar{e}$ will also be oriented away from the root following the pivot.   **Q.E.D.**

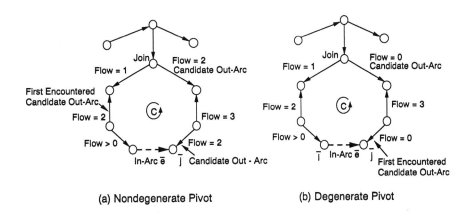

(a) Nondegenerate Pivot   **(b) Degenerate Pivot**

Figure 1.11   Maintaining a strongly feasible tree in the simplex method. Suppose that the in-arc $\bar{e} = (\bar{i}, \bar{j})$ is added to a strongly feasible T, closing the cycle C. Let $\hat{C}$ be the set of candidates for out-arc (the arcs of C^- attaining the minimum in $\delta = \min_{(i,j) \in C^-} x_{ij}$), and let e be the out-arc. The arcs of $\overline{T}$ with zero flow will be the arcs of $\hat{C} - e$ together with $\bar{e}$ if the pivot is degenerate. By choosing as out-arc the first encountered arc of $\hat{C}$ as C is traversed in the direction of $\bar{e}$ starting from the join, all of these arcs will be oriented away from the join and also from the root, so strong feasibility is maintained. Note that if the pivot is degenerate as in (b), then all arcs of $\hat{C}$ will be encountered after $\bar{e}$ (by strong feasibility of T), so the out-arc e must be encountered after $\bar{e}$. Thus, the in-arc $\bar{e}$ will be oriented away from the root in the case of a degenerate pivot, as required for strong feasibility of $\overline{T}$.

E X E R C I S E S

Exercise 1.1

Consider the tree of Fig. 1.11(a).

(a) Suppose that the in-arc is $(\bar{j}, \bar{i})$ [instead of $(\bar{i}, \bar{j})$]. Which arc should be the out-arc?

(b) Suppose that the in-arc is the arc starting at the join and ending at $\bar{j}$ [instead of $(\bar{i}, \bar{j})$]. Which arc should be the out-arc in order to preserve strong feasibility of the tree?

Exercise 1.2

Consider the minimum cost flow problem with nonnegativity constraints given in Fig. 1.12 (supplies are shown next to the nodes, arc costs are immaterial). Find all basic flow vectors and their associated trees. Specify which of these are feasible and which are strongly feasible (the root node is node 1).

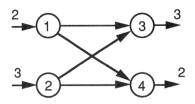

Figure 1.12   Graph for Exercise 1.2.

Exercise 1.3

Consider a feasible minimum cost flow problem such that the corresponding graph is connected. Suppose we are given a feasible flow vector x. Construct an algorithm that suitably modifies x to obtain a basic feasible flow vector and an associated spanning tree. *Hint:* For a feasible flow vector x there are two possibilities: (1) The subgraph S consisting of the set of arcs

$$\mathcal{A}_x = \{(i, j) \in \mathcal{A} \mid x_{ij} > 0\}$$

and the corresponding set of incident nodes is acyclic, in which case show that x is basic. (2) The subgraph S is not acyclic, in which case show how to construct a feasible flow vector x' differing from x by a simple cycle flow, and for which the arc set $\mathcal{A}_{x'}$ has at least one arc less than the set $\mathcal{A}_x$.

Exercise 1.4

Consider the following algorithm that tries to construct a flow vector that has a given divergence vector s, and is zero on arcs which are not in a given spanning tree T. For any vector x, define the surplus of each node i by

$$g_i = \sum_{\{j|(j,i)\in\mathcal{A}\}} x_{ji} - \sum_{\{j|(i,j)\in\mathcal{A}\}} x_{ij} + s_i.$$

The algorithm is initialized with $x = 0$. The typical iteration starts with a flow vector x and produces another flow vector $\overline{x}$ that differs from x along a simple path consisting of arcs of T. It operates as follows: a node i with $g_i > 0$ and a node j with $g_j < 0$ are selected, and the unique path P_{ij} that starts at i, ends at j, and has arcs in T is constructed (if no such nodes i and j can be found the algorithm stops). Then the flow of the forward arcs of P_{ij} are increased by δ and the flow of the backward arcs of P_{ij} are decreased by δ, where $\delta = \min\{g_i, -g_j\}$. Show that the algorithm terminates in a finite number of iterations, and that upon termination, we have $g_i = 0$ for all i if and only if $\sum_{i\in\mathcal{N}} s_i = 0$. *Hint:* Show that all the nodes with zero surplus with respect to x also have zero surplus with respect to $\overline{x}$. Furthermore, at least one node with nonzero surplus with respect to x has zero surplus with respect to $\overline{x}$.

Exercise 1.5

Consider a transportation problem involving the set of sources $\mathcal{S}$ and the set of sinks $\mathcal{T}$ (cf. Example 1.3 in Section 1.1). Suppose that there is no strict subset $\overline{\mathcal{S}}$ of $\mathcal{S}$ and strict subset $\overline{\mathcal{T}}$ of $\mathcal{T}$ such that

$$\sum_{i\in\overline{\mathcal{S}}} \alpha_i = \sum_{j\in\overline{\mathcal{T}}} \beta_j.$$

Show that for every feasible tree, the corresponding flow of every arc of the tree is positive. Conclude that if a feasible initial tree can be found, degeneracy never arises in the simplex method.

2.2   THE BASIC SIMPLEX ALGORITHM

We are now ready to state formally the simplex algorithm based on the ideas of the previous section.

At the beginning of each iteration we have a strongly feasible tree T and an associated basic flow vector x such that

$$x_{ij} = 0, \qquad \forall \, (i,j) \notin T \tag{2.1}$$

and a price vector p such that

$$r_{ij} = a_{ij} + p_j - p_i = 0, \qquad \forall \, (i,j) \in T. \tag{2.2}$$

The iteration has three possible outcomes:

(a) We will verify that x and p are primal and dual optimal, respectively.

(b) We will determine that the problem is unbounded.

(c) We will obtain by the method of Prop. 1.3 a strongly feasible tree $\overline{T} = T + \overline{e} - e$, differing from T by the in-arc $\overline{e}$ and the out-arc e.

Typical Simplex Iteration

Select an in-arc $\overline{e} = (\overline{i}, \overline{j}) \notin T$ such that

$$r_{\overline{i}\overline{j}} = a_{\overline{i}\overline{j}} + p_{\overline{j}} - p_{\overline{i}} < 0.$$

(If no such arc can be found, terminate; x is primal-optimal and p is dual-optimal.) Consider the cycle C formed by T and $\overline{e}$. If C^- is empty, terminate (the problem is unbounded); else, obtain the out-arc $e \in C^-$ as described in Prop. 1.3.

2.2.1 Justification of the Simplex Method

We now collect the facts already proved into a proposition that also deals with the integrality of the solutions obtained.

Proposition 2.1: Suppose that the simplex method is applied to the minimum cost flow problem with the nonnegativity constraints, starting with a strongly feasible tree.

(a) If the problem is not unbounded, the method terminates with an optimal primal solution x and an optimal dual solution p, and the optimal primal cost is equal to the optimal dual cost. Furthermore, if the supplies s_i are all integer, the optimal primal solution x is integer; if the starting price of the root node and the cost coefficients a_{ij} are all integer, the optimal dual solution p is integer.

(b) If the problem is unbounded, the method verifies this after a finite number of iterations.

Proof: (a) The trees generated by the method are strongly feasible, and by Prop. 1.2 these trees are all distinct, so the method terminates. Termination can only occur with either an optimal pair (x, p) or with the indication that the problem is unbounded. Thus, if the problem is not unbounded, the only possibility is termination with an optimal pair (x, p). Since upon termination x and p satisfy complementary slackness, the equality of the optimal primal and dual values follows from Prop. 2.3 in Section 1.2. Also, if the supplies s_i are all integer, from Prop. 1.1 it follows that all basic flow vectors are integer, including the one obtained at termination. If the starting price of the root node and the cost coefficients a_{ij} are all integer, it can be checked that all operations of the algorithm maintain the integrality of p.

(b) If the problem is unbounded, there is no optimal primal solution, so the simplex method cannot terminate with an optimal pair (x, p). The only other possibility is for the method to terminate with an indication that the problem is unbounded.   **Q.E.D.**

2.2.2   Choosing the Initial Strongly Feasible Tree – The Big-M Method

In the absence of an apparent choice for an initial strongly feasible tree, one may use the so called *big-M method*. In this method, some artificial variables are introduced to simplify the choice of an initial basic solution, but the cost coefficient M for these variables is chosen large enough so that the optimal solutions of the problem are not affected.

In particular, we modify the problem by introducing an extra node, labeled 0 and having zero supply $s_0 = 0$, together with a set of artificial arcs $\overline{\mathcal{A}}$ consisting of an arc $(i, 0)$ for each node i with $s_i > 0$, and an arc $(0, i)$ for each node i with $s_i \leq 0$. The cost coefficient of all these arcs is taken to be a scalar M, and its choice will be discussed shortly. We thus arrive at the following problem, referred to as the *big-M version* of the original problem:

$$\text{minimize} \quad \sum_{(i,j) \in \mathcal{A}} a_{ij} x_{ij} + M \left(\sum_{(i,0) \in \overline{\mathcal{A}}} x_{i0} + \sum_{(0,i) \in \overline{\mathcal{A}}} x_{0i} \right)$$

subject to   (2.3)

$$\sum_{\{j | (i,j) \in \mathcal{A} \cup \overline{\mathcal{A}}\}} x_{ij} - \sum_{\{j | (j,i) \in \mathcal{A} \cup \overline{\mathcal{A}}\}} x_{ji} = s_i, \quad \forall \, i \in \mathcal{N} \cup \{0\},$$

$$0 \leq x_{ij}, \quad \forall \, (i, j) \in \mathcal{A} \cup \overline{\mathcal{A}}.$$

The artificial arcs constitute a readily available initial spanning tree for the big-M version; see Fig. 2.1. It can be seen that the corresponding basic flow vector is given by

$$x_{i0} = s_i, \qquad \text{for each } i \text{ with } s_i > 0$$

$$x_{0i} = -s_i, \qquad \text{for each } i \text{ with } s_i \le 0$$

$$x_{ij} = 0, \qquad \forall \, (i,j) \in \mathcal{A}$$

and is therefore feasible. Let us choose the root to be the artificial node 0. The artificial arcs that carry zero flow are then oriented away from the root, so the tree is strongly feasible.

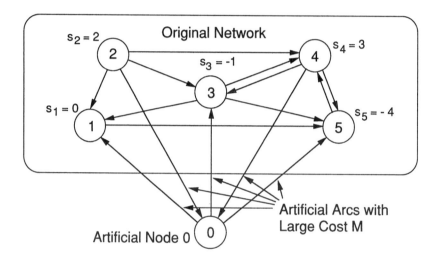

Figure 2.1   Artificial arcs used to modify the problem so as to facilitate the choice of an initial strongly feasible tree.

The cost M of the artificial arcs should be taken to be large enough so that these arcs will carry zero flow at every optimal solution of the big-M version. In this case, the flows of the nonartificial arcs define an optimal solution of the original problem. The following proposition quantifies the appropriate level of M for this to happen, and collects a number of related facts.

Proposition 2.2:   Consider the minimum cost flow problem with nonnegativity constraints (referred to as the original problem), and consider also its big-M version. Suppose that

$$2M > \sum_{(i,j) \in P^+} a_{ij} - \sum_{(i,j) \in P^-} a_{ij} \tag{2.4}$$

for all simple paths P of the original problem graph.

(a) If the original problem is feasible but not unbounded, the big-M version has optimal solutions $\bar{x}$, and each of these solutions is of the form

$$\bar{x}_{ij} = \begin{cases} x_{ij} & \text{if } (i,j) \in \mathcal{A} \\ 0 & \text{if } (i,j) \in \overline{\mathcal{A}}, \end{cases} \tag{2.5}$$

where x is an optimal solution of the original. Furthermore, every optimal solution x of the original problem gives rise to an optimal solution $\bar{x}$ of the big-M version via the preceding relation.

(b) If the original problem is unbounded, the big-M version is also unbounded.

(c) If the original problem is infeasible, then in every feasible solution of the big-M version some artificial arc carries positive flow.

Proof: (a) We first note that the big-M version cannot be unbounded unless the original problem is. To prove this, we argue by contradiction. If the big-M version is unbounded and the original problem is not, there would exist a simple forward cycle with negative cost in the big-M version. This cycle cannot consist of arcs of $\mathcal{A}$ exclusively, since the original is not unbounded. On the other hand, if the cycle consisted of the arcs $(m, 0)$ and $(0, n)$, and a simple path of the original graph, then by the condition (2.4) the cycle would have positive cost, arriving at a contradiction.

Having proved that the big-M version is not unbounded, we now note that, by Prop. 2.1(a), the simplex method starting with the strongly feasible tree of all the artificial arcs will terminate with optimal primal and dual solutions of the big-M version. Thus, optimal solutions of the big-M version exist, and for every optimal solution $\bar{x}$ of the form (2.5), the corresponding vector $x = \{x_{ij} \mid (i,j) \in \mathcal{A}\}$ with $x_{ij} = \bar{x}_{ij}$ for all $(i,j) \in \mathcal{A}$ is an optimal solution of the original problem.

To prove that all optimal solutions $\bar{x}$ of the big-M version are of the form (2.5), we argue by contradiction. Suppose that $\bar{x}$ is an optimal solution such that some artificial arcs carry positive flow. Let

$$\mathcal{N}^+ = \{m \mid s_m > 0, \bar{x}_{m0} > 0\},$$

$$\mathcal{N}^- = \{n \mid s_n \leq 0, \bar{x}_{0n} > 0\}.$$

We observe that $\mathcal{N}^+$ and $\mathcal{N}^-$ must be nonempty and that there is no unblocked simple path P with respect to $\bar{x}$ that starts at some $m \in \mathcal{N}^+$ and ends at some $n \in \mathcal{N}^-$; such a path, together with arcs $(m, 0)$ and $(0, n)$, would form an unblocked simple cycle, which would have negative cost in view of condition (2.4). Consider now the flow vector $x = \{x_{ij} \mid (i,j) \in \mathcal{A}\}$ with $x_{ij} = \bar{x}_{ij}$ for all $(i,j) \in \mathcal{A}$. Then, there is no path with respect to x of the original problem graph $(\mathcal{N}, \mathcal{A})$, that is unblocked with respect to x and that starts at a node of $\mathcal{N}^+$ and ends at a node of $\mathcal{N}^-$. By using a very similar argument as in the proof of Prop. 2.2 of Section 1.2, we can show (see Exercise 2.14 in Section 1.2) that there must exist a saturated cut $[\mathcal{S}, \mathcal{N} - \mathcal{S}]$ such that $\mathcal{N}^+ \subset \mathcal{S}$, $\mathcal{N}^- \subset \mathcal{N} - \mathcal{S}$. The capacity of this cut is equal to the sum of the divergences of the nodes $i \in \mathcal{S}$,

$$\sum_{i \in \mathcal{S}} y_i = \sum_{i \in \mathcal{S}} \left(\sum_{\{j | (i,j) \in \mathcal{A}\}} x_{ij} - \sum_{\{j | (j,i) \in \mathcal{A}\}} x_{ji} \right),$$

which is also equal to

$$\sum_{i \in \mathcal{S}} \left(s_i - \overline{x}_{i0} \right) = \sum_{i \in \mathcal{S}} s_i - \sum_{i \in \mathcal{N}^+} \overline{x}_{i0} < \sum_{i \in \mathcal{S}} s_i.$$

On the other hand, if the original problem is feasible, the capacity of any cut $[\mathcal{S}, \mathcal{N} - \mathcal{S}]$ cannot be less than $\sum_{i \in \mathcal{S}} s_i$, so we obtain a contradiction.

Finally, let x be an optimal solution of the original problem, and let $\overline{x}$ be given by Eq. (2.5). We will show that $\overline{x}$ is optimal for the big-M version. Indeed, every simple cycle that is unblocked with respect to $\overline{x}$ in the big-M version either consists of arcs in $\mathcal{A}$ and is therefore unblocked with respect to x in the original, or else consists of the arcs $(m, 0)$ and $(0, n)$, and a simple path $\overline{P}$ that starts at n and ends at m. In the former case, the cost of the cycle is nonnegative, since x is optimal for the original problem; in the latter case, the cost of the cycle is positive by condition (2.4) (with the path P being the reverse of path $\overline{P}$). Hence, $\overline{x}$ is optimal for the big-M version.

(b) Note that every feasible solution x of the original problem defines a feasible solution $\overline{x}$ of equal cost in the big-M version via Eq. (2.5). Therefore, if the cost of the original can be made arbitrarily large negative, the same is true of the big-M version.

(c) Observe that any feasible solution of the big-M version having zero flow on the artificial arcs defines a feasible solution x of the original via Eq. (2.5). **Q.E.D.**

Note that to satisfy the condition (2.4), it is sufficient to take

$$M > \frac{(N-1)C}{2},$$

where C is the arc cost range $C = \max_{(i,j) \in \mathcal{A}} |a_{ij}|$. Note also that if M does not satisfy the condition (2.4), then the big-M version may be unbounded, even if the original problem has an optimal solution (Exercise 2.2). Many practical simplex codes use an adaptive strategy for selecting M, whereby a moderate value of M is used initially, and this value is gradually increased if positive flows on the artificial arcs persist.

By combining the results of the preceding two propositions, we obtain the following proposition.

Proposition 2.3:   Assume that the minimum cost flow problem with non-negativity constraints is feasible and is not unbounded. Then there exists an optimal primal solution and an optimal dual solution, and the optimal primal cost is equal to the optimal dual cost. Furthermore, if the supplies s_i are all integer, there exists an optimal primal solution which is integer; if the cost coefficients a_{ij} are all integer, there exists an optimal dual solution which is integer.

Proof: Apply the simplex method to the big-M version with the initial strongly feasible tree of all the artificial arcs, and with M sufficiently large to satisfy condition (2.4). Then, by Prop. 2.2, the big-M version has optimal solutions, so by Prop. 2.1 the simplex method will provide an optimal pair $(\overline{x}, \overline{p})$, with $\overline{x}$ integer if the supplies are integer, and $\overline{p}$ integer if the cost coefficients are integer. By Prop. 2.2, the vector x defined by $x_{ij} = \overline{x}_{ij}$, for all $(i, j) \in \mathcal{A}$ will be an optimal solution of the original problem, while the price vector p defined by $p_i = \overline{p}_i$, for all $i \in \mathcal{N}$ will satisfy the CS conditions together with x. Hence, p will be an optimal dual solution.   **Q.E.D.**

A Shortest Path Example

Consider a single origin/all destinations shortest path problem involving the graph of Fig. 2.2. We will use this example to illustrate the simplex method and some of its special properties when applied to shortest path problems. The corresponding minimum cost flow problem is

$$\text{minimize} \quad \sum_{(i,j)\in\mathcal{A}} a_{ij}x_{ij}$$

$$\text{subject to}$$

$$\sum_{\{j|(1,j)\in\mathcal{A}\}} x_{1j} - \sum_{\{j|(j,1)\in\mathcal{A}\}} x_{j1} = 3,$$

$$\sum_{\{j|(i,j)\in\mathcal{A}\}} x_{ij} - \sum_{\{j|(j,i)\in\mathcal{A}\}} x_{ji} = -1, \qquad i = 2, 3, 4,$$

$$0 \le x_{ij}, \qquad \forall \, (i, j) \in \mathcal{A}.$$

We select as root the origin node 1. To deal with the problem of the initial choice of a strongly feasible tree, we use a variant of the big-M method. We introduce artificial arcs connecting the origin with each node $i \ne 1$ with very large cost M, and we use as an initial tree the set of artificial arcs with

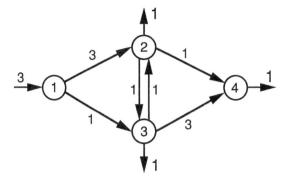

Figure 2.2 Example single origin/all destinations shortest path problem. The arc lengths are shown next to the arcs.

root node the origin (with this choice, there will be two arcs connecting the origin with each of its neighbors, but this should not cause any confusion). In the corresponding flow vector, every artificial arc carries unit flow, so the initial tree is strongly feasible (all arcs are oriented away from the root).

The corresponding price vector is $(0, -M, -M, -M)$ and the associated reduced costs of the nonartificial arcs are

$$r_{1j} = a_{1j} - M, \qquad \forall\, (1,j) \in \mathcal{A},$$

$$r_{ij} = a_{ij}, \qquad \forall\, (i,j) \in \mathcal{A},\ i \neq 1,\ j \neq 1.$$

One possible outcome of the first iteration is to select some arc $(1,j) \in \mathcal{A}$ as in-arc, and to select the artificial arc connecting 1 and j as out-arc. The process will then be continued, first obtaining the flow and price vectors corresponding to the new tree, then obtaining the out-arc, then the in-arc, etc.

Figures 2.3 and 2.4 show two possible sequences of pivots. The following can be noted:

(a) Each artificial arc eventually becomes the out-arc but never becomes the in-arc.

(b) In all trees, all the arcs are oriented away from the origin and carry unit flow.

(c) In Fig. 2.3, where the in-arc is selected to be the arc with minimum reduced cost, there are exactly $N - 1$ ($= 3$) pivots, and each time the out-arc is an artificial arc. In fact, in this case the simplex method works exactly like Dijkstra's method, permanently setting the label of one additional node with every pivot; here, node labels should be identified with the negative of node prices.

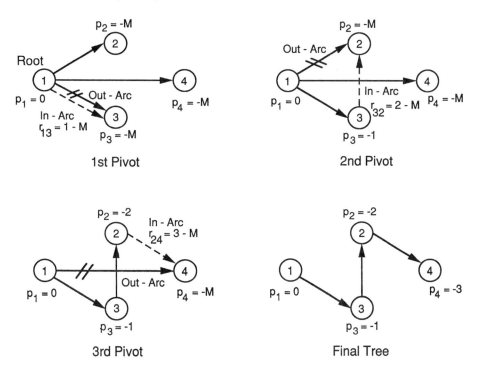

Figure 2.3   A possible sequence of pivots for the simplex method. The initial tree consists of the artificial arcs $(1,2)$, $(1,3)$, and $(1,4)$, each carrying one unit of flow. The in-arc is selected to be the arc with minimum reduced cost and the method behaves like Dijkstra's method, requiring only three $(= N - 1)$ pivots.

It can be shown that observations (a) and (b) above hold in general for the simplex method applied to feasible shortest path problems, and observation (c) also holds in general provided $a_{ij} \geq 0$ for all arcs (i, j). The proof of this is left as Exercise 2.8 for the reader.

The simplex method can also be used effectively to solve the all-pairs shortest path problem. In particular, one may first use the simplex method to solve the shortest path problem for a single origin, say node 1, and then modify the final tree T_1 to obtain an initial tree T_2 for applying the simplex method with another origin, say node 2. This can be done by deleting the unique arc of T_1 that is incoming to node 2, and replacing it with an artificial arc from 2 to 1 that has a very large cost; see Fig. 2.5.

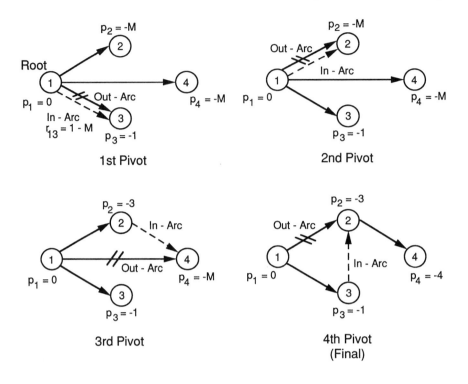

Figure 2.4 Another possible sequence of pivots for the simplex method. More than three pivots are required, in contrast with the sequence of Fig. 2.3.

EXERCISES

Exercise 2.1

Use the simplex method with the big-M initialization to solve the problem in Fig. 2.6.

Exercise 2.2

Construct an example where M does not satisfy the condition (2.4), and the original problem has an optimal solution, while the big-M version is unbounded. *Hint:* It is sufficient to consider a graph with two nodes.

Exercise 2.3

Construct an example where M satisfies the condition (2.4), and the original problem is infeasible, while the big-M version is unbounded. *Hint:* Consider

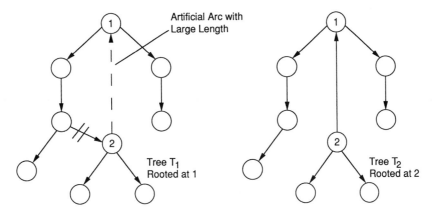

Figure 2.5   Obtaining an initial tree T_2 for the simplex method applied to the shortest path problem with origin 2, from the final tree T_1 of the simplex method applied for origin 1. We delete the unique arc of T_1 that is incoming to node 2, and replace it with an artificial arc from 2 to 1 that has a very large length.

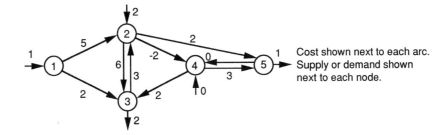

Figure 2.6   Minimum cost flow problem with nonnegativity constraints for Exercise 2.1.

problems that are infeasible and also contain a simple forward cycle of negative cost.

Exercise 2.4 (An Example of Cycling [Chv83])

Consider an assignment problem with sources 1, 2, 3, 4 and sinks 5, 6, 7, 8. There is an arc between each source and each sink. The arc costs are as follows:

$$a_{16} = a_{17} = a_{25} = a_{27} = a_{35} = a_{36} = a_{48} = 1, \qquad a_{ij} = 0 \text{ otherwise.}$$

Let the initial feasible tree consist of arcs (1,5), (1,6), (2,6), (2,8), (4,8), (4,7), (3,7), with corresponding arc flows

$$x_{15} = x_{26} = x_{37} = x_{48} = 1, \qquad x_{ij} = 0 \text{ otherwise.}$$

Suppose that the simplex method is applied without restriction on the choice of the out-arc (so the generated trees need not be strongly feasible). Verify that one possible sequence of in-arc/out-arc pairs is given by

$$\big((1,8),(2,8)\big), \big((3,6),(1,6)\big), \big((4,6),(4,7)\big),$$

$$\big((3,5),(3,6)\big), \big((3,8),(1,8)\big), \big((2,5),(3,5)\big),$$

$$\big((4,5),(4,6)\big), \big((2,7),(2,5)\big), \big((2,8),(3,8)\big),$$

$$\big((1,7),(2,7)\big), \big((4,7),(4,5)\big), \big((1,6),(1,7)\big),$$

and that after these twelve pivots we obtain the initial tree again.

Exercise 2.5 (Birchoff's Theorem for Doubly Stochastic Matrices)

A *doubly stochastic* $n \times n$ matrix $X = \{x_{ij}\}$ is a matrix such that the elements of each of its rows and columns are nonnegative, and add to one, that is, $x_{ij} \geq 0$ for all i and j, $\sum_{j=1}^{n} x_{ij} = 1$ for all i, and $\sum_{i=1}^{n} x_{ij} = 1$ for all j. A *permutation matrix* is a doubly stochastic matrix whose elements are either one or zero, so that there is a single one in each row and each column, with all other elements being zero.

(a) Show that given a doubly stochastic matrix X, there exists a permutation matrix X^* such that, for all i and j, if $x_{ij}^* = 1$, then $x_{ij} > 0$. *Hint:* View X as a feasible solution of the minimum cost flow version of an assignment problem, and view X^* as a feasible assignment.

(b) Use part (a) to show constructively that every doubly stochastic matrix X can be written as $\sum_{i=1}^{k} \gamma_i X_i^*$, where X_i^* are permutation matrices and $\gamma_i \geq 0$, $\sum_{i=1}^{k} \gamma_i = 1$. *Hint:* Define a sequence of matrices $X_0, X_1, \ldots, X_k$, which are nonnegative multiples of doubly stochastic matrices, such that $X_0 = X$, $X_k = 0$, and for all i, $X_i - X_{i+1}$ is a positive multiple of a permutation matrix.

Exercise 2.6 (Hall's Theorem for Perfect Matrices)

A *perfect* matrix is a matrix with nonnegative integer elements such that the elements of each of its rows and each of its columns add to the same integer k. Show that such a perfect matrix can be written as the sum of k permutation matrices. *Hint:* Use the hints and constructions of the preceding exercise.

Exercise 2.7 (Dual Feasibility Theorem)

Show that the dual problem is feasible, that is, there exists a price vector p with

$$p_i - p_j \le a_{ij}, \qquad \forall \ (i,j) \in \mathcal{A}$$

if and only if all forward cycles have nonnegative cost. *Hint:* Assume without loss of generality that the primal is feasible (take $s_i = 0$ if necessary), and note that all forward cycles have nonnegative cost if and only if the primal problem is not unbounded (see the discussion near the beginning of Section 2.1).

Exercise 2.8 (Relation of Dijkstra and Simplex for Shortest Paths)

Consider the single origin/all destinations shortest path problem

$$\text{minimize} \quad \sum_{(i,j)\in\mathcal{A}} a_{ij}x_{ij}$$

$$\text{subject to}$$

$$\sum_{\{j|(1,j)\in\mathcal{A}\}} x_{1j} - \sum_{\{j|(j,1)\in\mathcal{A}\}} x_{j1} = N - 1,$$

$$\sum_{\{j|(i,j)\in\mathcal{A}\}} x_{ij} - \sum_{\{j|(j,i)\in\mathcal{A}\}} x_{ji} = -1, \qquad \forall \ i \ne 1,$$

$$0 \le x_{ij}, \qquad \forall \ (i,j) \in \mathcal{A}.$$

Introduce an artificial arc $(1,i)$ for all $i \ne 1$ with very large cost M, and consider the simplex method starting with the strongly feasible tree of artificial arcs. Let the origin node 1 be the root node.

(a) Show that all the arcs of the trees generated by the simplex method are oriented away from the origin and carry unit flow.

(b) How can a negative length cycle be detected with the simplex method?

(c) Assume that $a_{ij} \ge 0$ for all $(i,j) \in \mathcal{A}$ and suppose that the in-arc is selected to have minimum reduced cost out of all arcs that are not in the tree. Use induction to show that after the kth pivot the tree consists of a shortest path tree from node 1 to the k closest nodes to node 1, together with the artificial arcs $(1,i)$ for all i that are not among the k closest nodes to node 1. Prove then that this implementation of the simplex method is equivalent to Dijkstra's method.

2.3   EXTENSION TO THE PROBLEM WITH UPPER AND LOWER BOUNDS

We now consider the extension of the simplex method of the previous section to the general minimum cost flow problem

$$\text{minimize} \quad \sum_{(i,j)\in\mathcal{A}} a_{ij}x_{ij} \tag{MCF}$$

subject to

$$\sum_{\{j|(i,j)\in\mathcal{A}\}} x_{ij} - \sum_{\{j|(j,i)\in\mathcal{A}\}} x_{ji} = s_i, \quad \forall\, i \in \mathcal{N}, \tag{3.1}$$

$$b_{ij} \leq x_{ij} \leq c_{ij}, \quad \forall\,(i,j) \in \mathcal{A}. \tag{3.2}$$

To simplify the presentation, we assume that $b_{ij} < c_{ij}$ for all arcs (i,j); any arc (i,j) with $b_{ij} = c_{ij}$ can be eliminated, and its flow, which is equal to the common bound, can be incorporated into the supplies s_i and s_j. A nice aspect of this problem is that we need not worry about unboundedness, since all arc flows are constrained to lie in a bounded interval.

The extension of the simplex method to the problem with upper and lower bounds is straightforward, and we will simply state the algorithm and the corresponding results without much elaboration. In fact, one may derive the simplex method for this problem by converting it to the minimum cost flow problem with nonnegativity constraints (cf. Fig. 1.7 in Section 1.1.3), applying the simplex method of the preceding section, and appropriately streamlining the computations. We leave the verification of this as Exercise 3.2 for the reader.

The method uses at each iteration a spanning tree T. Only arcs of T can have flows that are neither at the upper bound nor at the lower bound. However, to uniquely associate a basic flow vector with T, we must also specify for each arc $(i,j) \notin T$ whether $x_{ij} = b_{ij}$ or $x_{ij} = c_{ij}$. Thus, the simplex method maintains a triplet

$$(T, L, U),$$

where

> T is a spanning tree.

> L is the set of arcs $(i,j) \notin T$ with $x_{ij} = b_{ij}$.

> U is the set of arcs $(i,j) \notin T$ with $x_{ij} = c_{ij}$.

Such a triplet will be called a *basis*. It uniquely specifies a flow vector x, called the *basic flow vector* corresponding to (T, L, U). In particular, if the arc (i,j) belongs to T and separates T into the subtrees T_i and T_j, we have

$$x_{ij} = \sum_{n\in T_i} s_n - \sum_{\{(m,n)\in L|m\in T_i,n\in T_j\}} b_{mn} - \sum_{\{(m,n)\in U|m\in T_i,n\in T_j\}} c_{mn}$$

$$+ \sum_{\{(m,n)\in L|m\in T_j,n\in T_i\}} b_{mn} + \sum_{\{(m,n)\in U|m\in T_j,n\in T_i\}} c_{mn}.$$

If x is feasible, then the basis (T, L, U) is called feasible.

Similar to the previous section, we fix a root node r throughout the algorithm. A basis (T, L, U) specifies a price vector p using the same formula as in the previous section:

$$p_i = p_r - \sum_{(m,n) \in P_i^+} a_{mn} + \sum_{(m,n) \in P_i^-} a_{mn}, \qquad \forall \, i \in \mathcal{N},$$

where P_i is the unique simple path of T starting at the root node r and ending at i, and P_i^+ and P_i^- are the sets of forward and backward arcs of P_i, respectively.

We say that the feasible basis (T, L, U) is *strongly feasible* if all arcs $(i, j) \in T$ with $x_{ij} = b_{ij}$ are oriented away from the root and if all arcs $(i, j) \in T$ with $x_{ij} = c_{ij}$ are oriented toward the root (that is, the unique simple path from the root to i passes through j).

Given the strongly feasible basis (T, L, U) with a corresponding flow vector x and price vector p, an iteration of the simplex method produces another strongly feasible basis $(\overline{T}, \overline{L}, \overline{U})$ as follows.

Typical Simplex Iteration

Find an in-arc $\overline{e} = (\overline{i}, \overline{j}) \notin T$ such that either

$$r_{\overline{ij}} < 0 \qquad \text{if} \qquad \overline{e} \in L$$

or

$$r_{\overline{ij}} > 0 \qquad \text{if} \qquad \overline{e} \in U.$$

(If no such arc can be found, x is primal-optimal and p is dual-optimal.) Let C be the cycle closed by T and $\overline{e}$. Define the forward direction of C to be the same as the one of $\overline{e}$ if $\overline{e} \in L$ and opposite to $\overline{e}$ if $\overline{e} \in U$ (that is, $\overline{e} \in C^+$ if $\overline{e} \in L$ and $\overline{e} \in C^-$ if $\overline{e} \in U$). Also let

$$\delta = \min \left\{ \min_{(i,j) \in C^-} \{ x_{ij} - b_{ij} \}, \min_{(i,j) \in C^+} \{ c_{ij} - x_{ij} \} \right\},$$

and let $\hat{C}$ be the set of arcs where this minimum is obtained:

$$\hat{C} = \left\{ (i, j) \in C^- \mid x_{ij} - b_{ij} = \delta \right\} \cup \left\{ (i, j) \in C^+ \mid c_{ij} - x_{ij} = \delta \right\}.$$

Define the *join of* C as the first node of C that lies on the unique simple path of T that starts from the root and ends at $\overline{i}$. Select as out-arc the arc e of $\hat{C}$ that is encountered first as C is traversed in the forward direction starting from the join node. The new tree is $\overline{T} = T + \overline{e} - e$, and the corresponding flow vector $\overline{x}$ is obtained from x by

$$\overline{x}_{ij} = \begin{cases} x_{ij} & \text{if } (i,j) \notin C \\ x_{ij} + \delta & \text{if } (i,j) \in C^+ \\ x_{ij} - \delta & \text{if } (i,j) \in C^-. \end{cases}$$

Note that it is possible that the in-arc is the same as the out-arc, in which case T is unchanged. In this case, the flow of this arc will simply move from one bound to the other, affecting the sets L and U, and thus affecting the basis. The proofs of the preceding section can be modified to show that the algorithm maintains a strongly feasible tree.

The following proposition admits a very similar proof of Prop. 2.1.

Proposition 3.1:   Assume that the minimum cost flow problem (MCF) is feasible. The simplex method starting from a strongly feasible tree terminates with an optimal primal solution x and an optimal dual solution p. Furthermore, the optimal primal cost is equal to the optimal dual cost. If the supplies s_i and the flow bounds b_{ij}, c_{ij} are all integer, the optimal primal solution x is integer; if the starting price of the root node and the cost coefficients a_{ij} are all integer, the optimal dual solution p is integer.

If an initial strongly feasible tree is not readily available, we can solve instead a big-M version of the problem with suitably large value of M. This problem is

$$\text{minimize} \quad \sum_{(i,j)\in\mathcal{A}} a_{ij}x_{ij} + M\left(\sum_{(i,0)\in\overline{\mathcal{A}}} x_{i0} + \sum_{(0,i)\in\overline{\mathcal{A}}} x_{0i}\right)$$

subject to

$$\sum_{\{j|(i,j)\in\mathcal{A}\cup\overline{\mathcal{A}}\}} x_{ij} - \sum_{\{j|(j,i)\in\mathcal{A}\cup\overline{\mathcal{A}}\}} x_{ji} = s_i, \qquad \forall\, i \in \mathcal{N} \cup \{0\},$$

$$b_{ij} \le x_{ij} \le c_{ij}, \qquad \forall\, (i,j) \in \mathcal{A},$$

$$0 \le x_{i0} \le \overline{s}_i, \qquad \forall\, i \text{ with } s_i > 0,$$

$$0 \le x_{0i} \le \underline{s}_i, \qquad \forall\, i \text{ with } s_i \le 0,$$

where

$$\overline{s}_i = s_i - \sum_{\{j|(i,j)\in\mathcal{A}\}} b_{ij} + \sum_{\{j|(j,i)\in\mathcal{A}\}} b_{ji},$$

$$\underline{s}_i = -s_i + \sum_{\{j|(i,j)\in\mathcal{A}\}} b_{ij} - \sum_{\{j|(j,i)\in\mathcal{A}\}} b_{ji}.$$

The initial strongly feasible tree consists of the artificial arcs. The corresponding basic flow vector x is given by $x_{ij} = b_{ij}$ for all $(i,j) \in \mathcal{A}$, $x_{i0} = s_i$, for all i with $s_i > 0$, and $x_{0i} = -s_i$, for all i with $s_i \leq 0$.

Similar to the case of the problem with nonnegativity constraints, we obtain the following.

Proposition 3.2:   If the minimum cost flow problem (MCF) is feasible, then it has at least one optimal solution, and its dual problem also has at least one optimal solution. Furthermore, if the supplies s_i and the flow bounds b_{ij}, c_{ij} are all integer, there exists an optimal primal solution which is integer; if the cost coefficients a_{ij} are all integer, there exists an optimal dual solution which is integer.

E X E R C I S E S

Exercise 3.1

Use the simplex method to solve the minimum cost flow problem with the data of Fig. 2.6, and with the arc flow bounds $0 \leq x_{ij} \leq 1$ for all $(i,j) \in \mathcal{A}$.

Exercise 3.2

Suppose that the problem of this section is transformed to a minimum cost flow problem with nonnegativity constraints as in Fig. 1.7 of Section 1.1.3. Show that the simplex method of the previous section, when applied to the latter problem, is equivalent to the simplex method of the present section. In particular, relate feasible trees, basic flow vectors, and price vectors generated by the two methods, and show that they are in one-to-one correspondence.

2.4   IMPLEMENTATION ISSUES

To implement a network optimization algorithm efficiently it is essential to exploit the graph nature of the problem using appropriate data structures. There are two main issues here:

(a) Representing the problem in a way that facilitates the application of the algorithm.

(b) Using additional data structures that are well suited to the operations of the algorithm.

For simplex methods, the appropriate representations of the problem tend to be quite simple. However, additional fairly complex data structures are needed to implement efficiently the various operations related to flow and price computation, and tree manipulation. This is quite contrary to the situation with the methods that will be discussed in the next two chapters, where the appropriate problem representations are quite complex but the additional data structures are simple.

Problem Representation for Simplex Methods

For concreteness, consider the following problem with zero lower flow bounds

$$\text{minimize} \quad \sum_{(i,j)\in\mathcal{A}} a_{ij}x_{ij} \tag{4.1}$$

subject to

$$\sum_{\{j|(i,j)\in\mathcal{A}\}} x_{ij} - \sum_{\{j|(j,i)\in\mathcal{A}\}} x_{ji} = s_i, \qquad \forall\, i \in \mathcal{N},$$

$$0 \le x_{ij} \le c_{ij}, \qquad \forall\, (i,j) \in \mathcal{A}.$$

This has become the standard form for commonly available minimum cost flow codes. As was mentioned in Section 1.1.3, a problem with nonzero lower arc flow bounds b_{ij} can be converted to one with nonnegativity constraints by using a flow translation (replacing x_{ij} by $x_{ij} - b_{ij}$ and appropriately adjusting c_{ij}, s_i, and s_j).

One way to represent this problem, which is the most common in simplex codes, is to use four arrays of length A and one array of length N:

$START(a)$: The start node of arc a.

$END(a)$: The end node of arc a.

$COST(a)$: The cost coefficient of arc a.

$CAPACITY(a)$: The upper flow bound of arc a.

$SUPPLY(i)$: The supply of node i.

Figure 4.1 gives an example of a problem represented in this way.

An alternative representation is to store the costs a_{ij} and the upper flow bounds c_{ij} in two-dimensional $N \times N$ arrays (or in one-dimensional arrays of length N^2, with the elements of each row stored contiguously). This wastes memory and requires a lot of extra overhead when the problem is sparse $(A << N^2)$, but it may be a good choice for dense problems since it avoids the storage of the start and end nodes of each arc.

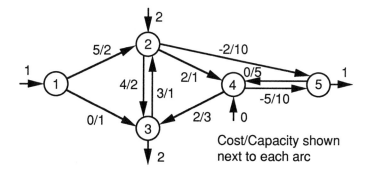

ARC	START	END	COST	CAPACITY
1	1	2	5	2
2	1	3	0	1
3	2	3	4	2
4	3	2	3	1
5	2	5	-2	10
6	2	4	2	1
7	3	4	2	3
8	5	4	0	5
9	4	5	-5	10

NODE	SUPPLY
1	1
2	2
3	-2
4	0
5	-1

Figure 4.1   Representation of a minimum cost flow problem in terms of the five arrays *START*, *END*, *COST*, *CAPACITY*, and *SUPPLY*.

Data Structures for Tree Operations

Taking a closer look at the operations of the simplex method, we see that the main computational steps at each iteration are the following:

(a) Finding an in-arc with negative reduced cost.

(b) Identifying the cycle formed by the current tree and the in-arc.

(c) Modifying the flows along the cycle and obtaining the out-arc.

(d) Recalculating the node prices.

As mentioned in Section 2.1.1, most codes maintain a candidate list, that is, a subset of arcs with negative reduced cost; the arc with most negative reduced cost from this list is selected as the in-arc at each iteration. The maximum size of the candidate list is set at some reasonable level (chosen heuristically), thereby avoiding a costly search and comparison of the reduced costs of all the arcs.

To identify the cycle and the associated flow increment at each iteration, simplex codes commonly use the following two arrays of length N:

(a) $PRED(i)$: The arc preceding node i on the unique path from the root to i on the current tree, together with an indication (such as a plus or a minus sign) of whether this is an incoming or outgoing arc of i.

(b) $DEPTH(i)$: The number of arcs of the unique path from the root to i on the current tree.

The $PRED$ array (together with the $START$ and END arrays) is sufficient both to represent the current tree and to construct the unique path on the tree from any node i to any other node j. (Construct the paths from i to the root and from j to the root, and subtract out the common portion of these paths.) In particular, if (i, j) is the in-arc, the cycle formed by (i, j) and the current tree could be obtained by finding the path joining i and j in this way. By using the $DEPTH$ array, however, the cycle can be constructed more quickly without having to go from i to j all the way to the root. In particular, one can start constructing the paths from i and j to the root simultaneously, adding a new node to the path whose current end node has greater $DEPTH$ (ties are broken arbitrarily). The join of the cycle can then be identified as the first encountered common node in the two paths. The following procedure starting with the in-arc (i, j) accomplishes this. In this procedure, $\bar{i}$ and $\bar{j}$ represent successive nodes of the paths starting at i and j, respectively, and ending at the join of the cycle.

Identifying the Join of the Cycle Corresponding to the In-Arc (i, j)

Set $\bar{i} = i, \bar{j} = j$.

Step 1: If $DEPTH(\bar{i}) \geq DEPTH(\bar{j})$, go to Step 2; else go to Step 3.

Step 2: Set $\bar{i} := START(PRED(\bar{i}))$ if $PRED(\bar{i})$ is an incoming arc to $\bar{i}$, and set $\bar{i} := END(PRED(\bar{i}))$ if $PRED(\bar{i})$ is an outgoing arc from $\bar{i}$. Go to Step 4.

Step 3: Set $\bar{j} := START(PRED(\bar{j}))$ if $PRED(\bar{j})$ is an incoming arc to $\bar{j}$, and set $\bar{i} := END(PRED(\bar{j}))$ if $PRED(\bar{j})$ is an outgoing arc from $\bar{j}$. Go to Step 4.

Step 4: If $\bar{i} = \bar{j}$, terminate; $\bar{i}$ is the join of the cycle corresponding to the in-arc (i, j). Else go to Step 1.

The cycle corresponding to the in-arc consists of the arcs $PRED(\bar{i})$ and $PRED(\bar{j})$ encountered during this procedure. With a simple modification of the procedure, we can simultaneously obtain the out-arc and calculate the flow increment. With little additional work, we can also change the flow along the cycle and update the $PRED$ and $DEPTH$ arrays consistently with the new tree.

We must still provide for a mechanism to calculate efficiently the prices corresponding to a given tree. This can be done iteratively, using the prices of the preceding tree as shown in Section 1.1; cf. Eqs. (1.11) and (1.12). To apply these equations, it is necessary to change the prices of the descendants of the endnode of the out-arc that has the larger value of $DEPTH$; cf. Fig. 4.2. Thus, it is sufficient to be able to calculate the descendants of a given node i in the current tree (the nodes whose unique path to the root passes through i). For this it is convenient to use one more array, called $THREAD$. It defines a traversal order of the nodes of the tree in depth-first fashion. To understand this order, it is useful to think of the tree laid out in a plane, and to consider visiting all nodes starting from the root, and going "top to bottom" and "left to right". An example is given in Fig. 4.3. It can be seen that every node i appears in the traversal order immediately before all of its descendants. Hence the descendants of i are all the nodes immediately following node i in the traversal order up to the first node j with $DEPTH(j) \leq DEPTH(i)$. The array $THREAD$ encodes the traversal order by storing in $THREAD(i)$ the node following node i; cf. Fig. 4.3. An important fact is that when the tree changes, the $THREAD$ array can be updated quite efficiently [with $O(N)$ operations]. The details, however, are too tedious and complicated to be included here; for a clear presentation, see [Chv83], p. 314.

2.5   NOTES AND SOURCES

2.1.   The first specialized version of the simplex method for the transportation problem problem was given in [Dan51]. This method was also described and extended to the minimum cost flow problem in [Dan63]. A general primal cost improvement algorithm involving flow changes along negative cost

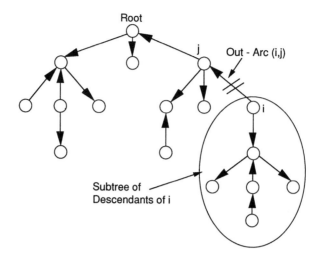

Figure 4.2   The two subtrees obtained when the out-arc is deleted from the current tree.   The subtree containing the endnode of the out-arc with larger *DEPTH* (node i in the example of the figure) consists of all the descendants of that endnode.

cycles was given in [Kle67]. Strongly feasible trees and their use in resolving degeneracy were introduced in [Cun76].

The subject of pivot selection has received considerable attention in the literature. Examples of poor performance of the simplex method are given in [Zad73a] and [Zad73b]. The performance of various pivot rules was studied empirically in [GSS77], [GoR77], [BBG77], [BGK77], [BGK78], [Mul78a], [Mul78b], and [GGK83]. Generally, even with the use of strongly feasible trees, it is possible that the number of successive degenerate pivots is not polynomial. Pivot rules with guaranteed polynomial upper bounds on the lengths of sequences of degenerate pivots are given in [Cun79] and [GHK87]. One of the simplest such rules maintains a strongly feasible tree and operates as follows: if the in-arc at some iteration has start node i, the in-arc at the next iteration must be the outgoing arc from node $(i+k)$ modulo N that has minimum reduced cost, where k is the smallest nonnegative integer such that node $(i+k)$ modulo N has at least one outgoing arc with negative reduced cost. For a textbook discussion of a variety of pivot rules under which the simplex method has polynomial running time, see [BJS90].

2.3.   Specialized simplex methods have been developed for the assignment problem; see [BGK77], [Hun83], [Akg86], [Bal85], [Gol85a], [Bal86]. For analysis and application of simplex methods in shortest path and max-flow problems, see [FuD55], [FNP81], [GKM84], [GHK86], and [GoH88].

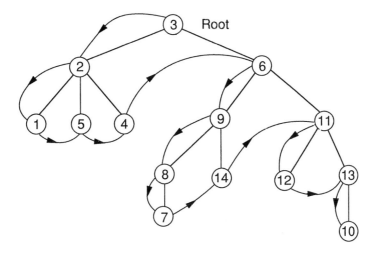

Traversal Order: 3, 2, 1, 5, 4, 6, 9, 8, 7, 14, 11, 12, 13, 10

i	1	2	3	4	5	6	7	8	9	10	11	12	13	14
$THREAD(i)$	5	1	2	6	4	9	14	7	8	0	12	13	10	11

Figure 4.3   Illustration of the *THREAD* array, which defines a depth-first traversal order of the nodes in the tree. Given the set S of already traversed nodes, the next node traversed is an immediate descendant of one of the nodes in S, which has maximum value of *DEPTH*. For each node i, *THREAD(i)* defines the successor of node i in this order (for the last node, *THREAD* is equal to 0).

2.4.   The development of good implementation techniques played a crucial role in the efficient use of the simplex method. Important contributions in this area include [Joh66], [SrT73], [GKK74a], [GKK74b], [BBG77], and [BGK79]. Textbook presentations of these techniques that supplement ours are given in [KeH80], [Chv83], and [BJS90].

3

Dual Ascent Methods

3.1 DUAL ASCENT

In this chapter we focus on the minimum cost flow problem

$$\text{minimize} \quad \sum_{(i,j)\in\mathcal{A}} a_{ij}x_{ij} \tag{MCF}$$

subject to

$$\sum_{\{j|(i,j)\in\mathcal{A}\}} x_{ij} - \sum_{\{j|(j,i)\in\mathcal{A}\}} x_{ji} = s_i, \quad \forall\, i \in \mathcal{N}, \tag{1.1}$$

$$b_{ij} \leq x_{ij} \leq c_{ij}, \quad \forall\, (i,j) \in \mathcal{A}. \tag{1.2}$$

Throughout the chapter we will assume that the scalars a_{ij}, b_{ij}, c_{ij}, and s_i are all integer. Usually, this is not an important practical restriction. However, there are extensions of the algorithms of this chapter that handle noninteger problem data, as will be discussed later.

The main idea of dual cost improvement (or dual ascent) algorithms is to start with a price vector and successively obtain new price vectors with improved dual cost value, with the aim of solving the dual problem. Recall from Section 1.2.2 that this problem is

$$\text{maximize } q(p)$$
$$\text{subject to no constraint on } p, \tag{1.3}$$

133

where the dual functional q is given by

$$q(p) = \sum_{(i,j)\in\mathcal{A}} q_{ij}(p_i - p_j) + \sum_{i\in\mathcal{N}} s_i p_i, \tag{1.4}$$

with

$$q_{ij}(p_i - p_j) = \min_{b_{ij}\leq x_{ij}\leq c_{ij}} \left\{ (a_{ij} + p_j - p_i)x_{ij} \right\}$$
$$= \begin{cases} (a_{ij} + p_j - p_i)b_{ij} & \text{if } p_i \leq a_{ij} + p_j, \\ (a_{ij} + p_j - p_i)c_{ij} & \text{if } p_i > a_{ij} + p_j. \end{cases} \tag{1.5}$$

It is helpful here to introduce some terminology. For any price vector p, we say that an arc (i, j) is

$$\text{inactive if} \quad p_i < a_{ij} + p_j,$$

$$\text{balanced if} \quad p_i = a_{ij} + p_j,$$

$$\text{active if} \quad p_i > a_{ij} + p_j.$$

The *complementary slackness* (CS) conditions for a flow–price vector pair (x, p), introduced in Section 1.2.2, can be restated as follows:

$$x_{ij} = b_{ij}, \quad \text{for all inactive arcs } (i, j), \tag{1.6}$$

$$b_{ij} \leq x_{ij} \leq c_{ij}, \quad \text{for all balanced arcs } (i, j), \tag{1.7}$$

$$x_{ij} = c_{ij}, \quad \text{for all active arcs } (i, j), \tag{1.8}$$

(see Fig. 1.1).

We restate for convenience the following basic duality result, proved in Section 1.2.2.

Proposition 1.1: If a feasible flow vector x^* and a price vector p^* satisfy the complementary slackness conditions (1.6)–(1.8), then x^* is an optimal solution of the minimum cost flow problem and p^* is an optimal solution of the dual problem (1.3).

The major dual ascent algorithms select at each iteration a connected subset of nodes $\mathcal{S}$, and change the prices of these nodes by equal amounts while leaving the prices of all other nodes unchanged. In other words, each iteration involves a price vector change along a direction of the form $d_{\mathcal{S}} = (d_1, \ldots, d_N)$, where

$$d_i = \begin{cases} 1 & \text{if } i \in \mathcal{S} \\ 0 & \text{if } i \notin \mathcal{S} \end{cases} \tag{1.9}$$

and $\mathcal{S}$ is a connected subset of nodes. Such directions will be called *elementary*.

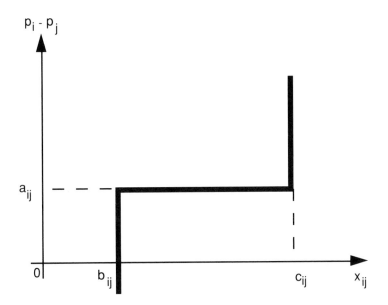

Figure 1.1   Illustration of the complementary slackness conditions. For each arc (i, j), the pair $(x_{ij}, p_i - p_j)$ should lie on the graph shown.

To check whether $d_{\mathcal{S}}$ is a direction of dual ascent, we need to calculate the corresponding directional derivative of the dual cost along $d_{\mathcal{S}}$ and check whether it is positive. From the dual cost expression (1.4)-(1.5), it is seen that this directional derivative is

$$q'(p; d_{\mathcal{S}}) = \lim_{\alpha \downarrow 0} \frac{q(p + \alpha d_{\mathcal{S}}) - q(p)}{\alpha}$$

$$= \sum_{(j,i)\,:\,\text{active, } j\notin\mathcal{S}, i\in\mathcal{S}} c_{ji} + \sum_{(j,i)\,:\,\text{inactive or balanced, } j\notin\mathcal{S}, i\in\mathcal{S}} b_{ji}$$

$$- \sum_{(i,j)\,:\,\text{active or balanced, } i\in\mathcal{S}, j\notin\mathcal{S}} c_{ij} - \sum_{(i,j)\,:\,\text{inactive, } i\in\mathcal{S}, j\notin\mathcal{S}} b_{ij}$$

$$+ \sum_{i\in\mathcal{S}} s_i. \tag{1.10}$$

In words, the directional derivative $q'(p; d_{\mathcal{S}})$ is the difference between inflow and outflow across the node set $\mathcal{S}$ when the flows of the inactive and active arcs are set at their lower and upper bounds, respectively, and the flow of each balanced arc incident to $\mathcal{S}$ is set to its lower or upper bound depending on whether the arc is incoming to $\mathcal{S}$ or outgoing from $\mathcal{S}$.

To obtain a suitable set $\mathcal{S}$, with positive directional derivative $q'(p, d_{\mathcal{S}})$, it is convenient to maintain a flow vector x satisfying CS together with p. This helps to organize the search for an ascent direction and to detect optimality, as will now be explained.

For a flow vector x, let us define the *surplus* g_i of node i as the difference between total inflow into i minus the total outflow from i, that is,

$$g_i = \sum_{\{j|(j,i)\in\mathcal{A}\}} x_{ji} - \sum_{\{j|(i,j)\in\mathcal{A}\}} x_{ij} + s_i. \tag{1.11}$$

We have

$$\sum_{i\in\mathcal{S}} g_i = \sum_{\{(j,i)\in\mathcal{A}|j\notin\mathcal{S},i\in\mathcal{S}\}} x_{ji} - \sum_{\{(i,j)\in\mathcal{A}|i\in\mathcal{S},j\notin\mathcal{S}\}} x_{ij} + \sum_{i\in\mathcal{S}} s_i, \tag{1.12}$$

and if x satisfies CS together with p, we obtain using Eqs. (1.10) and (1.12)

$$\sum_{i\in\mathcal{S}} g_i = q'(p;d_\mathcal{S}) + \sum_{(j,i)\,:\,\text{balanced},\,j\notin\mathcal{S},i\in\mathcal{S}} (x_{ji} - b_{ji})$$

$$+ \sum_{(i,j):\,\text{balanced},\,i\in\mathcal{S},j\notin\mathcal{S}} (c_{ij} - x_{ij}) \tag{1.13}$$

$$\geq q'(p;d_\mathcal{S}).$$

We see, therefore, that only a node set $\mathcal{S}$ that has positive total surplus is a candidate for generating a direction $d_\mathcal{S}$ of dual ascent. In particular, if there is no balanced arc (i,j) with $i\in\mathcal{S}$, $j\notin\mathcal{S}$, and $x_{ij} < c_{ij}$, and no balanced arc (j,i) with $j\notin\mathcal{S}$, $i\in\mathcal{S}$, and $b_{ij} < x_{ij}$, then

$$\sum_{i\in\mathcal{S}} g_i = q'(p;d_\mathcal{S}), \tag{1.14}$$

so if $\mathcal{S}$ has positive total surplus then $d_\mathcal{S}$ is an ascent direction. The following lemma expresses this idea and provides the basis for the subsequent algorithms.

Lemma 1.1:   Suppose that x and p satisfy the CS conditions, and let $\mathcal{S}$ be a subset of nodes. Let $d_\mathcal{S} = (d_1, d_2, \ldots, d_N)$ be the vector with $d_i = 1$ if $i \in \mathcal{S}$ and $d_i = 0$ otherwise, and assume that

$$\sum_{i\in\mathcal{S}} g_i > 0.$$

Then either $d_\mathcal{S}$ is a dual ascent direction, that is,

$$q'(p;d_\mathcal{S}) > 0,$$

or else there exist nodes $i \in \mathcal{S}$ and $j \notin \mathcal{S}$ such that either (i,j) is a balanced arc with $x_{ij} < c_{ij}$ or (j,i) is a balanced arc with $b_{ji} < x_{ji}$.

Proof: Follows from Eq. (1.13).   **Q.E.D.**

Overview of Dual Ascent Algorithms

The algorithms of this chapter start with an integer flow–price vector pair (x, p), satisfying CS, and operate in iterations. At the beginning of each iteration, we have a subset of nodes $\mathcal{S}$ such that

$$\sum_{i \in \mathcal{S}} g_i > 0;$$

initially $\mathcal{S}$ consists of one or more nodes with positive surplus. According to the preceding lemma, there are two possibilities:

(a) $\mathcal{S}$ defines a dual ascent direction $d_{\mathcal{S}} = (d_1, d_2, \ldots, d_N)$, where $d_i = 1$ if $i \in \mathcal{S}$, and $d_i = 0$ otherwise.

(b) $\mathcal{S}$ can be enlarged by adding a node $j \notin \mathcal{S}$ with the property described in Lemma 1.1, that is, for some $i \in \mathcal{S}$, either (i, j) is a balanced arc with $x_{ij} < c_{ij}$, or (j, i) is a balanced arc with $b_{ji} < x_{ji}$.

In case (b), there are two possibilities:

(1) $g_j \geq 0$, in which case,

$$\sum_{i \in \mathcal{S} \cup \{j\}} g_i > 0,$$

and the process can be continued with

$$\mathcal{S} \cup \{j\}$$

replacing $\mathcal{S}$.

(2) $g_j < 0$, in which case, it can be seen that there is a path originating at some node i of the starting set $\mathcal{S}$ and ending at node j that is *unblocked*, that is, all its arcs have room for a flow increase in the direction from i to j (see Fig. 1.2). Such a path is called an *augmenting path* (generalizing slightly the notion of an augmenting path used in the Ford-Fulkerson algorithm for the max-flow problem). By increasing the flow of the forward arcs (direction from i to j) of the path and by decreasing the flow of the backward arcs (direction from j to i) of the path, we can bring both surpluses g_i and g_j closer to zero by an integer amount while leaving the surplus of all other nodes unaffected and maintaining CS.

Since the total absolute surplus $\sum_{i \in \mathcal{N}} |g_i|$ cannot be indefinitely reduced by integer amounts, it is seen that starting from an integer flow–price vector pair satisfying CS, after at most a finite number of iterations in which flow augmentations occur without finding an ascent direction, one of three things will happen:

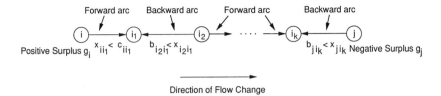

Direction of Flow Change

Figure 1.2   Illustration of an augmenting path. The initial node i and the final node j have positive and negative surplus, respectively. Furthermore, the path is unblocked, that is, each arc on the path has room for flow change in the direction from i to j. A flow change of magnitude $\delta > 0$ in this direction reduces the total absolute surplus $\sum_{m \in \mathcal{N}} |g_m|$ by 2δ provided $\delta \leq \min\{g_i, -g_j\}$.

(a) A dual ascent direction will be found; this direction can be used to improve the dual cost by an integer amount.

(b) $g_i = 0$ for all i; in this case the flow vector x is feasible, and since it satisfies CS together with p, by Prop. 1.1, x is primal-optimal and p is dual-optimal.

(c) $g_i \leq 0$ for all i but $g_i < 0$ for at least one i; since by adding Eq. (1.12) over all $i \in \mathcal{N}$ we have $\sum_{i \in \mathcal{N}} s_i = \sum_{i \in \mathcal{N}} g_i$ it follows that $\sum_{i \in \mathcal{N}} s_i < 0$, so the problem is infeasible.

Thus, for a feasible problem, the procedure just outlined can be used to find a dual ascent direction and improve the dual cost starting at any nonoptimal price vector. Figure 1.3 provides an illustration for a very simple problem.

In the next two sections, we discuss two different dual ascent methods. The first, known as *primal-dual*, in its classical form, tries at each iteration to use the *steepest ascent* direction, that is, the elementary direction with maximal directional derivative. This method can also be implemented by means of a shortest path computation. The second method, called *relaxation*, is usually faster in practice. It tries to use directions that are not necessarily steepest, but can be computed more quickly than the steepest ascent direction.

3.2   PRIMAL-DUAL (SEQUENTIAL SHORTEST PATH) METHODS

The primal-dual algorithm starts with any integer pair (x, p) satisfying CS. One possibility is to choose the integer vector p arbitrarily and to set $x_{ij} = b_{ij}$ if (i, j) is inactive or balanced, and $x_{ij} = c_{ij}$ otherwise. (Prior knowledge could be built into the initial choice of x and p using, for example, the results of an earlier optimization.) The algorithm preserves the integrality and CS property of the pair (x, p) throughout.

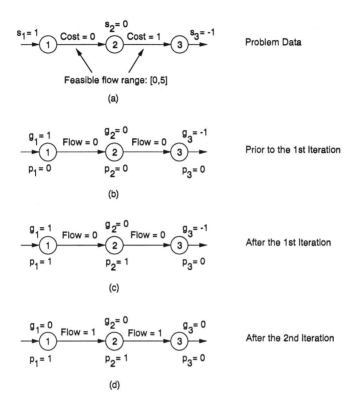

Figure 1.3   Illustration of a dual ascent method for the simple problem described in (a). Initially, $x = (0,0)$ and $p = (0,0,0)$ as shown in (b).

The first iteration starts with $\mathcal{S} = \{1\}$. It can be seen using Eq. (1.13), that the directional derivative $q'(p; d_{\mathcal{S}})$ is -4, so $d_{\mathcal{S}} = (1,0,0)$ is not a direction of ascent. We thus enlarge $\mathcal{S}$ by adding node 2 using the balanced arc $(1,2)$. Since there is no incident balanced arc to $\mathcal{S} = \{1,2\}$, the direction $d_{\mathcal{S}} = (1,1,0)$ is a direction of ascent [using Eq. (1.13), $q'(p; d_{\mathcal{S}}) = 1$]. We thus increase the prices of the nodes in $\mathcal{S}$ by a common increment γ, and we choose $\gamma = 1$ because this is the increment that maximizes the dual function along the direction $d_{\mathcal{S}}$ starting from p; this can be seen by checking the directional derivative of q at the price vector $(\gamma, \gamma, 0)$ along the direction $d_{\mathcal{S}}$ and finding that it switches from positive ($= 1$) to negative ($= -4$) at $\gamma = 1$ where the arc $(2,3)$ becomes balanced.

The second iteration starts again with $\mathcal{S} = \{1\}$. As in the first iteration, $\mathcal{S}$ is enlarged to $\mathcal{S} = \{1,2\}$. Since the corresponding direction $d_{\mathcal{S}} = (1,1,0)$ is not a direction of ascent [$q'(p; d_{\mathcal{S}}) = -4$], we explore the balanced incident arc $(2,3)$ and we discover the negative surplus node 3. The augmenting path $(1,2,3)$ has now been obtained, and the corresponding augmentation sets the flows of the arcs $(1,2)$ and $(2,3)$ to 1. Since now all node surpluses become zero, the algorithm terminates; $x = (1,1)$ is an optimal primal solution and $p = (1,1,0)$ is an optimal dual solution.

At the start of the typical iteration, we have an integer pair (x, p) satisfying CS. The iteration indicates that the primal problem is infeasible, or else indicates that (x, p) is optimal, or else transforms this pair into another pair satisfying CS. In particular, if $g_i \leq 0$ for all i, then in view of the fact $\sum_{i \in \mathcal{N}} g_i = \sum_{i \in \mathcal{N}} s_i$ [see Eq. (1.12) with $\mathcal{S} = \mathcal{N}$], there are two possibilities: (1) $g_i < 0$ for some i, in which case $\sum_{i \in \mathcal{N}} s_i < 0$ and the problem is infeasible, or (2) $g_i = 0$ for all i, in which case x is feasible and therefore also optimal, since it satisfies CS together with p. In either case, the algorithm terminates.

If on the other hand we have $g_i > 0$ for at least one node i, the iteration starts by selecting a nonempty subset I of nodes i with $g_i > 0$. The iteration maintains two sets of nodes $\mathcal{S}$ and $\mathcal{L}$, with $\mathcal{S} \subset \mathcal{L}$. Initially, $\mathcal{S}$ is empty and $\mathcal{L}$ consists of the subset I. We use the following terminology.

$\mathcal{S}$: Set of *scanned* nodes (these are the nodes whose incident arcs have been "examined" during the iteration).

$\mathcal{L}$: Set of *labeled* nodes (these are the nodes that have either been scanned during the iteration or are current candidates for scanning).

In the course of the iteration we continue to add nodes to $\mathcal{L}$ and $\mathcal{S}$ until either an augmenting path is found or $\mathcal{L} = \mathcal{S}$, in which case $d_{\mathcal{S}}$ will be shown to be an ascent direction. The iteration also maintains a *label* for every node $i \in \mathcal{L} - I$, which is an incident arc of i. The labels are useful for constructing augmenting paths (see Step 3 of the following iteration).

Typical Primal-Dual Iteration

> **Step 0 (Initialization):** Select a set I of nodes i with $g_i > 0$. [If no such node can be found, terminate; the pair (x, p) is optimal if $g_i = 0$ for all i; otherwise the problem is infeasible.] Set $\mathcal{L} := I$ and $\mathcal{S} :=$ empty, and go to Step 1.

> **Step 1 (Choose a Node to Scan):** If $\mathcal{S} = \mathcal{L}$, go to Step 4; else select a node $i \in \mathcal{L} - \mathcal{S}$, set $\mathcal{S} := \mathcal{S} \cup \{i\}$, and go to Step 2.

> **Step 2 (Label Neighbor Nodes of i):** Add to $\mathcal{L}$ all nodes $j \notin \mathcal{L}$ such that either (j, i) is balanced and $b_{ji} < x_{ji}$ or (i, j) is balanced and $x_{ij} < c_{ij}$; also for every such j, give to j the label "(j, i)" if (j, i) is balanced and $b_{ji} < x_{ji}$, and otherwise give to j the label "(i, j)." If for all the nodes j just added to $\mathcal{L}$ we have $g_j \geq 0$, go to Step 1. Else select one of these nodes j with $g_j < 0$ and go to Step 3.

> **Step 3 (Flow Augmentation):** An augmenting path P has been found that begins at a node i belonging to the initial set I and ends at the node j identified in Step 2. The path is constructed by tracing labels backward starting from j, and is such that we have
> $$x_{mn} < c_{mn}, \qquad \forall \, (m, n) \in P^+$$

$$x_{mn} > b_{mn}, \qquad \forall \ (m, n) \in P^-$$

where P^+ and P^- are the sets of forward and backward arcs of P, respectively. Let

$$\delta = \min\big\{g_i, -g_j, \big\{c_{mn} - x_{mn} \mid (m, n) \in P^+\big\}, \big\{x_{mn} - b_{mn} \mid (m, n) \in P^-\big\}\big\}.$$

Increase by δ the flows of all arcs in P^+, decrease by δ the flows of all arcs in P^-, and go to the next iteration.

Step 4 (Price Change): Let

$$\gamma = \min\big\{\{p_j + a_{ij} - p_i \mid (i, j) \in \mathcal{A}, x_{ij} < c_{ij}, i \in \mathcal{S}, j \notin \mathcal{S}\}, \tag{2.1}$$
$$\{p_j - a_{ji} - p_i \mid (j, i) \in \mathcal{A}, b_{ji} < x_{ji}, i \in \mathcal{S}, j \notin \mathcal{S}\}\big\}.$$

Set

$$p_i := \begin{cases} p_i + \gamma, & \text{if } i \in \mathcal{S} \\ p_i, & \text{otherwise.} \end{cases}$$

Add to $\mathcal{L}$ all nodes j for which the minimum in Eq. (2.1) is attained by an arc (i, j) or an arc (j, i); also for every such j, give to j the label "(i, j)" if the minimum in Eq. (2.1) is attained by an arc (i, j), and otherwise give to j the label "(j, i)." If for all the nodes j just added to $\mathcal{L}$ we have $g_j \geq 0$, go to Step 1. Else select one of these nodes j with $g_j < 0$ and go to Step 3. [*Note:* If there is no arc (i, j) with $x_{ij} < c_{ij}$, $i \in \mathcal{S}$, and $j \notin \mathcal{S}$, or arc (j, i) with $b_{ji} < x_{ji}$, $i \in \mathcal{S}$, and $j \notin \mathcal{S}$, the problem is infeasible and the algorithm terminates; see Prop. 2.1 that follows.]

Note the following regarding the primal-dual iteration:

(a) All operations of the iteration preserve the integrality of the flow–price vector pair.

(b) The iteration maintains CS of the flow–price vector pair. To see this, note that arcs with both ends in $\mathcal{S}$, which are balanced just before a price change, continue to be balanced after a price change. This means that a flow augmentation step, even if it occurs following several executions of Step 4, changes only flows of balanced arcs, so it cannot destroy CS. Also, a price change in Step 4 maintains CS because no arc flow is modified in this step and the price increment γ of Eq. (2.1) is such that no arc changes status from active to inactive or vice versa.

(c) At all times we have $\mathcal{S} \subset \mathcal{L}$. Furthermore, when Step 4 is entered, we have $\mathcal{S} = \mathcal{L}$ and $\mathcal{L}$ contains no node with negative surplus. Therefore, based on the logic of Step 2, there is no balanced arc (i, j) with $x_{ij} < c_{ij}$, $i \in \mathcal{S}$, and $j \notin \mathcal{S}$, and no balanced arc (j, i) with $b_{ji} < x_{ji}$, $i \in \mathcal{S}$, and $j \notin \mathcal{S}$. It follows from the discussion preceding Lemma 1.1 [cf. Eq. (1.14)] that $d_{\mathcal{S}}$ is an ascent direction.

(d) Only a finite number of price changes occur at each iteration, so each iteration executes to completion, either terminating with a flow augmentation in Step 3, or with an indication of infeasibility in Step 4. To see this, note that between two price changes, the set $\mathcal{L}$ is enlarged by at least one node, so there can be no more than N price changes per iteration.

(e) Only a finite number of flow augmentation steps are executed by the algorithm, since each of these reduces the total absolute surplus $\sum_{i \in \mathcal{N}} |g_i|$ by an integer amount [by (a) above], while price changes do not affect the total absolute surplus.

(f) The algorithm terminates. The reason is that each iteration will execute to completion [by (d) above], and will involve exactly one augmentation, while there will be only a finite number of augmentations [cf. (e) above].

The following proposition establishes the validity of the method.

Proposition 2.1:   Consider the minimum cost flow problem and assume that a_{ij}, b_{ij}, c_{ij}, and s_i are all integer.

(a) If the problem is feasible, then the primal-dual method terminates with an integer optimal flow vector x and an integer optimal price vector p.

(b) If the problem is infeasible, then the primal-dual method terminates either because $g_i \leq 0$ for all i and $g_i < 0$ for at least one i or because there is no arc (i, j) with $x_{ij} < c_{ij}$, $i \in \mathcal{S}$, and $j \notin \mathcal{S}$, or arc (j, i) with $b_{ji} < x_{ji}$, $i \in \mathcal{S}$, and $j \notin \mathcal{S}$ in Step 4.

Proof: The algorithm terminates as argued earlier, and there are three possibilities:

(1) The algorithm terminates because all nodes have zero surplus. In this case the flow–price vector pair obtained upon termination is feasible and satisfies CS, so it is optimal.

(2) The algorithm terminates because $g_i \leq 0$ for all i and $g_i < 0$ for at least one i. In this case the problem is infeasible, since for a feasible problem we must have $\sum_{i \in \mathcal{N}} g_i = 0$.

(3) The algorithm terminates because there is no arc (i, j) with $x_{ij} < c_{ij}$, $i \in \mathcal{S}$, and $j \notin \mathcal{S}$, or arc (j, i) with $b_{ji} < x_{ji}$, $i \in \mathcal{S}$, and $j \notin \mathcal{S}$ in Step 4. Then the flux across the cut $Q = [\mathcal{S}, \mathcal{N} - \mathcal{S}]$ is equal to the capacity $C(Q)$ and is also equal to the sum of the divergences of the nodes of $\mathcal{S}$, which is $\sum_{i \in \mathcal{S}}(s_i - g_i)$ [cf. Eq. (1.11)]. Since $g_i \geq 0$ for all $i \in \mathcal{S}$, $g_i > 0$ for the nodes $i \in I$, and $I \subset \mathcal{S}$, we see that

$$C(Q) < \sum_{i \in \mathcal{S}} s_i.$$

This implies that the problem is infeasible, since for any feasible flow vector we must have

$$\sum_{i \in S} s_i = F(Q) \leq C(Q),$$

where $F(Q)$ is the corresponding flux across Q. [Another way to show that the problem is infeasible in this case is to observe that d_S is a dual ascent direction, and if no arc (i, j) with the property stated exists, the rate of increase of the dual function remains unchanged as we move indefinitely along d_S starting from p. This implies that the dual optimal value is infinite or equivalently (by Prop. 3.2 in Section 2.3) that the primal problem is infeasible.]

Since termination can occur only under the above circumstances, the desired conclusion follows.   **Q.E.D.**

There are a number of variations of the primal-dual method, using different choices of the initial set I of positive surplus nodes. The two most common possibilities are:

(1) I consists of a *single* node i with $g_i > 0$.

(2) I consists of *all* nodes i with $g_i > 0$.

The primal-dual method was originally proposed with the latter choice. In this case, whenever there is a price change, the set S contains all nodes with positive surplus, and from the directional derivative formulas (1.13) and (1.14), it follows that the ascent direction used in Step 4 has the *maximum* possible directional derivative among elementary directions. This leads to the interpretation of the primal-dual method as a steepest ascent method.

Figure 2.1 traces the steps of the primal-dual method for a simple example.

The Shortest Path Implementation

We will now provide an alternative implementation of the primal-dual method in terms of a shortest path computation. This is known as the *sequential shortest path method*; it will be seen to be mathematically equivalent with the primal-dual method given earlier in the sense that it produces the same sequence of flow–price vector pairs.

Given a pair (x, p) satisfying CS, define the *reduced cost* of an arc (i, j) by

$$r_{ij} = a_{ij} + p_j - p_i. \tag{2.2}$$

Recall that an unblocked path P with respect to x is a path such that $x_{ij} < c_{ij}$ for all forward arcs $(i, j) \in P^+$ and $b_{ij} < x_{ij}$ for all backward arcs $(i, j) \in P^-$.

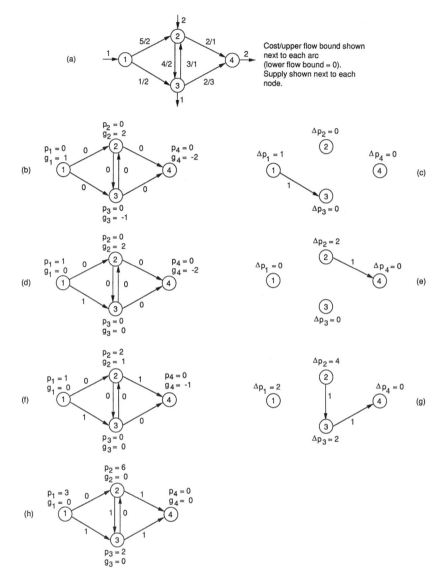

Figure 2.1   Example illustrating the primal-dual method, starting with zero prices.

(a) Problem data.

(b) Initial flows, prices, and surpluses.

(c) Augmenting path and price changes Δp_i of first iteration ($I = \{1\}$).

(d) Flows, prices, and surpluses after the first iteration.

(e) Augmenting path and price changes Δp_i of second iteration ($I = \{2\}$).

(f) Flows, prices, and surpluses after the second iteration.

(g) Augmenting path and price changes Δp_i of third iteration ($I = \{2\}$). There are two price changes here: first p_2 increases by 2, and then p_1, p_2, and p_3 increase by 2.

(h) Flows, prices, and surpluses after the third iteration. The algorithm terminates with an optimal flow–price pair, since all node surpluses are zero.

Furthermore, P is an augmenting path if its start and end nodes have positive and negative surplus, respectively. We define the *length* of an unblocked path P by

$$L_P = \sum_{(i,j)\in P^+} r_{ij} - \sum_{(i,j)\in P^-} r_{ij}. \tag{2.3}$$

Note that since (x,p) satisfies CS, all forward arcs of an unblocked path P must be inactive or balanced, while all backward arcs of P must be active or balanced [cf. Eqs. (1.6)-(1.8)], so we have

$$r_{ij} \geq 0, \qquad \forall\ (i,j) \in P^+, \tag{2.4}$$

$$r_{ij} \leq 0, \qquad \forall\ (i,j) \in P^-. \tag{2.5}$$

Thus, the length of P is nonnegative.

The sequential shortest path method starts each iteration with an integer pair (x,p) satisfying CS and with a set I of nodes i with $g_i > 0$, and proceeds as follows.

Sequential Shortest Path Iteration

Construct an augmenting path P with respect to x that has minimum length over all augmenting paths with respect to x that start at some node $i \in I$. Then, carry out an augmentation along P (cf. Step 3 of the primal-dual iteration) and modify the node prices as follows: let $\bar{d}$ be the length of P and for each node $m \in \mathcal{N}$, let d_m be the minimum of the lengths of the unblocked paths with respect to x that start at some node in I and end at m ($d_m = \infty$ if no such path exists). The new price vector $\bar{p}$ is given by

$$\bar{p}_m = p_m + \max\{0, \bar{d} - d_m\}, \qquad \forall\ m \in \mathcal{N}. \tag{2.6}$$

The method terminates under the following circumstances:

(a) All nodes i have zero surplus; in this case it will be seen that the current pair (x,p) is primal and dual optimal.

(b) $g_i \leq 0$ for all i and $g_i < 0$ for at least one i; in this case the problem is infeasible, since $\sum_{i\in\mathcal{N}} s_i = \sum_{i\in\mathcal{N}} g_i < 0$.

(c) There is no augmenting path with respect to x that starts at some node in I; in this case it will be seen that the problem is infeasible.

We will show shortly that the method preserves the integrality and the CS property of the pair (x,p), and that it terminates.

It is important to note that the shortest path computation can be executed using the standard shortest path algorithms described in Section 1.3.

The idea is to use r_{ij} as the length of each forward arc (i, j) of an unblocked path, and to reverse the direction of each backward arc (i, j) of an unblocked path and to use $-r_{ij}$ as its length [cf. the unblocked path length formula (2.3)]. In particular, the iteration can be executed using the following procedure.

Consider the *residual graph*, which has the same node set $\mathcal{N}$ of the original problem graph, and has

an arc (i, j) with length r_{ij} for every arc $(i, j) \in \mathcal{A}$ with $x_{ij} < c_{ij}$,

an arc (j, i) with length $-r_{ij}$ for every arc $(i, j) \in \mathcal{A}$ with $b_{ij} < x_{ij}$.

[If this creates two arcs in the same direction between two nodes, discard the arc with the larger length (in case of a tie, discard either arc).] Find a path P that is shortest among paths of the residual graph that start at some node in I and end at some node with negative surplus. Find also the shortest distances d_m from nodes of I to all other nodes m [or at least to those nodes m with d_m less than the length of P; cf. Eq. (2.6)].

Figure 2.2 illustrates the sequential shortest path method and shows the sequence of residual graphs for the example worked out earlier (cf. Fig. 2.1).

Note here that by Eqs. (2.4) and (2.5), the arc lengths of the residual graph are nonnegative, so Dijkstra's method can be used for the shortest path computation. Since all forward paths in the residual graph correspond to unblocked paths in the original problem graph, and corresponding paths have the same length, it is seen that the shortest path P is an augmenting path as required and that the shortest distances d_m yield the vector $\bar{p}$ defined by Eq. (2.6). We now prove the validity of the method.

Proposition 2.2:   Consider the minimum cost flow problem and assume that a_{ij}, b_{ij}, c_{ij}, and s_i are all integer. Then, for the sequential shortest path method, the following hold:

(a) Each iteration maintains the integrality and the CS property of the pair (x, p).

(b) If the problem is feasible, then the method terminates with an integer optimal flow vector x and an integer optimal price vector p.

(c) If the problem is infeasible, then the method terminates either because $g_i \leq 0$ for all i and $g_i < 0$ for at least one i, or because there is no augmenting path starting at some node of the set I and ending at some node with negative surplus.

Proof: (a) We will show that if the starting pair (x, p) of an iteration is integer and satisfies CS, the same is true for a pair $(\bar{x}, \bar{p})$ produced by the iteration. Indeed, a flow augmentation maintains the integrality of the flows, since the upper and lower flow bounds are assumed integer. Furthermore, the arc lengths of the residual graph are integer, so by Eq. (2.6), $\bar{p}$ is integer.

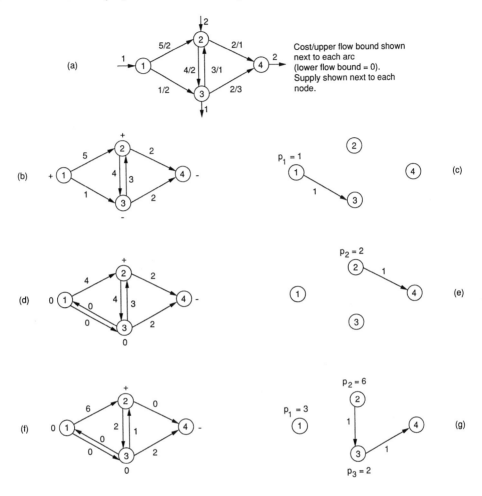

Figure 2.2   The sequential shortest path method applied to the problem of Fig. 2.1, starting with all zero prices. The sequences of flows, prices, and surpluses are the same as those generated by the primal-dual method.

(a) Problem data.

(b) Initial residual graph with the arc lengths shown next to the arcs. The nodes with positive, zero, and negative surplus are indicated by "+", "0", and "−", respectively.

(c) Shortest augmenting path and changed prices of first iteration $(I = \{1\})$.

(d) Residual graph with the arc lengths shown next to the arcs after the first iteration.

(e) Shortest augmenting path and changed prices of second iteration $(I = \{2\})$.

(f) Residual graph with the arc lengths shown next to the arcs after the second iteration.

(g) Shortest augmenting path and changed prices of third (and final) iteration $(I = \{2\})$.

To show that $(\overline{x}, \overline{p})$ satisfies CS, consider an arc (i, j) for which $\overline{x}_{ij} < c_{ij}$. We will show that $\overline{p}_i - \overline{p}_j \leq a_{ij}$. We distinguish two cases:

(1) $x_{ij} = c_{ij}$. In this case, we have $b_{ij} < x_{ij}$, the direction of (i, j) is reversed in the residual graph, and the reverse arc (j, i) lies on the shortest augmenting path P. Hence, we have

$$d_i \leq \overline{d}, \qquad d_j \leq \overline{d}, \qquad d_i = d_j - r_{ij}.$$

Using these equations, and Eqs. (2.2) and (2.6), we obtain

$$\overline{p}_i - \overline{p}_j = p_i - p_j + \max\{0, \overline{d} - d_i\} - \max\{0, \overline{d} - d_j\}$$
$$= p_i - p_j - (d_i - d_j) = p_i - p_j + r_{ij} = a_{ij}.$$

(2) $x_{ij} < c_{ij}$. In this case we have

$$d_j \leq d_i + r_{ij},$$

since (i, j) is an arc of the residual graph with length r_{ij}. Using this relation and the nonnegativity of r_{ij}, we see that

$$\max\{0, \overline{d} - d_i\} \leq \max\{0, \overline{d} - d_j + r_{ij}\}$$
$$\leq \max\{r_{ij}, \overline{d} - d_j + r_{ij}\} = \max\{0, \overline{d} - d_j\} + r_{ij}.$$

Hence, we have

$$\overline{p}_i - \overline{p}_j = p_i - p_j + \max\{0, \overline{d} - d_i\} - \max\{0, \overline{d} - d_j\} \leq p_i - p_j + r_{ij} = a_{ij}.$$

Thus, in both cases we have $\overline{p}_i - \overline{p}_j \leq a_{ij}$. We can similarly show that if $b_{ij} < \overline{x}_{ij}$, then $\overline{p}_i - \overline{p}_j \geq a_{ij}$, completing the proof of the CS property of the pair $(\overline{x}, \overline{p})$.

(b) and (c) Every completed iteration in which a shortest augmenting path is found reduces the total absolute surplus $\sum_{i \in \mathcal{N}} |g_i|$ by an integer amount, so termination must occur. Part (a) shows that at the start of each iteration, the pair (x, p) satisfies CS. There are two possibilities:

(1) $g_i \leq 0$ for all i. In this case, either $g_i = 0$ for all i in which case x is feasible, and x and p are primal and dual optimal, respectively, since they satisfy CS, or else $g_i < 0$ for some i, in which case the problem is infeasible.

(2) $g_i > 0$ for at least one i. In this case we can select a nonempty set I of nodes with positive surplus, form the residual graph, and attempt the corresponding shortest path computation. There are two possibilities: either a shortest augmenting path is found, in which case the iteration

will be completed with an attendant reduction of the total absolute surplus, or else there is no unblocked path with respect to x from a node of I to a node with negative surplus. In the latter case, we claim that the problem is infeasible. Indeed, by Prop. 2.2 in Section 1.2 (more accurately, the generalization given in Exercise 2.12 in Section 1.2), there exists a saturated cut $Q = [\mathcal{S}, \mathcal{N} - \mathcal{S}]$ such that all nodes of I belong to $\mathcal{S}$ and all nodes with negative surplus belong to $\mathcal{N} - \mathcal{S}$. The flux across Q is equal to the capacity $C(Q)$ of Q and is also equal to the sum of the divergences of the nodes of $\mathcal{S}$, which is $\sum_{i \in \mathcal{S}} (s_i - g_i)$ [cf. Eq. (1.11)]. Since $g_i \geq 0$ for all $i \in \mathcal{S}$, $g_i > 0$ for the nodes $i \in I$, and $I \subset \mathcal{S}$, we see that

$$C(Q) < \sum_{i \in \mathcal{S}} s_i.$$

This implies that the problem is infeasible, since for any feasible flow vector we must have $\sum_{i \in \mathcal{S}} s_i = F(Q) \leq C(Q)$, where $F(Q)$ is the corresponding flux across Q.

Thus, termination of the algorithm must occur in the manner stated in the proposition.   **Q.E.D.**

By appropriately adapting the shortest path algorithms of Section 1.3, one can obtain a variety of implementations of the sequential shortest path iteration. Here is an example, which adapts the generic single origin/single destination algorithm of Section 1.3.4 and supplements it with a labeling procedure that constructs the augmenting path. We introduce a candidate list V, a label d_i for each node i, a shortest distance estimate $\overline{d}$, and a node $\overline{j}$ whose initial choice is immaterial. Given a pair (x, p) satisfying CS and a set I of nodes with positive surplus, we set initially

$$V = I, \qquad \overline{d} = \infty,$$

$$d_i = 0, \qquad \forall \, i \in I, \qquad d_i = \infty, \qquad \forall \, i \notin I.$$

The shortest path computation proceeds in steps and terminates when V is empty. The typical step (assuming V is nonempty) is as follows:

Typical Shortest Path Step in a Sequential Shortest Path Iteration

Remove a node i from V. For each outgoing arc $(i, j) \in \mathcal{A}$, with $x_{ij} < c_{ij}$, if

$$d_i + r_{ij} < \min\{d_j, \overline{d}\},$$

give the label "(i, j)" to j, set

$$d_j := d_i + r_{ij},$$

add j to V if it does not already belong to V, and if $g_j < 0$, set $\overline{d} = d_i + r_{ij}$ and $\overline{j} = j$. Also, for each incoming arc $(j, i) \in \mathcal{A}$, with $b_{ji} < x_{ji}$, if

$$d_i - r_{ji} < \min\{d_j, \overline{d}\},$$

give the label "(j, i)" to j, set

$$d_j := d_i - r_{ji},$$

add j to V if it does not already belong to V, and if $g_j < 0$, set $\overline{d} = d_i - r_{ji}$ and $\overline{j} = j$.

When the shortest path computation terminates, an augmenting path of length $\overline{d}$ can be obtained by tracing labels backward from the node $\overline{j}$ to some node $i \in I$. The new price vector $\overline{p}$ is obtained via the equation $\overline{p}_m = p_m + \max\{0, \overline{d} - d_m\}$ for all $m \in \mathcal{N}$ [cf. Eq. (2.6)]. Note that if the node i removed from V has the minimum label property

$$d_i = \min_{j \in V} d_j,$$

the preceding algorithm corresponds to Dijkstra's method.

We finally note that the primal-dual method discussed earlier and the sequential shortest path method are mathematically equivalent in that they produce identical sequences of pairs (x, p), as shown by the following proposition (for an example, compare the calculations of Figs. 2.1 and 2.2). In fact with some thought, it can be seen that the primal-dual iteration amounts to the use of a form of Dijkstra's algorithm to calculate the shortest augmenting path and the corresponding distances.

Proposition 2.3:   Suppose that a primal-dual iteration starts with a pair (x, p), and let I be the initial set of nodes i with $g_i > 0$. Then:

(a) An augmenting path P may be generated in the augmentation Step 3 of the iteration (through some order of operations in Steps 1 and 2) if and only if P has minimum length over all augmenting paths with respect to x that start at some node in I.

(b) If $\overline{p}$ is the price vector produced by the iteration, then

$$\overline{p}_m = p_m + \max\{0, \overline{d} - d_m\}, \qquad \forall\, m \in \mathcal{N}, \tag{2.7}$$

where $\overline{d}$ is the length of the augmenting path P of the iteration and for each $m \in \mathcal{N}$, d_m is the minimum of the lengths of the unblocked paths with respect to x that start at some node in I and end at m.

Proof: Let $\overline{k} \geq 0$ be the number of price changes of the iteration. If $\overline{k} = 0$, i.e., no price change occurs, then any augmenting path P that can be produced by the iteration consists of balanced arcs, so its length is zero. Hence P has minimum length as stated in part (a). Furthermore, $\bar{p} = p$, which verifies Eq. (2.7).

Assume that $\bar{k} \geq 1$, let $\mathcal{S}_k$, $k = 1, \ldots, \bar{k}$, be the set of scanned nodes $\mathcal{S}$ when the kth price change occurs, and let γ_k, $k = 1, \ldots, \bar{k}$, be the corresponding price increment [cf. Eq. (2.1)]. Let also $\mathcal{S}_{\bar{k}+1}$ be the set $\mathcal{S}$ at the end of the iteration. We note that the sets $\mathcal{S}_k$ (and hence also γ_k) depend only on (x, p) and the set I, and are independent of the order of operations in Steps 1 and 2. In particular, $\mathcal{S}_1 - I$ is the set of all nodes j such that there exists an unblocked path of balanced arcs [with respect to (x, p)] that starts at some node $i \in I$ and ends at j. Thus, $\mathcal{S}_1$ and also γ_1, is uniquely defined by I and (x, p). Proceeding inductively, it is seen that $\mathcal{S}_{k+1} - \mathcal{S}_k$ is the set of all nodes j such that there exists an unblocked path of balanced arcs [with respect to (x, p^k), where p^k is the price vector after k price changes] that starts at some node $i \in \mathcal{S}_k$ and ends at j. Thus, $\mathcal{S}_{k+1}$ and γ_{k+1} are uniquely defined by I and (x, p) if $\mathcal{S}_1, \ldots, \mathcal{S}_k$ and $\gamma_1, \ldots, \gamma_k$ are.

It can be seen from Eq. (2.1) that for all k,

$\gamma_k =$minimum over the lengths of all (single arc) unblocked paths

starting at a node $i \in \mathcal{S}_k$ and ending at a node $j \notin \mathcal{S}_k$.

Using this property, and an induction argument (left for the reader), we can show that d_m, which is defined as the minimum over the lengths of all unblocked paths that start at some node $i \in I$ and end at node m, satisfies for all k,

$$d_m = \gamma_1 + \gamma_2 + \ldots + \gamma_k, \qquad \forall \, m \in \mathcal{S}_{k+1} - \mathcal{S}_k. \tag{2.8}$$

Furthermore, the length of any unblocked path that starts at some node $i \in I$ and ends at a node $m \notin \mathcal{S}_{k+1}$ is larger than $\gamma_1 + \gamma_2 + \ldots + \gamma_k$. In particular, the length of any augmenting path produced by the iteration is

$$\gamma_1 + \gamma_2 + \ldots + \gamma_{\bar{k}},$$

so it has the property stated in part (a). Also, the price vector $\bar{p}$ produced by the primal-dual iteration is given by

$$\bar{p}_m = \begin{cases} p_m + \gamma_1 + \gamma_2 + \ldots + \gamma_k & \text{if } m \in \mathcal{S}_{k+1} - \mathcal{S}_k, \; k = 1, \ldots, \bar{k}, \\ p_m & \text{otherwise}, \end{cases}$$

which in view of Eq. (2.8), agrees with Eq. (2.7).   **Q.E.D.**

EXERCISES

Exercise 2.1

Use the primal-dual method and the sequential shortest path method to solve the problem of Fig. 2.3. Verify that the two methods yield the same sequence of flows and prices (with identical initial data and appropriate choices of the initial sets I and augmenting paths).

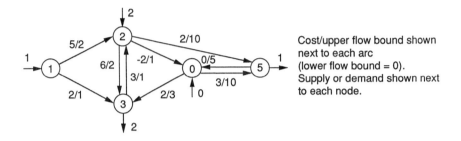

Figure 2.3   Minimum cost flow problem for Exercise 2.1.

Exercise 2.2 (Relation of Primal-Dual and Ford-Fulkerson)

Consider the Ford-Fulkerson algorithm for the max-flow problem, where $b_{ij} = 0$ for all $(i,j) \in \mathcal{A}$. Show that the method can be interpreted as an application of the primal-dual method to the minimum cost flow formulation of the max-flow problem of Example 1.2 in Section 1.1, starting with $p = 0$ and $x = 0$ [except for the flow of the artificial arc (t, s), which must be at its upper bound to satisfy CS]. Show in particular that all iterations of the primal-dual method start at s and terminate with an augmentation along a path ending at t. Furthermore, the method will execute only one price change, which will occur after a minimum cut is identified. The last iteration consists of an augmentation along the artificial arc (t, s).

Exercise 2.3 (Relation of Primal-Dual and Dijkstra)

Consider the shortest path problem with node 1 being the origin and all other nodes being destinations. Formulate this problem as a minimum cost flow problem with the origin having supply $N - 1$ and all destinations having supply -1. Assume that all arc lengths are nonnegative. Start with all flows and prices equal to zero, and apply the primal-dual method. Show that the method is equivalent to Dijkstra's algorithm. In particular, each augmentation uses a shortest path from the origin to some destination, the augmentations are done in the order of the destinations' proximity to the origin, and upon termination, $p_1 - p_i$ gives the shortest distance from 1 to each destination i that can be reached from the origin via a forward path.

Exercise 2.4 (Noninteger Problem Data)

Verify that the primal-dual method terminates even when the arc costs are noninteger. (Note, however, that the arc flow bounds must still be integer; the max-flow example of Exercise 2.9 in Section 1.2 applies to the primal-dual method as well, in view of the relation described in Exercise 2.2.) Modify the primal-dual method so that augmenting paths have as few arcs as possible. Show that with this modification, the arc flow bounds need not be integer for the method to terminate. How should the sequential shortest path method be modified so that it terminates even when the problem data are not integer?

3.3   THE RELAXATION METHOD

This method admits a similar implementation as the primal-dual method but computes ascent directions much faster. In particular, while in the primal-dual method we continue to enlarge the scanned set $\mathcal{S}$ until it is equal to the labeled set $\mathcal{L}$ (in which case we are sure that $d_{\mathcal{S}}$ is an ascent direction), in the relaxation method we stop adding nodes to $\mathcal{S}$ immediately after $d_{\mathcal{S}}$ becomes an ascent direction [this is done by computing the directional derivative $q'(p; d_{\mathcal{S}})$ using an efficient incremental method and by checking its sign]. In practice, $\mathcal{S}$ often consists of a single node, in which case the ascent direction is a single price coordinate, leading to the interpretation of the method as a *coordinate ascent method*. Unlike the primal-dual method, the relaxation method cannot be implemented using a shortest path computation.

As in the primal-dual method, at the start of the typical iteration we have an integer pair (x, p) satisfying CS. The iteration indicates that the primal problem is infeasible, or else indicates that (x, p) is optimal, or else transforms this pair into another pair satisfying CS. In particular, if $g_i \leq 0$ for all i, then there are two possibilities: (1) $g_i < 0$ for some i, in which case $\sum_{i \in \mathcal{N}} s_i < 0$ and the problem is infeasible, or (2) $g_i = 0$ for all i, in which case x is feasible and therefore also optimal, since it satisfies CS together with p. In either case, the algorithm terminates.

If on the other hand we have $g_i > 0$ for at least one node i, the iteration starts by selecting a node $\bar{i}$ with $g_{\bar{i}} > 0$. As in the primal-dual method, the iteration maintains two sets of nodes $\mathcal{S}$ and $\mathcal{L}$, with $\mathcal{S} \subset \mathcal{L}$. At the start of the iteration, $\mathcal{S}$ is empty and $\mathcal{L}$ consists of the node $\bar{i}$ with $g_{\bar{i}} > 0$. The iteration also maintains a *label* for every node $i \in \mathcal{L}$ except for the starting node $\bar{i}$; the label is an incident arc of i.

Typical Relaxation Iteration

Step 0 (Initialization): Select a node $\bar{i}$ with $g_{\bar{i}} > 0$. [If no such node can be found, terminate; the pair (x, p) is optimal if $g_i = 0$ for all i; otherwise the problem is infeasible.] Set $\mathcal{L} := \{\bar{i}\}$ and $\mathcal{S} :=$ empty, and go to Step 1.

Step 1 (Choose a Node to Scan): If $\mathcal{S} = \mathcal{L}$, go to Step 4; else select a node $i \in \mathcal{L} - \mathcal{S}$, set $\mathcal{S} := \mathcal{S} \cup \{i\}$, and go to Step 2.

Step 2 (Label Neighbor Nodes of i): If

$$q'(p; d_{\mathcal{S}}) > 0, \tag{3.1}$$

go to Step 4; else add to $\mathcal{L}$ all nodes $j \notin \mathcal{L}$ such that either (j, i) is balanced and $b_{ji} < x_{ji}$ or (i, j) is balanced and $x_{ij} < c_{ij}$; also for every such j, give to j the label "(j, i)" if (j, i) is balanced and $b_{ji} < x_{ji}$, and otherwise give to j the label "(i, j)." If for every node j just added to $\mathcal{L}$, we have $g_j \geq 0$, go to Step 1; else select one of these nodes j with $g_j < 0$ and go to Step 3.

Step 3 (Flow Augmentation): An augmenting path P has been found that begins at the starting node $\bar{i}$ and ends at the node j identified in Step 2. The path is constructed by tracing labels backward starting from j, and is such that we have

$$x_{mn} < c_{mn}, \qquad \forall \, (m, n) \in P^+, \tag{3.2}$$

$$x_{mn} > b_{mn}, \qquad \forall \, (m, n) \in P^-, \tag{3.3}$$

where P^+ and P^- are the sets of forward and backward arcs of P, respectively. Let

$$\delta = \min\Big\{ g_i, -g_j, \{c_{mn} - x_{mn} \mid (m, n) \in P^+\}, \{x_{mn} - b_{mn} \mid (m, n) \in P^-\} \Big\}.$$

Increase by δ the flows of all arcs in P^+, decrease by δ the flows of all arcs in P^-, and go to the next iteration.

Step 4 (Price Change): Set

$$x_{ij} = c_{ij}, \qquad \forall \text{ balanced arcs } (i, j) \text{ with } i \in \mathcal{S}, \ j \notin \mathcal{S}, \tag{3.4}$$

$$x_{ji} = b_{ji}, \qquad \forall \text{ balanced arcs } (j, i) \text{ with } i \in \mathcal{S}, \ j \notin \mathcal{S}. \tag{3.5}$$

Let

$$\gamma = \min\bigl\{\{p_j + a_{ij} - p_i \mid (i,j) \in \mathcal{A}, x_{ij} < c_{ij}, i \in \mathcal{S}, j \notin \mathcal{S}\},$$
$$\{p_j - a_{ji} - p_i \mid (j,i) \in \mathcal{A}, b_{ji} < x_{ji}, i \in \mathcal{S}, j \notin \mathcal{S}\}\bigr\}. \tag{3.6}$$

Set

$$p_i := \begin{cases} p_i + \gamma, & \text{if } i \in \mathcal{S} \\ p_i, & \text{otherwise.} \end{cases} \tag{3.7}$$

Go to the next iteration. [*Note:* As in the case of the primal-dual iteration, if after the flow adjustments of Eqs. (3.4) and (3.5) there is no arc (i,j) with $x_{ij} < c_{ij}$, $i \in \mathcal{S}$, and $j \notin \mathcal{S}$, or arc (j,i) with $b_{ji} < x_{ji}$, $i \in \mathcal{S}$, and $j \notin \mathcal{S}$, the problem is infeasible and the algorithm terminates.]

It can be seen that the relaxation iteration is quite similar to the primal-dual iteration. However, there are two important differences. First, in the relaxation iteration, after a price change in Step 4, we do not return to Step 1 to continue the search for an augmenting path like we do in the primal-dual method. Thus, the relaxation iteration terminates either with an augmentation as in Step 3 or with a price change as in Step 4, in contrast with the primal-dual iteration, which can only terminate with an augmentation. The second and more important difference is that in the relaxation iteration, a price change may be performed in Step 4 even if $\mathcal{S} \neq \mathcal{L}$ [cf. Eq. (3.1)]. It is because of this feature that the relaxation method identifies ascent directions faster than the primal-dual method. Note that in contrast with the primal-dual method, the total absolute surplus $\sum_{i \in \mathcal{N}} |g_i|$ may increase as a result of a relaxation iteration.

An important property of the method is that each time we enter Step 4, $d_{\mathcal{S}}$ is an ascent direction. To see this note that there are two possibilities: (1) we have $\mathcal{S} = \mathcal{L}$ (cf. Step 1) in which case $d_{\mathcal{S}}$ is an ascent direction similar to the corresponding situation in the primal-dual method, or (2) we have $\mathcal{S} \neq \mathcal{L}$ (cf. Step 2) in which case by Eq. (3.1) $d_{\mathcal{S}}$ is an ascent direction.

It is possible to "combine" several iterations of the relaxation method into a single iteration in order to save computation time, and this is done judiciously in the RELAX codes, which are public domain implementations of the relaxation method [BeT88], [BeT90]. Figure 3.1 traces the steps of the method for a simple example.

The following proposition establishes the validity of the method.

Proposition 3.1:   Consider the minimum cost flow problem and assume that a_{ij}, b_{ij}, c_{ij}, and s_i are all integer. If the problem is feasible, then the relaxation method terminates with an integer optimal flow vector x and an integer optimal price vector p.

Proof: The proof is similar to the corresponding proof for the primal-dual method (cf. Prop. 2.1). We first note that all operations of the iteration

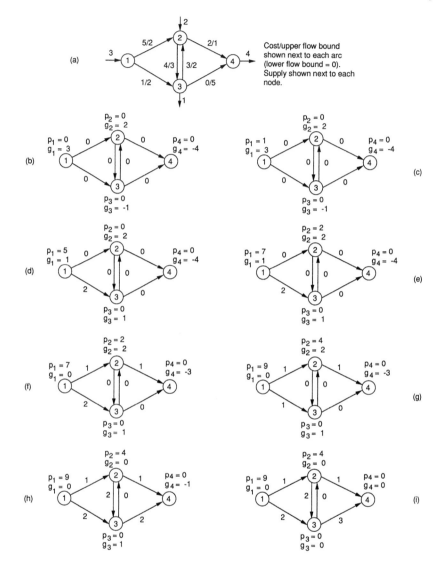

Figure 3.1   An illustration of the relaxation method, starting with all zero prices.

(a) Problem data.

(b) Initial flows, prices, and surpluses.

(c) After the first iteration, which consists of a price change of node 1.

(d) After the second iteration, which consists of another price change of node 1 [note the flow change of arc (1,3); cf. Eq. (3.4)].

(e) After the third iteration, which consists of a price change of nodes 1 and 2.

(f) After the fourth iteration, which consists of an augmentation along the path $(1, 2, 4)$.

(g) After the fifth iteration, which consists of a price change of nodes 1 and 2.

(h) After the sixth iteration, which consists of an augmentation along the path $(2, 3, 4)$.

(i) After the seventh iteration, which consists of an augmentation along the path $(3, 4)$.

preserve the integrality of the flow–price vector pair. To see that CS is also maintained, note that a flow augmentation step changes only flows of balanced arcs and therefore cannot destroy CS. Furthermore, the flow changes of Eqs. (3.4) and (3.5), and the price changes of Eqs. (3.6) and (3.7) maintain CS, because they set the flows of the balanced arcs that the price change renders active (or inactive) to the corresponding upper (or lower) bounds.

Every time there is a price change in Step 4, there is a strict improvement in the dual cost by the integer amount $\gamma q'(p; d_{\mathcal{S}})$ [using the CS property, it can be seen that $\gamma > 0$, and as argued earlier, $d_{\mathcal{S}}$ is an ascent direction so $q'(p; d_{\mathcal{S}}) > 0$]. Thus, for a feasible problem, we cannot have an infinite number of price changes. On the other hand, it is impossible to have an infinite number of flow augmentations between two successive price changes, since each of these reduces the total absolute surplus by an integer amount. It follows that the algorithm can execute only a finite number of iterations, and must terminate. Since upon termination x is feasible and satisfies CS together with p, it follows that x is primal-optimal and p is dual-optimal.   **Q.E.D.**

If the problem is infeasible, the method may terminate because $g_i \leq 0$ for all i and $g_i < 0$ for at least one i, or because after the flow adjustments of Eqs. (3.4) and (3.5) in Step 4, there is no arc (i, j) with $x_{ij} < c_{ij}$, $i \in \mathcal{S}$, and $j \notin \mathcal{S}$, or arc (j, i) with $b_{ji} < x_{ji}$, $i \in \mathcal{S}$, and $j \notin \mathcal{S}$. However, there is also the possibility that the method will execute an infinite number of iterations and price changes, with the prices of some of the nodes increasing to ∞. Exercise 3.2 shows that, when the problem is feasible, the node prices stay below a certain precomputable bound in the course of the algorithm. This fact can be used as an additional test to detect infeasibility.

It is important to note that the directional derivative $q'(p; d_{\mathcal{S}})$ needed for the ascent test (3.1) in Step 2 can be calculated *incrementally* (as new nodes are added one-by-one to $\mathcal{S}$) using the equation

$$q'(p; d_{\mathcal{S}}) = \sum_{i \in \mathcal{S}} g_i - \sum_{\substack{(j,i):\ \text{balanced},\ j \notin \mathcal{S},\ i \in \mathcal{S}}} (x_{ji} - b_{ji})$$
$$- \sum_{\substack{(i,j):\ \text{balanced},\ i \in \mathcal{S},\ j \notin \mathcal{S}}} (c_{ij} - x_{ij}); \tag{3.8}$$

cf. Eq. (1.13). Indeed, it follows from this equation that, given $q'(p; d_{\mathcal{S}})$ and a node $i \notin \mathcal{S}$, one can calculate the directional derivative corresponding to the enlarged set $\mathcal{S} \cup \{i\}$ using the formula

$$
\begin{aligned}
q'(p; d_{\mathcal{S} \cup \{i\}}) = q'(p; d_{\mathcal{S}}) + & \sum_{\{j | (i,j): \text{ balanced, } j \in \mathcal{S}\}} (x_{ij} - b_{ij}) \\
+ & \sum_{\{j | (j,i): \text{ balanced, } j \in \mathcal{S}\}} (c_{ji} - x_{ji}) \\
- & \sum_{\{j | (j,i): \text{ balanced, } j \notin \mathcal{S}\}} (x_{ji} - b_{ji}) \\
- & \sum_{\{j | (i,j): \text{ balanced, } j \notin \mathcal{S}\}} (c_{ij} - x_{ij}).
\end{aligned}
\tag{3.9}
$$

This formula is convenient because it involves only the incident balanced arcs of the new node i, which must be examined anyway while executing Step 2.

In practice, the method is implemented using iterations that start from both positive and negative surplus nodes. This seems to improve substantially the performance of the method. It can be shown that for a feasible problem, the algorithm terminates properly under these circumstances (Exercise 3.3). Another important practical issue has to do with the initial choice of flows and prices. One possibility is to try to choose an initial price vector that is as close to optimal as possible (for example, using the results of some earlier optimization); one can then choose the arc flows to satisfy the CS conditions.

Line Search and Coordinate Ascent Iterations

The stepsize γ of Eq. (3.6) corresponds to the first break point of the piecewise linear dual function along the ascent direction $d_{\mathcal{S}}$. It is also possible to calculate through a line search an optimal stepsize that maximizes the dual function along $d_{\mathcal{S}}$. We leave it for the reader to verify that this computation can be done quite economically, using Eq. (1.10) or Eq. (1.13) to test the sign of the directional derivative of the dual function at successive break points along $d_{\mathcal{S}}$. Computational experience shows that a line search is beneficial in practice. For this reason, it has been used in the RELAX codes [BeT88], [BeT90].

Consider now the case where there is a price change via Step 4 and the set $\mathcal{S}$ consists of just the starting node, say node i. This happens when the iteration scans the incident arcs of i at the first time Step 2 is entered and finds that the corresponding coordinate direction leads to a dual cost improvement $[q'(p; d_{\{i\}}) > 0]$. If line search of the type just described is performed, the price p_i is changed to a break point where the right derivative is nonpositive and the left derivative is nonnegative (cf. Fig. 3.2).

A precise description of this single-node relaxation iteration with line search, starting from a pair (x, p) satisfying CS, is as follows:

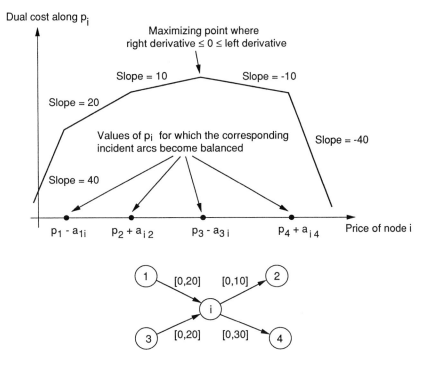

Figure 3.2 Illustration of single-node relaxation iteration. Here, node i has four incident arcs $(1, i)$, $(3, i)$, $(i, 2)$, and $(i, 4)$ with flow ranges $[0, 20]$, $[0, 20]$, $[0, 10]$, and $[0, 30]$, respectively, and supply $s_i = 0$. The arc costs and current prices are such that

$$p_1 - a_{1i} \leq p_2 + a_{i2} \leq p_3 - a_{3i} \leq p_4 + a_{i4},$$

as shown in the figure. The break points of the dual cost along the price p_i correspond to the values of p_i at which one or more incident arcs to node i become balanced. For values between two successive break points, there are no balanced arcs. For any price p_i to the left of the maximizing point, the surplus g_i must be positive to satisfy CS. A single-node iteration with line search increases p_i to the maximizing point.

Single-Node Relaxation Iteration

Choose a node i with $g_i > 0$. Let

$$B_i^+ = \{j \mid (i, j) : \text{ balanced}, x_{ij} < c_{ij}\}, \tag{3.10}$$

$$B_i^- = \{j \mid (j, i) : \text{ balanced}, b_{ji} < x_{ji}\}. \tag{3.11}$$

Step 1: If

$$g_i \geq \sum_{j \in B_i^+} (c_{ij} - x_{ij}) + \sum_{j \in B_i^-} (x_{ji} - b_{ji}),$$

go to Step 4. Otherwise, if $g_i > 0$, choose a node $j \in B_i^+$ with $g_j < 0$ and go to Step 2, or choose a node $j \in B_i^-$ with $g_j < 0$ and go to Step 3; if no such node can be found, or if $g_i = 0$, go to the next iteration.

Step 2 (Flow Adjustment on Outgoing Arc): Let

$$\delta = \min\{g_i, -g_j, c_{ij} - x_{ij}\}.$$

Set

$$x_{ij} := x_{ij} + \delta, \qquad g_i := g_i - \delta, \qquad g_j := g_j + \delta$$

and if $x_{ij} = c_{ij}$, delete j from B_i^+; go to Step 1.

Step 3 (Flow Adjustment on Incoming Arc): Let

$$\delta = \min\{g_i, -g_j, x_{ji} - b_{ji}\}.$$

Set

$$x_{ji} := x_{ji} - \delta, \qquad g_i := g_i - \delta, \qquad g_j := g_j + \delta$$

and if $x_{ji} = b_{ji}$, delete j from B_i^-; go to Step 1.

Step 4 (Increase Price of i): Set

$$g_i := g_i - \sum_{j \in B_i^+} (c_{ij} - x_{ij}) - \sum_{j \in B_i^-} (x_{ji} - b_{ji}), \tag{3.12}$$

$$x_{ij} = c_{ij}, \qquad \forall \, j \in B_i^+, \tag{3.13}$$

$$x_{ji} = b_{ji}, \qquad \forall \, j \in B_i^-, \tag{3.14}$$

$$p_i := \min\big\{\{p_j + a_{ij} \mid (i,j) \in \mathcal{A}, \, p_i < p_j + a_{ij}\},$$
$$\{p_j - a_{ji} \mid (j,i) \in \mathcal{A}, \, p_i < p_j - a_{ji}\}\big\}. \tag{3.15}$$

If after these changes $g_i > 0$, recalculate the sets B_i^+ and B_i^+ using Eqs. (3.10) and (3.11), and go to Step 1; else, go to the next iteration. [*Note:* If the set of arcs over which the minimum in Eq. (3.15) is calculated is empty, there are two possibilities: (a) $g_i > 0$, in which case it can be shown that the dual cost increases without bound along p_i and the primal problem is infeasible, or (b) $g_i = 0$, in which case the cost stays constant along p_i; in this case we leave p unchanged and go to the next iteration.]

Note that the single-node iteration may be unsuccessful in that it may fail to change either x or p. In this case, it should be followed by a regular relaxation iteration that labels the appropriate neighbors of node i, etc. Experience has shown that the most efficient way to implement the relaxation iteration is to first attempt its single-node version; if this fails to change x or p, then we proceed with the multiple node version, while salvaging whatever computation is possible from the single-node attempt. The RELAX codes [BeT88], [BeT90] make use of this idea. Experience shows that single-node iterations are very frequent in the early stages of the relaxation algorithm and account for most of the total dual cost improvement, but become much less frequent near the algorithm's termination.

A careful examination of the single-node iteration logic shows that in Step 4, after the surplus change of Eq. (3.12), the surplus g_i may be equal to zero; this will happen if $g_i = 0$ and simultaneously there is no balanced arc (i, j) with $x_{ij} < c_{ij}$, or balanced arc (j, i) with $b_{ji} < x_{ji}$. In this case, it can be shown (see also Fig. 3.2) that the price change of Eq. (3.15) leaves the dual cost unchanged, corresponding to movement of p_i along a flat segment to the next breakpoint of the dual cost, as shown in Fig. 3.3. This is known as a *degenerate ascent iteration*. Computational experience has shown that it is generally preferable to allow such iterations whenever possible. For special types of problems such as assignment, the use of degenerate ascent iterations can reduce dramatically the overall computation time.

We finally note that single-node relaxation iterations may be used to initialize the primal-dual method. In particular, one may start with several cycles of single-node iterations, where each node with nonzero surplus is taken up for relaxation once in each cycle. The resulting pair (x, p) is then used as a starting pair for the primal-dual method. Experience has shown that this initialization procedure is very effective.

EXERCISES

Exercise 3.1

Use the relaxation method to solve the problem of Fig. 2.3.

Exercise 3.2 (An Infeasibility Test for the Relaxation Method)

Consider the relaxation method, let p_i^0 be the initial price of node i, and let $\mathcal{M}$ be the set of nodes that have negative surplus initially. For every simple path P that ends at a node $j \in \mathcal{M}$, let H_P be the sum of the costs of the forward arcs of the path minus the sum of the costs of the backward arcs of the path, and let $H = \max_P H_P$. Show that, if the problem is feasible, then during the

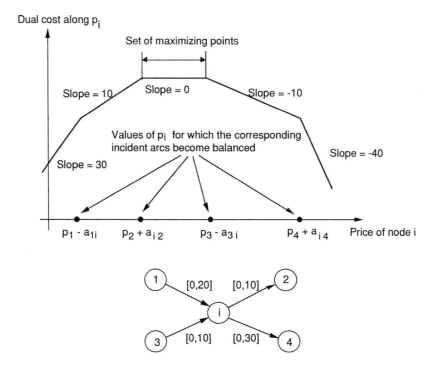

Figure 3.3 Illustration of a degenerate price increase. The difference between this example and the example of Fig. 3.2 is that the feasible flow range of arc $(3, i)$ is now $[0, 10]$ instead of $[0, 20]$. Here, there is a flat segment of the graph of the dual cost along p_i, corresponding to maximizing points. A degenerate price increase moves p_i from the extreme left maximizing point to the extreme right maximizing point.

course of the algorithm, the price of any positive surplus node cannot exceed its initial price by more than $H + \max_{j \in \mathcal{M}} p_j^0 - \min_{i \in \mathcal{N}} p_i^0$. Discuss how to use this bound to test for problem infeasibility in the relaxation method. *Hint:* Observe that at any point in the algorithm the prices of all nodes with negative surplus have not changed since the start of the algorithm. Show also that if i is a node with positive surplus, there must exist some node with negative surplus j and an unblocked path starting at i and ending at j.

Exercise 3.3

Write the form of the relaxation iteration starting from *both* positive and negative surplus nodes. Show that the method terminates at an optimal flow–price vector pair if a feasible solution exists. *Hint*: Show that each price change improves the dual cost by an integer amount, while there can be only a finite number of flow augmentations between successive price changes.

3.4   IMPLEMENTATION ISSUES

For the application of the methods of this chapter, one can represent the problem using the five arrays $START$, END, $COST$, $CAPACITY$, and $SUPPLY$, as in simplex methods (cf. Section 2.4). For an efficient implementation, however, it is essential to provide additional data structures that facilitate the labeling operations, the ascent steps of Step 4, and the shortest path computations. In particular, it is necessary to have easy access to the set of all incident arcs of each node. This can be done with the help of the following four additional arrays.

$FIRST\_IN(i)$: The first arc incoming to node i ($= 0$ if i has no incoming arcs).

$FIRST\_OUT(i)$: The first arc outgoing from node i ($= 0$ if i has no outgoing arcs).

$NEXT\_IN(a)$: The arc following arc a with the same end node as a ($= 0$ if a is the last incoming arc of the end node of a).

$NEXT\_OUT(a)$: The arc following arc a with the same start node as a ($= 0$ if a is the last outgoing arc of the start node of a).

Figure 4.1 illustrates these arrays. As an example of their use, suppose that we want to scan all the incoming arcs of node i. We first obtain the arc $a_1 = FIRST\_IN(i)$, then the arc $a_2 = NEXT\_IN(a_1)$, then the arc $a_3 = NEXT\_IN(a_2)$, etc., up to the arc a_k for which $NEXT\_IN(a_k) = 0$.

It is possible to forgo the use of the array $NEXT\_OUT$ if the arcs are stored in the order of their starting node, that is, the arcs outgoing from each node i are arcs $FIRST\_OUT(i)$ to $FIRST\_OUT(i + 1) - 1$. Then the array $FIRST\_OUT$ is sufficient to generate all arcs outgoing from any one node. Some codes (for example the assignment codes of Appendixes A.4 and A.5) use this device; they require that the arcs of the problem be ordered by starting node, thereby saving storage of one array (and usually some computation as well). The drawback to this idea is that it complicates sensitivity analysis. In particular, if the problem data are changed to add or remove some arcs, all the arrays describing the problem, except for $SUPPLY$, must be recompiled.

An additional data structure, useful primarily for the relaxation method, stores the *balanced* incident arcs of each node so as to facilitate the labeling step (Step 2). These arcs can be stored in two arrays of length N and two arrays of length A, much like the arrays $FIRST\_IN$, $FIRST\_OUT$, $NEXT\_IN$,

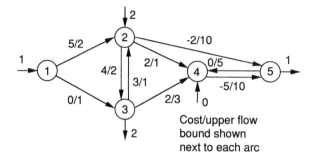

ARC	START	END	COST	CAPACITY	NEXT_IN	NEXT_OUT
1	1	2	5	2	4	2
2	1	3	0	1	3	0
3	2	3	4	2	0	5
4	3	2	3	1	0	7
5	2	5	-2	10	0	6
6	2	4	2	1	7	0
7	3	4	2	3	8	0
8	5	4	0	5	0	0
9	4	5	-5	10	5	0

NODE	SUPPLY	FIRST_IN	FIRST_OUT
1	1	0	1
2	2	1	3
3	-2	2	4
4	0	6	9
5	-1	9	8

Figure 4.1   Representation of the data of a minimum cost flow problem in terms of the nine arrays *START*, *END*, *COST*, *CAPACITY*, *SUPPLY*, *FIRST_IN*, *FIRST_OUT*, *NEXT_IN*, and *NEXT_OUT*.

and *NEXT_OUT*. However, as the set of balanced arcs changes in the course of the algorithm, the arrays used to store this set must be updated. We will not go into further details, but the interested reader can study the RELAX codes [BeT88], [BeT90] to see how this can be done efficiently.

Overall it can be seen that dual ascent methods require more arrays of length A than simplex methods, and therefore also more storage space (roughly twice as much).

3.5   NOTES AND SOURCES

3.1. A dual ascent method that we did not cover here is the dual simplex method. This is a general linear programming method that has been specialized to the minimum cost flow problem by several authors (see e.g. [HeK77], [JeB80]) but has not achieved much popularity.

3.2. The primal-dual method was first proposed in [Kuh55] for assignment problems under the name "Hungarian method." The method was generalized to the minimum cost flow problem in [FoF56a] and [FoF57]. A further generalization, the *out-of-kilter* method, was proposed independently in [FoF62] and [Min60]; see [Law76], [Roc84], and [BJS90] for detailed discussions. The out-of-kilter method can get started with any flow–price vector pair, not necessarily one that satisfies CS. It appears, however, that there isn't much that can be gained in practice by this extra flexibility, since for any given flow–price vector pair one can modify very simply the arc flows to satisfy CS. A method that is closely related to the primal-dual method and emphasizes the shortest path implementation was given by [BuG61]. An extension of the primal-dual method to network problems with gains was given in [Jew62], and extensions of the primal-dual and out-of-kilter methods to network flow problems with separable convex cost functions are given in [Roc84]. Primal-dual methods for the assignment problem are discussed in [Eng82], [McG83], [Der85], [CaS86], [CMT88]. Combinations of naive auction and sequential shortest path methods are discussed in [Ber81], [JoV86], [JoV87]; the code of Appendix A.5 is based on these references. Variations of the Hungarian and the primal-dual methods that are well suited for parallel computation have been developed in [BMP89], [BeC90a], and [BeC90b].

One can show a pseudopolynomial worst-case bound on the running time of the primal-dual method. The (practical) average running time of the method, however, is much better than the one suggested by this bound. It is possible to convert the algorithm to a polynomial one by using scaling procedures; see [EdK72] and [BlJ85]. Unfortunately, these procedures do not seem to improve the algorithm's performance in practice.

Despite the fundamentally different principles underlying the simplex and primal-dual methods (primal cost versus dual cost improvement), these methods are surprisingly related. It can be shown that the big-M version of the simplex method with a particular pivot selection rule is equivalent to the steepest ascent version of the primal-dual method [Zad79]. This suggests that the simplex method with the empirically best pivot selection rule should be more efficient in practice than the primal-dual method. Computational experience tends to agree with this conjecture. However, in many practical contexts, the primal-dual method has an advantage: it can easily use a good starting flow and price vector pair, obtained for example from the solution of a slightly different problem by modifying some of the arc flows to satisfy CS; this is true of all the methods of this chapter. Simplex methods are generally less capable of exploiting such prior knowledge; see also the discussion on sensitivity analysis in Section 5.5.

3.3. The relaxation method was first proposed in the context of the assignment problem by the author in [Ber81]. Its extension to the general minimum cost flow problem was given in [Ber82b]. References [BeT85] and [Tse86] consider the case where the problem data are noninteger. The relaxation method has been extended to network flow problems with gains ([BeT85] and [Tse86]), to general linear programs ([Tse86] and [TsB87a]), to network flow problems with convex arc cost functions [BHT87], and to monotropic programming problems [TsB87b]. When the arc cost functions are strictly convex, the method is particularly well suited for parallel implementation; see [BeE87a], [BHT87], [ElB89], [ChZ90], and [TBT90].

Extensive computational experience shows that the relaxation method typically outperforms primal-dual methods substantially for general minimum cost flow problems. In fact, primal-dual methods can often be speeded up considerably by initialization with a number of single-node relaxation iterations, although not to the point of challenging the relaxation method. The comparison between the relaxation method and simplex methods is less clear, although the relaxation method seems much faster for randomly generated problems. The relaxation method is also more capable of exploiting prior knowledge about an optimal solution; this advantage is shared with the primal-dual method. On the other hand, in contrast with the simplex method, the relaxation method requires that the problem data be integer; modified versions that can handle noninteger problem data ([BeT85] and [Tse86]), need not terminate, although they yield optimal solutions asymptotically.

3.4. The data structures for implementation of primal-dual methods briefly discussed in this section were proposed in [AaM76], and were used in the construction of an efficient out-of-kilter code. They are well suited for most types of dual ascent methods.

4

Auction Algorithms

In this chapter we will first focus on the assignment problem. We will discuss and analyze the auction algorithm described in Section 1.2.3, and some of its variations. We will then present an auction-like algorithm for shortest path problems. Finally, we will extend the auction algorithm to the minimum cost flow problem and some of its special cases.

4.1 THE AUCTION ALGORITHM FOR THE ASSIGNMENT PROBLEM

Recall the assignment problem where we want to match n persons and n objects on a one-to-one basis. We are given a value or benefit a_{ij} for matching person i with object j, and we want to assign persons to objects so as to maximize the total benefit. The set of objects to which person i can be assigned is a nonempty set denoted $A(i)$. An *assignment* S is a (possibly empty) set of person-object pairs (i, j) such that $j \in A(i)$ for all $(i, j) \in S$; for each person i there can be at most one pair $(i, j) \in S$; and for every object j there can be at most one pair $(i, j) \in S$. Given an assignment S, we say that person i is *assigned* if there exists a pair $(i, j) \in S$; otherwise we say that i is *unassigned*. We use similar terminology for objects. An assignment is said to be *feasible* if it contains n pairs, so that every person and every object is assigned; otherwise the assignment is called *partial*.

4.1.1   The Main Auction Algorithm

The auction algorithm, described somewhat loosely in Section 1.2.3, proceeds
iteratively and terminates when a feasible assignment is obtained. At the start
of the generic iteration we have a partial assignment S and a price vector p
satisfying ϵ-*complementary slackness* (ϵ-CS). This is the condition

$$a_{ij} - p_j \geq \max_{k \in A(i)} \{a_{ik} - p_k\} - \epsilon, \qquad \forall\, (i,j) \in S \tag{1.1}$$

introduced in Section 1.2.3. As an initial choice, one can use an arbitrary set of
prices together with the empty assignment, which trivially satisfies ϵ-CS. The
iteration consists of two phases: the *bidding phase* and the *assignment phase*
described in the following. We will show later that the iteration preserves the
ϵ-CS condition.

Bidding Phase

Let I be a nonempty subset of persons i that are unassigned under the assignment S. For each person $i \in I$:

1. Find a "best" object j_i having maximum value, that is,

$$j_i = \arg\max_{j \in A(i)} \{a_{ij} - p_j\},$$

and the corresponding value

$$v_i = \max_{j \in A(i)} \{a_{ij} - p_j\}, \tag{1.2}$$

and find the best value offered by objects other than j_i

$$w_i = \max_{j \in A(i), j \neq j_i} \{a_{ij} - p_j\}. \tag{1.3}$$

[If j_i is the only object in $A(i)$, we define w_i to be $-\infty$, or for computational purposes, a number that is much smaller than v_i.]

2. Compute the "bid" of person i given by

$$b_{ij_i} = p_{j_i} + v_i - w_i + \epsilon = a_{ij_i} - w_i + \epsilon. \tag{1.4}$$

[We characterize this situation by saying that person i bid for object j_i,
and that object j_i received a bid from person i. The algorithm works if
the bid has any value between $p_{j_i} + \epsilon$ and $p_{j_i} + v_i - w_i + \epsilon$, but it tends
to work fastest for the maximal choice of Eq. (1.4).]

Assignment Phase

For each object j, let $P(j)$ be the set of persons from which j received a bid in the bidding phase of the iteration. If $P(j)$ is nonempty, increase p_j to the highest bid,

$$p_j := \max_{i \in P(j)} b_{ij}, \tag{1.5}$$

remove from the assignment S any pair (i, j) (if j was assigned to some i under S), and add to S the pair (i_j, j), where i_j is a person in $P(j)$ attaining the maximum above.

Note that there is some freedom in choosing the subset of persons I that bid during an iteration. One possibility is to let I consist of a single unassigned person. This version, known as the *Gauss-Seidel version* because of its similarity with Gauss-Seidel methods for solving systems of nonlinear equations, usually works best in a serial computing environment. The version where I consists of all unassigned persons, is the one best suited for parallel computation; it is known as the *Jacobi version* because of its similarity with Jacobi methods for solving systems of nonlinear equations.

During an iteration, the objects whose prices are changed are the ones that received a bid during the iteration. Each price change involves an increace of at least ϵ. To see this, note that from Eqs. (1.2) to (1.4) we have

$$b_{ij_i} = a_{ij_i} - w_i + \epsilon \geq a_{ij_i} - v_i + \epsilon = p_{j_i} + \epsilon,$$

so each bid for an object, including the winning bid, exceeds the object's current price by at least ϵ. At the end of the iteration, we have a new assignment that differs from the preceding one in that each object that received a bid is now assigned to some person that was unassigned at the start of the iteration. However, the assignment at the end of the iteration need not have more pairs than the one at the start of the iteration, because it is possible that all objects that received a bid were assigned at the start of the iteration.

The choice of bidding increment $v_i - w_i + \epsilon$ for a person i [cf. Eq. (1.4)] is such that ϵ-CS is preserved by the algorithm, as shown by the following proposition (in fact, it can be seen that it is the largest bidding increment for which this is so).

Proposition 1.1:   The auction algorithm preserves ϵ-CS throughout its execution; that is, if the assignment and the price vector available at the start of an iteration satisfy ϵ-CS, the same is true for the assignment and the price vector obtained at the end of the iteration.

Proof: Suppose that object j^* received a bid from person i and was assigned to i during the iteration. Let p_j and p_j' be the object prices before and after the assignment phase, respectively. Then we have [see Eqs. (1.4) and (1.5)]

$$p_{j^*}' = a_{ij^*} - w_i + \epsilon.$$

Using this equation, we obtain

$$a_{ij^*} - p'_{j^*} = w_i - \epsilon = \max_{j \in A(i),\, j \neq j^*} \{a_{ij} - p_j\} - \epsilon.$$

Since $p'_j \geq p_j$ for all j, this equation implies that

$$a_{ij^*} - p'_{j^*} \geq \max_{j \in A(i)} \{a_{ij} - p'_j\} - \epsilon, \tag{1.6}$$

which shows that the ϵ-CS condition (1.1) continues to hold after the assignment phase of an iteration for all pairs (i, j^*) that entered the assignment during the iteration.

Consider also any pair (i, j^*) that belonged to the assignment just before the iteration, and also belongs to the assignment after the iteration. Then, j^* must not have received a bid during the iteration, so $p'_{j^*} = p_{j^*}$. Therefore, Eq. (1.6) holds in view of the ϵ-CS condition that held prior to the iteration and the fact $p'_j \geq p_j$ for all j. Hence, the ϵ-CS condition (1.1) holds for all pairs (i, j^*) that belong to the assignment after the iteration, proving the result. **Q.E.D.**

The next result establishes the validity of the algorithm. The proof relies on the following facts:

(a) Once an object is assigned, it remains assigned throughout the remainder of the algorithm's duration. Furthermore, except at termination, there will always exist at least one object that has never been assigned, and has a price equal to its initial price. The reason is that a bidding and assignment phase can result in a reassignment of an already assigned object to a different person, but cannot result in the object becoming unassigned.

(b) Each time an object receives a bid, its price increases by at least ϵ [see Eqs. (1.4) and (1.5)]. Therefore, if the object receives a bid an infinite number of times, its price increases to ∞.

(c) Every $|A(i)|$ bids by person i, where $|A(i)|$ is the number of objects in the set $A(i)$, the scalar v_i defined by the equation

$$v_i = \max_{j \in A(i)} \{a_{ij} - p_j\} \tag{1.7}$$

decreases by at least ϵ. The reason is that a bid by person i either decreases v_i by at least ϵ, or else leaves v_i unchanged because there is more than one object j attaining the maximum in Eq. (1.7). However, in the latter case, the price of the object j_i receiving the bid will increase by at least ϵ, and object j_i will not receive another bid by person i until

v_i decreases by at least ϵ. The conclusion is that if a person i bids an infinite number of times, v_i must decrease to $-\infty$.

Proposition 1.2:   If at least one feasible assignment exists, the auction algorithm terminates with a feasible assignment that is within $n\epsilon$ of being optimal (and is optimal if the problem data are integer and $\epsilon < 1/n$).

Proof: We argue by contradiction. If termination did not occur, the subset J^∞ of objects that received an infinite number of bids is nonempty. Also, the subset of persons I^∞ that bid an infinite number of times is nonempty. As argued in (b) above, the prices of the objects in J^∞ must tend to ∞, while as argued in (c) above, the scalars $v_i = \max_{j \in A(i)}\{a_{ij} - p_j\}$ must decrease to $-\infty$ for all persons $i \in I^\infty$. This implies that

$$A(i) \subset J^\infty, \qquad \forall \, i \in I^\infty. \tag{1.8}$$

The ϵ-CS condition (1.1) states that $a_{ij} - p_j \geq v_i - \epsilon$ for every assigned pair (i, j), so after a finite number of iterations, each object in J^∞ can only be assigned to a person from I^∞. Since after a finite number of iterations at least one person from I^∞ will be unassigned at the start of each iteration, it follows that the number of persons in I^∞ is strictly larger than the number of objects in J^∞. This contradicts the existence of a feasible assignment, since by Eq. (1.8), persons in I^∞ can only be assigned to objects in J^∞. Therefore, the algorithm must terminate. The feasible assignment obtained upon termination satisfies ϵ-CS by Prop. 1.1, so by Prop. 2.3 of Section 1.2.3, this assignment is within $n\epsilon$ of being optimal.   **Q.E.D.**

Consider now the case of an infeasible assignment problem. In this case, the auction algorithm cannot possibly terminate; it will keep on increasing the prices of some objects by increments of at least ϵ. Furthermore, some persons i will be submitting bids infinitely often, and the corresponding maximum values

$$v_i = \max_{j \in A(i)}\{a_{ij} - p_j\}$$

will be decreasing toward $-\infty$. One can detect this situation by making use of a precomputable lower bound on the above values v_i, which holds when the problem is feasible; see Exercise 1.5. Once v_i gets below this bound for some i, we know that the problem is infeasible. Unfortunately, it may take many iterations for some v_i to reach this bound. An alternative method to detect infeasibility is to convert the problem to a feasible problem by adding artificial arcs to the assignment graph. The values of these arcs should be very small (i.e. large negative), so that they never participate in an optimal assignment unless the problem is infeasible. Exercise 1.6 quantifies the appropriate threshold for the values of the artificial arcs.

4.1.2 The Approximate Coordinate Descent Interpretation

The Gauss-Seidel version of the auction algorithm resembles coordinate descent algorithms, and the relaxation method of the previous chapter in particular, because it involves the change of a single object price with all other prices held fixed. In contrast with the relaxation method, however, such a price change may worsen strictly the value of the dual function

$$q(p) = \sum_{i=1}^{n} \max_{j \in A(i)} \left\{ a_{ij} - p_j \right\} + \sum_{j=1}^{n} p_j,$$

which was introduced in Prop. 2.4 of Section 1.2.

Generally we can interpret the bidding and assignment phases as a simultaneous "approximate" coordinate descent step for all price coordinates that increase during the iteration. The coordinate steps are aimed at minimizing approximately the dual function. In particular, we claim that *the price p_j of each object j that received a bid during the assignment phase is increased to either a value that minimizes $q(p)$ when all other prices are kept constant or else exceeds the largest such value by no more than ϵ.* Figure 1.1 illustrates this property and outlines its proof.

Figure 1.1 suggests that the amount of deterioration of the dual cost is at most ϵ. Indeed, for the Gauss-Seidel version of the algorithm this can be deduced from the argument given in Figure 1.1 and is left for the reader as Exercise 1.1.

4.1.3 Computational Aspects – ϵ-Scaling

The auction algorithm can be shown to have an $O\big(A(n + nC/\epsilon)\big)$ worst-case running time, where A is the number of arcs of the assignment graph and

$$C = \max_{(i,j) \in \mathcal{A}} |a_{ij}|$$

is the maximum absolute object value; see [BeE88], [BeT89]. Thus, the amount of work to solve the problem can depend strongly on the value of ϵ as well as C. In practice, the dependence of the running time on ϵ and C is often significant, particularly for sparse problems; this dependence can also be seen in the example of Section 1.2.3 (cf. Fig. 2.14), and in Exercise 1.4.

The practical performance of the auction algorithm is often considerably improved by using ϵ-*scaling*, which consists of applying the algorithm several times, starting with a large value of ϵ and successively reducing ϵ up to an ultimate value that is less than $1/n$; cf. the discussion in Section 1.2.3. Each application of the algorithm, called a *scaling phase*, provides good initial prices for the next application. In the auction code of Appendix A.4, the integer

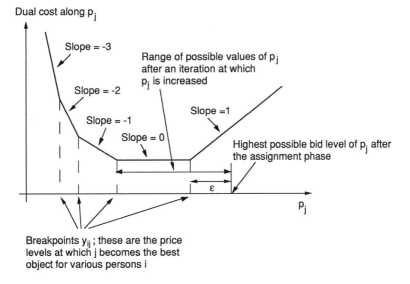

Figure 1.1   Form of the dual cost along the price coordinate p_j. From the definition of the dual cost q, the right directional derivative of q along p_j is

$$d_j^+ = 1 - (\text{number of persons } i \text{ with } j \in A(i) \text{ and } p_j < y_{ij}),$$

where

$$y_{ij} = a_{ij} - \max_{k \in A(i),\, k \neq j} \{a_{ik} - p_k\}$$

is the level of p_j below which j is the best person for person i. The break points are y_{ij} for all i such that $j \in A(i)$. Let $\overline{y} = \max_{\{i | j \in A(i)\}} \{a_{ij} - p_j\}$, let $\overline{i}$ be a person such that $\overline{y} = y_{\overline{i}j}$, let $\hat{y} = \max_{\{i | j \in A(i),\, i \neq \overline{i}\}} \{a_{ij} - p_j\}$, let $\hat{i}$ be a person such that $\hat{i} \neq \overline{i}$ and $\hat{y} = y_{\hat{i}j}$. Note that the interval $[\hat{y}, \overline{y}]$ is the set of points that minimize q along the coordinate p_j.

Let p_j be the price of j just before an iteration at which j receives a bid and let p_j' be the price of j after the iteration. We claim that $\hat{y} \leq p_j' \leq \overline{y} + \epsilon$. Indeed, if i is the person that bids and wins j during the iteration, then $p_j' = y_{ij} + \epsilon$, implying that $p_j' \leq \overline{y} + \epsilon$. To prove that $p_j' \geq \hat{y}$, we note that if $p_j \geq \hat{y}$, we must also have $p_j' \geq \hat{y}$, since $p_j' \geq p_j$. On the other hand, if $p_j' < \hat{y}$, there are two possibilities:
1. At the start of the iteration, $\overline{i}$ was not assigned to j. In this case, either $\overline{i}$ was unassigned in which case i will bid for j so that $p_j' = \overline{y} + \epsilon$, or else $\overline{i}$ was assigned to an object $\overline{j} \neq j$, in which case by ϵ-CS,

$$a_{\overline{i}j} - p_j - \epsilon \leq a_{\overline{i}\overline{j}} - p_{\overline{j}} \leq \max_{k \in A(\overline{i}),\, k \neq \overline{j}} \{a_{\overline{i}k} - p_k\} = a_{\overline{i}j} - \overline{y}.$$

Thus, $p_j \geq \overline{y} - \epsilon$, implying that $p_j' \geq \overline{y}$ (since a bid increases a price by at least ϵ). In both cases we have $p_j' \geq \overline{y} \geq \hat{y}$.
2. At the start of the iteration, $\overline{i}$ was assigned to j. In this case, $\hat{i}$ was not assigned to j, so by repeating the argument of the preceding paragraph with $\hat{i}$ and $\hat{y}$ replacing $\overline{i}$ and $\overline{y}$, respectively, we obtain $p_j' \geq \hat{y}$.

benefits a_{ij} are first multiplied by $n+1$ and the auction algorithm is applied with progressively lower values of ϵ, to the point where ϵ becomes 1 or smaller (because a_{ij} has been scaled by $n+1$, it is sufficient for optimality of the final assignment to have $\epsilon \leq 1$). The sequence of ϵ values used is

$$\epsilon(k) = \max\{1, \Delta/\theta^k\}, \qquad k = 0, 1, \ldots,$$

where Δ and θ are parameters set by the user with $\Delta > 0$ and $\theta > 1$. (Typical values for sparse problems are $C/5 \leq \Delta \leq C/2$ and $4 \leq \theta \leq 10$. For nonsparse problems, sometimes $\Delta = 1$, which in effect bypasses ϵ-scaling, works quite well.) The auction code of Appendix A.4 also uses an *adaptive* form of ϵ-scaling, whereby, within the kth scaling phase, the value of ϵ is gradually *increased* to the value $\epsilon(k)$ given above, starting from a relatively small value, based on the results of the computation.

For integer data, it can be shown that the worst-case running time of the auction algorithm using scaling and appropriate data structures is $O\bigl(nA\log(nC)\bigr)$; see [BeE88], [BeT89]. For randomly generated problems, the running time of the algorithm seems to grow proportionally to something like $A\log n$ or $A\log n \log(nC)$; see also Exercise 1.3.

EXERCISES

Exercise 1.1

Consider the Gauss-Seidel version of the auction algorithm, where only one person can bid at each iteration. Show that, as a result of a bid, the dual cost can be degraded by at most ϵ.

Exercise 1.2 (A Refinement of the Termination Tolerance [Ber79])

Show that the assignment obtained upon termination of the auction algorithm is within $(n-1)\epsilon$ of being optimal (rather than $n\epsilon$). Also, for every $n \geq 2$, construct an example of an assignment problem with integer data such that the auction algorithm terminates with a nonoptimal assignment when $\epsilon = 1/(n-1)$. (Try first $n = 2$ and $n = 3$, and generalize.) *Hint*: Modify slightly the algorithm so that when the last object is assigned, its price is increased by $v_i - w_i$ (rather than $v_i - w_i + \epsilon$). Then the assignment obtained upon termination satisfies the ϵ-CS condition for $n-1$ objects and the CS condition ($\epsilon = 0$) for the last object. Modify the proof of Prop. 2.6 in Section 1.2.

Exercise 1.3

This problem uses a rough (and flawed) argument to estimate the average complexity of the auction algorithm. We assume that at each iteration, only one person submits a bid (that is, the Gauss-Seidel version of the algorithm is used). Furthermore, every object is the recipient of a bid with equal probability $(1/n)$, independently of the results of earlier bids. (This assumption clearly does not hold, but seems to capture somewhat the real situation where the problem is fairly dense and ϵ-scaling is used.)

(a) Show that when k objects are unassigned the average number of iterations needed to assign a new object is n/k.

(b) Show that, on the average, the number of iterations is $n(1 + 1/2 + \cdots + 1/n)$, which can be estimated as $O(n \log n)$.

(c) Assuming that the average number of bids submitted by each person is the same for all persons, show that the average running time is $O(A \log n)$.

Exercise 1.4

Consider the auction algorithm applied to assignment problems with benefits in the range $[0, C]$, starting with zero prices.

(a) Show that for dense problems (every person can bid for every object) an object can receive a bid in at most $1 + C/\epsilon$ iterations.

(b) [Cas91] Use the example of Fig. 1.2 to show that, in general, some objects may receive a bid in a number of iterations that is proportional to nC/ϵ.

Exercise 1.5 (Detecting Infeasibility)

Consider application of the auction algorithm to a feasible assignment problem with initial object prices $\{p_j^0\}$. Let

$$v_i = \max_{j \in A(i)}\{a_{ij} - p_j\}$$

be the maximum object value for person i in the course of the algorithm. Show that for any unassigned person i we have at all times

$$v_i \geq -(2n-1)C - (n-1)\epsilon - \max_j\{p_j^0\},$$

where $C = \max_{(i,j) \in A}|a_{ij}|$, and describe how this lower bound can be used to detect that a problem is infeasible. *Hint*: Show that if the problem is feasible and i is unassigned, there must exist an augmenting path starting from i and ending at some unassigned object. Add the ϵ-CS condition along this path.

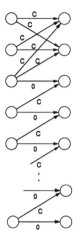

Figure 1.2 Assignment problem for which some objects receive a number of bids that is proportional to nC/ϵ. The arc values are shown next to the corresponding arcs.

Exercise 1.6 (Dealing with Infeasibility by Using Artificial Arcs)

Suppose that we add to the arc set $\mathcal{A}$ of an assignment problem a set $\overline{\mathcal{A}}$ of artificial arcs (possibly for the purpose of guaranteeing that the problem becomes feasible). Suppose also that we obtain an optimal assignment for the modified problem using the auction algorithm with initial object prices $\{p_j^0\}$. Show that if the original problem was feasible, no arc $(i,j) \in \overline{\mathcal{A}}$ will participate in the optimal assignment, provided

$$a_{ij} < -(2n-1)C - (n-1)\epsilon + p_j^0 - \max_k\{p_k^0\}, \qquad \forall \, (i,j) \in \overline{\mathcal{A}},$$

where $C = \max_{(i,j)\in\mathcal{A}} |a_{ij}|$. *Hint*: Use the result of Exercise 1.5.

Exercise 1.7 (Implementation of the Auction Algorithm [BeT91])

Frequently in the auction algorithm the two best objects for a given person do not change between two successive bids of that person. This exercise develops an implementation idea that attempts to exploit this fact by using a test to check whether the two best objects from the previous bid continue to be best. If the test is passed, the computation of the values $a_{ij} - p_j$ of the remaining objects is unnecessary. The implementation is used in the code for asymmetric assignment of Appendix A.4.

Suppose that at a given iteration, when we calculate the bid of the person i on the basis of a price vector p we compute the best value $v_i = \max_{j\in A(i)}\{a_{ij} -$

$p_j\}$, the best object $j_1 = \arg\max_{j \in A(i)}\{a_{ij} - p_j\}$, the second best value $w_i = \max_{j \in A(i), j \neq j_1}\{a_{ij} - p_j\}$, the second best object $j_2 = \arg\max_{j \in A(i), j \neq j_1}\{a_{ij} - p_j\}$, and the *third best value* $y_i = \max_{j \in A(i), j \neq j_1, j \neq j_2}\{a_{ij} - p_j\}$. Suppose that at a subsequent iteration when person i bids based on a price vector $\bar{p}$, we have $a_{ij_1} - \bar{p}_{j_1} \geq y_i$ and $a_{ij_2} - \bar{p}_{j_2} \geq y_i$. Show that j_1 and j_2 continue to be the two best objects for i (although j_1 need not be better than j_2).

4.2   REVERSE AUCTION AND INEQUALITY CONSTRAINED ASSIGNMENT PROBLEMS

In the auction algorithm, persons compete for objects by bidding and raising the price of their best object. It is possible to use an alternative form of the auction algorithm, called *reverse auction*, where, roughly, the *objects* compete for persons by essentially offering discounts.

To describe this algorithm, we introduce a *profit* variable π_i for each person i. Profits play for persons a role analogous to the role prices play for objects. We can describe reverse auction in two equivalent ways: one where unassigned objects lower their prices as much as possible to attract an unassigned person or lure a person away from its currently held object without violating ϵ-CS, and another where unassigned objects select a best person and raise his or her profit as much as possible without violating ϵ-CS. For analytical convenience, we will adopt the second description rather than the first, leaving the proof of their equivalence as Exercise 2.1 for the reader.

Let us consider the following ϵ-CS condition for a (partial) assignment S and a profit vector π:

$$a_{ij} - \pi_i \geq \max_{k \in B(j)}\{a_{kj} - \pi_k\} - \epsilon, \qquad \forall\,(i, j) \in S, \tag{2.1}$$

where $B(j)$ is the set of persons that can be assigned to object j,

$$B(j) = \{i \mid (i, j) \in \mathcal{A}\}.$$

For feasibility, we assume that this set is nonempty for all j. Note the symmetry of this condition with the corresponding one for prices; cf. Eq. (1.1). The reverse auction algorithm starts with and maintains an assignment and a profit vector π satisfying the above ϵ-CS condition. It terminates when the assignment is feasible. At the beginning of each iteration, we have an assignment S and a profit vector π satisfying the ϵ-CS condition (2.1).

Typical Iteration of Reverse Auction

Let J be a nonempty subset of objects j that are unassigned under the assignment S. For each object $j \in J$:

1. Find a "best" person i_j such that

$$i_j = \arg \max_{i \in B(j)} \{a_{ij} - \pi_i\},$$

and the corresponding value

$$\beta_j = \max_{i \in B(j)} \{a_{ij} - \pi_i\}, \tag{2.2}$$

and find

$$\omega_j = \max_{i \in B(j), i \neq i_j} \{a_{ij} - \pi_i\}. \tag{2.3}$$

[If i_j is the only person in $B(j)$, we define ω_j to be $-\infty$ or, for computational purposes, a number that is much smaller than β_j.]

2. Each object $j \in J$ bids for person i_j an amount

$$b_{i_j j} = \pi_{i_j} + \beta_j - \omega_j + \epsilon = a_{i_j j} - \omega_j + \epsilon. \tag{2.4}$$

3. For each person i that received at least one bid, increase π_i to the highest bid,

$$\pi_i := \max_{j \in P(i)} b_{ij}, \tag{2.5}$$

where $P(i)$ is the set of objects from which i received a bid; remove from the assignment S any pair (i, j) (if i was assigned to some j under S), and add to S the pair (i, j_i), where j_i is an object in $P(i)$ attaining the maximum above.

Note that reverse auction is identical to (forward) auction with the roles of persons and objects and those of profits and prices interchanged. Thus, by using the corresponding (forward) auction result (cf. Prop. 1.2), we have the following proposition.

Proposition 2.1: If at least one feasible assignment exists, the reverse auction algorithm terminates with a feasible assignment that is within $n\epsilon$ of being optimal (and is optimal if the problem data are integer and $\epsilon < 1/n$).

Combined Forward and Reverse Auction

One of the reasons we are interested in reverse auction is to construct algorithms that switch from forward to reverse auction and back. Such algorithms must simultaneously maintain a price vector p satisfying the ϵ-CS condition (1.1) and a profit vector π satisfying the ϵ-CS condition (2.1). To this end we introduce an ϵ-CS condition for the *pair* (π, p), which (as we will see) implies the other two. Maintaining this condition is essential for switching gracefully between forward and reverse auction.

Definition 2.1:   An assignment S and a pair (π, p) are said to satisfy ϵ-CS if

$$\pi_i + p_j \geq a_{ij} - \epsilon, \qquad \forall \, (i, j) \in \mathcal{A}, \tag{2.6a}$$

$$\pi_i + p_j = a_{ij}, \qquad \forall \, (i, j) \in S. \tag{2.6b}$$

We have the following proposition.

Proposition 2.2:   Suppose that an assignment S together with a profit-price pair (π, p) satisfy ϵ-CS. Then:

(a) S and π satisfy the ϵ-CS condition

$$a_{ij} - \pi_i \geq \max_{k \in B(j)} \{a_{kj} - \pi_k\} - \epsilon, \qquad \forall \, (i, j) \in S. \tag{2.7}$$

(b) S and p satisfy the ϵ-CS condition

$$a_{ij} - p_j \geq \max_{k \in A(i)} \{a_{ik} - p_k\} - \epsilon, \qquad \forall \, (i, j) \in S. \tag{2.8}$$

(c) If S is feasible, then S is within $n\epsilon$ of being an optimal assignment.

Proof: (a) In view of Eq. (2.6b), for all $(i, j) \in S$, we have $p_j = a_{ij} - \pi_i$, so Eq. (2.6a) implies that $a_{ij} - \pi_i \geq a_{kj} - \pi_k - \epsilon$ for all $k \in B(j)$. This shows Eq. (2.7).

(b) The proof is the same as the one of part (a) with the roles of π and p interchanged.

(c) Since by part (b) the ϵ-CS condition (2.8) is satisfied, by Prop. 2.6 of Section 1.2, S is within $n\epsilon$ of being optimal.   **Q.E.D.**

We now introduce a combined forward/reverse auction algorithm. The algorithm starts with and maintains an assignment S and a profit-price pair (π, p) satisfying the ϵ-CS condition (2.6). It terminates when the assignment is feasible.

Combined Forward/Reverse Auction Algorithm

Step 1 (Run forward auction): Execute several iterations of the forward auction algorithm (subject to the termination condition), and at the end of each iteration (after increasing the prices of the objects that received a bid) set

$$\pi_i = a_{ij_i} - p_{j_i} \qquad\qquad (2.9)$$

for every person-object pair (i, j_i) that entered the assignment during the iteration. Go to Step 2.

Step 2 (Run reverse auction): Execute several iterations of the reverse auction algorithm (subject to the termination condition), and at the end of each iteration (after increasing the profits of the persons that received a bid) set

$$p_j = a_{i_j j} - \pi_{i_j} \qquad\qquad (2.10)$$

for every person-object pair (i_j, j) that entered the assignment during the iteration. Go to Step 1.

Note that the additional overhead of the combined algorithm over the forward or the reverse algorithm is minimal; just one update of the form (2.9) or (2.10) is required per iteration for each object or person that received a bid during the iteration. An important property is that these updates maintain the ϵ-CS condition (2.6) for the pair (π, p), and therefore, by Prop. 2.2, maintain the required ϵ-CS conditions (2.7) and (2.8) for π and p, respectively. This is shown in the following proposition.

Proposition 2.3: If the assignment and the profit-price pair available at the start of an iteration of either the forward or the reverse auction algorithm satisfy the ϵ-CS condition (2.6), the same is true for the assignment and the profit-price pair obtained at the end of the iteration, provided Eq. (2.9) is used to update π (in the case of forward auction), and Eq. (2.10) is used to update p (in the case of reverse auction).

Proof: Assume for concreteness that forward auction is used, and let (π, p) and $(\overline{\pi}, \overline{p})$ be the profit-price pair before and after the iteration, respectively. Then, $\overline{p}_j \geq p_j$ for all j (with strict inequality if and only if j received a bid during the iteration). Therefore, we have $\overline{\pi}_i + \overline{p}_j \geq a_{ij} - \epsilon$ for all (i, j) such that $\pi_i = \overline{\pi}_i$. Furthermore, we have $\overline{\pi}_i + \overline{p}_j = \pi_i + p_j = a_{ij}$ for all (i, j) that belong to the assignment before as well as after the iteration. Also, in view of the update (2.9), we have $\overline{\pi}_i + \overline{p}_{j_i} = a_{ij_i}$ for all pairs (i, j_i) that entered the assignment during the iteration. What remains is to verify that the condition

$$\overline{\pi}_i + \overline{p}_j \geq a_{ij} - \epsilon, \qquad \forall\, j \in A(i) \qquad\qquad (2.11)$$

holds for all persons i that submitted a bid and were assigned to an object, say j_i, during the iteration. Indeed, for such a person i, we have, by Eq. (1.4),

$$\overline{p}_{j_i} = a_{ij_i} - \max_{j \in A(i), j \neq j_i} \{a_{ij} - p_j\} + \epsilon,$$

which implies that

$$\overline{\pi}_i = a_{ij_i} - \overline{p}_{j_i} \geq a_{ij} - p_j - \epsilon \geq a_{ij} - \overline{p}_j - \epsilon, \qquad \forall \, j \in A(i).$$

This shows the desired relation (2.11).   **Q.E.D.**

Note that during forward auction the object prices p_j increase while the profits π_i decrease, but exactly the opposite happens in reverse auction. For this reason, the termination proof that we used for forward and for reverse auction does not apply to the combined method. Indeed, it is possible to construct examples of feasible problems where the combined method never terminates if the switch between forward and reverse auctions is done arbitrarily. However, it is easy to guarantee that the combined algorithm terminates for a feasible problem; it is sufficient to ensure that some "irreversible progress" is made before switching between forward and reverse auction. One easily implementable possibility is to refrain from switching until the number of assigned person-object pairs increases by at least one.

The combined forward/reverse auction algorithm often works substantially faster than the forward version. It seems to to be affected less by "price wars," that is, protracted sequences of small price rises by a number of persons bidding for a smaller number of objects (cf. Fig. 2.13 in Section 1.2). Price wars can still occur in the combined algorithm, by they arise through more complex and unlikely problem structures than in the forward algorithm. For this reason the combined forward/reverse auction algorithm depends less on ϵ-scaling for good performance than its forward counterpart; in fact, starting with $\epsilon = 1/(n + 1)$, thus bypassing ϵ-scaling, is often the best choice.

4.2.1 Auction Algorithms for Asymmetric Assignment Problems

Reverse auction can be used in conjunction with forward auction to provide algorithms for solving the asymmetric assignment problem, where the number of objects n is larger than the number of persons m. Here we still require that each person be assigned to some object, but we allow objects to remain unassigned. As before, an assignment S is a (possibly empty) set of person-object pairs (i, j) such that $j \in A(i)$ for all $(i, j) \in S$; for each person i there can be at most one pair $(i, j) \in S$; and for every object j there can be at most one pair $(i, j) \in S$. The assignment S is said to be feasible if all persons are assigned under S.

The corresponding linear programming problem is

$$\text{maximize} \quad \sum_{(i,j)\in\mathcal{A}} a_{ij}x_{ij}$$

subject to

$$\sum_{j\in A(i)} x_{ij} = 1, \qquad \forall\, i = 1,\dots,m, \tag{2.12}$$

$$\sum_{i\in B(j)} x_{ij} \leq 1, \qquad \forall\, j = 1,\dots,n,$$

$$0 \leq x_{ij}, \qquad \forall\, (i,j) \in \mathcal{A}.$$

We can convert this program to the minimum cost flow problem

$$\text{minimize} \quad \sum_{(i,j)\in\mathcal{A}} \big(-a_{ij}\big)x_{ij}$$

subject to

$$\sum_{j\in A(i)} x_{ij} = 1, \qquad \forall\, i = 1,\dots,m, \tag{2.13}$$

$$\sum_{i\in B(j)} x_{ij} + x_{sj} = 1, \qquad \forall\, j = 1,\dots,n,$$

$$\sum_{j=1}^{n} x_{sj} = n - m,$$

$$0 \leq x_{ij}, \qquad \forall\, (i,j) \in \mathcal{A},$$

$$0 \leq x_{sj}, \qquad \forall\, j = 1,\dots,n,$$

by replacing maximization by minimization, by reversing the sign of a_{ij}, and by introducing a supersource node s, which is connected to each object node j by an arc (s,j) of zero cost and feasible flow range $[0,\infty)$ (see Fig. 2.1).

Using the theory of Section 1.2 (cf. Prop. 2.5 and Exercise 2.11 of that section), it can be seen that the corresponding dual problem is

$$\text{minimize} \quad \sum_{i=1}^{m} \pi_i + \sum_{j=1}^{n} p_j - (n-m)\lambda$$

subject to

$$\pi_i + p_j \geq a_{ij}, \qquad \forall\, (i,j) \in \mathcal{A}, \tag{2.14}$$

$$\lambda \leq p_j, \qquad \forall\, j = 1,\dots,n,$$

where we have converted maximization to minimization, we have used $-\pi_i$ in place of the price of each person node i, and we have denoted by λ the price of the supersource node s.

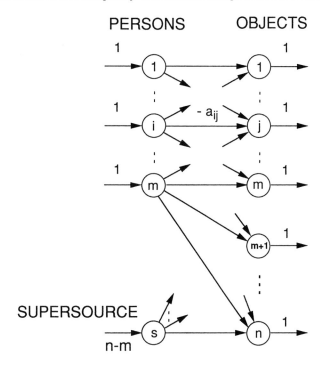

Figure 2.1   Converting an asymmetric assignment problem into a minimum cost flow problem involving a supersource node s and a zero cost artificial arc (s, j) with feasible flow range $[0, \infty)$ for each object j.

We now introduce an ϵ-CS condition for an assignment S and a pair (π, p).

Definition 2.2:   An assignment S and a pair (π, p) are said to satisfy ϵ-CS if

$$\pi_i + p_j \geq a_{ij} - \epsilon, \qquad \forall\ (i, j) \in \mathcal{A}, \tag{2.15a}$$

$$\pi_i + p_j = a_{ij}, \qquad \forall\ (i, j) \in S, \tag{2.15b}$$

$$p_j \leq \min_{k:\ \text{assigned under } S} p_k, \qquad \forall\ j:\ \text{unassigned under } S. \tag{2.15c}$$

The following proposition clarifies the significance of the preceding ϵ-CS condition.

Proposition 2.4:   If a feasible assignment S satisfies the ϵ-CS conditions (2.15) together with a pair (π, p), then S is within $m\epsilon$ of being optimal for the asymmetric assignment problem. The triplet $(\hat{\pi}, \hat{p}, \lambda)$, where

$$\lambda = \min_{k:\ \text{assigned under } S} p_k, \tag{2.16a}$$

$$\hat{\pi}_i = \pi_i + \epsilon, \qquad \forall\, i = 1, \ldots, m, \tag{2.16b}$$

$$\hat{p}_j = \begin{cases} p_j, & \text{if } j \text{ is assigned under } S, \\ \lambda, & \text{if } j \text{ is unassigned under } S \end{cases} \qquad \forall\, j = 1, \ldots, n, \tag{2.16c}$$

is within $m\epsilon$ of being an optimal solution of the dual problem (2.14).

Proof: For any feasible assignment $\{(i, k_i) \mid i = 1, \ldots, m\}$ and for any triplet $(\overline{\pi}, \overline{p}, \lambda)$ satisfying the dual feasibility constraints $\overline{\pi}_i + \overline{p}_j \geq a_{ij}$ for all $(i, j) \in \mathcal{A}$ and $\lambda \leq \overline{p}_j$ for all j, we have

$$\sum_{i=1}^m a_{ik_i} \leq \sum_{i=1}^m \overline{\pi}_i + \sum_{i=1}^m \overline{p}_{k_i} \leq \sum_{i=1}^m \overline{\pi}_i + \sum_{j=1}^n \overline{p}_j - (n-m)\lambda.$$

By maximizing over all feasible assignments $\{(i, k_i) \mid i = 1, \ldots, m\}$ and by minimizing over all dual-feasible triplets $(\overline{\pi}, \overline{p}, \lambda)$, we see that

$$A^* \leq D^*,$$

where A^* is the optimal assignment value and D^* is the minimal dual cost.

Let now $S = \{(i, j_i) \mid i = 1, \ldots, m\}$ be the given assignment satisfying ϵ-CS together with (π, p), and consider the triplet $(\hat{\pi}, \hat{p}, \lambda)$ defined by Eq. (2.16). Since for all i we have $\hat{\pi}_i + \hat{p}_{j_i} = a_{ij} + \epsilon$, we obtain

$$A^* \geq \sum_{i=1}^m a_{ij_i} = \sum_{i=1}^m \hat{\pi}_i + \sum_{i=1}^m \hat{p}_{j_i} - m\epsilon \geq \sum_{i=1}^m \hat{\pi}_i + \sum_{j=1}^n \hat{p}_j - (n-m)\lambda - m\epsilon$$

$$\geq D^* - m\epsilon,$$

where the last inequality holds because the triplet $(\hat{\pi}, \hat{p}, \lambda)$ is feasible for the dual problem. Since we showed earlier that $A^* \leq D^*$, the desired conclusion follows.   **Q.E.D.**

Consider now trying to solve the asymmetric assignment problem by means of auction. We can start with any assignment S and pair (π, p) satisfying the first two ϵ-CS conditions (2.15a) and (2.15b), and perform a forward auction (as defined earlier for the symmetric assignment problem) up to the point where each person is assigned to a distinct object. For a feasible problem, by essentially repeating the proof of Prop. 1.2 for the symmetric case, it can be seen that this will yield, in a finite number of iterations, a feasible assignment S satisfying the first two conditions (2.15a) and (2.15b). However, this assignment may not be optimal, because the prices of the unassigned objects j are not minimal; that is, they do not satisfy the third ϵ-CS condition (2.15c).

To remedy this situation, we use a modified form of reverse auction to lower the prices of the unassigned objects so that, after several iterations in which persons may be reassigned to other objects, the third condition, (2.15c), is satisfied. We will show that the assignment thus obtained satisfies all the ϵ-CS conditions (2.15a)-(2.15c), and by Prop. 2.4, is optimal within $m\epsilon$ (and thus optimal if the problem data are integer and $\epsilon < 1/m$).

The modified reversed auction starts with a feasible assignment S and with a pair (π, p) satisfying the first two ϵ-CS conditions (2.15a) and (2.15b). [For a feasible problem, such an S and (π, p) can be obtained by regular forward or reverse auction, as discussed earlier.] Let us denote by λ the minimal assigned object price under the initial assignment,

$$\lambda = \min_{j:\ \text{assigned under the initial assignment } S} p_j. \tag{2.17}$$

The typical iteration of modified reverse auction is the same as the one of reverse auction, except that only unassigned objects j with $p_j > \lambda$ participate in the auction. In particular, the algorithm maintains a feasible assignment S and a pair (π, p) satisfying Eqs. (2.15a) and (2.15b), and terminates when all unassigned objects j satisfy $p_j \leq \lambda$, in which case it will be seen that the third ϵ-CS condition (2.15c) is satisfied as well. The scalar λ is kept fixed throughout the algorithm.

Typical Iteration of Modified Reverse Auction for Asymmetric Assignment:

Select an object j that is unassigned under the assignment S and satisfies $p_j > \lambda$ (if no such object can be found, the algorithm terminates). Find a "best" person i_j such that

$$i_j = \arg\max_{i \in B(j)}\{a_{ij} - \pi_i\},$$

and the corresponding value

$$\beta_j = \max_{i \in B(j)}\{a_{ij} - \pi_i\}, \tag{2.18}$$

and find

$$\omega_j = \max_{i \in B(j), i \neq i_j}\{a_{ij} - \pi_i\}. \tag{2.19}$$

[If i_j is the only person in $B(j)$, we define ω_j to be $-\infty$.] If $\lambda \geq \beta_j - \epsilon$, set $p_j := \lambda$ and go to the next iteration. Otherwise, let

$$\delta = \min\{\beta_j - \lambda, \beta_j - \omega_j + \epsilon\}. \tag{2.20}$$

Set

$$p_j := \beta_j - \delta, \tag{2.21}$$

$$\pi_{i_j} := \pi_{i_j} + \delta, \tag{2.22}$$

add to the assignment S the pair (i_j, j), and remove from S the pair (i_j, j'), where j' is the object that was assigned to i_j under S at the start of the iteration.

Note that the formula (2.20) for the bidding increment δ is such that the object j enters the assignment at a price which is no less that λ [and is equal to λ if and only if the minimum in Eq. (2.20) is attained by the first term]. Furthermore, when δ is calculated (that is, when $\lambda > \beta_j - \epsilon$) we have $\delta \geq \epsilon$, so it can be seen from Eqs. (2.21) and (2.22) that, throughout the algorithm, prices are monotonically decreasing and profits are monotonically increasing. The following proposition establishes the validity of the method.

Proposition 2.5:   The modified reverse auction algorithm for the asymmetric assignment problem terminates with an assignment that is within $m\epsilon$ of being optimal.

Proof: In view of Prop. 2.4, the result will follow once we prove the following:

(a) The modified reverse auction iteration preserves the first two ϵ-CS conditions (2.15a) and (2.15b), as well as the condition

$$\lambda \leq \min_{j:\ \text{assigned under the current assignment } S} p_j, \tag{2.23}$$

so upon termination of the algorithm (necessarily with the prices of all unassigned objects less or equal to λ) the third ϵ-CS condition, (2.15c), is satisfied.

(b) The algorithm terminates.

We will prove these facts in sequence.

We assume that the conditions (2.15a), (2.15b), and (2.23) are satisfied at the start of an iteration, and we will show that they are also satisfied at the end of the iteration. First consider the case where there is no change in the assignment, which happens when $\lambda \geq \beta_j - \epsilon$. Then Eqs. (2.15b), and (2.23) are automatically satisfied at the end of the iteration; only p_j changes in the iteration according to

$$p_j := \lambda \geq \beta_j - \epsilon = \max_{i \in B(j)} \{a_{ij} - \pi_i\} - \epsilon,$$

so the condition (2.15a) is also satisfied at the end of the iteration.

Next consider the case where there is a change in the assignment during the iteration. Let (π, p) and $(\overline{\pi}, \overline{p})$ be the profit-price pair before and after the iteration, respectively, and let j and i_j be the object and person involved in the iteration. By construction [cf. Eqs. (2.21) and (2.22)], we have $\overline{\pi}_{i_j} + \overline{p}_j = a_{i_j j}$ and since $\overline{\pi}_i = \pi_i$ and $\overline{p}_k = p_k$ for all $i \neq i_j$ and $k \neq j$, we see that the condition (2.15b) ($\overline{\pi}_i + \overline{p}_k = a_{ik}$) is satisfied for all assigned pairs (i, k) at the end of the iteration.

To show that the condition (2.15a) is satisfied at the end of the iteration, that is,

$$\overline{\pi}_i + \overline{p}_k \geq a_{ik} - \epsilon, \qquad \forall \, (i, k) \in \mathcal{A}, \tag{2.24}$$

consider first objects $k \neq j$. Then, $\overline{p}_k = p_k$ and since $\overline{\pi}_i \geq \pi_i$ for all i, the above condition holds, since our hypothesis is that at the start of the iteration we have $\pi_i + p_k \geq a_{ik} - \epsilon$ for all (i, k). Consider next the case $k = j$. Then condition (2.24) holds for $i = i_j$, since $\overline{\pi}_{i_j} + \overline{p}_j = a_{i_j j}$. Also using Eqs. (2.18)-(2.21) and the fact $\delta \geq \epsilon$, we have for all $i \neq i_j$

$$\overline{\pi}_i + \overline{p}_j = \pi_i + \overline{p}_j \geq \pi_i + \beta_j - (\beta_j - \omega_j + \epsilon)$$
$$= \pi_i + \omega_j - \epsilon \geq \pi_i + (a_{ij} - \pi_i) - \epsilon = a_{ij} - \epsilon,$$

so condition (2.24) holds for $i \neq i_j$ and $k = j$, completing the proof of Eq. (2.24). To see that condition (2.23) is maintained by the iteration, note that by Eqs. (2.18), (2.19), and (2.21), we have

$$\overline{p}_j = \beta_j - \delta \geq \beta_j - (\beta_j - \lambda) = \lambda.$$

Finally, to show that the algorithm terminates, we note that in the typical iteration involving object j and person i_j there are two possibilities:

(1) The price of object j is set to λ without the object entering the assignment; this occurs if $\lambda \geq \beta_j - \epsilon$.

(2) The profit of person i_j increases by at least ϵ [this is seen from the definition (2.20) of δ; we have $\lambda < \beta_j - \epsilon$ and $\beta_j \geq \omega_j$, so $\delta \geq \epsilon$].

Since only objects j with $p_j > \lambda$ can participate in the auction, possibility (1) can occur only a finite number of times. Thus, if the algorithm does not terminate, the profits of some persons will increase to ∞. This is impossible, since when person i is assigned to object j we must have by Eqs. (2.15b) and (2.23)

$$\pi_i = a_{ij} - p_j \leq a_{ij} - \lambda,$$

so the profits are bounded from above by $\max_{(i,j) \in \mathcal{A}} a_{ij} - \lambda$. Thus the algorithm must terminate.   **Q.E.D.**

Note that one may bypass the modified reverse auction algorithm by starting the forward auction with all object prices equal to zero. Upon termination of the forward auction, the prices of the unassigned objects will still be at zero, while the prices of the assigned objects will be nonnegative. Therefore the ϵ-CS condition (2.15c) will be satisfied, and the modified reverse auction will be unnecessary (see Exercise 2.2).

Unfortunately the requirement of zero initial object prices is incompatible with ϵ-scaling. The principal advantage offered by the modified reverse auction algorithm is that it allows arbitrary initial object prices for the forward auction, thereby also allowing the use of ϵ-scaling. This can be shown to improve the theoretical worst-case complexity of the method, and is often beneficial in practice, particularly for sparse problems.

Reverse auction can be used also in the context of other types of network flow problems. One example is the variation of the asymmetric assignment problem where persons (as well as objects) need not be assigned if this degrades the assignment's value (see Exercise 2.3). Another class of assignment-like problems is described in the next subsection.

4.2.2 Auction Algorithms for Multiassignment Problems

An interesting type of assignment problem is described by the linear program

$$\text{maximize} \quad \sum_{(i,j)\in\mathcal{A}} a_{ij}x_{ij}$$

$$\text{subject to}$$

$$\sum_{j\in A(i)} x_{ij} \geq 1, \qquad \forall \ i = 1,\ldots,m, \tag{2.25}$$

$$\sum_{i\in B(j)} x_{ij} = 1, \qquad \forall \ j = 1,\ldots,n,$$

$$0 \leq x_{ij}, \qquad \forall \ (i,j) \in \mathcal{A},$$

where $m < n$. For feasibility, we assume that the sets $A(i)$ and $B(j)$ are nonempty for all i and j. This is known as the *multiassignment* problem, and is characterized by the possibility of assignment of more than one object to a single person. Problems of this type arise in military applications such as multi-target tracking with sensors of limited resolution [Bla86], [BaF88], where objects correspond to tracked moving objects and persons correspond to data points each representing at least one object (but possibly more than one because of the sensor's limited resolution). The multiassignment problem results when we try to associate data points with moving objects so as to match as closely as possible these data points with our prior knowledge of the objects' positions.

We can convert the multiassignment problem to the minimum cost flow problem

$$\text{minimize} \quad \sum_{(i,j)\in\mathcal{A}} \left(-a_{ij}\right)x_{ij}$$

$$\text{subject to}$$

$$\sum_{j \in A(i)} x_{ij} - x_{si} = 1, \qquad \forall\, i = 1, \ldots, m, \qquad (2.26)$$

$$\sum_{i \in B(j)} x_{ij} = 1, \qquad \forall\, j = 1, \ldots, n,$$

$$\sum_{i=1}^{m} x_{si} = n - m,$$

$$0 \le x_{ij}, \qquad \forall\, (i,j) \in \mathcal{A},$$

$$0 \le x_{si}, \qquad \forall\, i = 1, \ldots, n,$$

by replacing maximization by minimization, by reversing the sign of a_{ij}, and by introducing a supersource node s, which is connected to each person node i by an arc (s, i) of zero cost and feasible flow range $[0, \infty)$ (see Fig. 2.2).

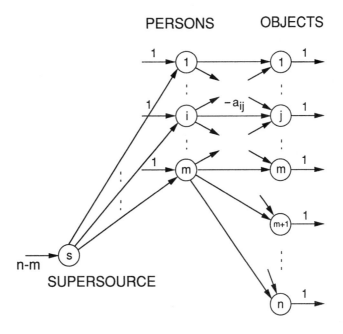

Figure 2.2   Converting a multiassignment problem into a minimum cost flow problem involving a supersource node s and a zero cost artificial arc (s, i) with feasible flow range $[0, \infty)$ for each person i.

Again using the theory of Section 1.2 and appropriately redefining the price variables corresponding to the nodes, it can be seen that the corresponding dual problem is

$$\text{minimize} \quad \sum_{i=1}^{m} \pi_i + \sum_{j=1}^{n} p_j + (n - m)\lambda$$

subject to

$$\pi_i + p_j \geq a_{ij}, \qquad \forall \ (i,j) \in \mathcal{A}, \tag{2.27}$$

$$\lambda \geq \pi_i, \qquad \forall \ i = 1, \ldots, m.$$

We define a *multiassignment* S to be a set of pairs $(i,j) \in \mathcal{A}$ such that for each object j, there is at most one pair (i,j) in S. A person i for which there are more than one pairs (i,j) in S is said to be *multiassigned* under S. We now introduce an ϵ-CS condition for a multiassignment S and a pair (π, p).

Definition 2.3:   A multiassignment S and a pair (π, p) are said to satisfy ϵ-CS if

$$\pi_i + p_j \geq a_{ij} - \epsilon, \qquad \forall \ (i,j) \in \mathcal{A}, \tag{2.28a}$$

$$\pi_i + p_j = a_{ij}, \qquad \forall \ (i,j) \in S, \tag{2.28b}$$

$$\pi_i = \max_{k=1,\ldots,m} \pi_k, \qquad \text{if } i \text{ is multiassigned under } S. \tag{2.28c}$$

We have the following result.

Proposition 2.6:   If a feasible multiassignment S satisfies the ϵ-CS conditions (2.28) together with a pair (π, p), then S is within $n\epsilon$ of being optimal for the multiassignment problem. The triplet $(\hat{\pi}, p, \hat{\lambda})$, where

$$\hat{\pi}_i = \pi_i + \epsilon, \qquad \forall \ i = 1, \ldots, m,$$

$$\hat{\lambda} = \max_{k=1,\ldots,m} \hat{\pi}_k,$$

is within $n\epsilon$ of being an optimal solution of the dual problem (2.27).

Proof: Very similar to the proof of Prop. 2.4 – left for the reader.   **Q.E.D.**

Consider now trying to solve the multiassignment problem by means of auction. We can start with any multiassignment S and profit-price pair (π, p) satisfying the first two ϵ-CS conditions (2.28a) and (2.28b), and perform a forward auction up to the point where each person is assigned to a (single) distinct object, while satisfying the conditions (2.28a) and (2.28b). However, this multiassignment will not be feasible, because some objects will still be unassigned.

To make further progress, we use a modified reverse auction that starts with the final results of the forward auction (that is, a multiassignment S, where each person is assigned to a single distinct object) and with a pair (π, p) satisfying the first two ϵ-CS conditions (2.28a) and (2.28b). Let us denote by λ the maximal initial person profit,

$$\lambda = \max_{i=1,\dots,m} \pi_i. \tag{2.29}$$

The typical iteration, given below, is the same as the one of reverse auction, except that unassigned objects j that bid for a person may not necessarily displace the object assigned to the person but may instead *share* the person with its already assigned object(s); this will happen if and only if the person's profit has reached the upper bound λ.

The algorithm maintains a multiassignment S, for which each person is assigned to at least one object, and a pair (π, p) satisfying Eqs. (2.28a) and (2.28b); it terminates when all unassigned objects j have been assigned. It will be seen that upon termination, the third ϵ-CS condition (2.28c) will be satisfied as well. The scalar λ is kept fixed throughout the algorithm.

Typical Iteration of Modified Reverse Auction for Multiassignment

Select an object j that is unassigned under the multiassignment S (if all objects are assigned, the algorithm terminates). Find a "best" person i_j such that

$$i_j = \arg \max_{i \in B(j)} \{a_{ij} - \pi_i\}, \tag{2.30}$$

and the corresponding value

$$\beta_j = \max_{i \in B(j)} \{a_{ij} - \pi_i\}, \tag{2.31}$$

and find

$$\omega_j = \max_{i \in B(j), i \neq i_j} \{a_{ij} - \pi_i\}. \tag{2.32}$$

[If i_j is the only person in $B(j)$, we define ω_j to be $-\infty$.] Let

$$\delta = \min\{\lambda - \pi_{i_j}, \beta_j - \omega_j + \epsilon\}. \tag{2.33}$$

Add (i_j, j) to the multiassignment S, set

$$p_j := \beta_j - \delta, \tag{2.34}$$

$$\pi_{i_j} := \pi_{i_j} + \delta, \tag{2.35}$$

and, if $\delta > 0$, remove from the multiassignment S the pair (i_j, j'), where j' was assigned to i_j under S.

Note that in an iteration the number of assigned objects increases by one if and only if $\delta = 0$ [which is equivalent to $\pi_{i_j} = \lambda$, since the second term $\beta_j - \omega_j + \epsilon$ in Eq. (2.33) is always greater or equal to ϵ]. The following proposition establishes the validity of the method.

Proposition 2.7:   The modified reverse auction algorithm for the multias-signment problem terminates with a feasible multiassignment that is within $n\epsilon$ of being optimal.

Proof: In view of Prop. 2.6, the result will follow once we prove the follow-ing:

(a) The modified reverse auction iteration preserves the ϵ-CS conditions (2.28), as well as the condition

$$\lambda = \max_{i=1,\ldots,m} \pi_i. \qquad (2.36)$$

(b) The algorithm terminates (necessarily with a feasible multiassignment).

To show (a) we use induction. In particular, we will show that if the conditions (2.28) and (2.36) are satisfied at the start of an iteration, they are also satisfied at the end of the iteration. This is easily seen to be true for Eqs. (2.28a) and (2.28b). Equations (2.28c) and (2.36) are preserved, since we have $\lambda = \max_{i=1,\ldots,m} \pi_i$ at the start of the iteration and the only profit that changes is π_{i_j}, which by Eqs. (2.33) and (2.35) is set to something that is less or equal to λ, and is set to λ if and only if i_j is multiassigned at the end of the iteration.

To show termination, we observe that a person i can receive a bid only a finite number of times after the profit π_i is set to λ, since at each of these times the corresponding object will get assigned to i without any object already assigned to i becoming unassigned. On the other hand, by Eqs. (2.33) and (2.35), at an iteration where a person receives a bid, his or her profit is either set equal to λ or else increases by at least ϵ. Since profits are bounded above by λ throughout the algorithm, it follows that each person can receive only a finite number of bids; this proves termination.   **Q.E.D.**

When the problem data are integer, Prop. 2.7 shows that the auction algorithm terminates with an optimal multiassignment provided $\epsilon < 1/n$. It is possible to strengthen this result and show that it is sufficient that $\epsilon < 1/m$ for optimality of the final multiassignment. This, however, requires a somewhat different proof argument than the one we have used so far; see Prop. 4.1 and Exercises 4.6 and 4.7 in Section 4.4.

E X E R C I S E S

Exercise 2.1 (Equivalence of Two Forms of Reverse Auction)

Show that the iteration of the Gauss-Seidel version of the reverse auction algo-rithm for the (symmetric) assignment problem can equivalently be described by the following iteration, which maintains an assignment and a pair (π, p) satisfying the ϵ-CS condition (2.6):

Step 1: Choose an unassigned object j.

Step 2: Decrease p_j to the highest level for which two or more persons will increase their profit by at least ϵ after assignment to j, that is, set p_j to the highest level for which $a_{ij} - p_j \geq \pi_i + \epsilon$ for at least two persons i, where π_i is the profit of i at the start of the iteration.

Step 3: From the persons in Step 2, assign to j a person i_j that experiences maximum profit increase after assignment to j, and cancel the prior assignment of i_j if he or she was assigned at the start of the iteration. Set the profit of i_j to $a_{i_j j} - p_j$.

Exercise 2.2

Consider the asymmetric assignment problem and apply forward auction starting with the zero price vector and the empty assignment. Show that, for a feasible problem, the algorithm terminates with a feasible assignment that is within $m\epsilon$ of being optimal. *Note:* Because this method must start with the zero price vector, it does not admit ϵ-scaling.

Exercise 2.3 (A Variation of the Asymmetric Assignment Problem)

Consider a problem which is the same as the asymmetric assignment problem with the exception that in a feasible assignment S there can be at most one incident arc for every person and at most one incident arc for every object (that is, there is no need for every person, as well as for every object, to be assigned). The corresponding linear program is

$$\text{maximize} \quad \sum_{(i,j)\in\mathcal{A}} a_{ij} x_{ij}$$

$$\text{subject to}$$

$$\sum_{j\in A(i)} x_{ij} \leq 1, \qquad \forall\, i = 1, \ldots, m,$$

$$\sum_{i\in B(j)} x_{ij} \leq 1, \qquad \forall\, j = 1, \ldots, n,$$

$$0 \leq x_{ij}, \qquad \forall\, (i,j) \in \mathcal{A}.$$

(a) Show that this problem can be converted to an asymmetric assignment problem where all persons must be assigned. *Hint:* For each person i introduce an artificial object i' and a zero cost arc (i, i').

(b) Adapt and streamline the auction algorithm of Section 4.2.1 to solve the problem.

Exercise 2.4

Consider the multiassignment problem. Derive a combined forward/reverse auction algorithm similar to the one for the symmetric assignment problem. Forward auction iterations should be used only when there are unassigned persons, and reverse auction iterations should be such that the quantity $\lambda = \max_i \pi_i$ is never increased.

Exercise 2.5 (A Refinement of the Optimality Conditions)

(a) Consider the asymmetric assignment problem with integer data, and suppose that we have a feasible assignment S and a pair (π, p) satisfying the first two ϵ-CS conditions (2.15a) and (2.15b) with $\epsilon < 1/m$. Show that in order for S to be optimal it is sufficient that

$$p_k \leq p_t$$

for all k and t such that k is unassigned under S, t is assigned under S, and there exists a path $(k, i_1, j_1, \ldots, i_q, j_q, i_{q+1}, t)$ such that $(i_r, j_r) \in S$ for $r = 1, \ldots, q$, and $(i_{q+1}, t) \in S$. *Hint:* Consider the existence of cycles with positive value along which S can be modified.

(b) Consider the multiassignment problem. Derive a result analogous to the one of part (a), with the condition $p_k \leq p_t$ replaced by the condition $\pi_k \geq \pi_t$, where k is any multiassigned person and t is any person for which there exists a path $(k, j_1, i_1, \ldots, j_q, i_q, j_{q+1}, t)$ such that $(k, j_1) \in S$ and $(i_r, j_{r+1}) \in S$ for $r = 1, \ldots, q$.

4.3   AN AUCTION ALGORITHM FOR SHORTEST PATHS

In this section we consider an algorithm for finding a shortest path from several origins to a single destination in a directed graph $(\mathcal{N}, \mathcal{A})$. We will see later that this algorithm can also be viewed as an application of the *naive* auction algorithm (this is the auction algorithm with $\epsilon = 0$, discussed in Section 1.2.4) to a special type of assignment problem that is equivalent to the shortest path problem.

We will assume throughout this section that *all cycles have positive length*. When all the arc lengths are nonnegative, the cycle positivity assumption can be weakened to a nonnegativity assumption at the expense of complicating the algorithm somewhat; see Exercise 3.3.

To simplify the presentation, we also assume that each node except for the destination has at least one outgoing incident arc; any node not satisfying this condition can be connected to the destination with a very high length arc without materially changing the problem and the subsequent algorithm.

For the single origin case the algorithm is very simple. It maintains a single path starting at the origin. At each iteration, the path is either *extended* by adding a new node or *contracted* by deleting its terminal node. When the destination becomes the terminal node of the path, the algorithm terminates.

To get an intuitive sense of the algorithm, think of a person moving in a graph-like maze, trying to reach a destination. The person criss-crosses the maze, either advancing or backtracking along the current path. Each time the person backtracks from a node, he or she records a measure of the desirability of revisiting and advancing from that node in the future (this will be implemented with the help of a price variable). The person revisits and proceeds forward from a node when the node's measure of desirability is judged superior to those of other nodes. The algorithm of this section emulates this search process efficiently, using simple data structures.

Similar to the algorithms of Section 1.3, complementary slackness conditions are fundamental for the algorithm of this section. However, it is helpful for our purposes to reformulate these conditions in terms of node prices p_i rather than the node labels d_i used in Section 1.3.

In particular, given a simple (forward) path P and a price vector p consisting of prices p_i, we say that the pair (P, p) satisfies *complementary slackness* (CS) if

$$p_i \leq a_{ij} + p_j, \qquad \forall \ (i,j) \in \mathcal{A}, \tag{3.1a}$$

$$p_i = a_{ij} + p_j, \qquad \text{for all pairs of successive nodes } i \text{ and } j \text{ of } P. \tag{3.1b}$$

[When we say that the pair (P, p) satisfies CS, we implicitly assume that P is simple.]

The CS conditions given above are equivalent to the CS conditions for the shortest path problem given in Prop. 3.1 in Section 1.3, with the labels d_i of that proposition replaced by the negative prices $-p_i$. It follows that if a pair (P, p) satisfies CS, then the portion of P between any node $i \in P$ and any node $k \in P$ is a shortest path from i to k, while $p_i - p_k$ is the corresponding shortest distance. This can also be seen directly by observing that by Eq. (3.1b), $p_i - p_k$ is the length of the portion of P between i and k, and every path connecting i to k must have length at least equal to $p_i - p_k$ [add Eq. (3.1a) along the arcs of the path].

There is an interesting interpretation of the CS conditions in terms of a mechanical model [Min57]. Think of each node as a ball, and for every arc $(i, j) \in \mathcal{A}$, connect i and j with a string of length a_{ij}. (This requires that $a_{ij} = a_{ji} > 0$, which we assume.) Let the resulting balls-and-strings model be at an arbitrary position in three-dimensional space, and let p_i be the vertical coordinate of node i. Then the CS condition $p_i - p_j \leq a_{ij}$ clearly holds for all arcs (i, j), as illustrated in Fig. 3.1(b). If the model is picked up and left to hang from the origin node (by gravity – strings that are tight are perfectly vertical), then for all the tight strings (i, j) we have $p_i - p_j = a_{ij}$, so any tight chain of strings corresponds to a shortest path between the endnodes of the chain, as illustrated in Fig. 3.1(c). In particular, the length of the tight chain connecting the origin node 1 to any other node i is $p_1 - p_i$ and is also equal to the shortest distance from 1 to i. (This result is essentially the min path/max tension theorem described in Exercise 3.5 of Chapter 1.)

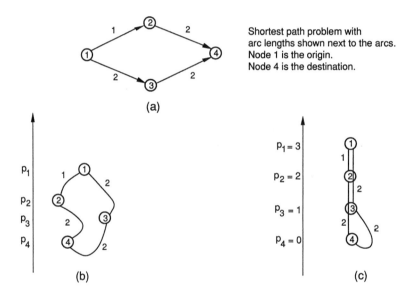

(a)

Shortest path problem with arc lengths shown next to the arcs. Node 1 is the origin. Node 4 is the destination.

(b)   (c)

Figure 3.1   Illustration of the CS conditions. If each node is a ball, and for every arc $(i, j) \in \mathcal{A}$, nodes i and j are connected with a string of length a_{ij}, the vertical coordinates p_i of the nodes satisfy $p_i - p_j \leq a_{ij}$, as shown in (b) for the problem given in (a). If the model is picked up and left to hang from the origin node 1, then $p_1 - p_i$ gives the shortest distance to each node i, as shown in (c).

The algorithm of this section can be interpreted in terms of the balls-and-strings model, as we will see shortly. As a prelude to this, it is interesting to note that Dijkstra's algorithm can also be interpreted in terms of this model, as shown in Fig. 3.2. At each iteration of the algorithm, the model is lifted by the origin node to the level where at least one more string becomes tight. Note that this interpretation leads to an interesting two-sided version of Dijkstra's algorithm for the single origin/single destination problem. In particular, it can be seen that a solution can be obtained by lifting the model upward from the origin, and simultaneously pulling the model downward from the destination. The corresponding algorithm is given in Exercise 3.5.

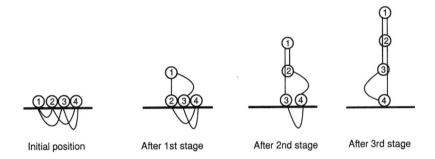

| Initial position | After 1st stage | After 2nd stage | After 3rd stage |

Figure 3.2   Interpretation of Dijkstra's algorithm in terms of the balls-and-strings model for the shortest path problem of Fig. 3.1. The model initially rests on a flat surface. It is then picked up from the origin and lifted in stages. At each stage the origin is raised to the next higher level at which one more node is ready to be lifted off the surface. Thus at each stage the shortest distance to at least one more node is found. Furthermore, the shortest distances of the nodes are obtained in the order of the nodes' proximity to the origin.

4.3.1   Algorithm Description and Analysis

We describe the algorithm in its simplest form for the case of a single origin and a single destination, and we defer the discussion of other and more efficient versions.

   Let node 1 be the origin node and let t be the destination node. The algorithm maintains at all times a simple path $P = (1, i_1, i_2, \ldots, i_k)$. (When we refer to a path in this section, we implicitly assume that the path is *forward*; that is, all the arcs of the path are forward arcs.) The node i_k is called the *terminal* node of P. The degenerate path $P = (1)$ may also be obtained in the course of the algorithm. If i_{k+1} is a node that does not belong to a path $P = (1, i_1, i_2, \ldots, i_k)$ and (i_k, i_{k+1}) is an arc, *extending* P by i_{k+1} means replacing P by the path $(1, i_1, i_2, \ldots, i_k, i_{k+1})$, called the *extension of P by i_{k+1}*. If P does not consist of just the origin node 1, *contracting* P means replacing P by the path $(1, i_1, i_2, \ldots, i_{k-1})$.

The algorithm maintains also a price vector p satisfying CS together with P. We assume that an initial pair (P,p) satisfying CS is available. This is not a restrictive assumption when all arc lengths are nonnegative, since then one can use the default pair

$$P = (1), \qquad p_i = 0, \ \forall \ i.$$

When some arcs have negative lengths, an initial choice of a pair (P,p) satisfying CS may not be obvious or available, but Exercise 3.2 provides a general method for finding such a pair.

We now describe the algorithm. Initially, (P,p) is any pair satisfying CS. The algorithm proceeds in iterations, transforming a pair (P,p) satisfying CS into another pair satisfying CS. At each iteration, the path P is either extended by a new node or else contracted by deleting its terminal node. In the latter case the price of the terminal node is increased strictly. A degenerate case occurs when the path consists by just the origin node 1; in this case the path is either extended or is left unchanged with the price p_1 being strictly increased. The iteration is as follows.

Typical Iteration

Let i be the terminal node of P. If

$$p_i < \min_{(i,j)\in\mathcal{A}} \big\{ a_{ij} + p_j \big\}, \tag{3.2}$$

go to Step 1; else go to Step 2.

Step 1 (Contract path): Set

$$p_i := \min_{(i,j)\in\mathcal{A}} \big\{ a_{ij} + p_j \big\}, \tag{3.3}$$

and if $i \neq 1$, contract P. Go to the next iteration.

Step 2 (Extend path): Extend P by node j_i where

$$j_i = \arg \min_{(i,j)\in\mathcal{A}} \big\{ a_{ij} + p_j \big\}. \tag{3.4}$$

If j_i is the destination t, stop; P is the desired shortest path. Otherwise, go to the next iteration.

Note that following an extension (Step 2), P is a simple path from 1 to j_i; if this were not so, then adding j_i to P would create a cycle, and for every arc (i,j) of this cycle we would have $p_i = a_{ij} + p_j$. By adding this condition along the cycle, we see that the cycle should have zero length, which is not possible by our assumptions.

Figure 3.3 illustrates the algorithm. As can be seen from the example of this figure, the terminal node traces the tree of shortest paths from the origin to the nodes that are closer to the origin than the given destination. This behavior is typical when the initial prices are all zero as we will show shortly. We now derive the properties of the algorithm and establish its validity.

Proposition 3.1:   The pairs (P, p) generated by the algorithm satisfy CS. Furthermore, for every pair of nodes i and j, and at all iterations, $p_i - p_j$ is an underestimate of the shortest distance from i to j.

Proof: We first show by induction that (P, p) satisfies CS. Indeed, the initial pair satisfies CS by assumption. Consider an iteration that starts with a pair (P, p) satisfying CS and produces a pair $(\bar{P}, \bar{p})$. Let i be the terminal node of P. If

$$p_i = \min_{(i,j) \in \mathcal{A}} \{a_{ij} + p_j\}, \tag{3.5}$$

then $\bar{P}$ is the extension of P by a node j_i and $\bar{p} = p$, implying that the CS condition (3.1b) holds for all arcs of P as well as arc (i, j_i) [since j_i attains the minimum in Eq. (3.5); cf. Eq. (3.4)].

Suppose next that

$$p_i < \min_{(i,j) \in \mathcal{A}} \{a_{ij} + p_j\}.$$

Then if P is the degenerate path (1), the CS condition holds vacuously. Otherwise, $\bar{P}$ is obtained by contracting P, we have $\bar{p}_i > p_i$, and for all nodes $j \in \bar{P}$, we have $\bar{p}_j = p_j$, implying the CS conditions (3.1a) and (3.1b) for arcs outgoing from nodes of $\bar{P}$. Also, for the terminal node i, we have

$$\bar{p}_i = \min_{(i,j) \in \mathcal{A}} \{a_{ij} + p_j\},$$

implying the CS condition (3.1a) for arcs outgoing from that node as well. Furthermore, since $\bar{p}_i > p_i$ and $\bar{p}_k = p_k$ for all $k \neq i$, we have $\bar{p}_k \leq a_{kj} + \bar{p}_j$ for all arcs (k, j) outgoing from nodes $k \notin P$. This completes the induction proof that (P, p) satisfies CS.

Finally consider any path from a node i to a node j. By adding the CS condition (3.1a) along that path, we see that the length of the path is at least $p_i - p_j$, proving the last assertion of the proposition.   **Q.E.D.**

Proposition 3.2:   If P is a path generated by the algorithm, then P is a shortest path from the origin to the terminal node of P.

Proof: This follows from the CS property of the pair (P, p) shown in Prop. 3.1; see the remarks following the CS conditions (3.1). In particular, by the CS condition (3.1b), P has length $p_1 - p_i$, and by the CS condition (3.1a),

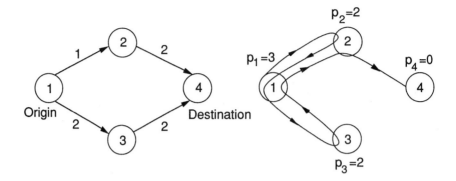

Shortest path problem with arc
lengths as shown

Trajectory of terminal node
and final prices generated by
the algorithm

Iteration #	Path P prior to the iteration	Price vector p prior to the iteration	Type of action during the iteration
1	(1)	$(0,0,0,0)$	contraction at 1
2	(1)	$(1,0,0,0)$	extension to 2
3	$(1,2)$	$(1,0,0,0)$	contraction at 2
4	(1)	$(1,2,0,0)$	contraction at 1
5	(1)	$(2,2,0,0)$	extension to 3
6	$(1,3)$	$(2,2,0,0)$	contraction at 3
7	(1)	$(2,2,2,0)$	contraction at 1
8	(1)	$(3,2,2,0)$	extension to 2
9	$(1,2)$	$(3,2,2,0)$	extension to 4
10	$(1,2,4)$	$(3,2,2,0)$	stop

Figure 3.3   An example illustrating the algorithm starting with $P = (1)$ and
$p = 0$.

every path connecting 1 and i must have length at least equal to $p_1 - p_i$.
Q.E.D.

Interpretations of the Algorithm

The algorithm can be interpreted in terms of a balls-and-strings model where nodes are raised in stages as illustrated in Fig. 3.4. All nodes are resting initially on a flat surface. At each stage, we raise the *last* node in a tight chain that starts at the origin to the level at which at least one more string becomes tight. This should be contrasted with Dijkstra's algorithm (cf. Fig. 3.2), where we raise the entire set of nodes that are connected with the origin via a tight chain.

For an alternative interpretation, denote for each node i,

$$D_i = \text{shortest distance from the origin 1 to node } i, \qquad (3.6)$$

with $D_1 = 0$ by convention. By Prop. 3.1, we have throughout the algorithm

$$p_1 - p_j \leq D_j, \qquad \forall\, j \in \mathcal{N},$$

while by Prop. 3.2, we have

$$p_1 - p_i = D_i, \qquad \text{for all } i \in P.$$

The preceding two relations imply that

$$D_i + p_i - p_t \leq D_j + p_j - p_t, \qquad \forall\, i \in P, \text{ and } j \in \mathcal{N}.$$

Since by Prop. 3.1 $p_j - p_t$ is an estimate of the shortest distance from j to t, we may view the quantity

$$D_j + p_j - p_t$$

as *an estimate of the shortest distance from 1 to t using only paths passing through j.* Thus, intuitively, it makes sense to consider a node j as "most desirable" for inclusion in the algorithm's path if $D_j + p_j - p_t$ is minimal.

Based on the preceding interpretation, it can be seen that:

  (a) The algorithm maintains a path consisting of "most desirable" candidates for participation in a shortest path from 1 to t.

  (b) The algorithm extends P by a node j if and only if j is a "most desirable" candidate.

  (c) The algorithm contracts P if the terminal node i has no neighbor that is "most desirable." Then, the estimate of i's shortest distance to t is

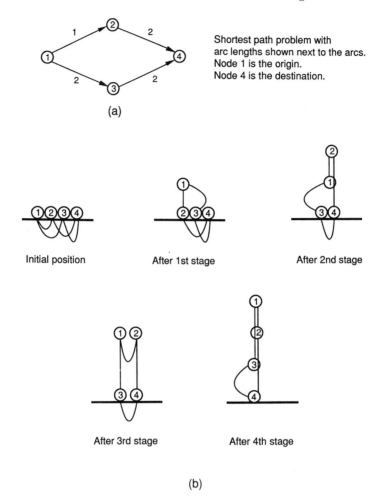

Figure 3.4   Illustration of the algorithm of this section in terms of the balls-and-strings model for the problem shown in (a). The model initially rests on a flat surface, and various balls are then raised in stages. At each stage we raise a single ball $i \neq t$, which is at a lower level than the origin and can be reached from the origin through a sequence of tight strings; i should not have any tight string connecting it to another ball, which is at a lower level, that is, i should be the last ball in a tight chain hanging from the origin. (If the origin does not have any tight string connecting it to another ball, which is at a lower level, we use $i =$ origin.) We then raise i to the first level at which one of the strings connecting it to a ball at a lower level becomes tight. Each stage corresponds to a contraction. The ball i, which is being raised, corresponds to the terminal node of the path.

improved (i.e., is increased), and i is not "most desirable" (since $D_i+p_i-p_t$ is not minimal anymore), thus justifying its deletion from P. Node i will be revisited only after $D_i + p_i - p_t$ becomes minimal again, after sufficiently large increases of the prices of the currently "most desirable" nodes.

The preceding interpretation suggests also that the nodes become terminal for the first time in the order of the initial values $D_j + p_j^0 - p_t^0$, where

$$p_i^0 = \text{initial price of node } i. \tag{3.7}$$

To formulate this property, denote for every node i

$$d_i = D_i + p_i^0. \tag{3.8}$$

Index the iterations by $1, 2, \ldots$, and let

$$k_i = \text{the first iteration at which node } i \text{ becomes the terminal node,} \tag{3.9}$$

where by convention, $k_1 = 0$ and $k_i = \infty$ if i never becomes a terminal node.

Proposition 3.3:

(a) At the end of iteration k_i we have $p_1 = d_i$.

(b) If $k_i < k_j$, then $d_i \le d_j$.

Proof: (a) At the end of iteration k_i, P is a shortest path from 1 to i by Prop. 3.2, while the length of P is $p_1 - p_i^0$.

(b) By part (a), at the end of iteration k_i we have $p_1 = d_i$, while at the end of iteration k_j we have $p_1 = d_j$. Since p_1 is monotonically nondecreasing during the algorithm and $k_i < k_j$, the result follows.   **Q.E.D.**

Note that the preceding proposition shows that when all arc lengths are nonnegative, and the default initialization $p = 0$ is used, the nodes become terminal for the first time in the order of their proximity to the origin. This property is also evident from the interpretation of the algorithm in terms of the balls-and-strings model; cf. Fig. 3.4.

Termination – Running Time of the Algorithm

The following proposition establishes the validity of the algorithm.

Proposition 3.4:   If there exists at least one path from the origin to the destination, the algorithm terminates with a shortest path from the origin to the destination. Otherwise the algorithm never terminates and $p_1 \to \infty$.

Proof: Assume first that there is a path from node 1 to the destination t. Since by Prop. 3.1 $p_1 - p_t$ is an underestimate of the (finite) shortest distance from 1 to t, p_1 is monotonically nondecreasing, and p_t is fixed throughout the algorithm, it follows that p_1 must stay bounded. We next claim that p_i must stay bounded for all i. Indeed, in order to have $p_i \to \infty$, node i must become the terminal node of P infinitely often, implying (by Prop. 3.1) that $p_1 - p_i$ must be equal to the shortest distance from 1 to i infinitely often, which is a contradiction since p_1 is bounded.

We next show that the algorithm terminates. Indeed, it can be seen with a straightforward induction argument that for every node i, either p_i is equal to its initial value or else p_i is the length of some path starting at i plus the initial price of the final node of the path; we call this the *modified length* of the path. Every path starting at i can be decomposed into a simple path and a finite number of cycles, each having positive length by assumption (Exercise 1.5 in Section 1.1), so the number of distinct modified path lengths within any bounded interval is bounded. Now, p_i was shown earlier to be bounded. Furthermore, each time i becomes the terminal node by extension of the path P, p_i is strictly larger over the preceding time i became the terminal node of P, corresponding to a strictly larger modified path length. It follows that the number of times i can become a terminal node by extension of the path P is bounded. Since the number of path contractions between two consecutive path extensions is bounded by the number of nodes in the graph, the number of iterations of the algorithm is bounded, implying that the algorithm terminates.

Assume now that there is no path from node 1 to the destination. Then the algorithm will never terminate, so by the preceding argument some node i will become the terminal node by extension of the path P infinitely often, and $p_i \to \infty$. At the end of iterations where this happens, $p_1 - p_i$ must be equal to the shortest distance from 1 to i, implying that $p_1 \to \infty$.   **Q.E.D.**

We will now estimate the running time of the algorithm, assuming that all the arc lengths and initial prices are integer. Our estimate involves the set of nodes

$$\mathcal{I} = \{i \mid d_i \le d_t\};   \tag{3.10}$$

by Prop. 3.3, these are the only nodes that ever become terminal nodes of the paths generated by the algorithm. Let us denote

$$I = \text{number of nodes in } \mathcal{I},   \tag{3.11}$$

$$G = \max_{i \in \mathcal{I}} g_i,   \tag{3.12}$$

where g_i is the number of outgoing incident arcs of node i, and let us also denote by E the product

$$E = I \cdot G.   \tag{3.13}$$

Proposition 3.5:   Assume that there exists at least one path from the origin 1 to the destination t, and that the arc lengths and initial prices are all integer. The worst case running time of the algorithm is $O\left(E\left(D_t + p_t^0 - p_1^0\right)\right)$.

Proof: Each time a node i becomes the terminal node of the path, we have $p_i = p_1 - D_i$ (cf. Prop. 3.2). Since at all times we have $p_1 \leq D_t + p_t^0$ (cf. Prop. 3.1), it follows that

$$p_i = p_1 - D_i \leq D_t + p_t^0 - D_i.$$

Using the definitions $d_t = D_t + p_t^0$ and $d_i = D_i + p_i^0$, and the fact $d_i \geq d_1$ (cf. Prop. 3.3), we see that throughout the algorithm we have

$$p_i - p_i^0 \leq d_t - d_i \leq d_t - d_1 = D_t + p_t^0 - p_1^0, \qquad \forall\, i \in \mathcal{I}.$$

Therefore, since prices increase by integer amounts, $D_t + p_t^0 - p_1^0 + 1$ bounds the number of times that each price p_i increases (with an attendant path contraction if $i \neq 1$). The computation per iteration is bounded by a constant multiple of the number of outgoing arcs of the terminal node of the path, so the computation corresponding to contractions and price increases is $O\left(E\left(D_t + p_t^0 - p_1^0\right)\right)$.

The number of path extensions with $i \in \mathcal{I}$ becoming the terminal node of the path is bounded by the number of increases of p_i, which in turn is bounded by $D_t + p_t^0 - p_1^0 + 1$. Thus the computation corresponding to extensions is also $O\left(E\left(D_t + p_t^0 - p_1^0\right)\right)$.   **Q.E.D.**

The actual running time of the algorithm can indeed, in the worst case, depend strongly on the shortest distance D_t, as suggested by the estimate of the preceding proposition. This is illustrated in Fig. 3.5 with a graph involving a cycle with relatively small length. It is possible to use scaling to turn the algorithm into one that is polynomial (see [Ber90]), but in practice this device does not seem particularly effective, because the practical performance of the algorithm is typically much better than suggested by the preceding running time estimate. In fact, for randomly generated problems, it appears that the number of iterations can be estimated quite reliably (within a small multiplicative factor) by

$$n_t - 1 + \sum_{i \in \mathcal{I}, i \neq t} (2n_i - 1), \tag{3.14}$$

where n_i is the number of nodes in a shortest path from 1 to i. For example, for the problem of Fig. 3.3 the above estimate is exact; see also Exercise 3.4. Note also that the number of iterations is reduced substantially when the algorithm is implemented in a forward/reverse mode, as discussed in the next subsection.

Assuming that the estimate (3.14) on the number of iterations is correct (within a constant factor) the running time of the algorithm depends critically on the number of nodes n_i in the shortest path to node i averaged over all nodes i. If the shortest paths are very long as in graphs with large diameter, the average number of arcs on a shortest path is $O(N)$, and the running time of the algorithm is usually $O(NA)$, where A is the number of arcs [a more accurate estimate is $O(NE)$, where E bounds the number of arcs in the subgraph of nodes that are closer to the origin than the destination t, cf. Eqs. (3.10)-(3.13)]. If on the other hand the shortest paths are short as in graphs with small diameter, the average number of arcs on a shortest path is $O(1)$, and the running time of the algorithm is usually $O(A)$ [a more accurate estimate is $O(E)$].

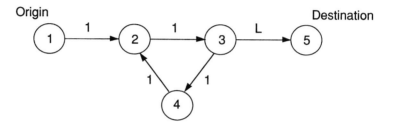

Figure 3.5   Example graph for which the number of iterations of the algorithm is not polynomially bounded. The lengths are shown next to the arcs and $L > 1$. By tracing the steps of the algorithm starting with $P = (1)$ and $p = 0$, we see that the price of node 3 will be first increased by 1 and then it will be increased by increments of 3 (the length of the cycle) as many times as is necessary for p_3 to reach or exceed L.

The Case of Multiple Destinations or Multiple Origins

To solve the problem with multiple destinations and a single origin, one can simply run the algorithm until every destination becomes the terminal node of the path at least once. Also, to solve the problem with multiple origins and a single destination, one can combine several versions of the algorithm – one for each origin. However, the different versions can share a common price vector, since regardless of the origin considered, the condition $p_i \leq a_{ij} + p_j$ is always maintained. There are several ways to operate such a method; they differ in the policy used for switching between different origins. One possibility is to run the algorithm for one origin and, after the shortest path is obtained, to switch to the next origin (without changing the price vector), and so on, until all origins are exhausted. Another possibility, which is probably preferable in most cases, is to rotate between different origins, switching from one origin to another, if a contraction at the origin occurs or the destination becomes the terminal node of the current path.

4.3.2 Efficient Implementation – Forward/Reverse Algorithm

The main computational bottleneck of the algorithm is the calculation of

$$\min_{(i,j)\in\mathcal{A}}\left\{a_{ij}+p_j\right\},$$

which is done every time node i becomes the terminal node of the path. We can reduce the number of these calculations using the following observation. Since the CS condition $p_i \le a_{ij}+p_j$ is maintained at all times for all arcs (i,j), if some (i,j_i) satisfies

$$p_i = a_{ij_i}+p_{j_i}$$

it follows that

$$a_{ij_i}+p_{j_i} = \min_{(i,j)\in\mathcal{A}}\left\{a_{ij}+p_j\right\},$$

so the path can be extended by j_i if i is the terminal node of the path. This suggests the following implementation strategy: each time a path contraction occurs with i being the terminal node, we calculate

$$\min_{(i,j)\in\mathcal{A}}\left\{a_{ij}+p_j\right\}$$

together with an arc (i,j_i) such that

$$j_i = \arg\min_{(i,j)\in\mathcal{A}}\left\{a_{ij}+p_j\right\}.$$

At the next time node i becomes the terminal node of the path, we check whether the condition $p_i = a_{ij_i}+p_{j_i}$ is satisfied, and if it is we extend the path by node j_i without going through the calculation of $\min_{(i,j)\in\mathcal{A}}\left\{a_{ij}+p_j\right\}$. In practice this device is very effective, typically saving from a third to a half of the calculations of the preceding expression. The reason is that the test $p_i = a_{ij_i}+p_{j_i}$ rarely fails; the only way it can fail is if the price p_{j_i} is increased between the two successive times i became the terminal node of the path.

The preceding idea can be strengthened further. Suppose that whenever we compute the "best neighbor"

$$j_i = \arg\min_{(i,j)\in\mathcal{A}}\left\{a_{ij}+p_j\right\}$$

we also compute the "second best neighbor" k_i, given by

$$k_i = \arg \min_{(i,j)\in\mathcal{A},\ j\neq j_i} \{a_{ij} + p_j\},$$

and the corresponding "second best level"

$$w_i = a_{ik_i} + p_{k_i}.$$

Then, at the next time node i becomes the terminal node of the path, we can check whether the condition $a_{ij_i} + p_{j_i} \leq w_i$ is satisfied, and if it is we know that j_i still attains the minimum in the expression

$$\min_{(i,j)\in\mathcal{A}} \{a_{ij} + p_j\},$$

thereby obviating the calculation of this minimum. If on the other hand we have $a_{ij_i} + p_{j_i} > w_i$ (due to an increase of p_{j_i} subsequent to the calculation of w_i), we can check to see whether we still have $w_i = a_{ik_i} + p_{k_i}$; if this is so, then k_i becomes the "best neighbor,"

$$k_i = \arg \min_{(i,j)\in\mathcal{A}} \{a_{ij} + p_j\},$$

thus again obviating the calculation of the minimum.

With proper implementation the devices outlined above can typically reduce the number of calculations of the expression $\min_{(i,j)\in\mathcal{A}}\{a_{ij} + p_j\}$ by a factor that is typically in the range from 3 to 5, thereby dramatically reducing the total computation time.

Forward/Reverse Algorithm

In shortest path problems, one can exchange the roles of origins and destinations by reversing the directions of all arcs. It is therefore possible to use a destination-oriented version of our algorithm that maintains a path R that *ends* at the destination and changes at each iteration by means of a contraction or an extension. This algorithm, presented below and called the *reverse algorithm*, is equivalent to the earlier algorithm, which will henceforth be referred to as the *forward algorithm*. The CS conditions for the problem with arc directions reversed are

$$\overline{p}_j \leq a_{ij} + \overline{p}_i, \qquad \forall\ (i,j) \in \mathcal{A},$$

$$\overline{p}_j = a_{ij} + \overline{p}_i, \qquad \text{for all pairs of successive nodes } i \text{ and } j \text{ of } R,$$

where $\overline{p}$ is the price vector. By replacing $\overline{p}$ by $-p$, we obtain the CS conditions in the form $p_i \leq a_{ij} + p_j$, thus maintaining a common CS condition for both the forward and the reverse algorithm. The following description of the reverse algorithm also replaces $\bar{p}$ by $-p$, with the result that the prices are *decreasing* instead of increasing. To be consistent with the assumptions made regarding the forward algorithm, we assume that each node except for the origin has at least one incoming arc.

In the reverse algorithm, initially, R is any path ending at the destination, and p is any price vector satisfying the CS conditions (3.1) together with R; for example,

$$R = (t), \qquad p_i = 0, \quad \forall\, i$$

if all arc lengths are nonnegative.

Typical Iteration of the Reverse Algorithm

Let j be the starting node of R. If

$$p_j > \max_{(i,j)\in\mathcal{A}}\left\{p_i - a_{ij}\right\},$$

go to Step 1; else go to Step 2.

Step 1 (Contract path): Set

$$p_j := \max_{(i,j)\in\mathcal{A}}\left\{p_i - a_{ij}\right\}$$

and, if $j \neq t$, contract R (that is, delete the starting node j of R). Go to the next iteration.

Step 2 (Extend path): Extend R by node i_j, (that is, make i_j the starting node of R, preceding j), where

$$i_j = \arg\max_{(i,j)\in\mathcal{A}}\left\{p_i - a_{ij}\right\}.$$

If i_j is the origin 1, stop; R is the desired shortest path. Otherwise, go to the next iteration.

The reverse algorithm is really the forward algorithm applied to a reverse shortest path problem, so by the results of Section 4.3.1, it is valid and terminates with a shortest path, if at least one path exists from 1 to t.

We now consider combining the forward and the reverse algorithms into one. In this combined algorithm, we initially have a price vector p, and two paths P and R, satisfying CS together with p, where P starts at the origin and R ends at the destination. The paths P and R are extended and contracted according to the rules of the forward and the reverse algorithms, respectively, and the combined algorithm terminates when P and R have a common node. Since P and R satisfy CS together with p throughout the algorithm, it is seen that when P and R meet, say at node i, the composite path consisting of the portion of P from 1 to i and the portion of R from i to t will be shortest.

Combined Algorithm

> **Step 1 (Run forward algorithm):** Execute several iterations of the forward algorithm (subject to the termination condition), at least one of which leads to an increase of the origin price p_1. Go to Step 2.

> **Step 2 (Run reverse algorithm):** Execute several iterations of the reverse algorithm (subject to the termination condition), at least one of which leads to a decrease of the destination price p_t. Go to Step 1.

To justify the combined algorithm, note that p_1 can only increase and p_t can only decrease during its course, and that the difference $p_1 - p_t$ can be no more than the shortest distance between 1 and t. Assume that the arc lengths and the initial prices are integer, and that there is at least one path from 1 to t. Then, p_1 and p_t can change only by integer amounts, and $p_1 - p_t$ is bounded. Hence, p_1 and p_t can change only a finite number of times, guaranteeing that there will be only a finite number of executions of Steps 1 and 2 of the combined algorithm. By the results of Section 4.3.1, each Step 1 and Step 2 must contain only a finite number of iterations of the forward and the reverse algorithms, respectively. It follows that the algorithm must terminate. Note that this argument relies on the requirement that p_1 increases at least once in Step 1 and p_t decreases at least once in Step 2. Without this requirement, one can construct examples showing that the combined algorithm may never terminate.

In practice, it appears that the combined algorithm is typically much faster than either the forward or the reverse algorithm (often by a factor of the order of ten or more). In particular, the running time of the (exclusively) forward algorithm is typically proportional to the product $m_F h_F$, where m_F is the number of nodes reached by the algorithm, and h_F is the average number of nodes on the shortest paths from the origin to these nodes [cf. Eq. (3.14)]. Similarly, the running time of the (exclusively) reverse algorithm is typically proportional to the product $m_R h_R$, where m_R is the number of nodes reached by the algorithm, and h_R is the average number of nodes on the shortest paths from these nodes to the destination. The running time of the forward/reverse algorithm is typically proportional to $\overline{m}_F \overline{h}_F + \overline{m}_R \overline{h}_R$, where the terms $\overline{m}_F$, $\overline{h}_F$, and $\overline{m}_R$, $\overline{h}_R$ are analogously defined, and correspond to the forward and the reverse portions of the algorithm, respectively. For many types of problems it appears that $\overline{m}_F + \overline{m}_R$ is much less than both m_F and m_R, while $\overline{h}_F + \overline{h}_R$ is roughly comparable to h_F and h_R. This explains the experimentally observed faster running time of the forward/reverse algorithm.

Note that the forward/reverse algorithm can also be interpreted in terms of the balls-and-strings model. Just as the forward algorithm can be viewed as a sequence of stages where some ball is lifted upward as in Fig. 3.4, the reverse algorithm can be viewed as a sequence of stages where some ball is pulled downward. In the forward/reverse algorithm, we switch from raising to lowering balls and reversely. It is apparent that the algorithm works provided we make sure that, once in a while, the vertical distance between the origin and the destination increases either because the origin is raised or because the destination is lowered.

Forward/Reverse Algorithm for Multiple Origins

One may use the combined algorithm for the problem with multiple origins and a single destination using an algorithm that combines a separate forward version of the algorithm for each origin, and a reverse algorithm, which is common for all origins. The same price vector can be used for all forward versions, since the condition $p_i \leq a_{ij} + p_j$ is always maintained. One possibility is to rotate between different origins and the destination, switching from a forward algorithm for one origin to the reverse algorithm, then to another origin, and so on. The switch is made if a contraction at the origin (in the forward algorithm case) or the destination (in the reverse algorithm case) occurs, or if the destination becomes the terminal node of the current path (in the forward algorithm case). The code given in Appendix A.2 uses this scheme.

4.3.3   Relation to Naive Auction and Dual Coordinate Ascent

We now explain how our (forward) single origin/single destination algorithm can be viewed as an instance of application of the naive auction algorithm to a special type of assignment problem.

The naive auction algorithm was described in Section 1.2.4 for maximization assignment problems, where we want to maximize the benefit of matching n persons and n objects on a one-to-one basis. It is convenient here to reformulate the problem and the algorithm in terms of minimization by reversing the signs of the cost coefficients and the prices, and by replacing maximization by minimization. In particular, suppose that there is a cost c_{ij} for assigning person i with object j and we want to assign persons to objects so as to minimize the total cost. Mathematically, we want to find a feasible assignment that minimizes the total cost $\sum_{i=1}^{n} c_{ij_i}$, where by a feasible assignment we mean a set of person-object pairs $(1, j_1), \ldots, (n, j_n)$ such that the objects $j_1, \ldots, j_n$ are all distinct and $(i, j_i) \in \mathcal{A}$ for all i.

The naive auction algorithm proceeds in iterations and generates a sequence of price vectors p and (partial) assignments. At the beginning of each iteration, the complementary slackness condition

$$c_{ij_i} + p_{j_i} = \min_{(i,j) \in \mathcal{A}} \{c_{ij} + p_j\} \tag{3.15}$$

is satisfied for all pairs (i, j_i) of the assignment [cf. Eq. (2.8) in Section 1.2.3]. The initial price vector–assignment pair is required to satisfy this condition, but is otherwise arbitrary. If all persons are assigned, the algorithm terminates. If not, some person who is unassigned, say i, is selected. This person finds an object j_i, which is best in the sense

$$j_i = \arg \min_{(i,j) \in \mathcal{A}} \{c_{ij} + p_j\},$$

and then:

(a) Gets assigned to the best object j_i; the person that was assigned to j_i at the beginning of the iteration (if any) becomes unassigned.

(b) Sets the price of j_i to the level at which he or she is indifferent between j_i and the second best object – that is, he or she sets p_{j_i} to

$$p_{j_i} + w_i - v_i,$$

where v_i is the cost for acquiring the best object (including payment of the corresponding price),

$$v_i = \min_{(i,j) \in \mathcal{A}} \{c_{ij} + p_j\},$$

and w_i is the cost for acquiring the second best object,

$$w_i = \min_{(i,j) \in \mathcal{A}, j \neq j_i} \{c_{ij} + p_j\}.$$

This process is repeated in a sequence of iterations until each person is assigned to an object.

The naive auction algorithm differs from the auction algorithm in the choice of the increment of the price increase. In the auction algorithm the price p_{j_i} is increased by $w_i - v_i + \epsilon$, where ϵ is a positive constant. Thus, the naive auction algorithm is the same as the auction algorithm, except that $\epsilon = 0$. This is, however, a significant difference. As shown in Section 1.2.4 (cf. Fig. 2.10), whereas the auction algorithm is guaranteed to terminate if at least one feasible assignment exists, the naive auction algorithm may cycle indefinitely, with some objects remaining unassigned. If, however, the naive auction algorithm terminates, the feasible assignment obtained upon termination is optimal (cf. Prop. 2.4 in Section 1.2.3).

Formulation of the Shortest Path Problem as an Assignment Problem

Given the shortest path problem of this section with node 1 as origin and node t as destination, we formulate the following assignment problem.

Let $2, \ldots, N$ be the "object" nodes, and for each node $i \neq t$ introduce a "person" node i'. For every arc (i, j) of the shortest path problem with $i \neq t$ and $j \neq 1$, introduce the arc (i', j) with cost a_{ij} in the assignment problem. Introduce also the zero cost arc (i', i) for each $i \neq 1, t$. Figure 3.6 illustrates the assignment problem and shows how, given the partial assignment that assigns object i to person i' for $i \neq 1, t$, paths from 1 to t can be associated with augmenting paths that start at $1'$ and end at t.

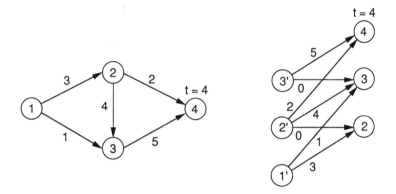

Figure 3.6   A shortest path problem (the origin is 1, the destination is $t = 4$) and its corresponding assignment problem. The arc lengths and the assignment costs are shown next to the arcs. Consider the partial assignment that assigns object i to person i' for $i \neq 1, t$. Then a shortest path can be associated with an optimal augmenting path that starts at $1'$ and ends at t.

Consider now applying the naive auction algorithm starting from a price vector p satisfying the CS condition (3.1a), that is,

$$p_i \leq a_{ij} + p_j, \qquad \forall\, (i, j) \in \mathcal{A} \tag{3.16}$$

and the partial assignment

$$(i', i), \qquad \forall\, i \neq 1, t.$$

This initial pair satisfies the corresponding complementary slackness condition (3.15), because the cost of the assigned arcs (i', i) is zero.

We impose an additional rule for breaking ties in the naive auction algorithm: if at some iteration involving the unassigned person i' the arc (i', i) is the best arc and is equally desirable with some other arc (i', j_i) (i.e., $p_i = a_{ij_i} + p_{j_i} = \min_{(i,j) \in \mathcal{A}} \{a_{ij} + p_j\}$), then the latter arc is preferred, that is, (i', j_i) is added to the assignment rather than (i', i). Furthermore, we introduce an inconsequential modification of the naive auction iteration involving a bid of person $1'$, in order to account for the special way of handling a contraction at the origin in the shortest path algorithm. In particular, the bid of $1'$ will consist of finding an object j_1 attaining the minimum in

$$\min_{(1,j)\in\mathcal{A}} \{a_{1j} + p_j\},$$

assigning j_1 to $1'$, and deassigning the person assigned to j_1 (in the case $j_1 \neq t$), but *not* changing the price p_{j_1}.

It can now be shown that the naive auction algorithm with the preceding modifications is equivalent to the (forward) shortest path algorithm of Section 4.3.1. In particular, the following can be verified by induction:

(a) The CS condition (3.16) is preserved by the naive auction algorithm.

(b) Each assignment generated by the naive auction algorithm consists of a sequence of the form

$$(1', i_1), (i_1', i_2), \dots, (i_{k-1}', i_k),$$

together with the additional arcs

$$(i', i), \quad \text{for } i \neq i_1, \dots, i_k, t;$$

this sequence corresponds to a path $P = (1, i_1, \dots, i_k)$ generated by the shortest path algorithm. As long as $i_k \neq t$, the (unique) unassigned person in the naive auction algorithm is person i_k', corresponding to the terminal node of the path. When $i_k = t$, a feasible assignment results, in which case the naive auction algorithm terminates, consistently with the termination criterion for the shortest path algorithm.

(c) In an iteration corresponding to an unassigned person i' with $i \neq 1$, the arc (i', i) is always a best arc; this is a consequence of the complementary slackness condition (3.16). Furthemore, there are three possibilities:

(1) (i', i) is the unique best arc, in which case (i', i) is added to the assignment, and the price p_i is increased by

$$\min_{(i,j)\in\mathcal{A}} \{c_{ij} + p_j\} - p_i;$$

this corresponds to contracting the current path by the terminal node i.

(2) There is an arc (i', j_i) with $j_i \neq t$, which is equally preferred to (i', i), that is,

$$p_i = a_{ij_i} + p_{j_i},$$

in which case, in view of the tie-breaking rule specified earlier, (i', j_i) is added to the assignment and the price p_{j_i} remains the same. Furthermore, the object j_i must have been assigned to j_i' at the start of the iteration, so adding (i', j_i) to the assignment [and removing (j_i', j_i)] corresponds to extending the current path by node j_i. (The positivity assumption on the cycle lengths is crucial for this property to hold.)

(3) The arc (i', t) is equally preferred to (i', i), in which case the heretofore unassigned object t is assigned to i', thereby terminating the naive auction algorithm; this corresponds to the destination t becoming the terminal node of the current path, thereby terminating the shortest path algorithm.

We have thus seen that the shortest path algorithm may be viewed as an instance of the naive auction algorithm. However, the properties of the former algorithm do not follow from generic properties of the latter. As shown in Section 1.2.4 (see Fig. 2.12), the naive auction algorithm need not terminate in general. In the present context it does terminate, thanks to the special structure of the corresponding assignment problem, and also thanks to the positivity assumption on all cycle lengths.

We finally note that the forward/reverse version of the shortest path algorithm is equivalent to a combined forward/reverse version of naive auction, with the minor modifications described earlier; see the algorithm of Section 4.2 with $\epsilon = 0$.

Relation to Dual Coordinate Ascent

We next explain how the single origin/single destination algorithm can be viewed as a dual coordinate ascent method.

As was seen in Section 1.3 [see Eq. (1.3) of that section], the shortest path problem can be written in the minimum cost flow format as follows:

$$\text{minimize} \quad \sum_{(i,j)\in\mathcal{A}} a_{ij} x_{ij}$$

subject to

$$\sum_{\{j|(i,j)\in\mathcal{A}\}} x_{ij} - \sum_{\{j|(j,i)\in\mathcal{A}\}} x_{ji} = s_i, \qquad \forall\, i \in \mathcal{N}, \tag{3.17}$$

$$0 \le x_{ij}, \qquad \forall\, (i,j) \in \mathcal{A},$$

where

$$s_1 = 1, \qquad s_t = -1$$
$$s_i = 0, \qquad \forall\, i \ne 1, t.$$

The dual problem is (cf. Exercise 2.11 in Section 1.2)

$$\text{maximize } p_1 - p_t$$
$$\text{subject to } p_i - p_j \le a_{ij}, \qquad \forall\, (i,j) \in \mathcal{A}.$$

Let us associate with a given path $P = (1, i_1, i_2, \ldots, i_k)$ the flow

$$x_{ij} = \begin{cases} 1 & \text{if } i \text{ and } j \text{ are successive nodes in } P \\ 0 & \text{otherwise.} \end{cases}$$

Then, the CS conditions (3.1a) and (3.1b) are equivalent to the complementary slackness conditions

$$p_i \leq a_{ij} + p_j, \qquad \forall \, (i, j) \in \mathcal{A},$$

$$p_i = a_{ij} + p_j, \qquad \text{for all } (i, j) \in \mathcal{A} \text{ with } 0 < x_{ij}$$

for the preceding minimum cost flow problem. For a pair (x, p), the above conditions together with primal feasibility [the conservation of flow constraint (3.17) for all $i \in \mathcal{N}$, which in our case translates to the terminal node of the path P being the destination node] are necessary and sufficient for x to be primal-optimal and p to be dual-optimal. Thus, upon termination of the shortest path algorithm, the price vector p is an optimal dual solution.

To interpret the algorithm as a dual ascent method, note that a path contraction and an attendant price increase of the terminal node i of P, corresponds to a step along the price coordinate p_i that leaves the dual cost $p_1 - p_t$ unchanged if $i \neq 1$. Furthermore, an increase of the origin price p_1 by an increment δ improves the dual cost by δ. Thus, the algorithm may be viewed as a dual coordinate ascent algorithm, except that true ascent steps occur only when the origin price increases; all other ascent steps are "degenerate," producing a price increase but no change in dual cost.

The above interpretation can also be visualized in terms of the balls-and-strings model of Fig. 3.4. The dual cost is the vertical distance $p_1 - p_t$ between the balls representing the origin and the destination. In the forward algorithm, the destination stays fixed at its initial position, and this vertical distance increases only at the stages where the origin is raised; these are the 1st, 3rd, and 4th stages in the example of Fig. 3.4. In the forward/reverse version of the algorithm, the vertical distance increases only at the stages where either the origin is raised or the destination is lowered; at all other stages it stays unchanged.

EXERCISES

Exercise 3.1

Apply the forward/reverse algorithm to the example of Fig. 3.5, and show that it terminates in a number of iterations that does not depend on the large arc length L. Construct a related example for which the number of iterations of the forward/reverse algorithm is not polynomially bounded.

Exercise 3.2 (Finding an Initial Price Vector [Ber90])

In order to initialize the shortest path algorithm of this section, one needs a price vector p satisfying the condition

$$p_i \le a_{ij} + p_j, \qquad \forall \, (i,j) \in \mathcal{A}. \tag{3.18}$$

Such a vector may not be available if some arc lengths are negative. Furthermore, even if all arc lengths are nonnegative, there are many cases where it is important to use a favorable initial price vector in place of the default choice $p = 0$. This possibility arises in a reoptimization context with slightly different arc length data, or with a different origin and/or destination. This exercise gives an algorithm to obtain a vector p satisfying the condition (3.18), starting from another vector $\bar{p}$ satisfying the same condition for a different set of arc lengths $\bar{a}_{ij}$.

Suppose that we have a vector $\bar{p}$ and a set of arc lengths $\{\bar{a}_{ij}\}$, satisfying $\bar{p}_i \le \bar{a}_{ij} + \bar{p}_j$ for all arcs (i,j), and we are given a new set of arc lengths $\{a_{ij}\}$. (For the case where some arc lengths a_{ij} are negative, this situation arises with $\bar{p} = 0$ and $\bar{a}_{ij} = \max\{0, a_{ij}\}$.) Consider the following algorithm that maintains a subset of arcs $\mathcal{E}$ and a price vector p, and terminates when $\mathcal{E}$ is empty. Initially

$$\mathcal{E} = \{(i,j) \in \mathcal{A} \mid a_{ij} < \bar{a}_{ij}, \ i \ne t\}, \qquad p = \bar{p}.$$

The typical iteration is as follows:

Step 1 (Select arc to scan): If $\mathcal{E}$ is empty, stop; otherwise, remove an arc (i,j) from $\mathcal{E}$ and go to Step 2.

Step 2 (Add affected arcs to $\mathcal{E}$): If $p_i > a_{ij} + p_j$, set

$$p_i := a_{ij} + p_j$$

and add to $\mathcal{E}$ every arc (k, i) with $k \ne t$ that does not already belong to $\mathcal{E}$.

Assuming that each node i is connected to the destination t with at least one path, and that all cycle lengths are positive, show that the algorithm terminates with a price vector p satisfying

$$p_i \le a_{ij} + p_j, \qquad \forall \, (i,j) \in \mathcal{A} \text{ with } i \ne t.$$

Exercise 3.3 (Extension for the Case of Zero Length Cycles)

Extend the algorithms of this section for the case where all arcs have nonnegative length but some cycles may consist exclusively of zero length arcs. *Hint:* Any cycle of zero length arcs generated by the algorithm can be treated as a single node.

Exercise 3.4

Consider the two single origin/single destination shortest path problems shown in Fig. 3.7.

(a) Show that the number of iterations required by the forward algorithm is estimated accurately by the formula given in Section 4.3.1,

$$n_t - 1 + \sum_{i \in \mathcal{I}, i \neq t} (2n_i - 1),$$

where n_i is the number of nodes in a shortest path from 1 to i. Show also that the corresponding running times are $O(N^2)$.

(b) Show that for the problem of Fig. 3.7(a) the running time of the forward/reverse algorithm (with a suitable "reasonable" rule for switching between the forward and reverse algorithms) is $O(N^2)$ (the number of iterations is roughly half the corresponding number for the forward algorithm). Show also that for the problem of Fig. 3.7(b) the running time of the forward/reverse algorithm is $O(N)$.

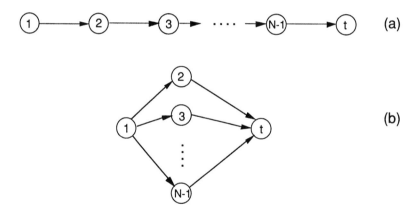

Figure 3.7   Shortest path problems for Exercise 3.4. In problem (a) arc lengths are equal to 1. In problem (b), the length of each arc $(1, i)$ is i, and the length of each arc (i, t) is N.

Exercise 3.5 (A Forward/Reverse Version of Dijkstra's Algorithm)

Consider the single origin/single destination shortest path problem and assume that all arc lengths are nonnegative. Let node 1 be the origin, let node t be the destination, and assume that there exists at least one path from 1 to

t. This exercise provides a forward/reverse version of Dijkstra's algorithm, which is motivated by the balls-and-strings model analogy of Figs. 3.1 and 3.2. In particular, the algorithm may be interpreted as alternately lifting the model upward from the origin (the following Step 1), and pulling the model downward from the destination (the following Step 2).

The algorithm maintains a price vector p and two node subsets W_1 and W_t. Initially, p satisfies the CS condition

$$p_i \le a_{ij} + p_j, \qquad \forall \ (i,j) \in \mathcal{A}, \tag{3.19}$$

$W_1 = \{1\}$, and $W_t = \{t\}$. One may view W_1 and W_t as the sets of permanently labeled nodes from the origin and from the destination, respectively. The algorithm terminates when W_1 and W_t have a node in common. The typical iteration is as follows:

Step 1 (Forward Step): Find

$$\gamma^+ = \min\{a_{ij} + p_j - p_i \mid (i,j) \in \mathcal{A}, \ i \in W_1, \ j \notin W_1\}$$

and let

$$V_1 = \{j \notin W_1 \mid \gamma^+ = a_{ij} + p_j - p_i \text{ for some } i \in W_1\}.$$

Set

$$p_i := \begin{cases} p_i + \gamma^+, & \text{if } i \in W_1 \\ p_i, & \text{if } i \notin W_1. \end{cases}$$

Set

$$W_1 := W_1 \cup V_1.$$

If W_1 and W_t have a node in common, terminate the algorithm; otherwise, go to Step 2.

Step 2 (Backward Step): Find

$$\gamma^- = \min\{a_{ji} + p_i - p_j \mid (j,i) \in \mathcal{A}, \ i \in W_t, \ j \notin W_t\}$$

and let

$$V_t = \{j \notin W_t \mid \gamma^+ = a_{ji} + p_i - p_j \text{ for some } i \in W_t\}.$$

Set

$$p_i := \begin{cases} p_i - \gamma^-, & \text{if } i \in W_t \\ p_i, & \text{if } i \notin W_t. \end{cases}$$

Set

$$W_t := W_t \cup V_t.$$

If W_1 and W_t have a node in common, terminate the algorithm; otherwise, go to Step 1.

(a) Show that throughout the algorithm, the condition (3.19) is maintained. Furthermore, for all $i \in W_1$, $p_1 - p_i$ is equal to the shortest distance from 1 to i. Similarly, for all $i \in W_t$, $p_i - p_t$ is equal to the shortest distance from i to t. *Hint*: Show that if $i \in W_1$, there exists a path from 1 to i such that $p_m = a_{mn} + p_n$ for all arcs (m, n) of the path.

(b) Show that the algorithm terminates and that upon termination, $p_1 - p_t$ is equal to the shortest distance from 1 to t.

(c) Show how the algorithm can be implemented so that its running time is $O(N^2)$. *Hint*: Let d_{mn} denote the shortest distance from m to n. Maintain the labels

$$v_j^+ = \min\{d_{1i} + a_{ij} \mid i \in W_1, \ (i, j) \in \mathcal{A}\}, \qquad \forall \ j \notin W_1,$$

$$v_j^- = \min\{a_{ji} + d_{it} \mid i \in W_t, \ (j, i) \in \mathcal{A}\}, \qquad \forall \ j \notin W_t.$$

Let p_j^0 be the initial price of node j. Show that

$$\gamma^+ = \min\left\{ \min_{j \notin W_1, j \notin W_t} \left(v_j^+ + p_j^0\right), \ p_t + \min_{j \notin W_1, j \in W_t} \left(v_j^+ + d_{jt}\right)\right\} - p_1, \qquad (3.20)$$

$$\gamma^- = \min\left\{ \min_{j \notin W_1, j \notin W_t} \left(v_j^- - p_j^0\right), \ -p_1 + \min_{j \in W_1, j \notin W_t} \left(v_j^- + d_{1j}\right)\right\} + p_t. \qquad (3.21)$$

Use these relations to calculate γ^+ and γ^- in $O(N)$ time.

(d) Show how the algorithm can be implemented using binary heaps so that its running time is $O(A \log N)$. *Hint*: One possibility is to use four heaps to implement the minimizations in Eqs. (3.20) and (3.21).

(e) Apply the two-sided version of Dijkstra's algorithm of Exercise 3.8 of Section 3.1 with arc lengths $a_{ij} + p_j - p_i$ and with the termination criterion of part (c) of that exercise. Show that the resulting algorithm is equivalent to the one of the present exercise.

Exercise 3.6 (A Generalized Auction Algorithm)

Consider the shortest path problem, and assume that all cycles have positive length and that there is at least one path from each node to each other node. Let p be a price vector satisfying the CS condition

$$p_i \leq a_{ij} + p_j, \qquad \forall \ (i, j) \in \mathcal{A} \qquad (3.22)$$

and let d_{mn} be the shortest distance from m to n. For each node m define the *chain of m* to be the subset of nodes

$$T_m(p) = \{m\} \cup \{n \mid p_m - p_n = d_{mn}\}.$$

(a) Show that $n \in T_m(p)$ if and only if either $n = m$ or else for every shortest path P from m to n we have

$$p_i = a_{ij} + p_j, \qquad \text{for all pairs of successive nodes } i \text{ and } j \text{ of } P.$$

Hint: Think in terms of the balls-and-strings model of Fig. 3.1.

(b) Define a *price rise* of node m to be the operation that increases the prices of the nodes in $T_m(p)$ by the increment

$$\gamma = \min\big\{a_{ij} + p_j - p_i \mid (i,j) \in \mathcal{A}, i \in T_m(p), j \notin T_m(p)\big\}.$$

Show that $\gamma > 0$ and that a price rise maintains the CS condition (3.22). Interpret a price rise in terms of the balls-and-strings model of Fig. 3.1.

(c) Let 1 be the origin node and let t be the destination node. Consider an algorithm that starts with a price vector satisfying Eq. (3.22), performs price rises of nodes m such that $t \notin T_m(p)$ (in any order), and terminates when $t \in T_1(p)$. Show that the algorithm terminates and that upon termination, $p_1 - p_t$ is the shortest distance from 1 to t.

(d) Show that the (forward) shortest path algorithm of this section is a special case of the algorithm of part (c).

(e) Adapt the algorithm of part (c) for the all origins/single destination problem, and discuss its potential for parallel computation. *Hint*: Note that if p^1 and p^2 are two price vectors satisfying

$$p_i^1 \le a_{ij} + p_j^1, \qquad p_i^2 \le a_{ij} + p_j^2, \qquad \forall\, (i,j) \in \mathcal{A},$$

then

$$\max\big\{p_i^1, p_i^2\big\} \le a_{ij} + \max\big\{p_j^1, p_j^2\big\}, \qquad \forall\, (i,j) \in \mathcal{A}.$$

(f) Develop an algorithm similar to the one of part (c) but involving price decreases in place of price increases. Develop also an algorithm involving both price increases and price decreases, which contains the forward/reverse algorithm of this section as a special case.

4.4   A GENERIC AUCTION ALGORITHM FOR THE MINIMUM COST FLOW PROBLEM

We will now generalize the auction idea and apply it to the minimum cost flow problem

$$\text{minimize} \quad \sum_{(i,j)\in\mathcal{A}} a_{ij} x_{ij} \qquad\qquad\qquad \text{(MCF)}$$

subject to

$$\sum_{\{j|(i,j)\in\mathcal{A}\}} x_{ij} - \sum_{\{j|(j,i)\in\mathcal{A}\}} x_{ji} = s_i, \qquad \forall\, i \in \mathcal{N}, \qquad (4.1)$$

$$b_{ij} \le x_{ij} \le c_{ij}, \qquad \forall\,(i,j)\in\mathcal{A}, \qquad\qquad (4.2)$$

where a_{ij}, b_{ij}, c_{ij}, and s_i are given integers. For a given flow vector x, the surplus of each node i is denoted by

$$g_i = \sum_{\{j|(j,i)\in\mathcal{A}\}} x_{ji} - \sum_{\{j|(i,j)\in\mathcal{A}\}} x_{ij} + s_i.$$

The algorithm to be described shortly maintains at all times a capacity-feasible flow vector x and a price vector p satisfying the ϵ-CS condition

$$p_i - p_j \le a_{ij} + \epsilon \qquad \text{for all } (i,j)\in\mathcal{A} \text{ with } x_{ij} < c_{ij}, \qquad (4.3a)$$

$$p_i - p_j \ge a_{ij} - \epsilon \qquad \text{for all } (i,j)\in\mathcal{A} \text{ with } b_{ij} < x_{ij}, \qquad (4.3b)$$

(see Fig. 4.1). The usefulness of ϵ-CS is due in large measure to the following proposition.

Proposition 4.1:   If $\epsilon < 1/N$, where N is the number of nodes, x is feasible, and x and p satisfy ϵ-CS, then x is optimal for the minimum cost flow problem (MCF).

Proof: If x is not optimal, then by Prop. 2.1 in Section 1.2, there exists a simple cycle Y that has negative cost, i.e.,

$$\sum_{(i,j)\in Y^+} a_{ij} - \sum_{(i,j)\in Y^-} a_{ij} < 0, \qquad\qquad (4.4)$$

and is unblocked with respect to x, i.e.,

$$x_{ij} < c_{ij}, \qquad \forall\,(i,j)\in Y^+,$$

$$b_{ij} < x_{ij}, \qquad \forall\,(i,j)\in Y^-.$$

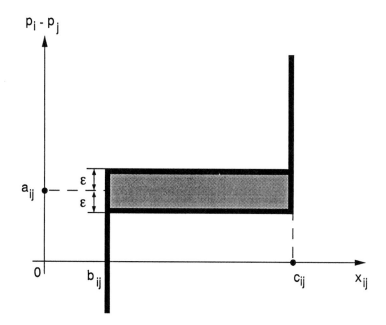

Figure 4.1   Illustration of ϵ-CS. All pairs of arc flows x_{ij} and price differences $p_i - p_j$ should either lie on the thick lines or in the shaded area between the thick lines.

By ϵ-CS [cf. Eq. (4.3)], the preceding relations imply that

$$p_i \leq p_j + a_{ij} + \epsilon, \qquad \forall \ (i, j) \in Y^+,$$

$$p_j \leq p_i - a_{ij} + \epsilon, \qquad \forall \ (i, j) \in Y^-.$$

By adding these relations over all arcs of Y (whose number is no more than N), and by using the hypothesis $\epsilon < 1/N$, we obtain

$$\sum_{(i,j)\in Y^+} a_{ij} - \sum_{(i,j)\in Y^-} a_{ij} \geq -N\epsilon > -1.$$

Since the arc costs a_{ij} are integer, we obtain a contradiction of Eq. (4.4). **Q.E.D.**

Exercises 4.5-4.7 provide various improvements of the tolerance $\epsilon < 1/N$ in some specific contexts.

Some Basic Algorithmic Operations

We now define some terminology and computational operations that can be used as building blocks in various algorithms. Each of these definitions assumes that (x, p) is a flow–price vector pair satisfying ϵ-CS, and will be used only in that context.

Definition 4.1:   An arc (i, j) is said to be ϵ^+-*unblocked* if

$$p_i = p_j + a_{ij} + \epsilon \qquad \text{and} \qquad x_{ij} < c_{ij}. \tag{4.5}$$

An arc (j, i) is said to be ϵ^--*unblocked* if

$$p_i = p_j - a_{ji} + \epsilon \qquad \text{and} \qquad b_{ji} < x_{ji}. \tag{4.6}$$

The *push list* of a node i is the (possibly empty) set of outgoing arcs (i, j) that are ϵ^+- unblocked, and incoming arcs (j, i) that are ϵ^--unblocked.

In the algorithms of this chapter, flow is allowed to increase only along ϵ^+-unblocked arcs and is allowed to decrease only along ϵ^--unblocked arcs. The next two definitions specify the type of flow changes considered.

Definition 4.2:   For an arc (i, j) [or arc (j, i)] of the push list of node i, let δ be a scalar such that $0 < \delta \leq c_{ij} - x_{ij}$ ($0 < \delta \leq x_{ji} - b_{ji}$, respectively). A *$\delta$-push at node i on arc* (i, j) [(j, i), respectively] consists of increasing the flow x_{ij} by δ (decreasing the flow x_{ji} by δ, respectively), while leaving all other flows, as well as the price vector unchanged.

In the context of the auction algorithm, a δ-push (with $\delta = 1$) corresponds to assigning an unassigned person to an object; this results in an increase of the flow on the corresponding arc from 0 to 1. The next operation consists of raising the prices of a subset of nodes by the maximum common increment γ that will not violate ϵ-CS.

Definition 4.3:   A *price rise* of a nonempty, strict subset of nodes I (i.e., $I \neq \emptyset$, $I \neq \mathcal{N}$) consists of leaving the flow vector x and the prices of nodes not belonging to I unchanged, and increasing the prices of the nodes in I by the amount γ given by

$$\gamma = \begin{cases} \min\{S^+, S^-\}, & \text{if } S^+ \cup S^- \neq \emptyset \\ 0, & \text{if } S^+ \cup S^- = \emptyset, \end{cases} \tag{4.7}$$

where S^+ and S^- are the sets of scalars given by

$$S^+ = \{p_j + a_{ij} + \epsilon - p_i \mid (i, j) \in \mathcal{A} \text{ such that } i \in I, j \notin I, x_{ij} < c_{ij}\}, \tag{4.8}$$

$$S^- = \{p_j - a_{ji} + \epsilon - p_i \mid (j, i) \in \mathcal{A} \text{ such that } i \in I, j \notin I, b_{ji} < x_{ji}\}. \tag{4.9}$$

In the case where the subset I consists of a single node i, a price rise of the singleton set $\{i\}$ is also referred to as a *price rise of node i*. If the price increment γ of Eq. (4.7) is positive, the price rise is said to be *substantive*; if $\gamma = 0$, the price rise is said to be *trivial*. (A trivial price rise changes nothing; it is introduced in order to facilitate the statement of some of the algorithms given below.)

Note that every scalar in the sets S^+ and S^- of Eqs. (4.8) and (4.9) is nonnegative by the ϵ-CS conditions (4.3a) and (4.3b), respectively, so we have $\gamma \geq 0$, and we are indeed dealing with price rises.

The generic algorithm to be described shortly consists of a sequence of δ-push and price rise operations. The following proposition lists some properties of these operations that are important in the context of this algorithm.

Proposition 4.2:   Let (x, p) be a flow–price vector pair satisfying ϵ-CS.

(a) The flow–price vector pair obtained after a δ-push or a price rise satisfies ϵ-CS.

(b) Let I be a subset of nodes such that $\sum_{i \in I} g_i > 0$. Then if the sets of scalars S^+ and S^- of Eqs. (4.8) and (4.9) are empty, the problem is infeasible.

Proof: (a) By the definition of ϵ-CS, the flow of an ϵ^+-unblocked and an ϵ^--unblocked arc can have any value within the feasible flow range. Since a δ-push only changes the flow of an ϵ^+-unblocked or ϵ^--unblocked arc, it cannot result in violation of ϵ-CS. Let p and p' be the price vectors before and after a price rise of a set I, respectively. For arcs (i, j) with $i \in I$, and $j \in I$, or with $i \notin I$ and $j \notin I$, the ϵ-CS condition (4.3) is satisfied by (x, p'), since it is satisfied by (x, p) and we have $p_i - p_j = p'_i - p'_j$. For arcs (i, j) with $i \in I$, $j \notin I$ and $x_{ij} < c_{ij}$ we have, using Eqs. (4.7) and (4.8),

$$p'_i - p'_j = p_i - p_j + \gamma \leq p_i - p_j + (p_j + a_{ij} + \epsilon - p_i) = a_{ij} + \epsilon, \qquad (4.10)$$

so the ϵ-CS condition (4.3a) is satisfied. For arcs (j, i) with $i \in I$, $j \notin I$ and $x_{ji} > b_{ji}$ the ϵ-CS condition (4.3b) is similarly satisfied.

(b) Since $S^+ \cup S^-$ is empty,

$$x_{ij} = c_{ij}, \qquad \text{for all } (i, j) \in \mathcal{A} \text{ with } i \in I, j \notin I, \qquad (4.11)$$

$$x_{ji} = b_{ji}, \qquad \text{for all } (j, i) \in \mathcal{A} \text{ with } i \in I, j \notin I. \qquad (4.12)$$

We have

$$0 < \sum_{i \in I} g_i = \sum_{i \in I} s_i - \sum_{\{(i,j) \in \mathcal{A} | i \in I, j \notin I\}} x_{ij} + \sum_{\{(j,i) \in \mathcal{A} | i \in I, j \notin I\}} x_{ji}, \qquad (4.13)$$

and by combining Eqs. (4.11)-(4.13), it follows that

$$0 < \sum_{i \in I} s_i - \sum_{\{(i,j) \in \mathcal{A} | i \in I, j \notin I\}} c_{ij} + \sum_{\{(j,i) \in \mathcal{A} | i \in I, j \notin I\}} b_{ji}.$$

For any feasible vector, the above relation implies that the sum of the divergences of nodes in I exceeds the capacity of the cut $[I, \mathcal{N} - I]$, which is a contradiction. Therefore, the problem is infeasible.   **Q.E.D.**

The Generic Algorithm

Suppose that the minimum cost flow problem (MCF) is feasible, and consider a pair (x, p) satisfying ϵ-CS. Suppose that for some node i we have $g_i > 0$. There are two possibilities:

(a) The push list of i is nonempty, in which case a δ-push at node i is possible.

(b) The push list of i is empty, in which case the set $S^+ \cup S^-$ corresponding to the set $I = \{i\}$ [cf. Eqs. (4.8) and (4.9)] is nonempty, since the problem is feasible [cf. Prop. 4.2(b)]. Therefore, from Eqs. (4.7)-(4.9), a price rise of node i will be substantive.

Thus, *if $g_i > 0$ for some i and the problem is feasible, then either a δ-push or a substantive price rise is possible at node i.*

The preceding observations motivate a method, called *generic algorithm*, which starts with a pair (x, p) satisfying ϵ-CS and performs a sequence of δ-pushes and substantive price rises. The algorithm keeps ϵ at a fixed positive value and terminates when $g_i \leq 0$ for all nodes i.

Typical Iteration of the Generic Algorithm

Perform in sequence and in any order a finite number of δ-pushes and substantive price rises; there should be at least one δ-push but not necessarily at least one price rise. Each δ-push should be performed at some node i with $g_i > 0$, and the flow increment δ must satisfy $\delta \leq g_i$. Furthermore, each price rise should be performed on a set I with $g_i \geq 0$ for all $i \in I$.

The following proposition establishes the validity of the generic algorithm.

Proposition 4.3:   Assume that the minimum cost flow problem (MCF) is feasible. If the increment δ of each δ-push is integer, then the generic algorithm terminates with a pair (x, p) satisfying ϵ-CS. The flow vector x is feasible, and is optimal if $\epsilon < 1/N$.

Proof: We first make the following observations.

(a) The algorithm preserves ϵ-CS; this is a consequence of Prop. 4.2.

(b) The prices of all nodes are monotonically nondecreasing during the algorithm.

(c) Once a node has nonnegative surplus, its surplus stays nonnegative thereafter. The reason is that a δ-push at a node i cannot drive the surplus of i below zero (since $\delta \leq g_i$), and cannot decrease the surplus of neighboring nodes.

(d) If at some time a node has negative surplus, its price must have never been increased up to that time, and must be equal to its initial price. This is a consequence of (c) above and of the assumption that only nodes with nonnegative surplus can be involved in a price rise.

Suppose, to arrive at a contradiction, that the algorithm does not terminate. Then, since there is at least one δ-push per iteration, an infinite number of δ-pushes must be performed at some node i on some arc (i, j). Since for each δ-push, δ is integer, an infinite number of δ-pushes must also be performed at node j on the arc (i, j). This means that arc (i, j) becomes alternately ϵ^+-unblocked with $g_i > 0$ and ϵ^--unblocked with $g_j > 0$ an infinite number of times, which implies that p_i and p_j must increase by amounts of at least 2ϵ an infinite number of times. Thus we have $p_i \to \infty$ and $p_j \to \infty$, while either $g_i > 0$ or $g_j > 0$ at the start of an infinite number of δ-pushes.

Let $\mathcal{N}^\infty$ be the set of nodes whose prices increase to ∞. To preserve ϵ-CS, we must have, after a sufficient number of iterations,

$$x_{ij} = c_{ij} \qquad \text{for all } (i, j) \in \mathcal{A} \text{ with } i \in \mathcal{N}^\infty, j \notin \mathcal{N}^\infty, \qquad (4.14)$$

$$x_{ji} = b_{ji} \qquad \text{for all } (j, i) \in \mathcal{A} \text{ with } i \in \mathcal{N}^\infty, j \notin \mathcal{N}^\infty. \qquad (4.15)$$

After some iteration, by (d) above, every node in $\mathcal{N}^\infty$ must have nonnegative surplus, so the sum of surpluses of the nodes in $\mathcal{N}^\infty$ must be positive at the start of the δ-pushes where either $g_i > 0$ or $g_j > 0$. It follows using the argument of the proof of Prop. 4.2(b) [cf. Eqs. (4.11)-(4.13)] that

$$0 < \sum_{i \in \mathcal{N}^\infty} s_i - \sum_{\{(i,j) \in \mathcal{A} | i \in \mathcal{N}^\infty, j \notin \mathcal{N}^\infty\}} c_{ij} + \sum_{\{(j,i) \in \mathcal{A} | i \in \mathcal{N}^\infty, j \notin \mathcal{N}^\infty\}} b_{ji}.$$

For any feasible vector, the above relation implies that the sum of the divergences of nodes in $\mathcal{N}^\infty$ exceeds the capacity of the cut $[\mathcal{N}^\infty, \mathcal{N} - \mathcal{N}^\infty]$, which is impossible. It follows that there is no feasible flow vector, contradicting the hypothesis. Thus the algorithm must terminate. Since upon ternination we have $g_i \leq 0$ for all i and the problem is assumed feasible, it follows that $g_i = 0$ for all i. Hence the final flow vector x is feasible and by (a) above it

satisfies ϵ-CS together with the final p. By Prop. 4.1, if $\epsilon < 1/N$, x is optimal.
Q.E.D.

The example of Fig. 4.2 shows how the generic algorithm may never terminate even for a feasible problem, if we do not require that it performs at least one δ-push per iteration.

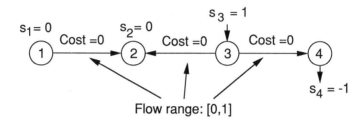

Flow range: [0,1]

Figure 4.2   Example of a feasible problem where the generic algorithm does not terminate, if it does not perform at least one δ-push per iteration. Initially, all flows and prices are zero. Here, the first iteration raises the price of node 1 by ϵ. Subsequent iterations consist of a price rise of node 2 by an increment of 2ϵ followed by a price rise of node 1 by an increment of 2ϵ.

Consider now what happens when the problem is infeasible. Let us assume that the generic algorithm is operated so that for each δ-push, δ is integer. Then either the algorithm will terminate with $g_i \leq 0$ for all i and $g_i < 0$ for at least one i, in which case infeasibility will be detected, or else it will perform an infinite number of iterations and, consequently, an infinite number of δ-pushes. In the latter case, from the proof of Prop. 4.3 it can be seen that the prices of the nodes involved in an infinite number of δ-pushes will diverge to infinity. This, together with a bound on the total price change of a node given in Exercise 4.9, can be used to detect infeasibility. It may also be possible to detect infeasibility by discovering in the course of the algorithm a subset of nodes I such that $\sum_{i \in I} g_i > 0$, and the sets of scalars S^+ and S^- of Eqs. (4.8) and (4.9) are empty [cf. Prop. 4.2(b)]. There is no guarantee, however, that such a set will be encountered during the algorithm's execution.

The generic algorithm can be applied in different ways to a variety of problems with special structure, yielding a variety of specific algorithms. In particular, it yields as a special case the auction algorithm for the symmetric assignment problem (see Exercise 4.1). The next section discusses an algorithm for the general minimum cost flow problem. We give here an example for an important class of transportation problems. Several related possibilities are explored in Exercises 4.1-4.4.

Example 4.1. Transportation Problems with Unit Sources

Consider a transportation problem where all the sources have unit supply. It has the form

$$\text{minimize} \quad \sum_{(i,j)\in\mathcal{A}} a_{ij}x_{ij}$$

subject to

$$\sum_{\{j|(i,j)\in\mathcal{A}\}} x_{ij} = 1, \quad \forall\, i = 1,\ldots,m,$$

$$\sum_{\{i|(i,j)\in\mathcal{A}\}} x_{ij} = \beta_j, \quad \forall\, j = 1,\ldots,n,$$

$$0 \le x_{ij} \le 1, \quad \forall\, (i,j)\in\mathcal{A}.$$

Here a_{ij} are integers, and β_j are positive integers satisfying $\sum_{j=1}^{n}\beta_j = m$.

The following algorithm is a special case of the generic algorithm. (With a little thought it can also be seen to be equivalent to the auction algorithm with similar objects, given in Exercise 4.2.) At the start of each iteration, we have a pair (x,p) satisfying ϵ-CS and also the following two properties:

(a) $x_{ij} = 0$ or $x_{ij} = 1$ for all arcs (i,j).

(b) $g_i = 0$ or $g_i = 1$ for all sources i, and $g_j \le 0$ for all sinks j.

During the typical iteration, we do the following.

Step 1: Select a source i with $g_i = 1$ and an arc (i,j_i) with $p_{j_i} + a_{ij_i} = \min_{(i,j)\in\mathcal{A}}\{p_j + a_{ij}\}$.

Step 2: Perform a price rise of i (to the level $p_{j_i} + a_{ij_i} + \epsilon$), then a 1-push operation at node i along the arc (i,j_i), then another price rise of i (to the level $\min_{(i,j)\in\mathcal{A},\, j\neq j_i}\{p_j + a_{ij}\} + \epsilon$).

Step 3: Let m_i be such that

$$m_i = \arg\min_{\{m|(m,j_i)\in\mathcal{A},\, x_{mj_i}=1\}}\{p_m - a_{mj_i}\},$$

perform a price rise of j_i (to the level $p_{m_i} - a_{m_ij_i} + \epsilon$); if $g_{j_i} = 1$ (after the 1-push operation of Step 2) perform a 1-push operation at node j_i along arc (m_i, j_i), and then perform a price rise of j_i.

It can be seen that the properties (a) and (b) mentioned above, as well as ϵ-CS, are preserved by the iteration. Furthermore, each iteration qualifies as an iteration of the generic algorithm, because a finite number of 1-pushes and price rises are performed, while at least one 1-push is performed. Therefore, Prop. 4.3 applies and asserts termination, if the problem is feasible. The flow vector obtained upon termination will be optimal if $\epsilon < 1/(m+n)$. (Actually, for optimality it is sufficient that $\epsilon < 1/2n$; see Exercise 4.6.)

It is possible to derive auction algorithms for other types of transportation problems similar to the one just given. For example, a generalization for the case where the supplies of the sources can be greater than 1 is given in Exercise 4.8. Other generalizations, based on the reverse auction ideas of Section 4.2, can be used to solve various transportation problems involving inequality constraints. Finally, algorithms for problems with unit sinks are possible (see [BeC90a] and Exercise 4.3), as well as algorithms for the general transportation problem (see [BeC90a] and Exercise 4.4).

EXERCISES

Exercise 4.1 (Relation to the Auction Algorithm for Assignment)

Describe how the auction algorithm for the symmetric assignment problem is a special case of the generic algorithm of this section. *Hint:* Introduce a price variable for each person. Show that a bid by a person i can be described as a price rise of i, followed by a 1-push operation along the arc (i, j) corresponding to the person's preferred object j, followed by another price rise of i, followed by a 1-push operation along arc (i', j) (if j is already assigned to i'), followed by a price rise of j.

Exercise 4.2 (Auction Algorithm with Similar Objects [BeC89a])

Given a symmetric assignment problem, we say that two objects j and j' are *similar*, and write $j \sim j'$, if for all persons $i = 1, \ldots, n$ we have

$$j \in A(i) \quad \Rightarrow \quad j' \in A(i) \quad \text{and} \quad a_{ij} = a_{ij'}.$$

For each object j, the set of all objects similar to j is called the *similarity class* of j and is denoted $M(j)$. Consider a variation of the auction algorithm that is the same as the one of Section 4.1 except for one difference: in the bidding phase, w_i is defined now as

$$w_i = \max_{j \in A(i), j \notin M(j_i)} \{a_{ij} - p_j\}$$

(instead of $w_i = \max_{j \in A(i), j \neq j_i} \{a_{ij} - p_j\}$).

(a) Show that if the initial assignment S satisfies ϵ-CS together with the initial vector $\hat{p}$ defined by

$$\hat{p}_j = \min_{k \in M(j)} p_k, \qquad j = 1, \ldots, n,$$

that is,

$$a_{ij} - \hat{p}_j \geq \max_{k \in A(i)} \{a_{ik} - \hat{p}_k\} - \epsilon, \qquad \forall\, (i,j) \in S,$$

the same is true of the assignment and the vector $\hat{p}$ obtained at the end of each assignment phase.

(b) Show also that the algorithm is equivalent to the algorithm of Example 4.1, and that for integer problem data it terminates with an optimal assignment if $\epsilon < 1/n$. (Actually, it is sufficient that $\epsilon < 1/m$, where m is the number of similarity classes, but proving this requires an argument of the type given in the proof of Prop. 4.1; see also the subsequent Exercise 4.6.)

Exercise 4.3

Derive an algorithm similar to the one of Example 4.1 for the transportation problem, where all sinks have unit demand. *Hint:* At the start of each iteration we must have $x_{ij} = 0$ or $x_{ij} = 1$ for all arcs (i,j), $g_i \geq 0$ for all sources i, and $g_j = 0$ or $g_j = -1$ for all sinks j.

Exercise 4.4 (Auction for Transportation Problems [BeC89a])

Consider the symmetric assignment problem. We say that two persons i and i' are *similar*, and write $i \sim i'$, if for all objects $j = 1, \ldots, N$ we have

$$j \in A(i) \quad \Rightarrow \quad j \in A(i') \quad \text{and} \quad a_{ij} = a_{i'j}.$$

The set of all persons similar to i is called the similarity class of i.

(a) Generalize the auction algorithm with similar objects given in Exercise 4.2 so that it takes into account both similar persons and similar objects. *Hint:* Consider simultaneous bids by all persons in the same similarity class.

(b) Show how the algorithm of part (a) can be applied to transportation problems.

Exercise 4.5 (Improved Optimality Condition [BeE87b])

Show that if x is feasible, and x and p satisfy ϵ-CS, then x is optimal for the minimum cost flow problem, provided

$$\epsilon < \min_{\text{All simple cycles } Y} \left\{ -\frac{\text{Cost of } Y}{\text{Number of arcs of } Y} \,\middle|\, \text{Cost of } Y < 0 \right\},$$

where

$$\text{Cost of } Y = \sum_{(i,j) \in Y^+} a_{ij} - \sum_{(i,j) \in Y^-} a_{ij}.$$

Show that this is true even if the problem data are not integer.

Exercise 4.6 (Termination Tolerance for Transportation Problems)

Consider a transportation problem with m sources and n sinks and integer data. Show that in order for a feasible x to be optimal it is sufficient that it satisfies ϵ-CS together with some p and

$$\epsilon < \frac{1}{2\min\{m,n\}}$$

[instead of $\epsilon < 1/(m+n)$]. *Hint*: Modify the proof of Prop. 4.1 or use the result of Exercise 4.5.

Exercise 4.7 (Termination Tolerance for Multiassignment)

Consider the multiassignment problem of Section 4.2.2, and assume that the problem data are integer. Show that in order for the modified reverse auction algorithm to yield an optimal multiassignment it is sufficient that $\epsilon < 1/m$ (instead of $\epsilon < 1/n$). *Hint*: Observe the similarity with Exercises 4.5 and 4.6.

Exercise 4.8 (Auction for Capacitated Transportation Problems)

Consider the transportation problem

$$\text{minimize} \quad \sum_{(i,j) \in \mathcal{A}} a_{ij} x_{ij}$$

subject to

$$\sum_{\{j | (i,j) \in \mathcal{A}\}} x_{ij} = \alpha_i, \qquad \forall\, i = 1, \ldots, m,$$

$$\sum_{\{i | (i,j) \in \mathcal{A}\}} x_{ij} = \beta_j, \qquad \forall\, j = 1, \ldots, n,$$

$$0 \le x_{ij} \le 1, \qquad \forall\, (i,j) \in \mathcal{A},$$

where the problem data are all integer, and $\alpha_i > 0$, $\beta_j > 0$ for all i and j, respectively. The following algorithm starts with a flow–price vector pair (x, p) such that ϵ-CS is satisfied, each x_{ij} is either 0 or 1, and

$$\sum_{\{j | (i,j) \in \mathcal{A}\}} x_{ij} \le \alpha_i, \qquad \forall\, i,$$

$$\sum_{\{i|(i,j)\in\mathcal{A}\}} x_{ij} \le \beta_j, \qquad \forall\ j.$$

In the typical iteration, we select a source i with $\sum_{\{j|(i,j)\in\mathcal{A}\}} x_{ij} < \alpha_i$ (if no such source can be found the algorithm terminates). Then, we find

$$\hat{p}_i = \min\{z \mid \text{the number of sinks } j \text{ with } z \ge a_{ij} + p_j + \epsilon \text{ is greater than } \alpha_i\},$$

$$\tilde{p}_i = \min\{z \mid \text{the number of sinks } j \text{ with } z \ge a_{ij} + p_j + \epsilon \text{ is no less than } \alpha_i\}.$$

We also consider sinks j with $x_{ij} = 0$ and $\tilde{p}_i \ge a_{ij} + p_j + \epsilon$, and we find a subset T, which consists of $\alpha_i - \sum_{\{j|(i,j)\in\mathcal{A}\}} x_{ij}$ such sinks and includes all sinks j with $\tilde{p}_i > a_{ij} + p_j + \epsilon$. We then set $p_i = \hat{p}_i$ and $x_{ij} = 1$ for all $j \in T$. After these changes, for each $j \in T$ with $\sum_{\{k|(k,j)\in\mathcal{A}\}} x_{kj} \ge \beta_j$, we find

$$\tilde{p}_j = \min_{\{k|x_{kj}=1\}} \{p_k - a_{kj} + \epsilon\},$$

and a source $\tilde{k}$ that attains the above minimum. If $\sum_{\{k|(k,j)\in\mathcal{A}\}} x_{kj} = \beta_j$, we set $p_j = \tilde{p}_j$; otherwise, we also find

$$\hat{p}_j = \min_{\{k|x_{kj}=1, k\ne\tilde{k}\}} \{p_k - a_{kj} + \epsilon\},$$

and we set $p_j = \hat{p}_j$ and $x_{\tilde{k}j} = 0$.

(a) Show that the algorithm is a special case of the generic algorithm, and for a feasible problem, it terminates with a pair (x, p) satisfying ϵ-CS. Show also that when $\alpha_i = 1$ and $\beta_j = 1$ for all i and j, respectively, the algorithm reduces to the (forward) auction algorithm for symmetric assignment problems.

(b) Derive a reverse and a combined forward/reverse version of the algorithm.

(c) Consider an asymmetric version of the problem where the equality constraints $\sum_{\{i|(i,j)\in\mathcal{A}\}} x_{ij} = \beta_j$ are replaced by the inequality constraints

$$\sum_{\{i|(i,j)\in\mathcal{A}\}} x_{ij} \le \beta_j.$$

Derive a forward/reverse auction algorithm along the lines of the asymmetric assignment algorithm of Section 4.2.

Exercise 4.9 (Dealing with Infeasibility)

Consider the generic algorithm applied to a feasible minimum cost flow problem with initial prices p_i^0.

(a) Show that the total price increase $(p_i - p_i^0)$ of any node i prior to termination of the algorithm satisfies

$$p_i - p_i^0 \leq (N-1)(C+\epsilon) + \max_{j \in \mathcal{N}} p_j^0 - \min_{j \in \mathcal{N}} p_j^0,$$

where $C = \max_{(i,j) \in \mathcal{A}} |a_{ij}|$. *Hint:* Let x^0 be a feasible flow vector and let (x, p) be the flow–price vector pair generated by the algorithm prior to its termination. Show that there exist nodes t and s such that $g_t > 0$ and $g_s < 0$, and a simple path H starting at s and ending at t such that $x_{ij} - x_{ij}^0 > 0$ for all $(i,j) \in H^+$ and $x_{ij} - x_{ij}^0 < 0$ for all $(i,j) \in H^-$. Now use ϵ-CS to assert that

$$p_j + a_{ij} \leq p_i + \epsilon, \qquad \forall \, (i,j) \in H^+,$$

$$p_i \leq p_j + a_{ij} + \epsilon, \qquad \forall \, (i,j) \in H^-.$$

Add these conditions along H to obtain

$$p_t - p_s \leq (N-1)(C+\epsilon).$$

Use the fact $p_s = p_s^0$ to conclude that

$$p_t - p_t^0 \leq (N-1)(C+\epsilon) + p_s - p_s^0 \leq (N-1)(C+\epsilon) + \max_{j \in \mathcal{N}} p_j^0 - \min_{j \in \mathcal{N}} p_j^0.$$

(b) Discuss how the result of part (a) can be used to detect infeasibility.

(c) Suppose we introduce some artificial arcs to guarantee that the problem is feasible. Discuss how to select the cost coefficients of the artificial arcs so that optimal solutions are not affected in the case where the original problem is feasible; cf. Exercise 1.6 in Section 4.1.

Exercise 4.10 (Suboptimality of a Feasible Flow Satisfying ϵ-CS)

Let x^* be an optimal flow vector for the minimum cost flow problem and let x be a feasible flow vector satisfying ϵ-CS together with a price vector p.

(a) Show that the cost of x is within $\epsilon \sum_{(i,j) \in \mathcal{A}} |x_{ij} - x_{ij}^*|$ from the optimal. *Hint:* Show that $(x - x^*)$ satisfies CS together with p for a minimum cost flow problem with arcs (i,j) having flow range $[b_{ij} - x_{ij}^*, c_{ij} - x_{ij}^*]$ and arc cost $\hat{a}_{ij}$ that differs from a_{ij} by no more than ϵ.

(b) Show by example that the suboptimality bound $\epsilon \sum_{(i,j) \in \mathcal{A}} |c_{ij} - b_{ij}|$ deduced from part (a) is tight. *Hint:* Consider a graph with two nodes and multiple arcs connecting these nodes. All the arcs have cost ϵ except for one that has cost $-\epsilon$.

4.5   THE ϵ-RELAXATION METHOD

We now describe the ϵ-relaxation method, which is a special case of the generic algorithm of the previous section, where, at each iteration, all δ-pushes and price rises involve a single node. The ϵ-relaxation method may also be viewed as a mathematically equivalent method to the auction algorithm for the assignment problem of Section 4.1. Indeed the auction algorithm can be obtained as a special case of ϵ-relaxation (see Exercise 5.3). Conversely, we can convert the minimum cost flow problem to a transportation problem (see Example 1.3 in Section 1.1), and then convert the latter problem to an assignment problem (by creating enough duplicate persons and objects). The reader can verify that when the auction algorithm is applied to this assignment problem, and the computation is appropriately streamlined, one obtains the ϵ-relaxation method.

We assume that the problem is feasible. In practice, the method could be supplemented with additional mechanisms to detect infeasibility, as discussed in the preceding section (see also Exercise 4.9).

We use a fixed positive value of ϵ, and we start with a pair (x, p) satisfying ϵ-CS. Furthermore, the starting arc flows are integer, and it will be seen that the integrality of the arc flows is preserved thanks to the integrality of the node supplies and the arc flow bounds. (Implementations that have good worst case complexity also require that all initial arc flows be at either their upper or their lower bound; see e.g. [BeT89]. This can be easily enforced, although it does not seem to be very important in practice.)

At the start of a typical iteration we have a flow–price vector pair (x, p) satisfying ϵ-CS and we select a node i with $g_i > 0$; if no such node can be found, the algorithm terminates. During the iteration we perform several δ-push and price rise operations of the type described in the previous section involving node i.

Typical Iteration of the ϵ-Relaxation Method

Step 1: If the push list of node i is empty, go to Step 3; else select an arc a from the push list of i and go to Step 2.

Step 2: Let j be the end-node of arc a, which is opposite to i. Let

$$\delta = \begin{cases} \min\{g_i, c_{ij} - x_{ij}\} & \text{if } a = (i, j) \\ \min\{g_i, x_{ji} - b_{ji}\} & \text{if } a = (j, i). \end{cases} \tag{5.1}$$

Perform a δ-push of i on arc a. If as a result of this operation we obtain $g_i = 0$, go to Step 3; else go to Step 1.

Step 3: Perform a price rise of node i. If $g_i = 0$, go to the next iteration; else go to Step 1.

Some insight into the ϵ-relaxation iteration can be obtained by noting that in the limit as $\epsilon \to 0$ it yields the single node relaxation iteration of Section 3.3. Figure 5.1 illustrates the sequence of price rises in an ϵ-relaxation iteration; this figure should be compared with the corresponding Fig. 3.2 in Section 3.3 for the single node relaxation iteration. As Fig. 5.1 illustrates, the ϵ-relaxation iteration can be interpreted as an approximate coordinate ascent or Gauss-Seidel relaxation iteration. This interpretation parallels the approximate coordinate descent interpretation of the mathematically equivalent auction algorithm, cf. Fig. 1.1 in Section 4.1.

We now establish the validity of the ϵ-relaxation method by using the analysis of the preceding section. In particular, we claim that the above iteration consists of a finite (but positive) number of δ-pushes with δ integer, and a finite (possibly zero) number of price rises at nodes with nonnegative surplus. Indeed, since the starting arc flows, the node supplies, and the arc flow bounds are integer, the flow increments δ of all δ-pushes will be positive integers throughout the algorithm. Furthermore, from Eq. (5.1) it is seen that the condition $\delta \leq g_i$ of the generic algorithm is satisfied. We also note that at most one δ-push per incident arc of node i is performed at each iteration because from Eq. (5.1) it is seen that a δ-push on arc a in Step 2 either sets the arc flow to the corresponding flow bound, which causes arc a to drop out of the push list of i through the end of the iteration, or else results in $g_i = 0$, which leads the iteration to branch to Step 3 and subsequently stop. Therefore, the number of δ-pushes per iteration is finite. In addition we have $g_i > 0$ at the start and $g_i = 0$ at the end of an iteration, so at least one δ-push must occur before an iteration can stop.

Regarding price rises, it is seen that Step 3 can be reached under two conditions:

(a) The push list of i is empty and $g_i > 0$, in which case the price rise in Step 3 will be substantive [in view of the assumption that the problem is feasible and Prop. 4.2(b)], and the iteration will branch to Step 1 with the push list of i having at least one new arc, or

(b) $g_i = 0$, in which case the iteration will stop after a (possibly trivial) price rise in Step 3.

Thus, all price rises involve a node with nonnegative surplus as required in the generic algorithm. Since after each substantive price rise with $g_i > 0$ at least one δ-push must be performed, it follows that the number of substantive price rises per iteration is finite.

From the preceding observations it is seen that, if the problem is feasible, the ϵ-relaxation method is a special case of the generic algorithm and satisfies the assumptions of Prop. 4.3. Therefore, it must terminate with a feasible flow vector, which is optimal if $\epsilon < 1/N$.

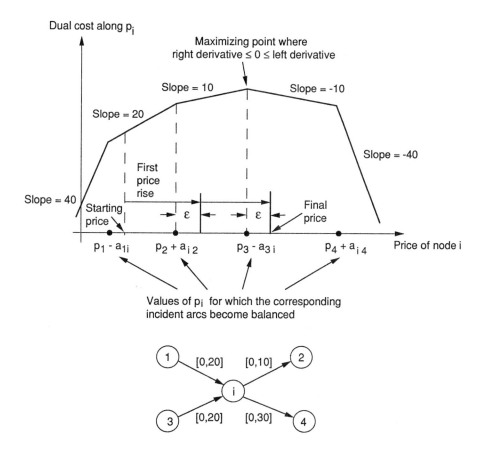

Figure 5.1   Illustration of the price rises of the ϵ-relaxation iteration. Here, node i has four incident arcs $(1, i)$, $(3, i)$, $(i, 2)$, and $(i, 4)$ with flow ranges $[0, 20]$, $[0, 20]$, $[0, 10]$, and $[0, 30]$, respectively, and supply $s_i = 0$. The arc costs and current prices are such that

$$p_1 - a_{1i} \leq p_2 + a_{i2} \leq p_3 - a_{3i} \leq p_4 + a_{i4},$$

as shown in the figure. The break points of the dual cost along the price p_i correspond to the values of p_i at which one or more incident arcs to node i become balanced. For values between two successive break points, there are no balanced arcs. Each price rise of the ϵ-relaxation iteration increases p_i to the point which is ϵ to the right of the next break point larger than p_i, (assuming that the starting price of node i is to the left of the maximizing point by more than ϵ). In the example of the figure, there are two price rises, the second of which sets p_i at the point which is ϵ to the right of the maximizing point, leading to the approximate (within ϵ) coordinate ascent interpretation.

Scaling

The ϵ-relaxation method, with the use of some fairly simple data structures (the so called sweep implementation), but without the use of scaling, can be shown to have an

$$O\big(N^3 + N^2L/\epsilon\big) \tag{5.2}$$

worst-case running time, where L is the maximum over the lengths of all simple paths, with the length of each arc (i,j) being the absolute reduced cost value $|p_j + a_{ij} - p_i|$, and p being the initial price vector. (The sweep implementation together with the above estimate were first given in [Ber86a]; see [BeE88] and [BeT89] for a detailed description and analysis.) Thus, the amount of work to solve the problem can depend strongly on the values of ϵ and L.

The ϵ-scaling technique discussed for the auction algorithm in Section 5.1 is also important in the context of the ϵ-relaxation method, and improves both the practical and the theoretical worst-case performance of the method. Although ϵ-scaling was first proposed in [Ber79] in connection with the auction algorithm, its first analysis was given in [Gol87] and [GoT90]. These references provided an $O\big(NA\log(N)\log(NC)\big)$ running time estimate for a scaled version of ϵ-relaxation that uses some complicated data structures called *dynamic trees*. By using ϵ-scaling and the sweep implementation referred to earlier, the worst-case running time of the algorithm for integer data can be shown to be $O\big(N^3\log(NC)\big)$, where $C = \max_{(i,j)\in\mathcal{A}}|a_{ij}|$; see [BeE87b], [BeE88], [BeT89]. These references actually analyze an alternative form of scaling, known as *cost scaling*, which is based on successively representing the cost coefficients by an increasing number of bits. Cost scaling and ϵ-scaling admit a very similar complexity analysis. Their practical performance is roughly comparable, although ϵ-scaling is somewhat easier to implement. For this reason, ϵ-scaling was used in the codes of Appendix A.4 and Appendix A.7.

Surplus Scaling

When applying the ϵ-scaling technique, except for the last scaling phase, it is not essential to reduce the surpluses of all nodes to zero; it is possible to terminate a scaling phase prematurely, and reduce ϵ further, in an effort to economize on computation. A technique that is typically quite effective is to iterate only with nodes whose surplus exceeds some threshold, which is gradually reduced to zero with each scaling phase. The threshold is usually set by some heuristic scheme.

Negative Surplus Node Iterations

It is possible to define a symmetric form of the ϵ-relaxation iteration that starts from a node with negative surplus and decreases (rather than increases) the price of that node. Furthermore, one can mix positive surplus and negative surplus iterations in the same algorithm; this is analogous to the combined forward/reverse auction algorithm for assignment and the forward/reverse auction algorithm for shortest paths. However, if the two types of iterations are mixed arbitrarily, the algorithm is not guaranteed to terminate even for a feasible problem; for an example, see [BeT89], p. 373. For this reason, some care must be exercised in mixing the two types of iterations in order to guarantee that the algorithm eventually makes progress.

Application to the Max-Flow Problem

The ϵ-relaxation method can be applied to the max-flow problem, once this problem is converted to the minimum cost flow format, involving a feedback arc connecting the sink with the source, and having cost -1 (see Example 1.2 in Section 1.2). Since all other arc costs are zero, the maximum path length L used in Eq. (5.2) is equal to 1, assuming a zero initial price vector. Therefore, the complexity estimate of Eq. (5.2) becomes

$$O\big(N^3 + N^2/\epsilon\big). \tag{5.3}$$

One can solve the problem without using scaling by taking $\epsilon = 1/(N+1)$, so in this case the preceding estimate yields an $O(N^3)$ worst-case running time. With the use of more sophisticated data structures, this running time can be considerably improved; see the references at the end of the chapter.

In practice, the ϵ-relaxation method initialized with zero flow and zero price vectors often finds a minimum cut very quickly. It may then work quite a bit more to set the remaining positive surpluses to zero. Thus, if one is interested in just a minimum cut or just the value of the maximum flow, it is worth testing periodically to see whether a minimum cut can be determined before the algorithm terminates. A method for detecting whether a minimum cut has been found is outlined in Exercise 5.4 and is used in the code of Appendix A.6. Given a minimum cut, one may find a maximum flow by continuing the algorithm until all node surpluses are zero, or by employing a version of the Ford-Fulkerson algorithm to return the positive surpluses to the source (see Exercise 5.4).

E X E R C I S E S

Exercise 5.1

Apply the ϵ-relaxation method to the problem of Fig. 2.3 of Section 3.2 with $\epsilon = 1$. Comment on the optimality of the solution obtained.

Exercise 5.2 (Degenerate Price Rises)

In this exercise, we consider a variation of the ϵ-relaxation method that involves *degenerate price rises*. A degenerate price rise changes the price of a node that currently has zero surplus to the maximum possible value that does not violate ϵ-CS with respect to the current flow vector (compare with degenerate price increases in the context of the single-node relaxation iteration where $\epsilon = 0$, as illustrated in Fig. 3.3 of Section 3.3). One example of such a price rise occurs when Step 3 of the ϵ-relaxation iteration is executed with $g_i = 0$.

Consider a variation of the ϵ-relaxation method where there are two types of iterations: (1) *regular* iterations, which are of the form described in the present section, and (2) *degenerate* iterations, which consist of a single degenerate price rise.

(a) Show that if the problem is feasible and the number of degenerate iterations is bounded by a constant times the number of regular iterations, then the method terminates with a pair (x, p) satisfying ϵ-CS.

(b) Show that the assumption of part (a) is essential for the validity of the method. *Hint*: Consider the example of Fig. 4.2.

Exercise 5.3 (Deriving Auction from ϵ-Relaxation)

Consider the assignment problem formulated as a minimum cost flow problem (see Example 1.1 in Section 1.1). We say that source i is assigned to sink j if (i, j) has positive flow. We consider a version of the ϵ–relaxation algorithm in which ϵ-relaxation iterations are organized as follows: between iterations (and also at initialization), only source nodes i can have positive surplus. Each iteration finds any unassigned source i (i.e., one with positive surplus), and performs an ϵ-relaxation iteration at i, and then takes the sink j to which i was consequently assigned and performs an ϵ-relaxation iteration at j, even if j has zero surplus. (If j has zero surplus, such an iteration will consist of just a degenerate price rise; see Exercise 5.2.)

More specifically, an iteration by an unassigned source i works as follows:

(1) Source node i sets its price to $p_j + a_{ij} + \epsilon$, where j minimizes $p_k + a_{ik} + \epsilon$ over all k for which $(i, k) \in \mathcal{A}$. It then sets $x_{ij} = 1$, assigning itself to j.

(2) Node i then raises its price to $p_{j'} + a_{ij'} + \epsilon$, where j' minimizes $p_k + a_{ik} + \epsilon$ for $k \neq j$, $(i, k) \in \mathcal{A}$.

(3) If sink j had a previous assignment $x_{i'j} = 1$, it breaks the assignment by setting $x_{i'j} := 0$. (One can show inductively that if this occurs, $p_j = p_{i'} - a_{i'j} + \epsilon$.)

(4) Sink j then raises its price p_j to

$$p_i - a_{ij} + \epsilon = p_{j'} + a_{ij'} - a_{ij} + 2\epsilon.$$

Show that the corresponding algorithm is equivalent to the Gauss-Seidel version of the auction algorithm.

Exercise 5.4 (Detecting a Minimum Cut Using ϵ-Relaxation)

Consider the max-flow problem with zero lower arc flow bounds. Suppose that we have a pair (x, p) satisfying the 1-CS condition

$$p_i - p_j \leq 1 \qquad \text{for all } (i, j) \in \mathcal{A} \text{ with } x_{ij} < c_{ij},$$

$$p_i - p_j \geq -1 \qquad \text{for all } (i, j) \in \mathcal{A} \text{ with } 0 < x_{ij},$$

$$p_s = p_t + N + 2.$$

[These are the 1-CS conditions for the equivalent minimum cost flow problem obtained by introducing an artificial arc (t, s) with cost $-(N + 1)$.] Suppose also that we have a cut $Q = [\mathcal{S}, \mathcal{N} - \mathcal{S}]$ with $s \in \mathcal{S}$ and $t \notin \mathcal{S}$, which is saturated with respect to x. Finally, suppose that the surplus of all nodes in $\mathcal{S}$ except s is nonnegative, while the surplus of all nodes in $\mathcal{N} - \mathcal{S}$ except t is nonpositive.

(a) Show that Q is a minimum cut. *Hint*: Apply the ϵ-relaxation method with $\epsilon = 1$ starting with (x, p). Argue that the flux across Q will not change.

(b) Given Q, show that a maximum flow can be found by solving two feasibility problems (which are in turn equivalent to some other max-flow problems; cf. Exercise 2.5 in Section 1.2). One feasibility problem should involve just the nodes of $\mathcal{S}$ and the other should involve just the nodes not in $\mathcal{S}$.

(c) Construct algorithms based on augmentations that solve the feasibility problems in part (b), thereby yielding a maximum flow.

4.6   IMPLEMENTATION ISSUES

The main operations of auction algorithms involve scanning the incident arcs of nodes; this is a shared feature with dual ascent methods. For this reason the data structures and implementation ideas discussed in connection with dual ascent methods, also apply to auction algorithms. In particular, for the max-flow and the minimum cost flow problems, using the *FIRST_IN*, *FIRST_OUT*, *NEXT_IN*, and *NEXT_OUT* arrays, described in Section 3.5, is convenient. In addition, a similar set of arrays can be used to store the arcs of the push lists in the ϵ-relaxation method; see the code given in Appendix A.7.

4.7   NOTES AND SOURCES

4.1. The auction algorithm, and the notions of ϵ-complementary slackness and ϵ-scaling were first proposed by the author in [Ber79] (see also [Ber85] and [Ber88]). Reference [BeE88] surveys coordinate step methods based on ϵ-complementary slackness and derives the worst-case complexity of the auction algorithm; see also [BeT89]. The parallel implementation aspects of the auction algorithm have been explored by several authors; see [BeC89c], [KKZ89], [PhZ88], [WeZ90], and [Zak90]. Exercise 1.3 that deals with the average complexity of the auction algorithm was inspired by [Sch90], which derives related results for the Jacobi version of the algorithm and its potential for parallelism.

4.2. The reverse auction algorithm and its application in inequality constrained assignment problems is due to [BCT91], which discusses additional related algorithms and gives computational results. Note that aside from faster convergence, the combined forward/reverse algorithm has potential for greater concurrency in a parallel machine than the forward algorithm.

4.3. The auction algorithm for shortest paths is due to the author [Ber90]. This reference also discusses an arc length scaling technique that can be used to make the algorithm polynomial. In practice, this scaling technique does not seem to be very useful, primarily because pseudopolynomial practical behavior appears to be unlikely, particularly for the forward/reverse version of the algorithm. The MS thesis [Pol91] discusses the parallelization aspects of the method. The interpretation of the forward/reverse version of Dijkstra's algorithm of Exercise 3.5 and the generalized auction algorithm of Exercise 3.6 are new.

4.4. The generic auction algorithm for minimum cost flow problems is due to [BeC89b]. Reference [BeC89a] describes various special cases involving bipartite graphs; see also Exercises 4.2 and 4.4.

4.5. The ϵ-relaxation method is due to the author; it was first published in [Ber86a] and [Ber86b], although it was known much earlier (since the development of the equivalent auction algorithm). Various implementations of the method aimed at improved worst-case complexity can be found in [BeE87b], [BeE88], [BeT89], [Gol87], and [GoT90]. The worst-case complexity of ϵ-

scaling was first analyzed in [Gol87] in connection with various implementations of the ϵ-relaxation method. Computational experience suggests, however, that the complexity analysis of the ϵ-relaxation method is not very useful in predicting practical behavior. In particular, despite its excellent polynomial complexity, the method is typically outperformed by the relaxation method of the previous chapter, which can be shown to have pseudopolynomial complexity. However, the ϵ-relaxation method is better suited for parallel computation than the other minimum cost flow methods described in this book; see [BeT89] for a discussion of related issues.

When the ϵ-relaxation method is applied to the max-flow problem, it bears a close resemblance with an $O(N^3)$ max-flow algorithm first proposed in [Gol85b]; see also [GoT86], which describes a similar max-flow algorithm that achieves a more favorable worst-case complexity using sophisticated data structures. These max-flow algorithms were derived from a different point of view that is unrelated to duality or ϵ-CS. They use node "labels," which in the context of the ϵ-relaxation approach can be viewed as prices. The max-flow version of the ϵ-relaxation method, first given in [Ber86a], is simpler than the algorithms of [Gol85] and [GoT86] in that it obtains a maximum flow in one phase rather than two. It can also be initialized with arbitrary prices, whereas in the max-flow algorithms of [Gol85], [GoT86] the initial prices must satisfy $p_i \leq p_j + 1$ for all arcs (i, j). Related max-flow algorithms are discussed in [AhO86], [ChM87], and [AMO89].

5

Performance and Comparisons

Several methods for solving minimum cost flow problems have been discussed, and it is important to know how they compare with one another in practice. Naturally, it is difficult to provide fully reliable guidelines, since one can only compare specific coded implementations of algorithms and not the algorithms themselves. Furthermore, the relative performance of various codes depends considerably on the sample problems used for testing, and also depends to some extent on the computer and the compiler used.

This chapter summarizes some of the computational experience using the codes of the appendixes and some other noncommercial codes, which are available from various sources. The codes were compiled and run on a 16 MHz Mac Plus using the widely available Absoft compiler. With the exception of assignment problems, the graphs of the test problems were randomly generated using the widely available public-domain generator NETGEN ([KNS74], version used is dated 1988). To reproduce these test problems, one should use the same random seed number as in [KNS74]. The results given are very limited but they are representative of a much broader experimentation with NETGEN problems.

The test problems are fairly similar to problems randomly generated with other generators that the author has tried. There seems to be nothing very peculiar about the way NETGEN generates problems. It obtains integer data using a uniform distibution over the specified range, and it tends to produce graphs with relatively small diameter. To guarantee that the problem is feasible, it builds the graph starting with a spanning tree of arcs with high capacity. These features are common in random problem generators.

On the other hand, special types of practical problems may have a structure that is not captured by random generators. As a result, two codes may compare quite differently for randomly generated problems and for specific types of practical problems. In particular, it should be mentioned that the graphs of some practical minimum cost flow problems tend to have a diameter that is much larger than the diameters of many types of randomly generated graphs. Practical experience has shown that such a structure enhances the performance of the primal-simplex method in comparison with the dual ascent and auction methods. A plausible conjecture here is that when the graph diameter is large, the cycles that the simplex method constructs, as well the augmenting paths that the dual ascent methods use, tend to have many arcs. This has an adverse effect on the amount of computation needed by both types of methods, but the effect on the dual ascent methods seems to be more serious. A related phenomenon may be conjectured for the case of auction algorithms.

Having warned the reader about the skepticism with which computational comparisons should be viewed, we give some running times obtained by several different methods on various types of randomly generated problems. In the last section of the chapter, we briefly discuss some issues of sensitivity analysis.

5.1   SHORTEST PATH PROBLEMS

We first consider shortest path problems with a single origin and with all other nodes being destinations. Table 1.1 gives times required to solve such problems with the following two codes due to Gallo and Pallotino [GaP88]:

(a) **HEAP-ALL-DEST:** This is an implementation of the binary heap label setting method given in [GaP88] as code SHEAP.

(b) **PAPE-ALL-DEST:** This is an implementation of a variation of the D'Esopo-Pape label correcting method given in [GaP88] as L2QUEUE. This code is included in Appendix A.2 with the kind permission of Professors Gallo and Pallotino.

We next consider shortest path problems with a single origin and a selected set of destinations. Tables 1.2 and 1.3 give times required to solve such problems with the following two codes given in Appendix A.2:

(a) **HEAP-SELECT-DEST:** This is the preceding binary heap label setting method, adapted to find shortest paths to a selected set of destinations.

N	A	HEAP-ALL-DEST	PAPE-ALL-DEST
1000	5000	0.417	0.333
2000	10000	0.883	0.700
3000	15000	1.400	1.150
4000	20000	1.900	1.367
5000	25000	2.400	3.350

Table 1.1   Times in secs required to solve single origin (node 1) to all destinations shortest path problems with arc lengths drawn from the range [1,100] using a uniform distribution.

(b) **AUCTION-SELECT-DEST:** This is a forward/reverse auction algorithm for finding shortest paths to a selected set of destinations (see Section 4.3).

N	A	HEAP-SELECT-DEST	AUCTION-SELECT-DEST
1000	5000	0.400	0.050
2000	10000	0.300	0.033
3000	15000	0.583	0.033
4000	20000	0.767	0.117
5000	25000	0.175	0.025

Table 1.2   Times in secs required to solve one origin to one destination shortest path problems with arc lengths drawn from the range [1,100] using a uniform distribution. The origin was node 1 and the destination was node N.

5.2   MAX-FLOW PROBLEMS

Here, we consider max-flow problems with node 1 being the source and node N being the sink. Table 2.1 gives times required to solve such problems with the following two codes given in Appendix A.6.

(a) **FORD-FULKERSON:** This is an implementation of the Ford-Fulkerson method (see Section 1.2.2).

N	A	HEAP-SELECT-DEST	AUCTION-SELECT-DEST
1000	5000	0.400	0.066
2000	10000	0.717	0.133
3000	15000	1.283	0.167
4000	20000	1.867	0.383
5000	25000	1.300	0.125

Table 1.3   Times in secs required to solve single origin to several destinations shortest path problems with arc lengths drawn from the range [1,100] using a uniform distribution. The origin was node 1. There were five destinations, nodes N, $N - 100$, $N - 200$, $N - 300$, $N - 400$.

(b) **ϵ-RELAX-MF:** This is an implementation of the ϵ-relaxation method for the max-flow problem (see Section 4.5). Here, $\epsilon = 1$ throughout the algorithm. The code may be operated so that it identifies a minimum cut but not necessarily a maximum flow.

N	A	FORD-FULKERSON	ϵ-RELAX-MF (C)	ϵ-RELAX-MF (F)
1000	5000	3.350	0.600	455.0
1000	15000	5.750	0.417	0.417
1500	10000	15.67	1.117	1397.0
1500	30000	29.03	0.767	0.767

Table 2.1   Times in secs required to solve max-flow problems with node 1 being the source and node N being the sink. For ϵ-RELAX-MF, we give the times needed to identify a minimum cut [column labeled ϵ-RELAX-MF (C)] and the total time needed to find a maximum flow [column labeled ϵ-RELAX-MF (F)]. The upper arc flow bounds were drawn from the range [10,1000] using a uniform distribution.

Table 2.1 shows that for very sparse problems, the ϵ-relaxation method can require a very long time to find a maximum flow after quickly finding a minimum cut. This is due to a price war induced by the lack of scaling ($\epsilon = 1$ throughout). Once ϵ-scaling is used, the uneven performance of the method is rectified, but then the time to find a minimum cut tends to increase to a level roughly competitive with that of the Ford-Fulkerson method. For reasonably dense randomly generated problems, scaling seems unnecessary;

the ϵ-relaxation method typically finds a maximum flow at roughly the same amount of time as a minimum cut, and substantially outperforms the Ford-Fulkerson method.

5.3   ASSIGNMENT PROBLEMS

Here we consider $n \times n$ symmetric assignment problems. Table 3.1 gives times required to solve such problems with the following four codes:

(a) **AUCTION-AS:** This is an implementation of the (forward) auction algorithm with ϵ-scaling given in Appendix A.4 (see Section 4.1). The starting ϵ was $\max_{(i,j)\in\mathcal{A}} |a_{ij}|/2$ and the reduction factor for ϵ was 5.

(b) **AUCTION-FR:** This is an implementation of the forward/reverse auction algorithm (see Section 4.2). The code is given in Appendix A.4. We used $\epsilon = 1$, so ϵ-scaling was bypassed.

(c) **AUCTION-SSP:** This is an implementation of the sequential shortest path method, preceded by a naive auction initialization phase given in Appendix A.5.

(d) **SSP:** This is the same as AUCTION-SSP with the naive auction part of the initialization discarded (that is, the parameter AUCTNUM in the code of Appendix A.5 was set to zero).

n	A	**AUCTION-AS**	**AUCTION-FR**	**AUCTION-SSP**	**SSP**
500	2500	1.600	0.400	2.033	2.283
1000	5000	5.467	0.967	8.450	8.933
2000	10000	6.233	2.883	20.03	22.22
3000	15000	10.87	3.050	51.10	54.70
4000	20000	12.97	3.650	70.05	77.07
5000	25000	20.53	5.583	119.5	127.9

Table 3.1   Times in secs required to solve symmetric assignment problems with arc costs drawn from the range [1,100] using a uniform distribution. The problems were generated using the built-in generators of the codes.

5.4   MINIMUM COST FLOW PROBLEMS

Here, we consider minimum cost flow problems of different types. Tables 4.1 and 4.2 give times required to solve such problems with the following codes:

(a) **RELAX:** This is an implementation of the relaxation method due to P. Tseng and the author. The code is available from the author; see the appendixes. An earlier version of this code may be found in [BeT88].

(b) **RELAX-SSP:** This is an implementation of the sequential shortest path method, preceded by a single-node relaxation initialization phase. The code is available from the author.

(c) **SSP:** This is the same as RELAX-SSP with the single node relaxation initialization discarded. The code is available from the author.

(d) ϵ-**RELAX:** This is the implementation of the ϵ-relaxation method of Appendix A.7. The starting ϵ was $\max_{(i,j)\in\mathcal{A}} |a_{ij}|/2$ and the reduction factor for ϵ was 5.

(e) ϵ-**RELAX-N:** This is an implementation of the ϵ-relaxation method that involves iterations from negative as well as positive surplus nodes. We used the same parameters in the ϵ-scaling procedure as for the preceding ϵ-RELAX code. The code is available from the author.

(f) **NETFLO:** This is the big-M primal-simplex code due to Kennington and Helgason. A listing of this code appears in [KeH80]. We used the most recent version that differs slightly from the code given in [KeH80].

5.5   SENSITIVITY ANALYSIS

In many practical situations, one may wish to vary slightly the problem data and observe the effect on the optimal solution. This is known as sensitivity analysis and may be motivated by a number of reasons. For example, one may wish to check if the optimal solution is "stable" with respect to parameter variations (small parameter variations result in small changes in the optimal cost or the optimal solution structure). In other cases, some of the problem parameters may be controllable and we may want to know if by changing them we can favorably influence the optimal solution. Still in other situations, the parameter values used may be estimates of some unknown true values, and we may want to evaluate the effect of the corresponding estimation errors.

In order to do sensitivity analysis efficiently, it is important to be able to use the computed optimal solution of a problem as a starting point for solving slightly different problems. The dual ascent and auction algorithms are generally much better suited for this purpose than the simplex method.

N	A	**RELAX**	**RELAX-SSP**	**SSP**	ϵ**-RELAX**	ϵ**-RELAX-N**	**NETFLO**
200	1300	1.700	5.417	13.03	5.967	7.083	3.317
200	1500	1.417	5.067	10.85	6.433	8.333	2.800
200	2000	2.033	7.517	14.70	7.317	9.150	3.883
200	2200	1.767	9.167	17.62	8.600	11.68	4.067
200	2900	2.383	8.633	20.98	9.500	14.42	5.150
1000	4800	5.433	21.53	43.33	20.35	23.57	20.20
1500	4342	8.650	44.95	73.85	35.42	40.03	24.88
1500	4385	8.750	44.27	50.73	41.00	41.37	32.57
1500	5107	9.317	36.82	49.27	36.63	36.98	37.57
1500	5730	9.433	45.03	62.37	40.02	34.25	40.52

Table 4.1   Times in secs required to solve minimum cost flow problems. These are the standard NETGEN problems 1 through 5 (first five problems in the table), and 31 through 35 (second five problems in the table), whose more detailed characteristics are given in the original source [KNS74]. The first five problems are symmetric transportation problems, and the second five problems are uncapacitated or lightly capacitated transshipment problems.

N	A	**RELAX**	**RELAX-SSP**	**SSP**	ϵ**-RELAX**	ϵ**-RELAX-N**	**NETFLO**
400	1000	2.950	13.12	19.75	17.37	14.72	6.283
1000	5000	9.867	112.2	217.9	68.68	58.40	51.72
2000	10000	23.18	551.2	801.1	251.9	178.2	212.0
3000	15000	37.38	724.5	1599.0	230.1	222.6	508.6

Table 4.2   Times in secs required to solve large symmetric transportation problems. The cost range is $[1,100]$ and the total supply is $500 \times N$.

For example, suppose we solve a problem and then modify it by changing a few arc capacities or costs, and/or some node supplies. To solve the modified problem using a dual ascent or auction algorithm, we can use as starting node prices the prices obtained from the earlier solution, and set to the appropriare bounds the arc flows that violate the new arc flow bounds or the CS or the ϵ-CS conditions. Typically, this starting flow-price vector pair is close to optimal, and solution of the modified problem is extremely fast. By contrast, to solve the modified problem using the simplex method one must provide a starting feasible tree. The optimal tree obtained from the previous problem will often be infeasible for the modified problem. As a result, a new starting tree must be constructed, and there are no simple ways to choose this tree to be nearly optimal.

APPENDIXES:
Codes

In these appendixes we describe briefly several FORTRAN codes for solving a variety of minimum cost flow problems. Unfortunately, due to space limitations, the listings of some of these codes cannot be included. The reader can obtain the full ASCII listings of all the codes described in the following appendixes (including the RELAX code of Appendix A.3 and the ϵ-RELAX-N code of Appendix A.7) in an IBM-PC or Macintosh readable diskette by sending \$25 to Prof. Dimitri P. Bertsekas, M.I.T., Rm 35-210, Cambridge, MA 02139.

All codes use integer arithmetic and can be compiled with the popular Absoft compiler on all Macintosh computers (subject to memory limitations). The cost range of the problem being solved must be sufficiently limited to avoid integer overflow. By changing a few input and output statements, the codes can be easily adapted for other computers and FORTRAN compilers.

A common format has been adopted whereby each of the codes (except for the assignment codes) does the following:

(a) Reads the problem in a common standard form.

(b) Converts the problem to a form suitable for the algorithm used.

(c) Calls the algorithm to solve the problem.

(d) Outputs the results.

[The assignment codes (Appendixes A.4 and A.5) include a built-in random problem generator.]

The standard form adopted is the one used for the simplex method (cf. Section 2.4). In particular, the problem is specified by:

The number of nodes N.

The number of arcs A.

The four A-length arrays $START$, END, $COST$, $CAPACITY$.

The N-length array $SUPPLY$.

As in Section 2.4, the arrays represent the following:

$START(a)$: The start node of arc a.

$END(a)$: The end node of arc a.

$COST(a)$: The cost coefficient of arc a.

$CAPACITY(a)$: The upper flow bound of arc a.

$SUPPLY(i)$: The supply of node i.

The standard form representation of the problem is the simplest. However, to avoid unnecessary conversions, it is more efficient to represent the problem in a format that is tailored to the method at hand. Thus, for long term use, the reader may wish to modify the input portion of the given codes.

A.1   PROBLEM GENERATOR AND CONVERSION CODES

A.1.1   GRIDGEN

To provide the reader with the means to create nonbipartite test problems, we give a simple generator, called GRIDGEN, which constructs random problems with an underlying two-dimensional grid with wraparound structure. The grid arcs form a "skeleton," guaranteeing problem feasibility. Additional arcs are added between randomly selected nodes, as specified by the user. The following problem parameters are required as input:

$DIM1$, $DIM2$: These are the two dimensions of the grid; the number of nodes is $N = DIM1 \times DIM2$.

$ADDARCS$: This is the number of arcs in addition to $6N$ arcs that are automatically generated. In particular, there are four arcs per node that form the grid, two arcs per node that start at the node and end at a randomly selected node, and $ADDARCS$ additional arcs that connect randomly selected pairs of nodes.

$TOTSUPPLY$: The total supply, that is, the sum of the supplies of the sources (nodes that have positive supply).

SOURCES, *SINKS*: The number of nodes that have positive supply, and the number of nodes that have negative supply, respectively. If both *SOURCES* and *SINKS* are less than $N/4$, the source nodes and sink nodes are selected randomly according to a uniform distribution; otherwise nodes 1 to *SOURCES* are the source nodes, and nodes are $(N + 1 - SINKS)$ to N are the sink nodes. In both cases the supply of a source is

$$\frac{TOTSUPPLY}{SOURCES}$$

and the supply of a sink is

$$\frac{TOTSUPPLY}{SINKS}$$

(to the greatest possible approximation).

MINCOST, *MAXCOST*: The cost coefficient of the $4N$ grid arcs is *MAXCOST*. All other arcs have cost coefficient selected according to a uniform distribution between *MINCOST* and *MAXCOST*. Thus, there is an incentive to avoid the grid arcs as much as possible in an optimal solution.

MINCAP, *MAXCAP*: The capacity of the grid arcs is *TOTSUPPLY*. The capacity of the other arcs is selected according to a uniform distribution between *MINCAP* and *MAXCAP*. The "skeleton" arcs of the grid guarantee that the problem is feasible (any source can be connected to any sink with a path of "capacity" *TOTSUPPLY*). However, these arcs have high cost, so at the optimum, they tend to carry little flow (if any). Thus, to generate a meaningful problem, the reader must specify a fairly large value for *ADDARCS*. Note that the generated problem cannot be unbounded since every arc has a real upper flow bound.

```
C ****************************************************
C MINCOST GRID PROBLEM GENERATOR
C BY DIMITRI P. BERTSEKAS
C SEPTEMBER 1990
C ****************************************************
C THIS CODE GENERATES A GRID MINCOST PROBLEM
C AND OUTPUTS THE PROBLEM IN STANDARD FORMAT
C IN THE FILE "FOR013.DAT".

        PARAMETER(MAXNODES=10000, MAXARCS=100000)
        IMPLICIT INTEGER (A-Z)
        LOGICAL MARK
        DIMENSION STARTN(MAXARCS),ENDN(MAXARCS)
        DIMENSION C(MAXARCS),U(MAXARCS)
        DIMENSION B(MAXNODES)
        DIMENSION MARK(MAXNODES)

C THIS CODE INCLUDES A UNIFORM RANDOM NUMBER GENERATOR
C WHICH RETURNS A VALUE IN (0,1)
C RANDOM GENERATOR STUFF
```

```
      COMMON /RANDM/ MULT,MODUL,I15,I16,JRAN
      REAL RAN

C INITIALIZE RANDOM GENERATOR

      ISEED=13502460
      CALL SETRAN(ISEED)

      PRINT*,'CREATING A 2-D GRID MINCOST FLOW PROBLEM GRAPH'
      PRINT*,'********************************************'
      PRINT*,'ENTER # OF NODES IN EACH OF THE TWO DIMENSIONS'
      READ*,DIM1,DIM2

      N=DIM1*DIM2

      PRINT*,'NUMBER OF ARCS SO FAR ',6*N
      PRINT*,'ENTER # OF ADDITIONAL ARCS'
      READ*,ADDARCS

      PRINT*,'TOTAL SUPPLY,# OF SOURCES,# OF SINKS'
      READ*,TOTSUPPLY,SOURCES,SINKS

      PRINT*,'ENTER MINIMUM AND MAXIMUM COST COEFFICIENT'
      READ*,MINCOST,MAXCOST
      PRINT*,'ENTER MIN AND MAX ARC CAPACITY'
      READ*,MINCAP,MAXCAP
      ARC=0

      DO 10 J=1,DIM2
      DO 15 I=1,DIM1
      NODE=I+(J-1)*DIM1

C CREATE HORIZONTAL ARCS

      IF ((I.GT.1).AND.(I.LT.DIM1)) THEN
      ARC=ARC+1
      STARTN(ARC)=NODE
      ENDN(ARC)=NODE+1
      C(ARC)=MAXCOST
      U(ARC)=TOTSUPPLY

      ARC=ARC+1
      STARTN(ARC)=NODE
      ENDN(ARC)=NODE-1
      C(ARC)=MAXCOST
      U(ARC)=TOTSUPPLY
      ELSE
      IF (I.EQ.1) THEN
      ARC=ARC+1
      STARTN(ARC)=NODE
      ENDN(ARC)=NODE+1
      C(ARC)=MAXCOST
      U(ARC)=TOTSUPPLY

      ARC=ARC+1
      STARTN(ARC)=NODE
      ENDN(ARC)=NODE+(DIM1-1)
```

```
C(ARC)=MAXCOST
U(ARC)=TOTSUPPLY
ELSE
ARC=ARC+1
STARTN(ARC)=NODE
ENDN(ARC)=NODE-(DIM1-1)
C(ARC)=MAXCOST
U(ARC)=TOTSUPPLY

ARC=ARC+1
STARTN(ARC)=NODE
ENDN(ARC)=NODE-1
C(ARC)=MAXCOST
U(ARC)=TOTSUPPLY
END IF
END IF

C CREATE VERTICAL ARCS

IF ((J.GT.1).AND.(J.LT.DIM2)) THEN
ARC=ARC+1
STARTN(ARC)=NODE
ENDN(ARC)=NODE+DIM1
C(ARC)=MAXCOST
U(ARC)=TOTSUPPLY

ARC=ARC+1
STARTN(ARC)=NODE
ENDN(ARC)=NODE-DIM1
C(ARC)=MAXCOST
U(ARC)=TOTSUPPLY
ELSE
IF (J.EQ.1) THEN
ARC=ARC+1
STARTN(ARC)=NODE
ENDN(ARC)=NODE+DIM1
C(ARC)=MAXCOST
U(ARC)=TOTSUPPLY

ARC=ARC+1
STARTN(ARC)=NODE
ENDN(ARC)=NODE+DIM1*(DIM2-1)
C(ARC)=MAXCOST
U(ARC)=TOTSUPPLY
ELSE
ARC=ARC+1
STARTN(ARC)=NODE
ENDN(ARC)=I
C(ARC)=MAXCOST
U(ARC)=TOTSUPPLY

ARC=ARC+1
STARTN(ARC)=NODE
ENDN(ARC)=NODE-DIM1
C(ARC)=MAXCOST
U(ARC)=TOTSUPPLY
END IF
END IF
```

```
C CREATE 2 ARCS WITH RANDOM END NODE

            DO 8 K=1,2
            ARC=ARC+1
            STARTN(ARC)=NODE
7            ENDN(ARC)=1+INT(RAN()*N)
            C(ARC)=MINCOST+RAN()*(MAXCOST-MINCOST)
            U(ARC)=MINCAP+RAN()*(MAXCAP-MINCAP)
            IF (ENDN(ARC).EQ.NODE) GOTO 7
8            CONTINUE
15          CONTINUE
10          CONTINUE

C CREATE ADDARCS NEW ARCS WITH RANDOM START AND END NODE

            DO 12 K=1,ADDARCS
            ARC=ARC+1
            NODE=1+INT(RAN()*N)
            STARTN(ARC)=NODE
13          ENDN(ARC)=1+INT(RAN()*N)
            C(ARC)=MINCOST+RAN()*(MAXCOST-MINCOST)
            U(ARC)=MINCAP+RAN()*(MAXCAP-MINCAP)
            IF (ENDN(ARC).EQ.NODE) GOTO 13
12          CONTINUE
            NA=ARC

C GENERATE THE SINKS AND SOURCES
            DO 17 I=1,N
            B(I)=0
            MARK(I)=.FALSE.
17          CONTINUE

            SUPL=0
            DO 20 I=1,SOURCES
18          NODE=1+INT(RAN()*N)
            IF (MARK(NODE)) THEN
            GOTO 18
            ELSE
            MARK(NODE)=.TRUE.
            B(NODE)=1+INT(TOTSUPPLY/SOURCES)
            SUPL=SUPL+B(NODE)
            END IF
20          CONTINUE
            DEM=0
            DO 25 I=1,SINKS
22          NODE=1+INT(RAN()*N)
            IF (MARK(NODE)) THEN
            GOTO 22
            ELSE
            MARK(NODE)=.TRUE.
            B(NODE)=-(1+INT(TOTSUPPLY/SINKS))
            DEM=DEM-B(NODE)
            END IF
25          CONTINUE

C EQUALIZE SUPPLY AND DEMAND
```

```
          IF (SUPL.GT.DEM) THEN
          DO 30 NODE=1,N
          IF (B(NODE).LT.0) THEN
          B(NODE)=B(NODE)-(SUPL-DEM)
          GOTO 38
          END IF
30        CONTINUE
          ELSE
          IF (SUPL.LT.DEM) THEN
          DO 35 NODE=1,N
          IF (B(NODE).GT.0) THEN
          B(NODE)=B(NODE)+(DEM-SUPL)
          GOTO 38
          END IF
35        CONTINUE
          END IF
          END IF

38        CONTINUE
          PRINT*,'*********************************************'
          PRINT*,'WRITING THE PROBLEM ON FILE FOR013.DAT'
          OPEN(13,FILE='FOR013.DAT',STATUS='NEW')
          REWIND(13)

C WRITE NUMBER OF NODES AND ARCS

          WRITE(13,1010) N,NA

C WRITE START, END, COST, AND CAPACITY OF EACH ARC

          DO 40 I=1,NA
          WRITE(13,1020) STARTN(I),ENDN(I),C(I),U(I)
40        CONTINUE

C WRITE SUPPLY OF EACH NODE

          DO 50 I=1,N
          WRITE(13,1000) B(I)
50        CONTINUE
          ENDFILE(13)
          REWIND(13)
          PRINT*,'END OF WRITING'
1000      FORMAT(1I8)
1010      FORMAT(2I8)
1020      FORMAT(4I8)
          STOP
          END

          SUBROUTINE SETRAN(ISEED)
          IMPLICIT REAL*8 (A-H,O-Z) , INTEGER*4 (I-N)

C**********************************************************************
C PORTABLE CONGRUENTIAL (UNIFORM) RANDOM NUMBER GENERATOR:
C NEXT_ VALUE = [(7**5) * PREVIOUS_ VALUE] MODULO[(2**31)-1]
C
C THIS GENERATOR CONSISTS OF TWO ROUTINES:
C (1) SETRAN - INITIALIZES CONSTANTS AND SEED
C (2) RRAN - GENERATES A REAL RANDOM NUMBER
```

```
C
C THE GENERATOR REQUIRES A MACHINE WITH
C AT LEAST 32 BITS OF PRECISION.
C THE SEED (ISEED) MUST BE IN THE RANGE (1,(2**31)-1).
C***********************************************************************
        COMMON /RANDM/ MULT,MODUL,I15,I16,JRAN
        IF(ISEED.LT.1) STOP 77
        MULT=16807
        MODUL=2147483647
        I15=2**15
        I16=2**16
        JRAN=ISEED
        RETURN
        END
C
        REAL FUNCTION RAN()
        IMPLICIT REAL*4 (A-H,O-Z) , INTEGER*4 (I-N)

C***********************************************************************
C RAN GENERATES A REAL RANDOM NUMBER BETWEEN 0 AND 1
C***********************************************************************

        COMMON /RANDM/ MULT,MODUL,I15,I16,JRAN
        IXHI=JRAN/I16
        IXLO=JRAN-IXHI*I16
        IXALO=IXLO*MULT
        LEFTLO=IXALO/I16
        IXAHI=IXHI*MULT
        IFULHI=IXAHI+LEFTLO
        IRTLO=IXALO-LEFTLO*I16
        IOVER=IFULHI/I15
        IRTHI=IFULHI-IOVER*I15
        JRAN=((IRTLO-MODUL)+IRTHI*I16)+IOVER
        IF(JRAN.LT.0) JRAN=JRAN+MODUL
        RAN = FLOAT(JRAN)/FLOAT(MODUL)
        RETURN
```

A.1.2   NGCONVERT: NETGEN to Stardard Format Conversion

There is in the public domain a popular random network problem generator called NETGEN [KNS74]. This generator uses a problem representation format that is different from the standard form described earlier. For the benefit of a reader who has access to NETGEN, we provide the conversion code NG-CONVERT, which reads a problem in the NETGEN format and writes it into the standard format.

```
C ****************** CONVERSION PROGRAM ******************
C THIS PROGRAM WILL READ A PROBLEM FILE CREATED VIA
C THE RANDOM PROBLEM GENERATOR NETGEN OR ANY GENERATOR THAT
C USES THE NETGEN FORMAT, AND CONVERT IT INTO THE STANDARD
C FORMAT.
C ************************************************
```

```
          PARAMETER(MAXNODES=10000, MAXARCS=100000)
          IMPLICIT NONE
          INTEGER START(MAXARCS),END(MAXARCS)
          INTEGER COST(MAXARCS),CAP(MAXARCS)
          INTEGER SUPPLY(MAXNODES)
          INTEGER I,N,IA,NA,NSORC,NSINK

          PRINT *,'READING NETGEN PROBLEM DATA'
          OPEN(12,FILE='FOR012.DAT',STATUS='OLD')
          REWIND(12)
          READ(12,1020) N,IA,NSORC,NSINK

          DO 10 I=1,IA
          READ(12,1020) START(I),END(I),COST(I),CAP(I)
10        CONTINUE
          DO 20 I=1,N
          SUPPLY(I)=0
20        CONTINUE
          NA=0
          DO 25 I=1,IA
          IF (START(I).EQ.N+1) THEN
          SUPPLY(END(I))=CAP(I)
          ELSE
          IF (END(I).EQ.N+2) THEN
          SUPPLY(START(I))=-CAP(I)
          ELSE
          NA=NA+1
          COST(NA)=COST(I)
          CAP(NA)=CAP(I)
          START(NA)=START(I)
          END(NA)=END(I)
          END IF
          END IF
25        CONTINUE
          PRINT*,'WRITING THE PROBLEM ON DISK IN STANDARD FORM'
          OPEN(13,FILE='FOR013.DAT',STATUS='NEW')
          REWIND(13)

C WRITE NUMBER OF NODES AND ARCS

          WRITE(13,1010) N,NA

C WRITE START, END, COST, AND CAPACITY OF EACH ARC

          DO 30 I=1,NA
          WRITE(13,1020) START(I),END(I),COST(I),CAP(I)
30        CONTINUE

C WRITE SUPPLY OF EACH NODE

          DO 40 I=1,N
          WRITE(13,1000) SUPPLY(I)
40        CONTINUE
          ENDFILE(13)
          REWIND(13)
          PRINT*,'END OF WRITING'
          STOP
1000      FORMAT(1I8)
```

```
1010    FORMAT(2I8)
1020    FORMAT(4I8)
        END
```

A.2   SHORTEST PATH CODES

A.2.1   PAPE-ALL-DEST

This code implements a variation of the D'Esopo-Pape single origin/all destinations label correcting method (cf. Section 1.3.3), given in [Pal84] and [GaP88]. The code is adapted from the L2QUEUE code of [GaP88].

```
C *** SAMPLE CALLING PROGRAM FOR SUBROUTINE L2QUEUE
C *** (SHORTEST PATH PROBLEM)
C *** THE PROGRAM IS BASED ON THE PAPER
C *** G. GALLO, S. PALLOTTINO "SHORTEST PATH ALGORITHMS",
C *** ANNALS OF OPERATIONS RESEARCH 7, 1988.
C
C *** INPUT AND OUTPUT PORTIONS MODIFIED AND
C *** THE FOUT DATA STRUCTURE INTRODUCED BY
C *** DIMITRI P. BERTSEKAS
C
C *** QUESTIONS AND COMMENTS SHOULD BE DIRECTED TO
C *** G. GALLO AND S. PALLOTTINO
C *** DEPT. OF COMP. SCI., UNIV. OF PISA, ITALY.
C *** FAX 39-50-510247
C *** EMAIL: PALLO@DIPISA.DI.UNIPI.IT
C ************************************************************
C FINDS SHORTEST PATH FROM ONE ORIGIN TO ALL DESTINATIONS
C ************************************************************
C ALL THE PARAMETERS ARE INTEGER
C THE ONLY MACHINE DEPENDENT CONSTANT USED IS INF
C**************************************************************************

        PARAMETER(MAXNODES=10000, MAXARCS=100000)
        INTEGER FOUT,NXTOUT,D,P,Q,R,HP,Y,X,T2,DEST
        REAL TT1,TT2,TCOST
        DIMENSION FOUT(MAXNODES),D(MAXNODES),P(MAXNODES),HP(MAXNODES)
        DIMENSION Q(MAXNODES)
        DIMENSION LNGT(MAXARCS),ND(MAXARCS),NXTOUT(MAXARCS)
        DATA INF/999999999/

        CALL READ(N,M,FOUT,NXTOUT,ND,LNGT)

        DO 10 I=1,N
        Q(I) = 0
        P(I) = 0
10      CONTINUE

C INITIALIZE ORIGIN AND QUEUE OF DESTINATIONS
```

```
      PRINT*,'THE NUMBER OF NODES IS = ',N
      PRINT*,'ENTER THE ORIGIN NODE'
      READ*,R

      PRINT *,'CALLING DESOPO-PAPE TO SOLVE THE PROBLEM'
      PRINT*,'******************************************'

C GET STARTING TIME FOR THE MAC II

      TT1 = LONG(362)/60.0

      CALL L2QUE(FOUT,NXTOUT,ND,LNGT,D,P,Q,N,INF,R)

C GET ENDING TIME FOR THE MAC II

      TT2 = LONG(362)/60.0 - TT1
      PRINT *,'FINISHED — TOTAL CPU TIME', TT2,' SECS'
      PRINT*,'******************************************'
      PRINT*,'THE ORIGIN NODE IS ',R
      PRINT*,'SH. DIST. OF DESTINATION ',N,' IS ',D(N)
45    PRINT*,'ENTER OTHER DESTINATION NODE (0 IF DONE)'
      READ*,DEST
      IF ((DEST.LT.0).OR.(DEST.GT.N)) GOTO 45
      IF (DEST.EQ.R) GOTO 45
      IF (DEST.NE.0) THEN
      PRINT*,'SHORTEST DISTANCE TO',DEST,' = ',D(DEST)
      GOTO 45
      END IF

      STOP
      END

      SUBROUTINE L2QUE(FOUT,NXTOUT,ND,LNGT,D,P,Q,N,INF,R)

C*****************************************************************
C ROUTINE L2QUE
C 1) FINDS A SHORTEST PATH TREE ROOTED AT NODE R AND THE SHORTEST
C DISTANCES
C 2) IS BASED ON THE D'ESOPO-PAPE METHOD WITH THE SET Q
C IMPLEMENTED AS A DOUBLE QUEUE Q(.)
C MEANING OF THE INPUT PARAMETERS:
C FOUT(I) = POINTER TO ARC-LIST OF NODE I, I=1,2,...,N+1
C ND(J) = ENDING NODE OF ARC J, J=1,2,...,M
C LNGT(J) = LENGTH OF ARC J, J=1,2,...,M
C NMAX = DIMENSION OF ARRAYS A(.), D(.), P(.), Q(.)
C MMAX = DIMENSION OF ARRAYS ND(.), LNGT(.)
C N = NUMBER OF NODES
C INF = VERY LARGE INTEGER VALUE (INFINITY)
C R = ROOT
C MEANING OF THE OUTPUT PARAMETERS:
C D(I) = SHORTEST DISTANCE FROM R TO I, I=1,2,...,N
C P(I) = PREDECESSOR NODE OF I IN THE SHORTEST PATH TREE, I=1,2,...,N
C OF THE MAIN INTERNAL PARAMETERS:
C Q(I) = LIST OF CANDIDATE NODES; Q(I) = -1 IF I IS NOT IN Q AND IT HAS
C ALREADY BEEN SCANNED
C = 0 IF I IS NOT IN Q AND IT HAS
C NOT BEEN SCANNED
C = J IF I PRECEDES NODE J IN THE
```

```
C LIST
C NN = N+1
C U = CURRENT NODE
C V = ENDING NODE OF THE CURRENT ARC
C INIT = START-POINTER TO THE ARC-LIST OF THE CURRENT NODE
C IFIN = END-POINTER TO THE ARC-LIST OF THE CURRENT NODE
C DV = TENTATIVE LABEL OF NODE V
C LAST = POINTER TO THE LAST NODE OF Q(.)
C PNTR = POINTER TO THE LAST NODE OF THE FIRST QUEUE OF Q(.)
C ALL THE PARAMETERS ARE INTEGER
C*****************************************************************

      PARAMETER(MAXNODES=10000, MAXARCS=100000)
      INTEGER FOUT,NXTOUT,D,P,Q,R,U,V,DV,PNTR
      DIMENSION FOUT(MAXNODES),D(MAXNODES),P(MAXNODES),Q(MAXNODES)
      DIMENSION ND(MAXARCS),LNGT(MAXARCS),NXTOUT(MAXARCS)

C INITIALIZE

      DO 10 I=1,N
      Q(I) = 0
      D(I) = INF
10        CONTINUE
      Q(R) = - 1
      D(R)=0
      P(R) = 0
      NN = N + 1
      Q(NN) = NN
      LAST = NN
      PNTR = NN
      U = R

C EXPLORE THE FORWARD STAR OF U

20        CONTINUE
      J=FOUT(U)
25        IF (J.GT.0) THEN
      V = ND(J)
      DV = D(U) + LNGT(J)

C CHECK WHETHER THE LABEL OF V CAN BE IMPROVED

      IF ( D(V) .GT. DV ) THEN
      D(V) = DV
      P(V) = U
      IF ( Q(V) ) 30,40,50

C IF V IS NOT IN Q AND IT HAS ALREADY BEEN SCANNED, IT IS INSERTED AT
C THE POSITION POINTED BY PNTR

30        Q(V) = Q(PNTR)
      Q(PNTR) = V
      IF ( LAST .EQ. PNTR ) LAST=V
      PNTR = V
      GO TO 50

C IF V IS NOT IN Q AND IT WAS NEVER SCANNED, IT IS INSERTED
C AT THE TAIL OF Q
```

```
40        Q(LAST) = V
          Q(V) = NN
          LAST = V
50        CONTINUE
          END IF
          J=NXTOUT(J)
          GOTO 25
          END IF

C REMOVE THE NEW CURRENT NODE U

60        U = Q(NN)
          Q(NN) = Q(U)
          Q(U) = - 1
          IF ( LAST .EQ. U ) LAST = NN
          IF ( PNTR .EQ. U ) PNTR = NN

C CHECK WHETHER THE LIST IS EMPTY

          IF ( U .LE. N ) GO TO 20

          RETURN
          END

          SUBROUTINE READ(N,M,FOUT,NXTOUT,END,LNGT)

C******************************************************************
C READS THE GRAPH DATA (STORED AS AN ADJACENCE LIST)
C AND THE ORIGINS LIST.
C******************************************************************

          PARAMETER(MAXNODES=10000, MAXARCS=100000)
          IMPLICIT INTEGER (A-Z)
          DIMENSION FOUT(MAXNODES),LAST(MAXNODES)
          DIMENSION START(MAXARCS),END(MAXARCS),LNGT(MAXARCS)
          DIMENSION NXTOUT(MAXARCS)
          PRINT*,'READING THE SHORTEST PATH PROBLEM DATA'
          OPEN(13,FILE='FOR013.DAT',STATUS='OLD')
          REWIND(13)

C READ NUMBER OF NODES AND ARCS

          READ(13,1010) N,M

C READ ENDNODE AND LENGTH OF EACH ARC

          DO 20 I=1,M
          READ(13,1020) START(I),END(I),LNGT(I),DUMMY
20        CONTINUE

          DO 30 I=1,N
          READ(13,1000) DUMMY
30        CONTINUE
          ENDFILE(13)
          REWIND(13)
          PRINT*,'END OF READING'
1000   FORMAT(1I8)
```

```
1010    FORMAT(2I8)
1020    FORMAT(4I8)
        PRINT *, 'RESTRUCTURING THE DATA '

C GENERATE FORWARD AND BACKWARD STARS FOR EACH NODE

        DO 60 I=1,N
        FOUT(I)=0
        LAST(I)=0
60      CONTINUE
        DO 65 ARC=1,M
        NXTOUT(ARC)=0
        NODE=START(ARC)
        IF (FOUT(NODE).NE.0) THEN
        NXTOUT(LAST(NODE))=ARC
        ELSE
        FOUT(NODE)=ARC
        END IF
        LAST(NODE)=ARC
65      CONTINUE

        RETURN
        END
```

A.2.2   HEAP-ALL-DEST

This is an implementation of the single origin/all destinations label setting method, using a binary heap to maintain the candidate list (cf. Section 1.3.2). This code is adapted from the SHEAP code of Gallo and Pallotino [GaP88]. The code is available from the author.

A.2.3   HEAP-SELECT-DEST

This code solves the shortest path problem with a single origin and a selected number of destinations. It is the same as the earlier code HEAP-ALL-DEST, except that it stops when all destinations have been permanently labeled.

```
C *** SAMPLE CALLING PROGRAM FOR SUBROUTINE SHEAP
C *** (SHORTEST PATH PROBLEM)
C
C *** THE PROGRAM IS BASED ON THE PAPER
C *** G. GALLO, S. PALLOTTINO "SHORTEST PATH ALGORITHMS",
C *** ANNALS OF OPERATIONS RESEARCH 7, 1988.
C
C *** INPUT AND OUTPUT PORTIONS MODIFIED AND
C *** THE FOUT DATA STRUCTURE INTRODUCED BY
C *** DIMITRI P. BERTSEKAS
C
C *** QUESTIONS AND COMMENTS SHOULD BE DIRECTED TO
C *** G. GALLO AND S. PALLOTTINO
C *****************************************************************
C *****************************************************************
C FINDS SHORTEST PATH FROM ONE ORIGIN TO SEVERAL DESTINATIONS
```

```
C *********************************************************
C ALL THE PARAMETERS ARE INTEGER
C THE ONLY MACHINE DEPENDENT CONSTANT USED IS INF
C***********************************************************************

      PARAMETER(MAXNODES=10000, MAXARCS=100000)
      INTEGER FOUT,D,P,Q,R,HP,Y,X,T2,DEST_COUNT,SH_DIST,DEST
      REAL TT1,TT2,TCOST
      DIMENSION FOUT(MAXNODES),D(MAXNODES),P(MAXNODES)
      DIMENSION HP(MAXNODES)
      DIMENSION Q(MAXNODES),SH_DIST(MAXNODES)
      DIMENSION LNGT(MAXARCS),ND(MAXARCS),NXTOUT(MAXARCS)
      DATA INF/999999999/

      CALL READ(N,M,FOUT,NXTOUT,ND,LNGT)

      DO 10 I=1,N
      Q(I) = 0
      P(I) = 0
      SH_DIST(I)=-1
10    CONTINUE

C INITIALIZE ORIGIN AND QUEUE OF DESTINATIONS

      PRINT*,'THE NUMBER OF NODES IS = ',N
      PRINT*,'ENTER THE ORIGIN NODE'
      READ*,R


42    PRINT*,'ENTER FIRST DESTINATION NODE'
      READ*,DEST

      IF ((DEST.LE.0).OR.(DEST.GT.N)) GOTO 42
      IF (DEST.EQ.R) GOTO 42

      IF ((DEST.LE.0).OR.(DEST.GE.N)) DEST =N
      SH_DIST(DEST)=0
      DEST_COUNT=1

45    PRINT*,'ENTER NEXT DESTINATION NODE (0 IF DONE)'
      READ*,DEST
      IF ((DEST.LT.0).OR.(DEST.GT.N).OR.(DEST.EQ.R)) GOTO 45
      IF (DEST.NE.0) THEN
      IF (SH_DIST(DEST).LT.0) THEN
      DEST_COUNT=DEST_COUNT+1
      SH_DIST(DEST)=0
      END IF
      GOTO 45
      END IF

50    CONTINUE

      PRINT*,'TOTAL NUMBER OF DESTINATIONS = ',DEST_COUNT
      PRINT *,'CALLING DIJKSTRA/HEAP TO SOLVE THE PROBLEM'
      PRINT*,'*******************************************'

C GET STARTING TIME FOR THE MAC II
```

```
        TT1 = LONG(362)/60.0

        CALL SHEAP(FOUT,NXTOUT,ND,LNGT,D,P,Q,HP,N,INF,R,
       &DEST_COUNT,SH_DIST)

C GET ENDING TIME FOR THE MAC II

        TT2 = LONG(362)/60.0 - TT1
        PRINT *,'FINISHED — TOTAL CPU TIME', TT2,' SECS'
        PRINT*,'*****************************************'
        PRINT*,'THE ORIGIN NODE IS ',R
        DO 200 I=1,N
        IF (SH_DIST(I).GE.0) THEN
        IF (SH_DIST(I).NE.D(I)) THEN
        PRINT*,'ERROR'
        END IF
        PRINT*,'SH. DIST. OF DESTINATION ',I,' IS ',SH_DIST(I)
        END IF
200     CONTINUE

        PRINT*,'*****************************************'
        PRINT *, 'PROGRAM ENDED; PRESS <CR>'
        PAUSE

        STOP
        END

        SUBROUTINE SHEAP(FOUT,NXTOUT,ND,LNGT,D,P,Q,HP,N,INF,R,
       &DEST_COUNT,SH_DIST)

C***********************************************************************
C ROUTINE SHEAP
C 1) FINDS A SHORTEST PATH TREE ROOTED AT NODE R AND THE SHORTEST
C DISTANCES
C 2) IS BASED ON DIJKSTRA'S METHOD, WITH PRIORITY QUEUE Q IMPLE-
MENTED
C AS A BINARY HEAP
C MEANING OF THE INPUT PARAMETERS:
C FOUT(I) = POINTER TO ARC-LIST OF NODE I, I=1,2,...,N+1
C ND(J) = ENDING NODE OF ARC J, J=1,2,...,M
C LNGT(J) = LENGTH OF ARC J, J=1,2,...,M
C N = NUMBER OF NODES
C INF = VERY LARGE INTEGER VALUE (INFINITY)
C R = ROOT
C MEANING OF THE OUTPUT PARAMETERS:
C D(I) = SHORTEST DISTANCE FROM R TO I, I=1,2,...,N
C I IN THE SHORTEST PATH TREE, I=1,2,...,N
C MEANING OF THE MAIN INTERNAL PARAMETERS:
C Q(I) = DICTIONARY OF THE HEAP: Q(I) GIVES THE POSITION OF NODE
C I IN THE HEAP HP(.), I=1,2,...,N
C HP(I)= I-TH NODE IN THE HEAP, I=1,2,...,NHP
C NHP = NUMBER OF NODES IN THE HEAP (NHP<=N)
C NN = N+1
C U = CURRENT NODE
C V = ENDING NODE OF THE CURRENT ARC
C INIT = START-POINTER TO THE ARC-LIST OF THE CURRENT NODE
C IFIN = END-POINTER TO THE ARC-LIST OF THE CURRENT NODE
C DV = TENTATIVE LABEL OF NODE V
```

```
C ALL THE PARAMETERS ARE INTEGER
C***********************************************************************

      PARAMETER(MAXNODES=10000, MAXARCS=100000)
      INTEGER FOUT,D,P,Q,R,U,V,DV,HP,DP1
      INTEGER HP1,HP2,HP3,DEST_COUNT,SH_DIST
      DIMENSION FOUT(MAXNODES),D(MAXNODES),P(MAXNODES)
      DIMENSION Q(MAXNODES),HP(MAXNODES)
      DIMENSION ND(MAXARCS),LNGT(MAXARCS),NXTOUT(MAXARCS)
      DIMENSION SH_DIST(MAXNODES)

C INITIALIZE

      DO 10 I=1,N
      D(I) = INF
10    CONTINUE
      NHP = 0
      D(R) = 0
      P(R) = 0
      NN = N + 1
      U = R

C EXPLORE THE FORWARD STAR OF U

20    CONTINUE
      J=FOUT(U)
25    IF (J.GT.0) THEN
      V = ND(J)
      DV = D(U) + LNGT(J)

C CHECK WHETHER THE LABEL OF V CAN BE IMPROVED

      IF ( D(V) .GT. DV ) THEN
      D(V) = DV
      P(V) = U
      IF ( Q(V) .NE. 0 ) GO TO 30

C INSERT NODE V INTO THE HEAP

      NHP = NHP + 1
      Q(V) = NHP

C UPDATE THE HEAP

30    K = Q(V)
40    K2 = K/2
      IF ( K2 .LE. 0 ) GO TO 50
      HP2 = HP(K2)
      IF ( DV .GE. D(HP2) ) GO TO 50
      HP(K) = HP2
      Q(HP2) = K
      K = K2
      GOTO 40
50    HP(K) = V
      Q(V) = K
      END IF
      J=NXTOUT(J)
      GOTO 25
```

```
         END IF

C REMOVE THE NEW CURRENT NODE U FROM THE HEAP
C CHECK IF IT IS A DESTINATION

70       U= HP(1)
         IF (SH_DIST(U).GE.0) THEN
         SH_DIST(U)=D(U)
         DEST_COUNT=DEST_COUNT-1
         IF (DEST_COUNT.EQ.0) GOTO 130
         END IF
         Q(U) = 0
         NHP = NHP - 1

C CHECK WHETHER THE HEAP IS EMPTY

         IF ( NHP ) 130,20,80

C UPDATE THE HEAP

80       HP1 = HP(NHP+1)
         DP1 = D(HP1)
         K = 1
90       K2 = 2*K
         HP2 = HP(K2)
         IF ( K2-NHP ) 100,110,120
100      HP3 = HP(K2+1)
         IF ( D(HP2) .LT. D(HP3) ) GO TO 110
         HP2 = HP3
         K2 = K2 + 1
110      IF ( DP1 .LE. D(HP2) ) GO TO 120
         HP(K) = HP2
         Q(HP2) = K
         K = K2
         GO TO 90
120      HP(K)=HP1
         Q(HP1) = K
         GO TO 20
130      CONTINUE
         RETURN
         END

         SUBROUTINE READ(N,M,FOUT,NXTOUT,END,LNGT)
         SAME AS IN CODE PAPE-ALL-DEST
```

A.2.4 AUCTION-SELECT-DEST

This code also solves the shortest path problem with a single origin and a selected number of destinations. It implements the combined forward/backward
auction algorithm of Section 4.3.

```
C ************************************************************
C *** SAMPLE CALLING PROGRAM FOR SUBROUTINE AUCTION_SP
C *** (FORWARD AND BACKWARD VERSION)
C *** SHORTEST PATH PROBLEM FROM ONE ORIGIN TO A SELECTED
C *** SET OF DESTINATIONS
```

```
C *** ASSUMING ALL ARC LENGTHS ARE NONNEGATIVE
C
C *** BY DIMITRI BERTSEKAS, AUGUST '90
C *** READS PROBLEM FILES IN STANDARD FORM
C
C ********************************************************
        PARAMETER(MAXNODES=10000, MAXARCS=100000)
        IMPLICIT NONE
        INTEGER FOUT,P,LNGT,PRD,END,R,DEST,START,T2,LARGE,I,N,NA
        INTEGER PRDARC,COUNT,ITER,TERM,NUM_ORIG,NUM_EXT,NUM_SUCC
        INTEGER DPRDARC,FIN,NXTIN,NXTOUT,DTERM,DCOUNT
        INTEGER EXTEND_ARC,DEXTEND_ARC,NODE,ARC
        INTEGER FRSTQUEUE,NXTQUEUE,SH_DIST,CUR_DEST
        INTEGER PREVNODE,DEST_COUNT,DUMMY
        REAL*8 TT1,TT2
        COMMON /SCALARS/ N,LARGE,R,DEST
        COMMON /STATS/ ITER,NUM_ORIG,NUM_EXT,NUM_SUCC
        COMMON /BLK1/ START
        COMMON /BLK2/ END
        COMMON /LENGTH/ LNGT
        COMMON /FRSTOUT/ FOUT
        COMMON /FRSTIN/ FIN
        COMMON /NEXTOUT/ NXTOUT
        COMMON /NEXTIN/ NXTIN
        COMMON /PRICES/ P
        COMMON /PREDARC/ PRDARC
        COMMON /PRECARC/ DPRDARC
        COMMON /EXTARC/ EXTEND_ARC
        COMMON /DEXTARC/ DEXTEND_ARC
        COMMON /DTERM/ FRSTQUEUE,PREVNODE,DEST_COUNT
        COMMON /NXTQUEUE/ NXTQUEUE
        COMMON /SH_DIST/ SH_DIST
        DIMENSION FOUT(MAXNODES),NXTOUT(MAXARCS)
        DIMENSION P(MAXNODES),LNGT(MAXARCS)
        DIMENSION START(MAXARCS),END(MAXARCS),PRDARC(MAXNODES)
        DIMENSION EXTEND_ARC(MAXNODES),DEXTEND_ARC(MAXNODES)
        DIMENSION FIN(MAXNODES),NXTIN(MAXARCS),DPRDARC(MAXNODES)
        DIMENSION NXTQUEUE(MAXNODES),SH_DIST(MAXNODES)

        PRINT*,'AUCTION/SHORT. PATHS (1 ORIG., SEVERAL DEST.)'
        PRINT*,'*******************************************'
        PRINT *,'READING PROBLEM DATA'
        OPEN(13,FILE='FOR013.DAT',STATUS='OLD')
        REWIND(13)

C READ NUMBER OF NODES AND ARCS

        READ(13,1010) N,NA

C READ START, END, COST, AND CAPACITY OF EACH ARC

        DO 20 I=1,NA
        READ(13,1020) START(I),END(I),LNGT(I),DUMMY
20      CONTINUE

C READ SUPPLY OF EACH NODE
```

```
         DO 30 I=1,N
         READ(13,1000) DUMMY
30       CONTINUE
         ENDFILE(13)
         REWIND(13)
         PRINT*,'END OF READING'
1000     FORMAT(1I8)
1010     FORMAT(2I8)
1020     FORMAT(4I8)
         PRINT *, 'RESTRUCTURING THE DATA '

C GENERATE FORWARD AND BACKWARD STARS FOR EACH NODE

         DO 60 I=1,N
         PRDARC(I)=0
         FOUT(I)=0
60       CONTINUE
         DO 65 ARC=1,NA
         NXTOUT(ARC)=0
         NODE=START(ARC)
         IF (FOUT(NODE).NE.0) THEN
         NXTOUT(PRDARC(NODE))=ARC
         ELSE
         FOUT(NODE)=ARC
         END IF
         PRDARC(NODE)=ARC
65       CONTINUE
         DO 125 I=1,N
         FIN(I)=0
         PRDARC(I)=0
125      CONTINUE
         DO 130 ARC=1,NA
         NXTIN(ARC)=0
         NODE=END(ARC)
         IF (FIN(NODE).NE.0) THEN
         NXTIN(PRDARC(NODE))=ARC
         ELSE
         FIN(NODE)=ARC
         END IF
         PRDARC(NODE)=ARC
130      CONTINUE

C SET LARGE TO A LARGE INTEGER FOR YOUR MACHINE

         LARGE=200000000

C INITIALIZE PRICES AND PREDECESSOR ARCS

         DO 140 I=1,N
         P(I) = 0
         PRDARC(I)=-1
         DPRDARC(I)=-1
         EXTEND_ARC(I)=-1
         DEXTEND_ARC(I)=-1
         NXTQUEUE(I)=-1
         SH_DIST(I)=-1
140      CONTINUE
```

```
C INITIALIZE ORIGIN AND QUEUE OF DESTINATIONS

            PRINT*,'THE NUMBER OF NODES IS = ',N
150         PRINT*,'ENTER THE ORIGIN NODE'
            READ*,R
            IF ((R.LE.0).OR.(R.GT.N)) GOTO 150

41          CONTINUE
42          PRINT*,'ENTER FIRST DESTINATION NODE'
            READ*,DEST
            IF ((DEST.LE.0).OR.(DEST.GT.N)) GOTO 42
            IF (DEST.EQ.R) GOTO 42
            CUR_DEST=DEST
            FRSTQUEUE=DEST
            DEST_COUNT=1
            NXTQUEUE(DEST)=0

45          PRINT*,'ENTER NEXT DESTINATION NODE (0 IF DONE)'
            READ*,DEST
            IF ((DEST.LT.0).OR.(DEST.GT.N)) GOTO 45
            IF (DEST.EQ.R) GOTO 45
            IF (DEST.NE.0) THEN
            IF (NXTQUEUE(DEST).LT.0) THEN
            NXTQUEUE(CUR_DEST)=DEST
            CUR_DEST=DEST
            DEST_COUNT=DEST_COUNT+1
            NXTQUEUE(DEST)=0
            END IF
            GOTO 45
            ELSE
            NXTQUEUE(CUR_DEST)=FRSTQUEUE
            PREVNODE=CUR_DEST
            END IF

50          CONTINUE
            PRINT*,'TOTAL NUMBER OF DESTINATIONS = ',DEST_COUNT
            PRINT *,'CALLING SHORTEST PATH AUCTION'
            PRINT*,'*****************************************'

C GET STARTING TIME FOR THE MAC II

            TT1 = LONG(362)/60.0
            CALL AUCTION_SP

C GET ENDING TIME FOR THE MAC II

            TT2 = LONG(362)/60.0 - TT1
            PRINT *,'FINISHED — TOTAL CPU TIME', TT2,' SECS'
            PRINT*,'*****************************************'
            PRINT*,'THE ORIGIN NODE IS ',R
            DO 200 I=1,N
            IF (SH_DIST(I).GE.0) THEN
            PRINT*,'SH. DIST. OF DESTINATION ',I,' IS ',SH_DIST(I)
            END IF
200         CONTINUE
            PRINT*,'*****************************************'
            COUNT=0
            DCOUNT=0
```

```
          DO 100 I=1,N
          IF (PRDARC(I).GT.0) COUNT=COUNT+1
          IF (DPRDARC(I).GT.0) DCOUNT=DCOUNT+1
100       CONTINUE
          PRINT *, '# OF NODES REACHED FROM ORIGIN =',COUNT
          PRINT *, '# OF NODES REACHED FROM DESTINATIONS =',DCOUNT
X         PRINT *, '# OF EXTENSIONS AT THE ORIGIN =',NUM_ORIG
X         PRINT *, '# OF SPECULATIVE EXTENSION ATTEMPTS =',NUM_EXT
X         PRINT *, '# OF SPECULATIVE EXTENSION SUCCESSES =',NUM_SUCC
X         PRINT *, '# OF NODE SCANS =',ITER
          PRINT*,'******************************************'
          PRINT*,'ENTER <0> TO STOP; <1> TO RUN FURTHER'
          READ*,DEST
          IF (DEST.EQ.1) THEN
          DO 400 I=1,N
          NXTQUEUE(I)=-1
          SH_DIST(I)=-1
400       CONTINUE
          GOTO 41
          END IF

          STOP
          END


          SUBROUTINE AUCTION_SP
C******************************************************************
C ROUTINE AUCTION_SP
C FINDS A SHORTEST PATH FROM NODE R TO SEVERAL NODES
C ASSUMING ALL ARC LENGTHS ARE NONNEGATIVE
C MEANING OF VARIOUS VARIABLES:
C FOUT(I) = FIRST OUTGOING ARC FROM NODE I
C FIN(I) = FIRST INCOMING ARC TO NODE I
C NXTOUT(J) = NEXT ARC WITH THE SAME END NODE AS J (=0 IF J IS LAST)
C NXTIN(J) = NEXT ARC WITH THE SAME END NODE AS J (=0 IF J IS LAST)
C START(J) = STARTING NODE OF ARC J
C END(J) = ENDING NODE OF ARC J
C LNGT(J) = LENGTH OF ARC J
C N = NUMBER OF NODES
C M = NUMBER OF ARCS
C LARGE = VERY LARGE INTEGER VALUE (INFINITY)
C R = ORIGIN
C DEST = CURRENT DESTINATION
C P(I) = PRICE OF I
C PRDARC(I) = PREDECESSOR OF I IN THE CURRENT FORWARD PATH
C TERM = TERMINAL NODE OF CURRENT FORWARD PATH
C DPRDARC(I) = PREDECESSOR OF I IN THE CURRENT BACKWARD PATH
C DTERM = TERMINAL NODE OF CURRENT BACKWARD PATH
C ENDNODE = ENDING NODE OF THE CURRENT ARC
C FRSTQUEUE = FIRST NODE IN THE QUEUE OF DESTINATIONS
C NXTQUEUE(I) = DESTINATION NEXT TO I IN THE QUEUE OF DESTINATIONS
C SH_DIST(I) = SHORTEST DISTANCE FROM ORIGIN TO NODE I
C EXTEND_ARC(I) = LIKELY CANDIDATE FOR OUTGOING ARC FROM I
C ON SHORTEST PATH
C DEXTEND_ARC(I) = LIKELY CANDIDATE FOR INCOMING ARC TO I
C ON SHORTEST PATH
C ALL THE VARIABLES ARE INTEGER
C******************************************************************
          PARAMETER(MAXNODES=10000, MAXARCS=100000)
```

```
            IMPLICIT NONE
            INTEGER FOUT,P,LNGT,PRD,SB,W,R,DEST,LARGE,N,M
            INTEGER TERM,ENDNODE,INIT,IFIN,LEVEL,NEW_LEVEL
            INTEGER I,J,START,END,ITER,NUM_ORIG,NUM_EXT,NUM_SUCC
            INTEGER EXTEND_ARC,BSTLEVEL,PTERM,PRDARC,EXTARC
            INTEGER DEXTEND_ARC,DTERM,DBSTLEVEL,DPTERM,DPRDARC,DEXTARC
            INTEGER FIN,NXTIN,NXTOUT,STARTNODE
            INTEGER FRSTQUEUE,NXTQUEUE,SH_DIST,PREVNODE,DEST_COUNT
            COMMON /SCALARS/ N,LARGE,R,DEST
            COMMON /STATS/ ITER,NUM_ORIG,NUM_EXT,NUM_SUCC
            COMMON /BLK1/ START
            COMMON /BLK2/ END
            COMMON /LENGTH/ LNGT
            COMMON /FRSTOUT/ FOUT
            COMMON /FRSTIN/ FIN
            COMMON /NEXTOUT/ NXTOUT
            COMMON /NEXTIN/ NXTIN
            COMMON /PRICES/ P
            COMMON /PREDARC/ PRDARC
            COMMON /PRECARC/ DPRDARC
            COMMON /EXTARC/ EXTEND_ARC
            COMMON /DEXTARC/ DEXTEND_ARC
            COMMON /DTERM/ FRSTQUEUE,PREVNODE,DEST_COUNT
            COMMON /NXTQUEUE/ NXTQUEUE
            COMMON /SH_DIST/ SH_DIST
            DIMENSION FOUT(MAXNODES),NXTOUT(MAXARCS)
            DIMENSION P(MAXNODES),LNGT(MAXARCS)
            DIMENSION START(MAXARCS),END(MAXARCS),PRDARC(MAXNODES)
            DIMENSION FIN(MAXNODES),NXTIN(MAXARCS),DPRDARC(MAXNODES)
            DIMENSION EXTEND_ARC(MAXNODES),DEXTEND_ARC(MAXNODES)
            DIMENSION NXTQUEUE(MAXNODES),SH_DIST(MAXNODES)

X           ITER=0
X           NUM_ORIG=0
X           NUM_EXT=0
X           NUM_SUCC=0
            DEST=FRSTQUEUE
            TERM=R
            DTERM=DEST
            GOTO 110

C *********** MAIN FORWARD ALGORITHM **********

C START OF A NEW ITERATION

20          CONTINUE
            PTERM=P(TERM)
            EXTARC=EXTEND_ARC(TERM)
            IF (EXTARC.LT.0) THEN
            EXTARC=DPRDARC(TERM)
            IF (EXTARC.LT.0) GO TO 100
            END IF

C SPECULATIVE PATH EXTENSION ATTEMPT

X           NUM_EXT=NUM_EXT+1
            ENDNODE=END(EXTARC)
            BSTLEVEL=LNGT(EXTARC)+P(ENDNODE)
```

```
        IF (PTERM.EQ.BSTLEVEL) THEN
X       NUM_SUCC=NUM_SUCC+1
        TERM=ENDNODE
        PRDARC(TERM)=EXTARC

C IF NEW DESTINATION FOUND, SWITCH TO THE BACKWARD ALGORITHM

        IF (NXTQUEUE(TERM).GE.0) THEN
        IF (SH_DIST(TERM).LT.0) THEN
        SH_DIST(TERM)=P(R)-P(TERM)
        GOTO 110
        END IF
        END IF

C RETURN FOR ANOTHER ITERATION

        GO TO 20
        END IF

C EXTENSION ATTEMPT WAS UNSUCCESSFUL, SO SCAN TERMINAL NODE

100     CONTINUE
X       ITER=ITER+1
        BSTLEVEL=LARGE
        J=FOUT(TERM)
200     IF (J.GT.0) THEN
        NEW_LEVEL = P(END(J)) + LNGT(J)
        IF (NEW_LEVEL.LT.BSTLEVEL) THEN
        BSTLEVEL=NEW_LEVEL
        EXTARC=J
        END IF
        J=NXTOUT(J)
        GOTO 200
        END IF
        EXTEND_ARC(TERM)=EXTARC
        IF (BSTLEVEL.GT.PTERM) THEN

C PATH CONTRACTION

        P(TERM)=BSTLEVEL
        IF (TERM.NE.R) THEN
        TERM=START(PRDARC(TERM))

C RETURN FOR ANOTHER ITERATION BUT SKIP
C THE SPECULATIVE EXTENSION ATTEMPT

        PTERM=P(TERM)
        GO TO 100
        ELSE

C ORIGIN REACHED; SWITCH TO THE BACKWARD ALGORITHM

X       NUM_ORIG=NUM_ORIG+1
        IF (PTERM.GE.LARGE) THEN
        PRINT *,'NO PATH TO THE DESTINATION'
        PAUSE
        STOP
        END IF
```

```
            GO TO 110
            END IF
            ELSE

C PATH EXTENSION

            TERM=END(EXTARC)
            PRDARC(TERM)=EXTARC

C IF NEW DESTINATION FOUND, SWITCH TO THE BACKWARD ALGORITHM

            IF (NXTQUEUE(TERM).GE.0) THEN
            IF (SH_DIST(TERM).LT.0) THEN
            SH_DIST(TERM)=P(R)-P(TERM)
            GOTO 110
            END IF
            END IF

C RETURN FOR ANOTHER ITERATION

            GO TO 20
            END IF

C *********** MAIN BACKWARD ALGORITHM **********

C CLEANUP THE QUEUE

110         CONTINUE
115         IF (SH_DIST(DEST).GE.0) THEN
            DTERM=NXTQUEUE(DEST)
            NXTQUEUE(DEST)=-1
            DEST=DTERM
            NXTQUEUE(PREVNODE)=DEST
            DEST_COUNT=DEST_COUNT-1

C IF THE DESTINATIONS HAVE BEEN EXHAUSTED RETURN

            IF (DEST_COUNT.EQ.0) THEN
            RETURN
            ELSE
            GOTO 115
            END IF
            END IF

C START OF A NEW ITERATION

120         CONTINUE
            DPTERM=P(DTERM)
            DEXTARC=DEXTEND_ARC(DTERM)
            IF (DEXTARC.LT.0) THEN
            DEXTARC=PRDARC(DTERM)
            IF (DEXTARC.LT.0) GO TO 1100
            END IF

C PATH EXTENSION

X           NUM_EXT=NUM_EXT+1
            STARTNODE=START(DEXTARC)
```

```
            DBSTLEVEL=P(STARTNODE)-LNGT(DEXTARC)
            IF (DPTERM.EQ.DBSTLEVEL) THEN
X           NUM_SUCC=NUM_SUCC+1
            DTERM=STARTNODE
            DPRDARC(DTERM)=DEXTARC

C IF THE ORIGIN IS FOUND, SWITCH TO THE FORWARD ALGORITHM

            IF (DTERM.EQ.R) THEN
            SH_DIST(DEST)=P(R)-P(DEST)
            DEST_COUNT=DEST_COUNT-1

C IF THE DESTINATIONS HAVE BEEN EXHAUSTED RETURN

            IF (DEST_COUNT.EQ.0) THEN
            RETURN
            ELSE
            DTERM=NXTQUEUE(DEST)
            NXTQUEUE(DEST)=-1
            DEST=DTERM
            NXTQUEUE(PREVNODE)=DEST
            GOTO 20
            END IF
            END IF

C RETURN FOR ANOTHER ITERATION

            GO TO 120
            END IF

C SCAN TERMINAL NODE

1100        CONTINUE
X           ITER=ITER+1
            DBSTLEVEL=-LARGE
            J=FIN(DTERM)
1200        IF (J.GT.0) THEN
            STARTNODE = START(J)
            NEW_LEVEL = P(STARTNODE) - LNGT(J)
            IF (NEW_LEVEL.GT.DBSTLEVEL) THEN
            DBSTLEVEL=NEW_LEVEL
            DEXTARC=J
            END IF
            J=NXTIN(J)
            GOTO 1200
            END IF
            DEXTEND_ARC(DTERM)=DEXTARC
            IF (DBSTLEVEL.LT.DPTERM) THEN

C PATH CONTRACTION

            P(DTERM)=DBSTLEVEL
            IF (DTERM.NE.DEST) THEN
            DTERM=END(DPRDARC(DTERM))

C RETURN FOR ANOTHER SCAN

            DPTERM=P(DTERM)
```

```
              GO TO 1100
              ELSE

C DESTINATION REACHED; SWITCH TO THE ORIGIN

X        NUM_ORIG=NUM_ORIG+1
              IF (DPTERM.LE.-LARGE) THEN
              PRINT *,'NO PATH TO THE ORIGIN'
              PAUSE
              STOP
              END IF
              PREVNODE=DEST
              DEST=NXTQUEUE(DEST)
              DTERM=DEST
              GO TO 20
              END IF
              ELSE

C PATH EXTENSION

              DTERM=START(DEXTARC)
              DPRDARC(DTERM)=DEXTARC

C IF THE ORIGIN IS FOUND, SWITCH TO THE FORWARD ALGORITHM

              IF (DTERM.EQ.R) THEN
              SH_DIST(DEST)=P(R)-P(DEST)
              DEST_COUNT=DEST_COUNT-1
              IF (DEST_COUNT.EQ.0) THEN
              RETURN
              ELSE
              DTERM=NXTQUEUE(DEST)
              NXTQUEUE(DEST)=-1
              DEST=DTERM
              NXTQUEUE(PREVNODE)=DEST
              GOTO 20
              END IF
              END IF

C RETURN FOR ANOTHER ITERATION

              GO TO 120
              END IF

              END
```

A.3   RELAXATION CODE

This code (RELAX) implements the relaxation method of Section 3.3. The code was written by the author in collaboration with Paul Tseng (with contributions by Jon Eckstein in the initialization part of the code). There are small differences between the code given here and similar codes of the RE-

LAX family that have been released to the research community since 1987 ([BeT88], [BeT90]). The code is available from the author.

A.4   AUCTION CODES FOR ASSIGNMENT PROBLEMS

Since assignment problems cannot be generated by the GRIDGEN program, the assignment codes include a built-in random problem generator. This generator can be replaced by other code that reads an assignment problem from a file.

A.4.1   AUCTION-AS

This code implements the forward/reverse auction algorithm with ϵ-scaling for the asymmetric assignment problem; cf. Section 4.2.1. It can also solve as a special case the symmetric assignment problem. In this case as well as in the case where ϵ-scaling is bypassed ($\epsilon = 1$ throughout the algorithm), only the forward part of the algorithm is used. Note also that this code uses the "third best" object implementation described in Exercise 1.7 of Section 4.1.

```
C ****************************************************************
C SAMPLE CALLING PROGRAM FOR AUCTION ALGORITHM
C FOR ASSIGNMENT PROBLEMS
C THIS DRIVER CREATES AN ASSIGNMENT PROBLEM
C WITH LESS OR EQUAL NUMBER OF ROWS THAN COLUMNS,
C AND CALLS THE AUCTION_AS SUBROUTINE TO FIND AN
C ASSIGNMENT OF MAXIMAL VALUE.
C THIS VERSION USES A THIRD BEST VALUE
C ****************************************************************
        PARAMETER(MAXNODES=10000, MAXARCS=100000)
        IMPLICIT NONE
        INTEGER M,N,NA,A,K,ILARGE,BEGEPS,ENDEPS,CYCLES
        INTEGER NUMPHASES,STARTINCR,AVERAGE,LAMBDA
        INTEGER I,J,ARC,NOASS,ICOST,ABSCOST,CURARC
        INTEGER CURCOL,FSTARC,LSTARC,MINCOST,MAXCOST
        INTEGER EXTRA,REMAINDER,INDEX,COUNT
        INTEGER COL_ASSIGNED_TO(MAXNODES),ROW_ASSIGNED_TO(MAXNODES)
        INTEGER FOUT(MAXNODES),FIN(MAXNODES),NXTIN(MAXARCS)
        INTEGER COST(MAXARCS),START(MAXARCS),END(MAXARCS)
        INTEGER PCOL(MAXNODES),PROW(MAXNODES)
        INTEGER PRDARC(MAXNODES)
        REAL FACTOR,TT1,TT2,TCOST
        COMMON/ARRAYC/COST/ARRAYS/START/ARRAYE/END
        COMMON/ARRAYFO/FOUT/ARRAYFI/FIN/ARRAYNI/NXTIN
        COMMON/ARRAYRA/ROW_ASSIGNED_TO/ARRAYCA/COL_ASSIGNED_TO
        COMMON/ARRAYPC/PCOL/ARRAYPR/PROW
        COMMON/BK1/M,N,A,ILARGE
        COMMON/BK2/CYCLES,AVERAGE,NUMPHASES,LAMBDA
C ****************************************************************
C PROBLEM GENERATION CODE STARTS HERE
```

```
C THE USER MAY REPLACE THIS CODE WITH A CODE THAT READS
C HIS/HER PROBLEM FROM A FILE
C ***********************************************************
C THIS CODE INCLUDES A UNIFORM RANDOM NUMBER GENERATOR
C WHICH RETURNS A VALUE IN (0,1)
C INITIALIZE RANDOM GENERATOR

        INTEGER MULT,MODUL,I15,I16,JRAN,ISEED
        REAL RAN
        COMMON /RANDM/ MULT,MODUL,I15,I16,JRAN
        ISEED=13502460
        CALL SETRAN(ISEED)

        PRINT*,'GENERATING AN ASYMMETRIC ASSIGNMENT PROBLEM'
        PRINT*,'*******************************************'

C **** READ THE NUMBER OF ROWS M, COLUMNS N, AND ARCS A ****

        PRINT*,'ENTER THE NUMBER OF ROWS'
        READ*,M

2        PRINT*,'ENTER THE NUMBER OF COLUMNS (>= # OF ROWS)'
        READ*,N
        IF (N.LT.M) GO TO 2
5        PRINT*,'ENTER THE NUMBER OF ARCS PER ROW (>1)'
        READ*,NA
        IF (NA.LT.2) GOTO 5

        PRINT*,'ENTER THE MINIMUM AND THE MAXIMUM COST'
        READ*,MINCOST,MAXCOST

C THE NUMBER OF ARCS IS M*NA+N-M

        A=M*NA+N-M
        PRINT*,'THE NUMBER OF ARCS IS ',A

C THE ARCS INCIDENT TO ROW I ARE FOUT(I) TO FOUT(I+1)-1
C ALSO, FOR FEASIBILITY EACH ROW IS DIRECTLY CONNECTED
C WITH THE CORRESPONDING COLUMN;
C ALSO EACH COLUMN HAS AT LEAST ONE ARC

        EXTRA=INT((N-M)/M)
        DO 20 I=1,M
        FOUT(I)=1+(I-1)*(NA+EXTRA)
20       CONTINUE
        FOUT(M+1)=A+1

        DO 22 I=1,M
        DO 23 ARC=FOUT(I),FOUT(I+1)-1
        START(ARC)=I
23       CONTINUE
22       CONTINUE

C GENERATE THE END(ARC) AND COST(ARC) WHICH ARE THE COLUMN
C AND THE COST COEFFICIENT ASSOCIATED WITH ARC

        DO 25 ARC=1,A
        END(ARC)=1+RAN()*N
```

```
           IF ((END(ARC).GT.N).OR.(END(ARC).LT.1)) THEN
           PRINT*,'ERROR IN PROBLEM GENERATION'
           PAUSE
           STOP
           END IF
           COST(ARC)=MINCOST+RAN()*(MAXCOST-MINCOST)
25         CONTINUE

C MODIFY THE END OF THE LAST ARC OUT OF EACH ROW FOR FEASIBILITY
C AND SET ITS COST TO -MAXCOST

           DO 30 I=1,M
           END(FOUT(I+1)-1)=I
           COST(FOUT(I+1)-1)=-MAXCOST
30         CONTINUE

C MODIFY THE END OF SOME ARCS
C SO THAT EACH COLUMN HAS AT LEAST ONE ARC

           IF (EXTRA.GE.1) THEN
           DO 32 I=1,M
           DO 33 K=1,EXTRA
           END(FOUT(I)+K-1)=K*M+I
33         CONTINUE
32         CONTINUE
           END IF

           REMAINDER=N-M*(1+EXTRA)
           IF (REMAINDER.GE.1) THEN
           INDEX=FOUT(M)+EXTRA-1
           DO 35 J=1,REMAINDER
           END(INDEX+J)=(1+EXTRA)*M+J
35         CONTINUE
           END IF

C CONSTRUCT THE FIN() AND NXTIN() ARRAYS

           DO 42 J=1,N
           FIN(J)=0
           PRDARC(J)=0
42         CONTINUE
           DO 43 ARC=1,A
           NXTIN(ARC)=0
           J=END(ARC)
           IF (FIN(J).NE.0) THEN
           NXTIN(PRDARC(J))=ARC
           ELSE
           FIN(J)=ARC
           END IF
           PRDARC(J)=ARC
43         CONTINUE

C ***********************************************************
C PROBLEM GENERATION CODE ENDS HERE
C ***********************************************************
C SCALE THE COST TO WORK WITH INTEGER EPSILON

           MAXCOST=0
```

```
         DO 45 ARC=1,A
         COST(ARC)=COST(ARC)*(M+1)
         ABSCOST=IABS(COST(ARC))
         IF (ABSCOST.GT.MAXCOST) MAXCOST=ABSCOST
45       CONTINUE

C *** ILARGE IS A VERY LARGE INTEGER FOR YOUR MACHINE ***
C THE SCALED COSTS SHOULD BE SIGNIFICANTLY SMALLER THAN
C ILARGE AND SIGNIFICANTLY LARGER THAN -ILARGE

         ILARGE=2000000000
         LAMBDA=-ILARGE

C THE FOLLOWING PARAMETERS BEGEPS, FACTOR, ENDEPS, AND STARTINCR
C ARE PASSED TO THE AUCTION ALGORITHM. VALUES BETWEEN
C (A) MAXCOST/5 AND MAXCOST/2 FOR BEGEPS
C (B) 4 AND 6 FOR FACTOR
C (C) M/10 AND 1 FOR ENDEPS
C (D) 1 AND BEGEPS FOR STARTINCR
C HAVE WORKED WELL FOR LARGE SPARSE PROBLEMS.
C FOR DENSE PROBLEMS AND FOR VERY ASYMMETRIC PROBLEMS
C IT IS RECOMMENDED THAT
C BEGEPS BE SET TO A SMALLER VALUE (POSSIBLY 1),
C ENDEPS BE SET TO 1,
C STARTINCR BE SET TO 1.
C FOR VERY ASYMMETRIC PROBLEMS, BEGEPS=1, CORRESPONDING TO
C NO E-SCALING, MAY WORK BEST AND SHOULD BE AT LEAST TRIED.

         PRINT*,'MAXIMUM COST IS ',MAXCOST
         PRINT*,'ENTER THE STARTING EPSILON'
         READ*,BEGEPS
         IF (BEGEPS.LT.1) BEGEPS=1
         PRINT*,'ENTER THE EPSILON REDUCTION FACTOR'
         READ*,FACTOR
         ENDEPS=M/10
         IF (ENDEPS.LT.1) ENDEPS=1
         IF (ENDEPS.GT.BEGEPS) ENDEPS=BEGEPS
         STARTINCR=BEGEPS/10
         IF (STARTINCR.LT.1) STARTINCR=1
         PRINT*,'****************************************'
         PRINT*,'STARTING EPSILON = ',BEGEPS
         PRINT*,'EPSILON REDUCTION FACTOR = ',FACTOR
         PRINT*,'THRESHOLD EPSILON BEFORE IT IS SET TO 1 = ',ENDEPS
         PRINT*,'STARTING MIN BIDDING INCREMENT = ',STARTINCR
         PRINT*,'CALLING ASYMMETRIC ASSIGNMENT AUCTION'
         PRINT*,'****************************************'

C GET STARTING TIME FOR THE MAC II

         TT1 = LONG(362)/60.0

         CALL AUCTION_AS(BEGEPS,FACTOR,ENDEPS,STARTINCR)

C GET ENDING TIME FOR THE MAC II

         TT2 = LONG(362)/60.0 - TT1
         PRINT *,'FINISHED — TOTAL CPU TIME', TT2,' SECS'
         PRINT*,'****************************************'
```

```
C *** DISPLAY RESULTS ***
X      WRITE(9,2010) CYCLES
X2010  FORMAT(' NO OF AUCTION CYCLES',I7)
X      WRITE(9,2020) AVERAGE
X2020  FORMAT(' AVERAGE NUMBER OF BIDS PER CYCLE',F9.3)
       WRITE(9,2030) NUMPHASES
2030   FORMAT('NO OF EPSILON SUBPROBLEMS SOLVED =',I7)

C CHECK OPTIMALITY & CALCULATE COST

       DO 48 J=1,N
       I=ROW_ASSIGNED_TO(J)
       IF (N.GT.M) THEN
       ROW_ASSIGNED_TO(J)=0
       ELSE
       IF (I.GT.0) THEN
       COL_ASSIGNED_TO(I)=J
       END IF
       END IF
48     CONTINUE
       TCOST=0
       DO 50 I=1,M
       J=COL_ASSIGNED_TO(I)
       ROW_ASSIGNED_TO(J)=I
       IF (J.EQ.0) THEN
       PRINT*,'ROW ',I,' IS UNASSIGNED'
       END IF
       IF (PCOL(J).LT.LAMBDA) THEN
       PRINT*,'CS VIOLATION AT ASSIGNED COLUMN ',J
       END IF
       FSTARC=FOUT(I)
       LSTARC=FOUT(I+1)-1
       MAXCOST=-ILARGE
       DO 55 ARC=FSTARC,LSTARC
       CURCOL=END(ARC)
       IF (PROW(I)+PCOL(CURCOL).LT.COST(ARC)-1) THEN
       PRINT*,'1-CS VIOLATED AT ARC ',ARC
       END IF
       IF (CURCOL.EQ.J) THEN
       IF (MAXCOST.LT.COST(ARC)) THEN
       MAXCOST=COST(ARC)
       END IF
       END IF
55     CONTINUE
       TCOST=TCOST+MAXCOST/(M+1)
       IF (PROW(I)+PCOL(J).NE.MAXCOST) THEN
       PRINT*,'1-CS VIOLATED AT ROW ',I
       END IF
50     CONTINUE
       COUNT=0
       DO 60 J=1,N
       IF (ROW_ASSIGNED_TO(J).EQ.0) THEN
       IF (PCOL(J).GT.LAMBDA) THEN
       PRINT*,'CS VIOLATION AT UNASSIGNED COLUMN ',J
       END IF
       ELSE
       COUNT=COUNT+1
       END IF
```

```
60        CONTINUE
          IF (COUNT.LT.M) THEN
          PRINT*,'THE NUMBER OF ASSIGNED COLUMNS IS WRONG'
          END IF
          WRITE(9,2100) TCOST
2100      FORMAT(' ASSIGNMENT COST=',F14.2)
          PRINT *, ' PROGRAM ENDED; <CR> TO EXIT '

          PAUSE
          END


C ******************************************************************
C AUCTION CODE FOR ASYMMETRIC M BY N ASSIGNMENT PROBLEMS
C WRITTEN BY DIMITRI P. BERTSEKAS
C DEC. 1990
C THIS CODE IMPLEMENTS A FORWARD/REVERSE AUCTION ALGORITHM
C WITH E-SCALING FOR THE ASYMMETRIC ASSIGNMENT PROBLEM.
C IT SOLVES A SEQUENCE OF SUBPROBLEMS AND DECREASES
C EPSILON BY A CONSTANT FACTOR BETWEEN SUBPROBLEMS.
C THIS VERSION CORRESPONDS TO A GAUSS-SEIDEL MODE.
C THE CODE TREATS THE PROBLEM AS A MAXIMIZATION PROBLEM.
C TO SOLVE A MINIMIZATION PROBLEM, REVERSE THE SIGN OF THE
C ARC COSTS PRIOR TO CALLING AUCTION, AND REVERSE AGAIN
C THE SIGN OF THE OPTIMAL COST UPON RETURN FROM AUCTION.
C THIS CODE ALLOWS MULTIPLE ARCS BETWEEN A ROW AND A COLUMN.
C THIS VERSION OF THE AUCTION ALGORITHM IS ADAPTIVE. THE MINIMAL
C BIDDING INCREMENT (STORED IN THE VARIABLE INCR)
C MAY BE SMALLER THAN EPSILON. FOR EVERY SUBPROBLEM, INCR STARTS
C AT THE PARAMETER VALUE STARTINCR
C (WHICH IS PASSED TO THE AUCTION ROUTINE) AND IS INCREASED
C BY A FACTOR OF 2 AT THE END OF EACH CYCLE, UP TO A MAXIMUM VALUE
C OF EPSILON. THIS ADAPTIVE FEATURE IS PARTICULARLY EFFECTIVE FOR
C DENSE PROBLEMS. IT CAN BE DEFEATED BY SELECTING STARTINCR=BEGEPS
C ******************************************************************
C THE USER MUST SUPPLY THE FOLLOWING PROBLEM DATA
C IN FORWARD STAR FORMAT
C (THAT IS, ALL ARCS OF THE SAME ROW ARE NUMBERED CONSECUTIVELY):
C M=NUMBER OF ROWS
C N=NUMBER OF COLUMNS
C A=NUMBER OF ARCS
C FOUT(ROW)=FIRST ARC COMING OUT OF ROW
C FIN(COL)=FIRST ARC COMING INTO COL
C NXTIN(ARC)=NEXT ARC INCIDENT TO THE SAME COLUMN AS ARC
C COST(ARC)=COST OF ARC
C START(ARC)=ROW CORRESPONDING TO ARC
C END(ARC)=COLUMN CORRESPONDING TO ARC
C AND THE FOLLOWING PARAMETERS FOR THE AUCTION ALGORITHM:
C BEGEPS=STARTING VALUE OF EPSILON (MUST BE NO LESS THAN 1)
C ENDEPS=FINAL VALUE OF EPSILON BEFORE IT IS SET TO 1
C FACTOR=EPSILON REDUCTION FACTOR BETWEEN SUBPROBLEMS
C STARTINCR=THE STARTING VALUE OF THE BIDDING INCREMENT
C ENDEPS SHOULD NOT EXCEED BEGEPS.
C FACTOR MUST BE GREATER THAN 1.
C FOUT(.) IS AN ARRAY OF LENGTH N.
C COST(.),END(.) ARE ARRAYS OF LENGTH A.
C THE SOLUTION IS CONTAINED IN THE ARRAY ROW_ASSIGNED_TO(.) WHERE
C ROW_ASSIGNED_TO(COL) GIVES THE ROW ASSIGNED TO COL.
C ALSO COL_ASSIGNED_TO(ROW) GIVES THE COLUMN ASSIGNED TO ROW.
```

```
C THIS ALGORITHM DOES NOT CHECK FOR INFEASIBILITY OF THE PROBLEM.
C TO MAKE SURE THE PROBLEM IS FEASIBLE THE USER MAY ADD
C ADDITIONAL VERY SMALL (I.E., LARGE NEGATIVE) COST ARCS.
C ****************************************************************
C ALL PROBLEM DATA ARE INTEGER
C ****************************************************************
       SUBROUTINE AUCTION_AS(BEGEPS,FACTOR,ENDEPS,STARTINCR)
       PARAMETER(MAXNODES=10000, MAXARCS=100000)
       IMPLICIT NONE
       INTEGER A,K,N,I,J,M,CURARC,CURCOL,CURROW,LAMBDA,DELTA
       INTEGER THRESH,INCR,STARTINCR,INCRFACTOR,EPS_THRESH
       INTEGER NOLIST,RNOLIST,NONEWLIST,RNONEWLIST
       INTEGER ROW,COLUMN, BSTROW,BSTCOL
       INTEGER FSTARC,FSTCOL,NXTARC,NXTROW,LSTARC,SNDARC,SNDCOL
       INTEGER MAX1,MAX2,TMAX,TMIN,TRDARC,EPSILON,BEGEPS,ENDEPS
       INTEGER ISMALL,ILARGE,LARGEINCR,CYCLES
       INTEGER NUMPHASES,OLDROW,OLDCOL
       INTEGER MAX3,BSTARC,SBSTARC
       INTEGER CUR_BARC,TRDVAL(MAXNODES)
       LOGICAL INIT,REVERSE
       INTEGER BEST_ARC(MAXNODES),SECD_ARC(MAXNODES)
       INTEGER COL_ASSIGNED_TO(MAXNODES),ROW_ASSIGNED_TO(MAXNODES)
       INTEGER FOUT(MAXNODES),FIN(MAXNODES),NXTIN(MAXARCS)
       INTEGER COST(MAXARCS),START(MAXARCS),END(MAXARCS)
       INTEGER LIST(MAXNODES),REV_LIST(MAXNODES)
       INTEGER PCOL(MAXNODES),PROW(MAXNODES)
       REAL AVERAGE,FACTOR
       COMMON/ARRAYC/COST/ARRAYS/START/ARRAYE/END
       COMMON/ARRAYFO/FOUT/ARRAYFI/FIN/ARRAYNI/NXTIN
       COMMON/ARRAYRA/ROW_ASSIGNED_TO/ARRAYCA/COL_ASSIGNED_TO
       COMMON/ARRAYPC/PCOL/ARRAYPR/PROW
       COMMON/BK1/M,N,A,ILARGE
       COMMON/BK2/CYCLES,AVERAGE,NUMPHASES,LAMBDA

C ******* CHECK VALIDITY OF PARAMETERS PASSED *******

       IF (BEGEPS.LT.1) THEN
       PRINT*,'STARTING VALUE OF EPSILON IS LESS THAN 1'
       PRINT*,'EXECUTION ABORTED'
       STOP
       END IF
       IF (ENDEPS.GT.BEGEPS) THEN
       PRINT*,'PARAMETER ENDEPS IS GREATER THAN PARAMETER BEGEPS'
       PRINT*,'ENDEPS IS SET AT THE DEFAULT VALUE OF 1'
       ENDEPS=1
       END IF
       IF ((FACTOR.LE.1).AND.(BEGEPS.GT.1)) THEN
       PRINT*,'EPSILON REDUCTION FACTOR IS NOT GREATER THAN 1'
       PRINT*,'EXECUTION ABORTED'
       STOP
       END IF
       IF (STARTINCR.LT.1) THEN
       PRINT*,'MIN BIDDING INCREMENT IS LESS THAN 1'
       PRINT*,'STARTINCR IS SET AT THE DEFAULT VALUE OF 1'
       STARTINCR=1
       END IF
```

```
C ******* INITIALIZATION *******

        EPSILON=BEGEPS
        IF ((EPSILON.EQ.1).OR.(M.EQ.N)) THEN
        REVERSE=.FALSE.
        ELSE
        REVERSE=.TRUE.
        END IF
        ISMALL=-ILARGE
        LARGEINCR=INT(ILARGE/10)
        THRESH=INT(0.2*M)
        INCRFACTOR=2
        EPS_THRESH=BEGEPS/(FACTOR**3)
        IF (EPS_THRESH.LT.2) EPS_THRESH=2
        INIT=.FALSE.
        IF (THRESH.GT.100) THRESH=100
X       CYCLES=1
X       AVERAGE=N
        NUMPHASES=1
        DO 10 I=1,N
        PCOL(I)=ISMALL
10      CONTINUE
        FOUT(M+1)=A+1


C *************************************************************
C THIS IMPLEMENTATION OF AUCTION OPERATES IN CYCLES.
C EACH CYCLE CONSISTS OF ONE BID BY EACH OF THE ROWS THAT ARE
C UNASSIGNED AT THE START OF THE CYCLE (THESE ROWS ARE STORED IN
C THE ARRAY LIST(.)). AS THE CYCLE PROGRESSES NEW
C ROWS BECOME UNASSIGNED; THESE ARE STORED IN LIST(.)
C AND WILL SUBMIT A BID AT THE NEXT CYCLE.
C THE ALGORITHM FIRST FINDS A FEASIBLE ASSIGNMENT, WHERE ALL
C PERSONS ARE ASSIGNED, USING A FORWARD AUCTION. THEN THE
C ALGORITHM USES A MODIFIED REVERSE AUCTION TO SATISFY
C THE REMAINING E-CS CONDITIONS.
C *************************************************************
C START SUBPROBLEM (SCALING PHASE) W/ NEW EPSILON
C *************************************************************

12      CONTINUE

C INITIALIZE ROW ASSIGNMENT LISTS

        NOLIST=M
        DO 20 I=1,M
        LIST(I)=I
20      CONTINUE
        DO 22 J=1,N
        ROW_ASSIGNED_TO(J)=0
22      CONTINUE
        INCR=STARTINCR
        IF (INCR.GT.EPSILON) INCR=EPSILON
        IF (EPSILON.EQ.1) THRESH=0

        IF (EPSILON.LT.EPS_THRESH) THEN

C START FORWARD AUCTION CYCLE W/ THIRD BEST IMPLEMENTATION
C FEATURE. OTHERWISE START A "REGULAR" FORWARD AUCTION CYCLE
```

```
C AT LABEL NUMBERED 15

17      CONTINUE

C INITIALIZE COUNT OF NEXT LIST OF UNASSIGNED ROWS

        NONEWLIST=0

C CYCLE THROUGH THE CURRENT LIST OF UNASSIGNED ROWS

        DO 103 I=1,NOLIST
        ROW=LIST(I)
        FSTARC=FOUT(ROW)
        LSTARC=FOUT(ROW+1)-1
        FSTCOL=END(FSTARC)

C FIRST TAKE CARE OF THE EXCEPTIONAL CASE
C WHERE ROW HAS ONLY ONE ARC

        IF (FSTARC.EQ.LSTARC) THEN
        PCOL(FSTCOL)=PCOL(FSTCOL)+LARGEINCR
        PROW(ROW)=COST(FSTARC)-PCOL(FSTCOL)
        OLDROW=ROW_ASSIGNED_TO(FSTCOL)
        ROW_ASSIGNED_TO(FSTCOL)=ROW
        IF (OLDROW.GT.0) THEN
        NONEWLIST=NONEWLIST+1
        LIST(NONEWLIST)=OLDROW
        END IF
        GO TO 103
        END IF

C NEXT TAKE CARE OF THE REGULAR CASE
C WHERE ROW HAS MULTIPLE ARCS

        IF (((FSTARC+2).LE.LSTARC).AND.(INIT)) THEN
        BSTARC=BEST_ARC(ROW)
        SBSTARC=SECD_ARC(ROW)
        BSTCOL=END(BSTARC)
        SNDCOL=END(SECD_ARC(ROW))
        MAX1=COST(BSTARC)-PCOL(BSTCOL)
        MAX2=COST(SBSTARC)-PCOL(SNDCOL)
        IF((MAX1.GE.TRDVAL(ROW)).AND.(MAX2.GE.TRDVAL(ROW))) THEN
        IF (MAX1.LT.MAX2) THEN
        TMAX=MAX1
        MAX1=MAX2
        MAX2=TMAX
        BSTCOL=SNDCOL
        END IF
        GO TO 70
        END IF
        END IF

        SNDARC=FSTARC+1
        SNDCOL=END(SNDARC)
        MAX1=COST(FSTARC)-PCOL(FSTCOL)
        MAX2=COST(SNDARC)-PCOL(SNDCOL)
        IF (MAX1.GE.MAX2) THEN
        BSTARC=FSTARC
```

```
          SBSTARC=SNDARC
          ELSE
          TMAX=MAX1
          MAX1=MAX2
          MAX2=TMAX
          BSTARC=SNDARC
          SBSTARC=FSTARC
          END IF
          IF (SNDARC.LT.LSTARC) THEN
          TRDARC=SNDARC+1
          MAX3=ISMALL
          DO 43 CURARC=TRDARC,LSTARC
          CURCOL=END(CURARC)
          TMAX=COST(CURARC)-PCOL(CURCOL)
          IF (TMAX.GT.MAX2) THEN
          IF (TMAX.GT.MAX1) THEN
          SBSTARC=BSTARC
          BSTARC=CURARC
          MAX3=MAX2
          MAX2=MAX1
          MAX1=TMAX
          ELSE
          SBSTARC=CURARC
          MAX3=MAX2
          MAX2=TMAX
          END IF
          ELSE
          IF (MAX3.LT.TMAX) MAX3=TMAX
          END IF
43        CONTINUE
          END IF
          BEST_ARC(ROW)=BSTARC
          BSTCOL=END(BSTARC)
          SECD_ARC(ROW)=SBSTARC
          TRDVAL(ROW)=MAX3
70        CONTINUE

C ROW BIDS FOR BSTCOL INCREASING ITS PRICE, AND GETS ASSIGNED
C TO BSTCOL; ANY ROW ASSIGNED TO BSTCOL BECOMES UNASSIGNED

          PCOL(BSTCOL)=PCOL(BSTCOL)+MAX1-MAX2+INCR
          PROW(ROW)=MAX2-INCR
          OLDROW=ROW_ASSIGNED_TO(BSTCOL)
          ROW_ASSIGNED_TO(BSTCOL)=ROW
          IF (OLDROW.GT.0) THEN
          NONEWLIST=NONEWLIST+1
          LIST(NONEWLIST)=OLDROW
          END IF
103       CONTINUE

C END OF A FORWARD AUCTION CYCLE W/ THIRD BEST IMPLEMENTATION
C OPTIONALLY COLLECT STATISTICS

X         AVERAGE=(CYCLES*AVERAGE+NOLIST)/(CYCLES+1)
X         CYCLES=CYCLES+1

C CHECK IF A SWITCH TO MODIFIED REVERSE AUCTION
C SHOULD BE MADE (IF NONEWLIST EQUALS ZERO).
```

```
C ALSO INCREASE THE MINIMAL BIDDING INCREMENT UP TO A MAXIMUM
C VALUE OF EPSILON (THIS IS THE ADAPTIVE FEATURE)

         INCR=INCR*INCRFACTOR
         IF (INCR.GT.EPSILON) INCR=EPSILON
         IF (NONEWLIST.GT.THRESH) THEN
         NOLIST=NONEWLIST
         INIT=.TRUE.
         GO TO 17
         END IF

         ELSE

C START "REGULAR" FORWARD AUCTION CYCLE

15       CONTINUE

C INITIALIZE COUNT OF NEXT LIST OF UNASSIGNED ROWS

         NONEWLIST=0


C CYCLE THROUGH THE CURRENT LIST OF UNASSIGNED ROWS

         DO 100 I=1,NOLIST
         ROW=LIST(I)
         FSTARC=FOUT(ROW)
         LSTARC=FOUT(ROW+1)-1
         FSTCOL=END(FSTARC)

C FIRST TAKE CARE OF THE EXCEPTIONAL CASE
C WHERE ROW HAS ONLY ONE ARC

         IF (FSTARC.EQ.LSTARC) THEN
         PCOL(FSTCOL)=PCOL(FSTCOL)+LARGEINCR
         PROW(ROW)=COST(FSTARC)-PCOL(FSTCOL)
         OLDROW=ROW_ASSIGNED_TO(FSTCOL)
         ROW_ASSIGNED_TO(FSTCOL)=ROW
         IF (OLDROW.GT.0) THEN
         NONEWLIST=NONEWLIST+1
         LIST(NONEWLIST)=OLDROW
         END IF
         GO TO 100
         END IF

C NEXT TAKE CARE OF THE REGULAR CASE
C WHERE ROW HAS MULTIPLE ARCS

         SNDARC=FSTARC+1
         SNDCOL=END(SNDARC)
         MAX1=COST(FSTARC)-PCOL(FSTCOL)
         MAX2=COST(SNDARC)-PCOL(SNDCOL)
         IF (MAX1.GE.MAX2) THEN
         BSTCOL=FSTCOL
         ELSE
         TMAX=MAX1
         MAX1=MAX2
         MAX2=TMAX
```

```
            BSTCOL=SNDCOL
            END IF
            IF (SNDARC.LT.LSTARC) THEN
            TRDARC=SNDARC+1
            DO 40 CURARC=TRDARC,LSTARC
            CURCOL=END(CURARC)
            TMAX=COST(CURARC)-PCOL(CURCOL)
            IF (TMAX.GT.MAX2) THEN
            IF (TMAX.GT.MAX1) THEN
            MAX2=MAX1
            MAX1=TMAX
            BSTCOL=CURCOL
            ELSE
            MAX2=TMAX
            END IF
            END IF
  40        CONTINUE
            END IF

C ROW BIDS FOR BSTCOL INCREASING ITS PRICE, AND GETS ASSIGNED
C TO BSTCOL; ANY ROW ASSIGNED TO BSTCOL BECOMES UNASSIGNED

            PCOL(BSTCOL)=PCOL(BSTCOL)+MAX1-MAX2+INCR
            PROW(ROW)=MAX2-INCR
            OLDROW=ROW_ASSIGNED_TO(BSTCOL)
            ROW_ASSIGNED_TO(BSTCOL)=ROW
            IF (OLDROW.GT.0) THEN
            NONEWLIST=NONEWLIST+1
            LIST(NONEWLIST)=OLDROW
            END IF
  100       CONTINUE

C ********* END OF A REGULAR FORWARD AUCTION CYCLE **********
C OPTIONALLY COLLECT STATISTICS

X           AVERAGE=(CYCLES*AVERAGE+NOLIST)/(CYCLES+1)
X           CYCLES=CYCLES+1
C CHECK IF A SWITCH TO MODIFIED REVERSE AUCTION
C SHOULD BE MADE (IF NONEWLIST IS NO MORE THAN THE THRESHOLD).
C ALSO INCREASE THE MINIMAL BIDDING INCREMENT UP TO A MAXIMUM
C VALUE OF EPSILON (THIS IS THE ADAPTIVE FEATURE)

            INCR=INCR*INCRFACTOR
            IF (INCR.GT.EPSILON) INCR=EPSILON
            IF (NONEWLIST.GT.THRESH) THEN
            NOLIST=NONEWLIST
            GO TO 15
            END IF

            END IF

C *************************************************************
C START OF MODIFIED REVERSE AUCTION
C *************************************************************

C IF THE PROBLEM IS SYMMETRIC SKIP THE REVERSE AUCTION

            IF (NOT.REVERSE) GOTO 400
```

```
C IF EPSILON IS NOT YET ONE SKIP THE REVERSE AUCTION

      IF (EPSILON.GT.1) GOTO 400

      INCR=EPSILON

C COMPUTE LAMBDA WHICH IS THE MINIMUM COLUMN PRICE OVER ALL
C ASSIGNED COLUMNS, AND COMPILE THE LIST OF UNASSIGNED COLUMNS

      LAMBDA=ILARGE
      RNOLIST=0
      DO 310 J=1,N
      ROW=ROW_ASSIGNED_TO(J)
      IF (ROW.GT.0) THEN
      COL_ASSIGNED_TO(ROW)=J
      IF (LAMBDA.GT.PCOL(J)) LAMBDA=PCOL(J)
      ELSE
      RNOLIST=RNOLIST+1
      REV_LIST(RNOLIST)=J
      END IF
310   CONTINUE
      IF (RNOLIST.NE.N-M) THEN
      PRINT*,'NUMBER OF UNASSIGNED ROWS IS WRONG'
      PAUSE
      STOP
      END IF

C START OF A NEW MODIFIED REVERSE AUCTION CYCLE

315   CONTINUE

C INITIALIZE COUNT OF NEXT LIST OF UNASSIGNED COLUMNS

      RNONEWLIST=0

C CYCLE THROUGH THE CURRENT LIST OF UNASSIGNED COLUMNS

      DO 340 J=1,RNOLIST
      COLUMN=REV_LIST(J)
      IF (PCOL(COLUMN).LE.LAMBDA) GO TO 340
      CURARC=FIN(COLUMN)
      NXTARC=NXTIN(CURARC)
      CURROW=START(CURARC)

C FIRST TAKE CARE OF THE EXCEPTIONAL CASE
C WHERE ROW HAS ONLY ONE ARC

      IF (NXTARC.EQ.0) THEN
      MAX1=COST(CURARC)-PROW(CURROW)
      IF (LAMBDA.GE.MAX1-INCR) THEN
      PCOL(COLUMN)=LAMBDA
      GO TO 340
      END IF
      PCOL(COLUMN)=LAMBDA
      PROW(CURROW)=COST(CURARC)-LAMBDA
      OLDCOL=COL_ASSIGNED_TO(CURROW)
      COL_ASSIGNED_TO(CURROW)=COLUMN
```

```
          IF (PCOL(OLDCOL).GT.LAMBDA) THEN
          RNONEWLIST=RNONEWLIST+1
          REV_LIST(RNONEWLIST)=OLDCOL
          END IF
          GO TO 340
          END IF

C NEXT TAKE CARE OF THE REGULAR CASE
C WHERE ROW HAS MULTIPLE ARCS

          NXTROW=START(NXTARC)
          MAX1=COST(CURARC)-PROW(CURROW)
          MAX2=COST(NXTARC)-PROW(NXTROW)
          IF (MAX1.GE.MAX2) THEN
          BSTROW=CURROW
          ELSE
          TMAX=MAX1
          MAX1=MAX2
          MAX2=TMAX
          BSTROW=NXTROW
          END IF

          CURARC=NXTIN(NXTARC)

330    IF (CURARC.GT.0) THEN
          CURROW=START(CURARC)
          TMAX=COST(CURARC)-PROW(CURROW)
          IF (TMAX.GT.MAX2) THEN
          IF (TMAX.GT.MAX1) THEN
          MAX2=MAX1
          MAX1=TMAX
          BSTROW=CURROW
          ELSE
          MAX2=TMAX
          END IF
          END IF
          CURARC=NXTIN(CURARC)
          GO TO 330
          END IF

C COLUMN BIDS FOR BSTROW INCREASING ITS PRICE, AND GETS ASSIGNED
C TO BSTROW; ANY COLUMN ASSIGNED TO BSTROW BECOMES UNASSIGNED

          IF (LAMBDA.GE.MAX1-INCR) THEN
          PCOL(COLUMN)=LAMBDA
          GO TO 340
          END IF
          DELTA=MAX1-MAX2+INCR
          IF (DELTA.GT.MAX1-LAMBDA) DELTA=MAX1-LAMBDA
          PROW(BSTROW)=PROW(BSTROW)+DELTA
          PCOL(COLUMN)=MAX1-DELTA
          OLDCOL=COL_ASSIGNED_TO(BSTROW)
          COL_ASSIGNED_TO(BSTROW)=COLUMN
          IF (PCOL(OLDCOL).GT.LAMBDA) THEN
          RNONEWLIST=RNONEWLIST+1
          REV_LIST(RNONEWLIST)=OLDCOL
          END IF
340    CONTINUE
```

```
C ********** END OF A MODIFIED REVERSE AUCTION CYCLE ***********
C OPTIONALLY COLLECT STATISTICS

X      AVERAGE=(CYCLES*AVERAGE+RNOLIST)/(CYCLES+1)
X      CYCLES=CYCLES+1
       IF (RNONEWLIST.GT.0) THEN
       RNOLIST=RNONEWLIST
       GO TO 315
       END IF

C **************************************************************
C END OF SUBPROBLEM (SCALING PHASE)
C **************************************************************

400    CONTINUE

C ****** IF EPSILON IS 1 TERMINATE ******

       IF (EPSILON.EQ.1) THEN
       RETURN
       ELSE

C ELSE REDUCE EPSILON AND UPDATE PARAMETERS
C FOR THE NEXT SCALING PHASE

       NUMPHASES=NUMPHASES+1
       EPSILON=INT(EPSILON/FACTOR)
       IF (EPSILON.GT.INCR) EPSILON=INT(EPSILON/FACTOR)
       IF ((EPSILON.LT.1).OR.(EPSILON.LT.ENDEPS)) EPSILON=1
       IF (STARTINCR.LT.EPSILON) STARTINCR=FACTOR*STARTINCR
       THRESH=INT(THRESH/FACTOR)

X       PRINT*,'*** END OF A SCALING PHASE; NEW EPSILON=',EPSILON
       GO TO 12
       END IF
       END

       SUBROUTINE SETRAN(ISEED)
       SAME AS IN CODE GRIDGEN
```

A.4.2   AUCTION-FR

This code implements the combined forward/reverse auction algorithm with
ϵ-scaling for the symmetric assignment problem; cf. Section 4.2. For good
performance, it is frequently not essential to use ϵ-scaling in this code. It is
therefore recommended that the code be tried without ϵ-scaling by setting the
starting ϵ to 1.

```
C **************************************************************
C SAMPLE CALLING PROGRAM FOR COMBINED FORWARD/REVERSE
C AUCTION ALGORITHM
C THIS DRIVER CREATES A SYMMETRIC ASSIGNMENT PROBLEM
C WITH EQUAL NUMBER OF ROWS AND COLUMNS,
C AND CALLS THE AUCTION_FR SUBROUTINE TO FIND AN
```

```
C ASSIGNMENT OF MAXIMAL VALUE.
C ****************************************************************

      PARAMETER(MAXNODES=10000, MAXARCS=100000)
      IMPLICIT NONE
      INTEGER N,NA,A,ILARGE,BEGEPS,ENDEPS,CYCLES
      INTEGER NUMPHASES,STARTINCR,AVERAGE
      INTEGER I,J,ARC,NOASS,ICOST,ABSCOST,CURARC
      INTEGER CURCOL,FSTARC,LSTARC,MINCOST,MAXCOST
      INTEGER COL_ASSIGNED_TO(MAXNODES),ROW_ASSIGNED_TO(MAXNODES)
      INTEGER FOUT(MAXNODES),FIN(MAXNODES),NXTIN(MAXARCS)
      INTEGER COST(MAXARCS),START(MAXARCS),END(MAXARCS)
      INTEGER PCOL(MAXNODES),PROW(MAXNODES)
      INTEGER PRDARC(MAXNODES)
      REAL FACTOR,TT1,TT2,TCOST
      COMMON/ARRAYC/COST/ARRAYS/START/ARRAYE/END
      COMMON/ARRAYFO/FOUT/ARRAYFI/FIN/ARRAYNI/NXTIN
      COMMON/ARRAYRA/ROW_ASSIGNED_TO/ARRAYCA/COL_ASSIGNED_TO
      COMMON/ARRAYPC/PCOL/ARRAYPR/PROW
      COMMON/BK1/N,A,ILARGE/BK2/CYCLES,AVERAGE,NUMPHASES


C ***********************************************************
C PROBLEM GENERATION CODE STARTS HERE
C THE USER MAY REPLACE THIS CODE WITH A CODE THAT READS
C HIS/HER PROBLEM FROM A FILE
C ***********************************************************
C THIS CODE INCLUDES A UNIFORM RANDOM NUMBER GENERATOR
C WHICH RETURNS A VALUE IN (0,1)
C INITIALIZE RANDOM GENERATOR

      INTEGER MULT,MODUL,I15,I16,JRAN,ISEED
      REAL RAN
      COMMON /RANDM/ MULT,MODUL,I15,I16,JRAN
      ISEED=13502460
      CALL SETRAN(ISEED)

      PRINT*,'GENERATING A SYMMETRIC ASSIGNMENT PROBLEM'
      PRINT*,'*****************************************'

C **** READ THE NUMBER OF ROWS N & THE NUMBER OF ARCS A ****

      PRINT*,'ENTER THE NUMBER OF ROWS (AND COLUMNS)'
      READ*,N
5     PRINT*,'ENTER THE NUMBER OF ARCS PER ROW (>1)'
      READ*,NA
      IF (NA.LT.2) GOTO 5
      PRINT*,'ENTER THE MINIMUM AND THE MAXIMUM COST'
      READ*,MINCOST,MAXCOST

C THE NUMBER OF ARCS IS N*NA

      A=N*NA

C THE ARCS INCIDENT TO ROW I ARE FOUT(I) TO FOUT(I+1)-1
C ALSO, FOR FEASIBILITY EACH ROW IS DIRECTLY CONNECTED
C WITH THE CORRESPONDING COLUMN

      DO 20 I=1,N
```

```
                    FOUT(I)=1+(I-1)*NA
20          CONTINUE
                    FOUT(N+1)=A+1

                    DO 22 I=1,N
                    DO 23 ARC=FOUT(I),FOUT(I+1)-1
                    START(ARC)=I
23          CONTINUE
22          CONTINUE

C GENERATE THE END(ARC) AND COST(ARC) WHICH ARE THE COLUMN
C AND THE COST COEFFICIENT ASSOCIATED WITH ARC

                    DO 25 ARC=1,A
                    END(ARC)=1+RAN()*N
                    IF ((END(ARC).GT.N).OR.(END(ARC).LT.1)) THEN
                    PRINT*,'ERROR IN PROBLEM GENERATION'
                    PAUSE
                    STOP
                    END IF
                    COST(ARC)=MINCOST+RAN()*(MAXCOST-MINCOST)
25          CONTINUE

C MODIFY THE END OF THE LAST ARC OUT OF EACH ROW FOR FEASIBILITY
C AND SET ITS COST TO -MAXCOST

                    DO 30 I=1,N
                    END(FOUT(I+1)-1)=I
                    COST(FOUT(I+1)-1)=-MAXCOST
30          CONTINUE

C CONSTRUCT THE FIN() AND NXTIN() ARRAYS

                    DO 32 J=1,N
                    FIN(J)=0
                    PRDARC(J)=0
32          CONTINUE
                    DO 33 ARC=1,A
                    NXTIN(ARC)=0
                    J=END(ARC)
                    IF (FIN(J).NE.0) THEN
                    NXTIN(PRDARC(J))=ARC
                    ELSE
                    FIN(J)=ARC
                    END IF
                    PRDARC(J)=ARC
33          CONTINUE

C **************************************************************
C PROBLEM GENERATION CODE ENDS HERE
C **************************************************************
C SCALE THE COST TO WORK WITH INTEGER EPSILON

                    MAXCOST=0
                    DO 35 ARC=1,A
                    COST(ARC)=COST(ARC)*(N+1)
                    ABSCOST=IABS(COST(ARC))
                    IF (ABSCOST.GT.MAXCOST) MAXCOST=ABSCOST
```

```
35      CONTINUE

C *** ILARGE IS A VERY LARGE INTEGER FOR YOUR MACHINE ***
C THE SCALED COSTS SHOULD BE SIGNIFICANTLY SMALLER THAN
C ILARGE AND SIGNIFICANTLY LARGER THAN -ILARGE

        ILARGE=2000000000

C THE FOLLOWING PARAMETERS BEGEPS, FACTOR, ENDEPS, AND STARTINCR
C ARE PASSED TO THE AUCTION ALGORITHM. VALUES BETWEEN
C (A) MAXCOST/2 AND 1 FOR BEGEPS
C (B) 4 AND 6 FOR FACTOR
C (C) N AND 1 FOR ENDEPS
C (D) 1 AND BEGEPS FOR STARTINCR
C HAVE WORKED WELL FOR LARGE SPARSE PROBLEMS.
C FOR DENSE PROBLEMS IT IS RECOMMENDED THAT
C BEGEPS BE SET TO A SMALLER VALUE,
C ENDEPS BE SET TO 1,
C STARTINCR BE SET TO 1.
C GENERALLY, THE COMBINED FORWARD/REVERSE ALGORITHM
C WORKS BEST WITH A SMALLER VALUE OF BEGEPS THAN THE
C FORWARD ALGORITHM.
C IT IS WORTH TRYING BEGEPS=1, IN WHICH CASE THERE IS
C ONLY ONE SCALING PHASE (THAT IS, NO E-SCALING IS USED).

        PRINT*,'****************************************'
        PRINT*,'MAXIMUM COST IS ',MAXCOST
        PRINT*,'ENTER THE STARTING EPSILON'
        READ*,BEGEPS
        IF (BEGEPS.LT.1) BEGEPS=1
        PRINT*,'ENTER THE EPSILON REDUCTION FACTOR'
        READ*,FACTOR
        ENDEPS=N/10
        IF (ENDEPS.LT.1) ENDEPS=1
        IF (ENDEPS.GT.BEGEPS) ENDEPS=BEGEPS
        STARTINCR=1
        IF (STARTINCR.LT.1) STARTINCR=1
        PRINT*,'****************************************'
        PRINT*,'STARTING EPSILON = ',BEGEPS
        PRINT*,'EPSILON REDUCTION FACTOR = ',FACTOR
        PRINT*,'THRESHOLD EPSILON BEFORE IT IS SET TO 1 = ',ENDEPS
        PRINT*,'STARTING MIN BIDDING INCREMENT = ',STARTINCR
        PRINT*,'CALLING FORWARD/REVERSE AUCTION'
        PRINT*,'****************************************'

C GET STARTING TIME FOR THE MAC II

        TT1 = LONG(362)/60.0

        CALL AUCTION_FR(BEGEPS,FACTOR,ENDEPS,STARTINCR)

C GET ENDING TIME FOR THE MAC II

        TT2 = LONG(362)/60.0 - TT1
        PRINT *,'FINISHED — TOTAL CPU TIME', TT2,' SECS'
        PRINT*,'****************************************'

C *** DISPLAY RESULTS ***
```

```
X           WRITE(9,2010) CYCLES
X2010    FORMAT(' NO OF AUCTION CYCLES',I7)
X           WRITE(9,2020) AVERAGE
X2020    FORMAT(' AVERAGE NUMBER OF BIDS PER CYCLE',F9.3)
           WRITE(9,2030) NUMPHASES
2030     FORMAT('NO OF EPSILON SUBPROBLEMS SOLVED =',I7)

C CHECK OPTIMALITY & CALCULATE COST

           TCOST=0
           DO 40 I=1,N
           J=COL_ASSIGNED_TO(I)
           IF (J.EQ.0) THEN
           PRINT*,'ROW ',I,' IS UNASSIGNED'
           END IF
           IF (ROW_ASSIGNED_TO(J).NE.I) THEN
           PRINT*,'ASSIGNMENT MIXUP: ROW ',I,' COLUMN ',J
           END IF
           FSTARC=FOUT(I)
           LSTARC=FOUT(I+1)-1
           MAXCOST=-ILARGE
           DO 45 ARC=FSTARC,LSTARC
           CURCOL=END(ARC)
           IF (PROW(I)+PCOL(CURCOL).LT.COST(ARC)-1) THEN
           PRINT*,'1-CS VIOLATED AT ARC ',ARC
           END IF
           IF (CURCOL.EQ.J) THEN
           IF (MAXCOST.LT.COST(ARC)) THEN
           MAXCOST=COST(ARC)
           END IF
           END IF
45         CONTINUE
           TCOST=TCOST+MAXCOST/(N+1)
           IF (PROW(I)+PCOL(J).NE.MAXCOST) THEN
           PRINT*,'1-CS VIOLATED AT ROW ',I
           END IF
40         CONTINUE
           DO 50 J=1,N
           IF (ROW_ASSIGNED_TO(J).EQ.0) THEN
           PRINT*,'COLUMN ',J,' IS UNASSIGNED'
           END IF
50         CONTINUE
           WRITE(9,2100) TCOST
2100     FORMAT(' ASSIGNMENT COST=',F14.2)
           PRINT *, ' PROGRAM ENDED; <CR> TO EXIT '

           PAUSE
           END


C ****************************************************************
C FORWARD/REVERSE AUCTION CODE FOR N BY N ASSIGNMENT PROBLEMS
C WRITTEN BY DIMITRI P. BERTSEKAS
C DEC. 1990
C THIS CODE IMPLEMENTS THE FORWARD/REVERSE AUCTION ALGORITHM
C WITH E-SCALING FOR SYMMETRIC N BY N ASSIGNMENT PROBLEMS.
C IT SOLVES A SEQUENCE OF SUBPROBLEMS AND DECREASES
C EPSILON BY A CONSTANT FACTOR BETWEEN SUBPROBLEMS.
```

```
C THIS VERSION CORRESPONDS TO A GAUSS-SEIDEL MODE
C AND SOLVES EPSILON SUBPROBLEMS INEXACTLY.
C THE CODE IS AN IMPROVED VERSION OF AN EARLIER (SEPT. 1985)
C AUCTION CODE WITH E-SCALING WRITTEN BY DIMITRI P. BERTSEKAS
C THE CODE TREATS THE PROBLEM AS A MAXIMIZATION PROBLEM.
C TO SOLVE A MINIMIZATION PROBLEM, REVERSE THE SIGN OF THE
C ARC COSTS PRIOR TO CALLING AUCTION, AND REVERSE AGAIN
C THE SIGN OF THE OPTIMAL COST UPON RETURN FROM AUCTION.
C THIS CODE ALLOWS MULTIPLE ARCS BETWEEN A ROW AND A COLUMN.
C THIS VERSION OF THE AUCTION ALGORITHM IS ADAPTIVE.
C ********************************************************************
C THE USER MUST SUPPLY THE FOLLOWING PROBLEM DATA
C IN FORWARD STAR FORMAT
C (THAT IS, ALL ARCS OF THE SAME ROW ARE NUMBERED CONSECUTIVELY):
C N=NUMBER OF ROWS (EQUALS NUMBER OF COLUMNS)
C A=NUMBER OF ARCS
C FOUT(ROW)=FIRST ARC COMING OUT OF ROW
C FIN(COL)=FIRST ARC COMING INTO COL
C NXTIN(ARC)=NEXT ARC INCIDENT TO THE SAME COLUMN AS ARC
C COST(ARC)=COST OF ARC
C START(ARC)=ROW CORRESPONDING TO ARC
C END(ARC)=COLUMN CORRESPONDING TO ARC
C AND THE FOLLOWING PARAMETERS FOR THE AUCTION ALGORITHM:
C BEGEPS=STARTING VALUE OF EPSILON (MUST BE NO LESS THAN 1)
C ENDEPS=FINAL VALUE OF EPSILON BEFORE IT IS SET TO 1
C FACTOR=EPSILON REDUCTION FACTOR BETWEEN SUBPROBLEMS
C STARTINCR=THE STARTING VALUE OF THE BIDDING INCREMENT
C ENDEPS SHOULD NOT EXCEED BEGEPS.
C FACTOR MUST BE GREATER THAN 1 (UNLESS BEGEPS=1).
C FOUT(.) IS AN ARRAY OF LENGTH N.
C COST(.),END(.) ARE ARRAYS OF LENGTH A.
C THE SOLUTION IS CONTAINED IN THE ARRAY ROW_ASSIGNED_TO(.) WHERE
C ROW_ASSIGNED_TO(COL) GIVES THE ROW ASSIGNED TO COL.
C ALSO COL_ASSIGNED_TO(ROW) GIVES THE COLUMN ASSIGNED TO ROW.
C THIS ALGORITHM DOES NOT CHECK FOR INFEASIBILITY OF THE PROBLEM.
C TO MAKE SURE THE PROBLEM IS FEASIBLE THE USER MAY ADD
C ADDITIONAL VERY SMALL (I.E., LARGE NEGATIVE) COST ARCS.
C ********************************************************************
C ALL PROBLEM DATA ARE INTEGER
C ********************************************************************

        SUBROUTINE AUCTION_FR(BEGEPS,FACTOR,ENDEPS,STARTINCR)
        PARAMETER(MAXNODES=10000, MAXARCS=100000)
        IMPLICIT NONE
        INTEGER A,K,N,I,J,M,CURARC,CURCOL,CURROW
        INTEGER THRESH,INCR,STARTINCR,INCRFACTOR
        INTEGER NOLIST,RNOLIST,NONEWLIST,RNONEWLIST
        INTEGER ROW,COLUMN, BSTROW,BSTCOL
        INTEGER FSTARC,FSTCOL,NXTARC,NXTROW,LSTARC,SNDARC,SNDCOL
        INTEGER MAX1,MAX2,TMAX,TMIN,TRDARC,EPSILON,BEGEPS,ENDEPS
        INTEGER ISMALL,ILARGE,LARGEINCR,CYCLES
        INTEGER NUMPHASES,OLDROW,OLDCOL
        INTEGER COL_ASSIGNED_TO(MAXNODES),ROW_ASSIGNED_TO(MAXNODES)
        INTEGER FOUT(MAXNODES),FIN(MAXNODES),NXTIN(MAXARCS)
        INTEGER COST(MAXARCS),START(MAXARCS),END(MAXARCS)
        INTEGER LIST(MAXNODES),REV_LIST(MAXNODES)
        INTEGER PCOL(MAXNODES),PROW(MAXNODES)
        REAL AVERAGE,FACTOR
```

```
      LOGICAL READY_SWITCH,SWITCH
      COMMON/ARRAYC/COST/ARRAYS/START/ARRAYE/END
      COMMON/ARRAYFO/FOUT/ARRAYFI/FIN/ARRAYNI/NXTIN
      COMMON/ARRAYRA/ROW_ASSIGNED_TO/ARRAYCA/COL_ASSIGNED_TO
      COMMON/ARRAYPC/PCOL/ARRAYPR/PROW
      COMMON/BK1/N,A,ILARGE/BK2/CYCLES,AVERAGE,NUMPHASES

C ************************************************************
C ******* CHECK VALIDITY OF PARAMETERS PASSED *******

      IF (BEGEPS.LT.1) THEN
      PRINT*,'STARTING VALUE OF EPSILON IS LESS THAN 1'
      PRINT*,'EXECUTION ABORTED'
      STOP
      END IF
      IF (ENDEPS.GT.BEGEPS) THEN
      PRINT*,'PARAMETER ENDEPS IS GREATER THAN PARAMETER BEGEPS'
      PRINT*,'ENDEPS IS SET AT THE DEFAULT VALUE OF 1'
      ENDEPS=1
      END IF
      IF ((FACTOR.LE.1).AND.(BEGEPS.GT.1)) THEN
      PRINT*,'EPSILON REDUCTION FACTOR IS NOT GREATER THAN 1'
      PRINT*,'EXECUTION ABORTED'
      STOP
      END IF
      IF (STARTINCR.LT.1) THEN
      PRINT*,'MIN BIDDING INCREMENT IS LESS THAN 1'
      PRINT*,'STARTINCR IS SET AT THE DEFAULT VALUE OF 1'
      STARTINCR=1
      END IF

C ******* INITIALIZATION *******

      EPSILON=BEGEPS
      ISMALL=-ILARGE
      LARGEINCR=INT(ILARGE/10)
      THRESH=INT(0.2*N)
      INCRFACTOR=2
      IF (THRESH.GT.100) THRESH=100
X        CYCLES=1
X        AVERAGE=N
      NUMPHASES=1

C INITIALIZE FORWARD/REVERSE SWITCH PARAMETERS

      READY_SWITCH=.FALSE.
      SWITCH=.TRUE.

      DO 10 J=1,N
      PCOL(J)=0
10    CONTINUE
      FOUT(N+1)=A+1

C ************************************************************
C THIS IMPLEMENTATION OF THE AUCTION ALGORITHM OPERATES IN
C CYCLES. EACH FORWARD AUCTION CYCLE CONSISTS OF ONE BID BY EACH
C OF THE ROWS THAT ARE UNASSIGNED AT THE START OF THE CYCLE
C (THESE ROWS ARE STORED IN THE ARRAY LIST(.)).
```

```
C AS THE CYCLE PROGRESSES NEW
C ROWS BECOME UNASSIGNED; THESE ARE STORED IN LIST(.)
C AND WILL SUBMIT A BID AT THE NEXT CYCLE.
C REVERSE AUCTION CYCLES ARE STRUCTURED SIMILARLY.
C **************************************************************
C START SUBPROBLEM (SCALING PHASE) W/ NEW EPSILON
C **************************************************************

12        CONTINUE

C INITIALIZE ROW AND COLUMN ASSIGNMENT LISTS

          NOLIST=N
          DO 20 I=1,N
          COL_ASSIGNED_TO(I)=0
          LIST(I)=I
20        CONTINUE
          RNOLIST=N
          DO 22 J=1,N
          ROW_ASSIGNED_TO(J)=0
          REV_LIST(J)=J
22        CONTINUE
          INCR=STARTINCR
          IF (INCR.GT.EPSILON) INCR=EPSILON
          IF (EPSILON.EQ.1) THRESH=0


C **************************************************************
C START FORWARD AUCTION CYCLE
C **************************************************************

15        CONTINUE

C INITIALIZE COUNT OF NEXT LIST OF UNASSIGNED ROWS

          NONEWLIST=0

C CYCLE THROUGH THE CURRENT LIST OF UNASSIGNED ROWS

          DO 100 I=1,NOLIST
          ROW=LIST(I)
          IF (COL_ASSIGNED_TO(ROW).GT.0) GO TO 100
          FSTARC=FOUT(ROW)
          LSTARC=FOUT(ROW+1)-1
          FSTCOL=END(FSTARC)

C FIRST TAKE CARE OF THE EXCEPTIONAL CASE
C WHERE ROW HAS ONLY ONE ARC

          IF (FSTARC.EQ.LSTARC) THEN
          PCOL(FSTCOL)=PCOL(FSTCOL)+LARGEINCR
          PROW(ROW)=COST(FSTARC)-PCOL(FSTCOL)
          OLDROW=ROW_ASSIGNED_TO(FSTCOL)
          ROW_ASSIGNED_TO(FSTCOL)=ROW
          COL_ASSIGNED_TO(ROW)=FSTCOL
          IF (OLDROW.GT.0) THEN
          COL_ASSIGNED_TO(OLDROW)=0
          NONEWLIST=NONEWLIST+1
          LIST(NONEWLIST)=OLDROW
```

```
            END IF
            GO TO 100
            END IF

C NEXT TAKE CARE OF THE REGULAR CASE
C WHERE ROW HAS MULTIPLE ARCS

            SNDARC=FSTARC+1
            SNDCOL=END(SNDARC)
            MAX1=COST(FSTARC)-PCOL(FSTCOL)
            MAX2=COST(SNDARC)-PCOL(SNDCOL)
            IF (MAX1.GE.MAX2) THEN
            BSTCOL=FSTCOL
            ELSE
            TMAX=MAX1
            MAX1=MAX2
            MAX2=TMAX
            BSTCOL=SNDCOL
            END IF
            IF (SNDARC.LT.LSTARC) THEN
            TRDARC=SNDARC+1
            DO 40 CURARC=TRDARC,LSTARC
            CURCOL=END(CURARC)
            TMAX=COST(CURARC)-PCOL(CURCOL)
            IF (TMAX.GT.MAX2) THEN
            IF (TMAX.GT.MAX1) THEN
            MAX2=MAX1
            MAX1=TMAX
            BSTCOL=CURCOL
            ELSE
            MAX2=TMAX
            END IF
            END IF
40          CONTINUE
            END IF

C ROW BIDS FOR BSTCOL INCREASING ITS PRICE, AND GETS ASSIGNED
C TO BSTCOL; ANY ROW ASSIGNED TO BSTCOL BECOMES UNASSIGNED

            PCOL(BSTCOL)=PCOL(BSTCOL)+MAX1-MAX2+INCR
            PROW(ROW)=MAX2-INCR
            COL_ASSIGNED_TO(ROW)=BSTCOL
            OLDROW=ROW_ASSIGNED_TO(BSTCOL)
            ROW_ASSIGNED_TO(BSTCOL)=ROW
            IF (OLDROW.GT.0) THEN
            COL_ASSIGNED_TO(OLDROW)=0
            NONEWLIST=NONEWLIST+1
            LIST(NONEWLIST)=OLDROW
            END IF
100         CONTINUE

C ************* END OF A FORWARD AUCTION CYCLE **************
C OPTIONALLY COLLECT STATISTICS

X           AVERAGE=(CYCLES*AVERAGE+NOLIST)/(CYCLES+1)
X           CYCLES=CYCLES+1

C CHECK IF THERE ARE STILL 'MANY' UNASSIGNED ROWS, THAT IS, IF THE
```

```
C NUMBER OF UNASSIGNED ROWS IS GREATER THAN
C THE PARAMETER THRESH. IF NOT, REPLACE CURRENT LIST
C WITH THE NEW LIST, AND GO FOR ANOTHER CYCLE.

        INCR=INCR*INCRFACTOR
        IF (INCR.GT.EPSILON) INCR=EPSILON
        IF (NONEWLIST.GT.THRESH) THEN
        IF (SWITCH) THEN
        NOLIST=NONEWLIST
        GO TO 115
        END IF
        IF (NONEWLIST.LT.NOLIST) READY_SWITCH=.TRUE.
        IF ((NONEWLIST.EQ.NOLIST).AND.(READY_SWITCH)) THEN
        READY_SWITCH=.FALSE.
        GO TO 115
        ELSE
        NOLIST=NONEWLIST
        GO TO 15
        END IF
        ELSE
        GO TO 300
        END IF


C ****************************************************************
C START REVERSE AUCTION CYCLE
C ****************************************************************


115    CONTINUE

C INITIALIZE COUNT OF NEXT LIST OF UNASSIGNED COLUMNS

        RNONEWLIST=0

C CYCLE THROUGH THE CURRENT LIST OF UNASSIGNED COLUMNS

        DO 200 J=1,RNOLIST
        COLUMN=REV_LIST(J)
        IF (ROW_ASSIGNED_TO(COLUMN).GT.0) GO TO 200
        CURARC=FIN(COLUMN)
        NXTARC=NXTIN(CURARC)
        CURROW=START(CURARC)

C FIRST TAKE CARE OF THE EXCEPTIONAL CASE
C WHERE ROW HAS ONLY ONE ARC

        IF (NXTARC.EQ.0) THEN
        PROW(CURROW)=PROW(CURROW)+LARGEINCR
        PCOL(COLUMN)=COST(CURARC)-PROW(CURROW)
        OLDCOL=COL_ASSIGNED_TO(CURROW)
        COL_ASSIGNED_TO(CURROW)=COLUMN
        ROW_ASSIGNED_TO(COLUMN)=CURROW
        IF (OLDCOL.GT.0) THEN
        ROW_ASSIGNED_TO(OLDCOL)=0
        RNONEWLIST=RNONEWLIST+1
        REV_LIST(RNONEWLIST)=OLDCOL
        END IF
        GO TO 200
        END IF
```

```
C NEXT TAKE CARE OF THE REGULAR CASE
C WHERE ROW HAS MULTIPLE ARCS

        NXTROW=START(NXTARC)
        MAX1=COST(CURARC)-PROW(CURROW)
        MAX2=COST(NXTARC)-PROW(NXTROW)
        IF (MAX1.GE.MAX2) THEN
        BSTROW=CURROW
        ELSE
        TMAX=MAX1
        MAX1=MAX2
        MAX2=TMAX
        BSTROW=NXTROW
        END IF

        CURARC=NXTIN(NXTARC)

130     IF (CURARC.GT.0) THEN
        CURROW=START(CURARC)
        TMAX=COST(CURARC)-PROW(CURROW)
        IF (TMAX.GT.MAX2) THEN
        IF (TMAX.GT.MAX1) THEN
        MAX2=MAX1
        MAX1=TMAX
        BSTROW=CURROW
        ELSE
        MAX2=TMAX
        END IF
        END IF
        CURARC=NXTIN(CURARC)
        GO TO 130
        END IF

C COLUMN BIDS FOR BSTROW INCREASING ITS PRICE, AND GETS ASSIGNED
C TO BSTROW; ANY COLUMN ASSIGNED TO BSTROW BECOMES UNASSIGNED

        PROW(BSTROW)=PROW(BSTROW)+MAX1-MAX2+INCR
        PCOL(COLUMN)=MAX2-INCR
        ROW_ASSIGNED_TO(COLUMN)=BSTROW
        OLDCOL=COL_ASSIGNED_TO(BSTROW)
        COL_ASSIGNED_TO(BSTROW)=COLUMN
        IF (OLDCOL.GT.0) THEN
        ROW_ASSIGNED_TO(OLDCOL)=0
        RNONEWLIST=RNONEWLIST+1
        REV_LIST(RNONEWLIST)=OLDCOL
        END IF
200     CONTINUE

C ************* END OF A REVERSE AUCTION CYCLE ***************
C OPTIONALLY COLLECT STATISTICS

X       AVERAGE=(CYCLES*AVERAGE+RNOLIST)/(CYCLES+1)
X       CYCLES=CYCLES+1

C CHECK IF THERE ARE STILL 'MANY' UNASSIGNED COLUMNS, THAT IS,
C IF THE NUMBER OF UNASSIGNED COLUMNS IS GREATER THAN
C THE PARAMETER THRESH. IF NOT, REPLACE CURRENT LIST
```

```
C WITH THE NEW LIST, AND GO FOR ANOTHER CYCLE.

      INCR=INCR*INCRFACTOR
      IF (INCR.GT.EPSILON) INCR=EPSILON
      IF (RNONEWLIST.GT.THRESH) THEN
      IF (SWITCH) THEN
      SWITCH=.FALSE.
      RNOLIST=RNONEWLIST
      GO TO 15
      END IF
      IF (RNONEWLIST.LT.RNOLIST) READY_SWITCH=.TRUE.
      IF ((RNONEWLIST.EQ.RNOLIST).AND.(READY_SWITCH)) THEN
      READY_SWITCH=.FALSE.
      GO TO 15
      ELSE
      RNOLIST=RNONEWLIST
      GO TO 115
      END IF
      ELSE
      GO TO 300
      END IF

C ************************************************************
C END OF SUBPROBLEM (SCALING PHASE)
C ************************************************************

300   CONTINUE

C ****** IF EPSILON IS 1 TERMINATE ******

      IF (EPSILON.EQ.1) THEN
      RETURN
      ELSE

C ELSE REDUCE EPSILON AND
C UPDATE PARAMETERS FOR THE NEXT SCALING PHASE

      NUMPHASES=NUMPHASES+1
      EPSILON=INT(EPSILON/FACTOR)
      IF (EPSILON.GT.INCR) EPSILON=INT(EPSILON/FACTOR)
      IF ((EPSILON.LT.1).OR.(EPSILON.LT.ENDEPS)) EPSILON=1
      IF (STARTINCR.LT.EPSILON) STARTINCR=FACTOR*STARTINCR
      THRESH=INT(THRESH/FACTOR)
X     PRINT*,'*** END OF A SCALING PHASE; NEW EPSILON=',EPSILON
      GO TO 12
      END IF
      END

      SUBROUTINE SETRAN(ISEED)
      SAME AS IN CODE GRIDGEN
```

A.5   COMBINED NAIVE AUCTION AND SEQUENTIAL SHORTEST PATH CODE

This code implements the sequential shortest path method for the assignment problem, preceded by an extensive initialization using the naive auction algorithm (cf. Section 1.2.4). The code is quite similar in structure and performance to a code of the author [Ber81] and to the code of [JoV86] and [JoV87]. These codes also combined a naive auction initialization with the sequential shortest path method.

```
C ****************************************************************
C COMBINED NAIVE AUCTION AND SEQUENTIAL SHORTEST PATH METHOD
C FOR SYMMETRIC N X N ASSIGNMENT PROBLEMS
C FINDS AN OPTIMAL ASSIGNMENT
C WRITTEN BY DIMITRI P. BERTSEKAS
C
C ****************************************************************
C USER MUST SUPPLY THE FOLLOWING PROBLEM DATA
C N=NUMBER OF ROWS AND NUMBER OF COLUMNS
C A=NUMBER OF ARCS
C FOUT(ROW)=1ST ARC COMING OUT OF ROW
C COST(ARC)=COST OF ARC
C END(ARC)=COLUMN CORRESPONDING TO ARC
C FOUT(.) IS AN N - LENGTH ARRAY
C COST(.),END(.),NXTEND(.) ARE ARRAYS OF LENGTH A
C THE OPTIMAL ASSIGNMENT IS CONTAINED IN THE ARRAY ASSIGN(.) WHERE
C ASSIGN(COL) IS THE ROW ASSIGNED TO COL
C THIS ALGORITHM DOES NOT CHECK FOR INFEASIBILITY OF THE PROBLEM
C TO MAKE SURE THE PROBLEM IS FEASIBLE THE USER MAY ADD
C ADDITIONAL VERY HIGH COST ARCS
C THIS CODE ALLOWS MULTIPLE ARCS BETWEEN A ROW AND A COLUMN.
C ****************************************************************
C ALL PROBLEM DATA ARE INTEGER
C ****************************************************************

        PARAMETER(MAXNODES=10000, MAXARCS=100000)
        IMPLICIT INTEGER (A-Z)
        INTEGER AUCTNUM,A,STARC,ENDARC,CURROW,ARC,COUNT
        INTEGER HCOUNT,ROW,FSTARC,FSTCOL,SNDARC,SNDCOL,TMAX,BSTCOL
        INTEGER TMARG,TA,ROWPR,OLMARG,PRICE,TPRICE,CURCOL,DUMMY
        INTEGER FOUT(MAXNODES),PCOL(MAXNODES)
        INTEGER PROW(MAXNODES),MARG(MAXNODES)
        INTEGER ASSIGN(MAXNODES),COLLAB(MAXNODES),ROWLAB(MAXNODES)
        INTEGER LIST(MAXNODES),SCAN(MAXNODES)
        INTEGER COST(MAXARCS),END(MAXARCS)
        LOGICAL MAXSET
        REAL THRESH,RAND,TT,TIMER,TCOST

C ****************************************************************
C PROBLEM GENERATION CODE STARTS HERE
C THE USER MAY REPLACE THIS CODE WITH A CODE THAT READS
C HIS/HER PROBLEM FROM A FILE
C ****************************************************************
C RANDOM GENERATOR STUFF

        INTEGER MULT,MODUL,I15,I16,JRAN,ISEED
        REAL RAN
        COMMON /RANDM/ MULT,MODUL,I15,I16,JRAN

C UNIFORM RANDOM NUMBER GENERATOR
```

```
C WHICH RETURNS A VALUE IN (0,1)
C INITIALIZE RANDOM GENERATOR

      ISEED=13502460
      CALL SETRAN(ISEED)

      PRINT*,'GENERATING A SYMMETRIC ASSIGNMENT PROBLEM'
      PRINT*,'*****************************************'

C **** READ THE NUMBER OF ROWS N & THE NUMBER OF ARCS A ****

      PRINT*,'ENTER THE NUMBER OF ROWS (AND COLUMNS)'
      READ*,N
5     PRINT*,'ENTER THE NUMBER OF ARCS PER ROW (>1)'
      READ*,NA
      IF (NA.LT.2) GOTO 5
      PRINT*,'ENTER THE MINIMUM AND THE MAXIMUM COST'
      READ*,MINCOST,MAXCOST

C THE NUMBER OF ARCS IS N*NA

      A=N*NA

C THE ARCS INCIDENT TO ROW I ARE FOUT(I) TO FOUT(I+1)-1
C FOR FEASIBILITY EACH ROW IS DIRECTLY CONNECTED
C WITH THE CORRESPONDING COLUMN

      DO 20 I=1,N
      FOUT(I)=1+(I-1)*NA
20    CONTINUE

C **** GENERATE THE END(IA) AND COST(IA) WHICH ARE THE COLUMN
C AND THE COST COEFFICIENT ASSOCIATED WITH ARC IA ****

      DO 25 IA=1,A
      END(IA)=1+RAN()*N
      IF ((END(IA).GT.N).OR.(END(IA).LT.1)) THEN
      PRINT*,'ERROR IN PROBLEM GENERATION'
      PAUSE
      STOP
      END IF
      COST(IA)=MINCOST+RAN()*(MAXCOST-MINCOST)
25    CONTINUE

C MODIFY THE END OF THE LAST ARC OUT OF EACH ROW
C FOR FEASIBILITY AND SET ITS COST TO -MAXCOST

      DO 30 I=1,N
      END(FOUT(I+1)-1)=I
      COST(FOUT(I+1)-1)=-MAXCOST
30    CONTINUE

C **************************************************************
C PROBLEM GENERATION CODE ENDS HERE
C **************************************************************
C MAIN ALGORITHM BEGINS HERE
C THE ALGORITHM INTERNALLY TREATS THE PROBLEM AS A
C MINIMIZATION PROBLEM.
```

```
C TO SOLVE AN ASSIGNMENT MAXIMIZATION PROBLEM, SET
C THE FOLLOWING PARAMETER MAXSET TO TRUE, ELSE SET IT TO FALSE

            MAXSET=.TRUE.
            IF (MAXSET) THEN
            DO 35 IA=1,A
            COST(IA)=-COST(IA)
35          CONTINUE
            END IF
            PRINT*,'NO OF ROWS (AND COLUMNS):',N
            PRINT*,'NO OF ARCS:',A
            PRINT*,'COMBINED NAIVE AUCTION AND SEQ. SH. PATH METHOD'
            PRINT *,'*********************************************'
            TIMER = LONG(362)
            ISIMPL=0
            IPRC=0
            ISMALL=-20000000
            ILARGE=-ISMALL
            COUNT=0
            HCOUNT=0
            FOUT(N+1)=A+1

C THE FOLLOWING INITIALIZATION UP TO THE START OF THE
C NAIVE AUCTION CYCLES WAS SUGGESTED BY JONKER AND VOLGENANT
C INITIALIZE COLUMN PRICES

            DO 105 J=1,N
            PCOL(J)=ILARGE
105         CONTINUE

C FIND BEST ROW FOR EACH COLUMN

            DO 120 I=1,N
            PROW(I)=0
            ROWLAB(I)=0
            FSTARC=FOUT(I)
            LSTARC=FOUT(I+1)-1
            DO 110 ARC=FSTARC,LSTARC
            J=END(ARC)
            IF (COST(ARC).LT.PCOL(J)) THEN
            PCOL(J)=COST(ARC)
            ASSIGN(J)=I
            END IF
110         CONTINUE
120         CONTINUE

C CONSTRUCT ROW ASSIGNMENT AND DEASSIGN MULTIPLY ASSIGNED ROWS

            DO 130 J=1,N
            J0=N-J+1
            I=ASSIGN(J0)
            IF (ROWLAB(I).NE.0) THEN
            ROWLAB(I)=-ABS(ROWLAB(I))
            ASSIGN(J0)=0
            ELSE
            ROWLAB(I)=J0
            END IF
130         CONTINUE
```

```
C CONSTRUCT CANDIDATE LIST AND CORRECT COLUMN PRICES

         NEWNOL=0
         DO 150 I=1,N
         CURCOL=ROWLAB(I)
         IF (CURCOL.EQ.0) THEN
         NEWNOL=NEWNOL+1
         LIST(NEWNOL)=I
         GOTO 150
         END IF
         IF (CURCOL.LT.0) THEN
         ROWLAB(I)=-CURCOL
         ELSE
         MAX2=ISMALL
         FSTARC=FOUT(I)
         LSTARC=FOUT(I+1)-1
         DO 140 ARC=FSTARC,LSTARC
         J=END(ARC)
         IF (J.NE.CURCOL) THEN
         IF (PCOL(J)-COST(ARC).GT.MAX2) THEN
         MAX2=PCOL(J)-COST(ARC)
         END IF
         END IF
140   CONTINUE
         PROW(I)=MAX2
         PCOL(CURCOL)=PCOL(CURCOL)+MAX2
         END IF
150   CONTINUE
         IF (NEWNOL.EQ.0) GO TO 2000

C ***********************************************************
C END OF INITIALIZATION; DO A NUMBER OF AUCTION CYCLES
C WHICH IS SET BELOW IN THE PARAMETER AUCTNUM BASED ON THE
C SPARSITY OF THE PROBLEM
C TO RUN A PURE SEQUENTIAL SHORTEST PATH METHOD SET AUCTNUM=0

         IF (N*N.LT.10*A) AUCTNUM=2
         IF ((N*N.GE.10*A).AND.(N*N.LT.25*A)) AUCTNUM=3
         IF ((N*N.GE.25*A).AND.(N*N.LT.50*A)) AUCTNUM=4
         IF ((N*N.GE.50*A).AND.(N*N.LT.100*A)) AUCTNUM=5
         IF (N*N.GE.100*A) AUCTNUM=6

C START OF A NEW CYCLE

80    NOLIST=NEWNOL
         I=1
         NEWNOL=0

C TAKE UP A ROW FOR ITERATION

100   ROW=LIST(I)
         I=I+1
         FSTARC=FOUT(ROW)
         LSTARC=FOUT(ROW+1)-1
         BSTCOL=END(FSTARC)
         IF (FSTARC.EQ.LSTARC) THEN
         OLDROW=ASSIGN(BSTCOL)
```

```
         ASSIGN(BSTCOL)=ROW
         ROWLAB(ROW)=BSTCOL
         PROW(ROW)=ISMALL
         PCOL(BSTCOL)=ISMALL+COST(FSTARC)
         IF (OLDROW.GT.0) THEN
         I=I-1
         LIST(I)=OLDROW
         ROWLAB(OLDROW)=0
         END IF
         ISIMPL=ISIMPL+1
         GO TO 100
         END IF
         SNDARC=FSTARC+1
         SNDCOL=END(SNDARC)
         MAX1=PCOL(BSTCOL)-COST(FSTARC)
         MAX2=PCOL(SNDCOL)-COST(SNDARC)
         IF (MAX1.LT.MAX2) THEN
         TMAX=MAX1
         MAX1=MAX2
         MAX2=TMAX
         FSTCOL=BSTCOL
         BSTCOL=SNDCOL
         SNDCOL=FSTCOL
         END IF
         IF (SNDARC.LT.LSTARC) THEN
         TRDARC=SNDARC+1
         DO 108 ARC=TRDARC,LSTARC
         CURCOL=END(ARC)
         TMAX=PCOL(CURCOL)-COST(ARC)
         IF (TMAX.GT.MAX2) THEN
         IF (TMAX.GT.MAX1) THEN
         MAX2=MAX1
         MAX1=TMAX
         SNDCOL=BSTCOL
         BSTCOL=CURCOL
         ELSE
         MAX2=TMAX
         SNDCOL=CURCOL
         END IF
         END IF
108   CONTINUE
         END IF
         PROW(ROW)=MAX2
         OLDROW=ASSIGN(BSTCOL)
         INCR=MAX1-MAX2
         IF (INCR.GT.0) THEN
         PCOL(BSTCOL)=PCOL(BSTCOL)-INCR
         ASSIGN(BSTCOL)=ROW
         ROWLAB(ROW)=BSTCOL
         IF (OLDROW.GT.0) THEN
         I=I-1
         LIST(I)=OLDROW
         ROWLAB(OLDROW)=0
         ISIMPL=ISIMPL+1
         GOTO 100
         END IF
         ELSE
         IF (OLDROW.GT.0) THEN
```

```
           BSTCOL=SNDCOL
           OLDROW=ASSIGN(BSTCOL)
           END IF
           IF (OLDROW.EQ.0) THEN
           ASSIGN(BSTCOL)=ROW
           ROWLAB(ROW)=BSTCOL
           ELSE
           NEWNOL=NEWNOL+1
           LIST(NEWNOL)=ROW
           END IF
           END IF
           ISIMPL=ISIMPL+1
           IF (I.LE.NOLIST) GOTO 100

C END OF A NAIVE AUCTION CYCLE

           COUNT=COUNT+1
           IF (NEWNOL.EQ.0) THEN
           NASSIH=NEWNOL
           GOTO 2000
           END IF
           IF (COUNT.LT.AUCTNUM) GOTO 80

C ************************************
C END OF NAIVE AUCTION PART
C START OF SEQ. SH. PATH METHOD
C ************************************

1000       NASSIH=NEWNOL
X          IHPRC=0
1020       DO 180 I=1,NEWNOL
           SCAN(I)=LIST(I)
180        CONTINUE
           DO 190 J=1,N
           MARG(J)=1
190        CONTINUE
           NOSCAN=NEWNOL
           IL1=1
           IL2=NOSCAN
1030       DO 1060 I=IL1,IL2
           CURROW=SCAN(I)
           ROWPR=PROW(CURROW)
           FSTARC=FOUT(CURROW)
           LSTARC=FOUT(CURROW+1)-1
           DO 1050 ARC=FSTARC,LSTARC
           CURCOL=END(ARC)
           OLMARG=MARG(CURCOL)
           IF (OLMARG.EQ.0) GO TO 1050
           TMARG=PCOL(CURCOL)-ROWPR-COST(ARC)
           IF (TMARG.EQ.0) THEN
           IF (ASSIGN(CURCOL).EQ.0) THEN
           GO TO 1500

C PERFORM AUGMENTATION

           ELSE
           MARG(CURCOL)=0
           NOSCAN=NOSCAN+1
```

```
            SCAN(NOSCAN)=ASSIGN(CURCOL)
            COLLAB(CURCOL)=CURROW
            END IF
            ELSE
            IF ((OLMARG.GT.0).OR.(TMARG.GT.OLMARG)) THEN
            MARG(CURCOL)=TMARG
            COLLAB(CURCOL)=CURROW
            END IF
            END IF
1050    CONTINUE
1060    CONTINUE

C CURRENT SCAN PHASE COMPLETE; CHECK FOR MORE ROWS TO SCAN

            IF (IL2.LT.NOSCAN) THEN
            IL1=IL2+1
            IL2=NOSCAN
            GO TO 1030
            END IF

C PRICE CHANGE

            IPRC=IPRC+1
X           IHPRC=IHPRC+1
            INCR=ISMALL
            DO 200 J=1,N
            TMARG=MARG(J)
            IF ((TMARG.LT.0).AND.(TMARG.GT.INCR)) INCR=TMARG
200     CONTINUE
            DO 210 I=1,NOSCAN
            PROW(SCAN(I))=PROW(SCAN(I))+INCR
210     CONTINUE
            DO 220 J=1,N
            IF (MARG(J).EQ.0) PCOL(J)=PCOL(J)+INCR
220     CONTINUE
            DO 1400 J=1,N
            IF (MARG(J).GE.0) GO TO 1400
            MARG(J)=MARG(J)-INCR
            IF (MARG(J).EQ.0) THEN
            IF (ASSIGN(J).EQ.0) THEN
            CURCOL=J
            CURROW=COLLAB(CURCOL)

C PERFORM AUGMENTATION

            GO TO 1500
            ELSE
            NOSCAN=NOSCAN+1
            SCAN(NOSCAN)=ASSIGN(J)
            END IF
            END IF
1400    CONTINUE
            IL1=IL2+1
            IL2=NOSCAN
            GO TO 1030

C END PRICE CHANGE
C AUGMENTATION STARTS HERE
```

```
1500   IF (ROWLAB(CURROW).EQ.0) THEN
         ASSIGN(CURCOL)=CURROW
         ROWLAB(CURROW)=CURCOL
         GO TO 1700
         END IF
         TA=ROWLAB(CURROW)
         ASSIGN(CURCOL)=CURROW
         ROWLAB(CURROW)=CURCOL
         CURCOL=TA
         CURROW=COLLAB(CURCOL)
         GO TO 1500
1700   IF (NEWNOL.EQ.1) GO TO 2000
         DO 240 I=1,NEWNOL-1
         IF (LIST(I).EQ.CURROW) THEN
         DO 250 K=I+1,NEWNOL
         LIST(K-I)=LIST(K)
250    CONTINUE
         DO 260 K=1,I-1
         LIST(NEWNOL-I+K)=SCAN(K)
260    CONTINUE
         NEWNOL=NEWNOL-1
         GO TO 1020
         END IF
240    CONTINUE
         NEWNOL=NEWNOL-1
         GO TO 1020


C END AUGMENTATION
C ****************************************************
C EXIT ROUTINE. CHECKS FOR OPTIMALITY OF THE SOLUTION
C CALCULATES THE OPTIMAL COST, AND COMPILES SOLUTION
C STATISTICS. THE USER MAY REPLACE THIS BY CODE THAT
C WRITES AT THE APPROPRIATE DEVICE THE OPTIMAL SOLUTION
C CONTAINED IN THE ARRAY ASSIGN(.).
C ****************************************************

2000   CONTINUE
         TT =(LONG(362) - TIMER)/60
         PRINT*, 'TOTAL TIME = ',TT, ' secs.'
         PRINT*,'NO OF NAIVE AUCTION ITERATIONS:',ISIMPL
         PRINT*,'NO OF SH. PATH ITERATIONS:',NASSIH
X        PRINT*,'NO OF PRICE CHANGES:',IHPRC

C CHECK FEASIBILITY OF SOLUTION & CALCULATE COST

         DO 265 I=1,N
         ROWLAB(I)=0
265    CONTINUE
         NOASS=0
         DO 280 J=1,N
         IF (ASSIGN(J).GT.0) THEN
         ROWLAB(ASSIGN(J))=J
         NOASS=NOASS+1
         END IF
280    CONTINUE
         IF (NOASS.LT.N) THEN
         PRINT*,'THE NUMBER OF ASSIGNED COLUMNS IS',NOASS,'(TOO SMALL)'
```

```
              END IF
              TCOST=0
              DO 300 I=1,N
              J=ROWLAB(I)
              IF (J.EQ.0) THEN
              PRINT*,'ROW ',I,' IS UNASSIGNED'
              END IF
              FSTARC=FOUT(I)
              LSTARC=FOUT(I+1)-1
              MINCOST=ILARGE
              DO 310 ARC=FSTARC,LSTARC
              CURCOL=END(ARC)
              TMARG=PROW(I)-PCOL(CURCOL)+COST(ARC)
              IF (TMARG.LT.0) THEN
              PRINT*,'COMPL. SLACKNESS VIOLATION: ROW',I,' COLUMN',CURCOL
              END IF
              IF (CURCOL.EQ.J) THEN
              IF (MINCOST.GT.COST(ARC)) THEN
              MINCOST=COST(ARC)
              ROWMARG=TMARG
              END IF
              END IF
310           CONTINUE
              IF (ROWMARG.NE.0) THEN
              PRINT*,'COMPL. SLACK. VIOLATION AT ASSIGNED ARC OF ROW',I
              END IF
              IF (MAXSET) THEN
              TCOST=TCOST-MINCOST
              ELSE
              TCOST=TCOST+MINCOST
              END IF
300           CONTINUE
              WRITE(9,2100) TCOST
2100   FORMAT(' ASSIGNMENT COST=',F14.2)
              PRINT *,'********************************************'
              PRINT *, 'PROGRAM ENDED; PRESS <CR>'

              PAUSE
              STOP
              END


              SUBROUTINE SETRAN(ISEED)
              SAME AS IN CODE GRIDGEN
```

A.6   MAX-FLOW CODES

A.6.1   FORD-FULKERSON

This code implements the Ford-Fulkerson method for solving the max-flow problem (cf. Section 1.2.2).

```
C ******* SAMPLE CALLING PROGRAM FOR FORD-FULKERSON *******
        PARAMETER (MAXNODES=10000, MAXARCS=40000)
        IMPLICIT INTEGER (A-Z)
        COMMON /SCALARS/ N,NA,LARGE,SOURCE,SINK
        COMMON /STATS/ NITER
        COMMON /UBOUND/ U
        COMMON /FLOW/ F
        COMMON /BLK1/ STARTN
        COMMON /BLK2/ ENDN
        COMMON /BLK3/ PRDCSR
        COMMON /BLK4/ FIN
        COMMON /BLK5/ FOUT
        COMMON /BLK6/ NXTIN
        COMMON /BLK7/ NXTOU
        COMMON /LABELS/ LABEL
        COMMON /MARKS/ MARK
        INTEGER STARTN(MAXARCS)
        INTEGER ENDN(MAXARCS)
        INTEGER U(MAXARCS)
        INTEGER F(MAXARCS)
        INTEGER PRDCSR(MAXNODES)
        INTEGER FIN(MAXNODES)
        INTEGER FOUT(MAXNODES)
        INTEGER NXTIN(MAXARCS)
        INTEGER NXTOU(MAXARCS)
        INTEGER LABEL(MAXNODES)
        LOGICAL MARK(MAXNODES)
        REAL*8 TT,TIMER
        PRINT*,'FORD-FULKERSON METHOD FOR MAX-FLOW'
        PRINT*,'********************************'
        PRINT *,'READING PROBLEM DATA'
        OPEN(13,FILE='FOR013.DAT',STATUS='OLD')
        REWIND(13)

C READ NUMBER OF NODES AND ARCS

        READ(13,1010) N,NA

C READ START, END, COST, AND CAPACITY OF EACH ARC

        DO 20 I=1,NA
        READ(13,1020) STARTN(I),ENDN(I),DUMMY,U(I)
20      CONTINUE

        ENDFILE(13)
        REWIND(13)
1000    FORMAT(1I8)
1010    FORMAT(2I8)
1020    FORMAT(4I8)
        PRINT*,'THE NUMBER OF NODES IS = ',N
41      PRINT*,'ENTER THE SUPERSOURCE NODE'
        READ*,SOURCE
        IF ((SOURCE.LE.0).OR.(SOURCE.GT.N)) GOTO 41

42      PRINT*,'ENTER THE SUPERSINK NODE'
        READ*,SINK
```

```
                IF ((SINK.LE.0).OR.(SINK.GT.N)) GOTO 42
                IF (SINK.EQ.R) GOTO 42

C THE SOURCE AND SINK NODES WILL NOT BE ITERATED ON

                PRINT *, 'RESTRUCTURING THE DATA '
                CALL INIDAT


C SET FLOWS TO ZERO

                DO 50 ARC=1,NA
                F(ARC)=0
50              CONTINUE
                PRINT*,'INITIALIZING DATA STRUCTURES'
                CALL INIDAT
                PRINT *,'********************************'
                TIMER = LONG(362)
                CALL FORD_FULK
                TT = FLOAT(LONG(362) - TIMER)/60
                PRINT*, 'TOTAL TIME = ',TT, ' secs.'

C ***** COMPUTE MAX-FLOW *****

                MAX_FLOW=0
                DO 60 ARC=1,NA
                IF (STARTN(ARC).EQ.SOURCE) MAX_FLOW=MAX_FLOW+F(ARC)
60              CONTINUE
                MAX_FLOW2=0
                DO 70 ARC=1,NA
                IF (ENDN(ARC).EQ.SINK) MAX_FLOW2=MAX_FLOW2+F(ARC)
70              CONTINUE
                PRINT *,'# OF ITERATIONS = ',NITER
                PRINT *, 'MAX-FLOW = ',MAX_FLOW2
                PRINT *,'********************************'
                IF (MAXFLOW.NE.MAXFLOW2) THEN
                PRINT*,'SOURCE FLOW NOT EQUAL TO SINK FLOW'
                ENDIF
                PRINT *, 'PROGRAM ENDED; PRESS ¡CR¿ TO EXIT'
                PAUSE
                END


                SUBROUTINE INIDAT

C THIS SUBROUTINE USES THE DATA ARRAYS STARTN AND ENDN
C TO CONSTRUCT AUXILIARY DATA ARRAYS FOUT, NXTOU, FIN, AND
C NXTIN. IN THIS SUBROUTINE WE
C ARBITRARILY ORDER THE ARCS LEAVING EACH NODE AND STORE
C THIS INFORMATION IN FOUT AND NXTOU. SIMILARLY, WE ARBITRA-
C RILY ORDER THE ARCS ENTERING EACH NODE AND STORE THIS
C INFORMATION IN FIN AND NXTIN. AT THE COMPLETION OF THE
C CONSTRUCTION, WE HAVE
C FOUT(I) = FIRST ARC LEAVING NODE I.
C NXTOU(J) = NEXT ARC LEAVING THE HEAD NODE OF ARC J.
C FIN(I) = FIRST ARC ENTERING NODE I.
C NXTIN(J) = NEXT ARC ENTERING THE TAIL NODE OF ARC J.
```

```
      PARAMETER (MAXNODES=10000, MAXARCS=40000)
      IMPLICIT INTEGER (A-Z)
      COMMON /SCALARS/ N,NA,LARGE
      COMMON /BLK1/ STARTN
      COMMON /BLK2/ ENDN
      COMMON /BLK4/ FIN
      COMMON /BLK5/ FOUT
      COMMON /BLK6/ NXTIN
      COMMON /BLK7/ NXTOU
      INTEGER STARTN(MAXARCS)
      INTEGER ENDN(MAXARCS)
      INTEGER FIN(MAXNODES)
      INTEGER FOUT(MAXNODES)
      INTEGER NXTIN(MAXARCS)
      INTEGER NXTOU(MAXARCS)
      INTEGER FINALIN(MAXNODES)
      INTEGER FINALOU(MAXNODES)
      DO 20 NODE=1,N
      FIN(NODE)=0
      FOUT(NODE)=0
      FINALIN(NODE)=0
      FINALOU(NODE)=0
20    CONTINUE
      DO 30 ARC=1,NA
      START=STARTN(ARC)
      END=ENDN(ARC)
      IF (FOUT(START).NE.0) THEN
      NXTOU(FINALOU(START))=ARC
      ELSE
      FOUT(START)=ARC
      END IF
      IF (FIN(END).NE.0) THEN
      NXTIN(FINALIN(END))=ARC
      ELSE
      FIN(END)=ARC
      END IF
      FINALOU(START)=ARC
      FINALIN(END)=ARC
      NXTIN(ARC)=0
      NXTOU(ARC)=0
30    CONTINUE
      RETURN
      END


      SUBROUTINE FORD_FULK
      IMPLICIT INTEGER (A-Z)
      COMMON /SCALARS/ N,NA,LARGE,SOURCE,SINK
      COMMON /STATS/ NITER
      COMMON /UBOUND/ U
      COMMON /FLOW/ F
      COMMON /BLK1/ STARTN
      COMMON /BLK2/ ENDN
      COMMON /BLK3/ PRDCSR
      COMMON /BLK4/ FIN
      COMMON /BLK5/ FOUT
      COMMON /BLK6/ NXTIN
      COMMON /BLK7/ NXTOU
```

```
                COMMON /MARKS/ MARK
                COMMON /LABELS/ LABEL
                INTEGER STARTN(1),ENDN(1),U(1),F(1),FIN(1),FOUT(1)
                INTEGER NXTIN(1),NXTOU(1),PRDCSR(1),LABEL(1)
                LOGICAL MARK(1)

                NITER=0
                DO 10 I=1,N
                MARK(I)=.FALSE.
10              CONTINUE

C START OF NEW ITERATION

15              NLABEL=1
                NSCAN=1
                MARK(SOURCE)=.TRUE.
                LABEL(1)=SOURCE


20              CONTINUE

C SCAN A NEW NODE

                NODE=LABEL(NSCAN)

C SCAN OUTGOING ARCS OF NODE

                ARC=FOUT(NODE)
30              IF (ARC.GT.0) THEN
                NODE2=ENDN(ARC)
                IF ((.NOT.MARK(NODE2)).AND.(F(ARC).LT.U(ARC))) THEN
                PRDCSR(NODE2)=ARC
                IF (NODE2.EQ.SINK) THEN
                CALL AUGMENT
                NITER=NITER+1
                DO 40 I=1,NLABEL
                MARK(LABEL(I))=.FALSE.
40              CONTINUE
                GOTO 15
                ELSE
                MARK(NODE2)=.TRUE.
                NLABEL=NLABEL+1
                LABEL(NLABEL)=NODE2
                END IF
                END IF
                ARC=NXTOU(ARC)
                GOTO 30
                END IF

C SCAN INCOMING ARCS OF NODE

                ARC=FIN(NODE)
50              IF (ARC.GT.0) THEN
                NODE2=STARTN(ARC)
                IF ((.NOT.MARK(NODE2)).AND.(F(ARC).GT.0)) THEN
                PRDCSR(NODE2)=-ARC
                IF (NODE2.EQ.SINK) THEN
                CALL AUGMENT
```

```
                NITER=NITER+1
                DO 60 I=1,NLABEL
                MARK(LABEL(I))=.FALSE.
60              CONTINUE
                GOTO 15
                ELSE
                MARK(NODE2)=.TRUE.
                NLABEL=NLABEL+1
                LABEL(NLABEL)=NODE2
                END IF
                END IF
                ARC=NXTIN(ARC)
                GOTO 50
                END IF

C CHECK FOR TERMINATION; SCAN A NEW NODE

                IF (NSCAN.EQ.NLABEL) THEN
                RETURN
                END IF
                NSCAN=NSCAN+1
                GOTO 20
                END

                SUBROUTINE AUGMENT
                IMPLICIT INTEGER (A-Z)
                COMMON /SCALARS/ N,NA,LARGE,SOURCE,SINK
                COMMON /UBOUND/ U
                COMMON /FLOW/ F
                COMMON /BLK1/ STARTN
                COMMON /BLK2/ ENDN
                COMMON /BLK3/ PRDCSR
                INTEGER STARTN(1),ENDN(1),U(1),F(1),PRDCSR(1)

                DX=LARGE
                CURNODE=SINK
10              IF (CURNODE.NE.SOURCE) THEN
                ARC=PRDCSR(CURNODE)
                IF (ARC.GT.0) THEN
                INCR=U(ARC)-F(ARC)
                IF (DX.GT.INCR) DX=INCR
                CURNODE=STARTN(ARC)
                ELSE
                ARC=-ARC
                INCR=F(ARC)
                IF (DX.GT.INCR) DX=INCR
                CURNODE=ENDN(ARC)
                END IF
                GOTO 10
                END IF

                CURNODE=SINK
20              IF (CURNODE.NE.SOURCE) THEN
                ARC=PRDCSR(CURNODE)
                IF (ARC.GT.0) THEN
                F(ARC)=F(ARC)+DX
                CURNODE=STARTN(ARC)
```

```
      ELSE
      ARC=-ARC
      F(ARC)=F(ARC)-DX
      CURNODE=ENDN(ARC)
      END IF
      GOTO 20
      END IF

      RETURN

      END
```

A.6.2 ϵ-RELAX-MF

This code implements the ϵ-relaxation method for the max-flow problem (cf.
Section 4.5). Here, $\epsilon = 1$ throughout the algorithm. By toggling an input
parameter, the code may be directed to stop after it identifies a minimum
cut, or to proceed to find a maximum flow.

```
C ******* SAMPLE CALLING PROGRAM FOR E-RELAX/MAX-FLOW *******
C THIS VERSION USES A CYCLIC QUEUE, A SHORTEST PATH
C (BREADTH FIRST) INITIALIZATION
C AND A ROUTINE THAT DETECTS A SATURATED CUT AND
C OPTIONALLY TERMINATES EARLY
C **************************************************
      PARAMETER (MAXNODES=10000, MAXARCS=40000)
      IMPLICIT INTEGER (A-Z)
      COMMON /SCALARS/ N,NA,LARGE,SOURCE,SINK,CUTFLAG
      COMMON /STATS/ NCYC,NITER
      COMMON /BLK1/ STARTN
      COMMON /BLK2/ ENDN
      COMMON /UBOUND/ U
      COMMON /FLOW/ F
      COMMON /PRICES/ P
      COMMON /BLK3/ SURPLUS
      COMMON /BLK4/ FIN
      COMMON /BLK5/ FOUT
      COMMON /BLK6/ NXTIN
      COMMON /BLK7/ NXTOU
      COMMON /BLK11/ FPUSHF
      COMMON /BLK12/ NXTPUSHF
      COMMON /BLK13/ FPUSHB
      COMMON /BLK14/ NXTPUSHB
      COMMON /LABELS/ LABEL
      COMMON /MARKS/ MARK
      COMMON /QUEUE/ NXTQUEUE
      INTEGER NXTQUEUE(MAXNODES)
      INTEGER STARTN(MAXARCS)
      INTEGER ENDN(MAXARCS)
      INTEGER U(MAXARCS)
      INTEGER F(MAXARCS)
      INTEGER SURPLUS(MAXNODES)
      INTEGER FIN(MAXNODES)
```

```
            INTEGER FOUT(MAXNODES)
            INTEGER NXTIN(MAXARCS)
            INTEGER NXTOU(MAXARCS)
            INTEGER P(MAXNODES)
            INTEGER FPUSHF(MAXNODES)
            INTEGER NXTPUSHF(MAXARCS)
            INTEGER FPUSHB(MAXNODES)
            INTEGER NXTPUSHB(MAXARCS)
            INTEGER LABEL(MAXNODES)
            LOGICAL MARK(MAXNODES)
            REAL*8 TT,TIMER

            PRINT*,'SPECIALIZED E-RELAXATION METHOD FOR MAX-FLOW'
            PRINT*,'*****************************************'
            PRINT *,'READING PROBLEM DATA'
            OPEN(13,FILE='FOR013.DAT',STATUS='OLD')
            REWIND(13)

C READ NUMBER OF NODES AND ARCS

            READ(13,1010) N,NA

C READ START, END, COST, AND CAPACITY OF EACH ARC

            DO 20 I=1,NA
            READ(13,1020) STARTN(I),ENDN(I),DUMMY,U(I)
20          CONTINUE

C READ SUPPLY OF EACH NODE

            DO 30 I=1,N
            READ(13,1000) DUMMY
30          CONTINUE
            ENDFILE(13)
            REWIND(13)
1000        FORMAT(1I8)
1010        FORMAT(2I8)
1020        FORMAT(4I8)
            PRINT*,'THE NUMBER OF NODES IS = ',N
41          PRINT*,'ENTER THE SUPERSOURCE NODE'
            READ*,SOURCE
            IF ((SOURCE.LE.0).OR.(SOURCE.GT.N)) GOTO 41

42          PRINT*,'ENTER THE SUPERSINK NODE'
            READ*,SINK

            IF ((SINK.LE.0).OR.(SINK.GT.N)) GOTO 42
            IF (SINK.EQ.R) GOTO 42

C THE SOURCE AND SINK NODES WILL NOT BE ITERATED ON
C INITIALIZE PRICES & SURPLUSES

            DO 10 NODE=1,N
            FPUSHF(NODE)=0
            FPUSHB(NODE)=0
            P(NODE)=0
            SURPLUS(NODE)=0
10          CONTINUE
```

```
C SET THE PRICES OF THE SOURCE AND SINK:
C HERE THE NUMBER OF NODES IS N, SO, FOR E=1,
C THE COST OF THE IMPLICIT FEEDBACK ARC SHOULD BE -(N+1).
C HENCE TO MAKE THE IMPLICIT FEEDBACK ARC E- - BALANCED
C WE TAKE THE PRICE OF THE SOURCE TO BE N+2.

        P(SOURCE)=N+2

C SET FLOWS TO UPPER BOUND OR LOWER BOUND TO SATISFY E-CS

        DO 50 ARC=1,NA
        IF (STARTN(ARC).EQ.SOURCE) THEN
        F(ARC)=U(ARC)
        SURPLUS(ENDN(ARC))=SURPLUS(ENDN(ARC))+F(ARC)
        SURPLUS(SOURCE)=SURPLUS(SOURCE)-F(ARC)
        ELSE
        F(ARC)=0
        END IF
50      CONTINUE
        LARGE=2000000
        PRINT*,'INITIALIZING DATA STRUCTURES'
        CALL INIDAT

C SET THE VARIABLE CUTFLAG TO 1 IF YOU WISH THE ALGORITHM
C TO TERMINATE WITH A MINIMUM CUT WITHOUT NECESSARILY
C HAVING FOUND THE MAXIMUM FLOW

        CUTFLAG=1
        IF (CUTFLAG.EQ.1) THEN
        PRINT*,'THE CODE MAY FIND A MIN-CUT BUT NOT A MAX-FLOW'
        END IF
        PRINT *,'**********************************************'
        TIMER = LONG(362)
        CALL E_RELAX_MF
        TT = FLOAT(LONG(362) - TIMER)/60
        PRINT*, 'TOTAL TIME = ',TT, ' secs.'

C COMPUTE MAX-FLOW

        MAX_FLOW=0
        DO 60 ARC=1,NA
        IF (STARTN(ARC).EQ.SOURCE) MAX_FLOW=MAX_FLOW+F(ARC)
60      CONTINUE
        MAX_FLOW2=0
        DO 70 ARC=1,NA
        IF (ENDN(ARC).EQ.SINK) MAX_FLOW2=MAX_FLOW2+F(ARC)
70      CONTINUE
        PRINT *,'# OF CYCLES = ',NCYC
        PRINT *,'# OF ITERATIONS = ',NITER
        PRINT *, 'MAX-FLOW = ',MAX_FLOW2
        PRINT *,'**********************************************'
        IF (MAXFLOW.NE.MAXFLOW2) THEN
        PRINT*,'FLOW FROM SUPERSOURCE =',MAX_FLOW
        PRINT*,'FLOW TO SUPERSINK =',MAX_FLOW2
        PRINT*,'SATURATED CUT FOUND EARLY'
        ENDIF
        DO 90 ARC=1,NA
```

```
          IF (F(ARC).GT.0) THEN
          IF (P(STARTN(ARC))-P(ENDN(ARC)).LT.-1) THEN
          PRINT*,'E-CS VIOLATED AT ARC ',ARC
          ENDIF
          ENDIF
          IF (F(ARC).LT.U(ARC)) THEN
          IF (P(STARTN(ARC))-P(ENDN(ARC)).GT.1) THEN
          PRINT*,'E-CS VIOLATED AT ARC ',ARC
          ENDIF
          ENDIF
90        CONTINUE
          PRINT *, ' '
          PRINT *, 'PROGRAM ENDED; PRESS <CR> TO EXIT'
          PAUSE
          END


          SUBROUTINE INIDAT

C THIS SUBROUTINE USES THE DATA ARRAYS STARTN AND ENDN
C TO CONSTRUCT AUXILIARY DATA ARRAYS FOUT, NXTOU, FIN, AND
C NXTIN THAT ARE REQUIRED BY E-RELAX-MF. IN THIS SUBROUTINE WE
C ARBITRARILY ORDER THE ARCS LEAVING EACH NODE AND STORE
C THIS INFORMATION IN FOUT AND NXTOU. SIMILARLY, WE ARBITRA-
C RILY ORDER THE ARCS ENTERING EACH NODE AND STORE THIS
C INFORMATION IN FIN AND NXTIN. AT THE COMPLETION OF THE
C CONSTRUCTION, WE HAVE
C FOUT(I) = FIRST ARC LEAVING NODE I.
C NXTOU(J) = NEXT ARC LEAVING THE HEAD NODE OF ARC J.
C FIN(I) = FIRST ARC ENTERING NODE I.
C NXTIN(J) = NEXT ARC ENTERING THE TAIL NODE OF ARC J.

          PARAMETER (MAXNODES=10000, MAXARCS=40000)
          IMPLICIT INTEGER (A-Z)
          COMMON /SCALARS/ N,NA,LARGE
          COMMON /BLK1/ STARTN
          COMMON /BLK2/ ENDN
          COMMON /BLK4/ FIN
          COMMON /BLK5/ FOUT
          COMMON /BLK6/ NXTIN
          COMMON /BLK7/ NXTOU
          INTEGER STARTN(MAXARCS)
          INTEGER ENDN(MAXARCS)
          INTEGER FIN(MAXNODES)
          INTEGER FOUT(MAXNODES)
          INTEGER NXTIN(MAXARCS)
          INTEGER NXTOU(MAXARCS)
          INTEGER FINALIN(MAXNODES),FINALOU(MAXNODES)
          DO 20 NODE=1,N
          FIN(NODE)=0
          FOUT(NODE)=0
          FINALIN(NODE)=0
          FINALOU(NODE)=0
20        CONTINUE
          DO 30 ARC=1,NA
          START=STARTN(ARC)
          END=ENDN(ARC)
          IF (FOUT(START).NE.0) THEN
```

```
            NXTOU(FINALOU(START))=ARC
            ELSE
            FOUT(START)=ARC
            END IF
            IF (FIN(END).NE.0) THEN
            NXTIN(FINALIN(END))=ARC
            ELSE
            FIN(END)=ARC
            END IF
            FINALOU(START)=ARC
            FINALIN(END)=ARC
            NXTIN(ARC)=0
            NXTOU(ARC)=0
30          CONTINUE
            RETURN
            END


C *************************************************************
C BASIC E-RELAXATION FOR MAX-FLOW.
C THIS VERSION USES A QUEUE TO SELECT NODES TO ITERATE ON,
C AND MAINTAINS PUSH LISTS. NODES JOIN THE QUEUE AT THE BOTTOM.
C *************************************************************

            SUBROUTINE E_RELAX_MF
            IMPLICIT INTEGER (A-Z)
            COMMON /SCALARS/ N,NA,LARGE,SOURCE,SINK,CUTFLAG
            COMMON /STATS/ NCYC,NITER
            COMMON /BLK1/ STARTN
            COMMON /BLK2/ ENDN
            COMMON /UBOUND/ U
            COMMON /FLOW/ F
            COMMON /PRICES/ P
            COMMON /BLK3/ SURPLUS
            COMMON /BLK4/ FIN
            COMMON /BLK5/ FOUT
            COMMON /BLK6/ NXTIN
            COMMON /BLK7/ NXTOU
            COMMON /BLK11/ FPUSHF
            COMMON /BLK12/ NXTPUSHF
            COMMON /BLK13/ FPUSHB
            COMMON /BLK14/ NXTPUSHB
            COMMON /MARKS/ MARK
            COMMON /LABELS/ LABEL
            COMMON /QUEUE/ NXTQUEUE
            INTEGER NXTQUEUE(1)
            INTEGER STARTN(1),ENDN(1),U(1),F(1),SURPLUS(1),FIN(1),FOUT(1)
            INTEGER NXTIN(1),NXTOU(1),P(1)
            INTEGER FPUSHF(1),NXTPUSHF(1),FPUSHB(1),NXTPUSHB(1)
            INTEGER LABEL(1)
            LOGICAL MARK(1)

C INITIALIZE COUNT OF NUMBER OF UP ITERATIONS PERFORMED

            NITER = 0
            NCYC=0
            COUNT=0

C INITIALIZE PRICES BY A BREADTH FIRST SEARCH METHOD
```

```
          DO 51 NODE=1,N
          MARK(NODE)=.FALSE.
51        CONTINUE
          MARK(SOURCE)=.TRUE.
          NLABEL=1
          LABEL(1)=SINK
          NSCAN=0
55        CONTINUE
          NSCAN=NSCAN+1
          NODE=LABEL(NSCAN)
          MARK(NODE)=.TRUE.
          ARC=FIN(NODE)
58        IF (ARC.GT.0) THEN
          START=STARTN(ARC)
          IF (.NOT.MARK(START)) THEN
          NLABEL=NLABEL+1
          LABEL(NLABEL)=START
          P(START)=P(NODE)+1
          MARK(START)=.TRUE.
          END IF
          ARC=NXTIN(ARC)
          GOTO 58
          END IF
          IF (NLABEL.GT.NSCAN) GOTO 55

C ***** QUEUE INITIALIZATION *****

          FIRST=0
          DO 82 NODE=1,N
          IF ((NODE.NE.SOURCE).AND.(NODE.NE.SINK)) THEN
          IF (FIRST.EQ.0) THEN
          FIRST=NODE
          ELSE
          NXTQUEUE(LAST)=NODE
          END IF
          LAST=NODE
          ELSE
          NXTQUEUE(NODE)=-1
          END IF
82        CONTINUE
          NXTQUEUE(LAST)=FIRST
          I=FIRST
          PREVNODE=LAST
          LASTQUEUE=LAST

C ********************************************************
C DO A CYCLE: REPEAT UNTIL NO MORE NODES.
C ********************************************************

100    CONTINUE

C TAKE UP NEXT NODE (NODE I) FOR ITERATION

          SURPI=SURPLUS(I)
          IF (SURPI .GT. 0) THEN
          PRICE = P(I)
```

```
C PRINT*,'NODE ',I,' START PRICE = ',PRICE

         NITER = NITER + 1
         ARCF = FPUSHF(I)
         ARCB = FPUSHB(I)

C ******************** D - PUSHES ************************
C START BY TRYING TO PUSH AWAY FLOW ON ARCS THAT WERE
C ADMISSIBLE AT THE END OF THE LAST ITERATION (IF ANY)
C AT THIS NODE. WE MUST CHECK THAT THEY ARE STILL ADMISSIBLE.

120      IF ((SURPI .GT. 0) .AND. (ARCF .GT. 0)) THEN
         RESID = U(ARCF) - F(ARCF)
         J = ENDN(ARCF)
         IF ((PRICE-P(J).EQ.1).AND.(RESID.GT.0)) THEN
         IF (SURPI .GE. RESID) THEN
         F(ARCF) = U(ARCF)
         SURPI = SURPI - RESID
         SURPLUS(J) = SURPLUS(J) + RESID
         IF (NXTQUEUE(J).EQ.0) THEN
         IF (SURPLUS(J).GT.0) THEN
         NXTQUEUE(PREVNODE)=J
         NXTQUEUE(J)=I
         PREVNODE=J
         END IF
         END IF
         ARCF = NXTPUSHF(ARCF)
         ELSE
         F(ARCF) = F(ARCF) + SURPI
         SURPLUS(J) = SURPLUS(J) + SURPI
         IF (NXTQUEUE(J).EQ.0) THEN
         IF (SURPLUS(J).GT.0) THEN
         NXTQUEUE(PREVNODE)=J
         NXTQUEUE(J)=I
         PREVNODE=J
         END IF
         END IF
         SURPI = 0
         ENDIF
         ELSE
         ARCF = NXTPUSHF(ARCF)
         ENDIF
         GOTO 120
         ENDIF

121      IF ((SURPI .GT. 0) .AND. (ARCB .GT. 0)) THEN
         J = STARTN(ARCB)
         IF ((PRICE-P(J).EQ.1).AND.(F(ARCB).GT.0)) THEN
         IF (SURPI .GE. F(ARCB)) THEN
         SURPI = SURPI - F(ARCB)
         SURPLUS(J) = SURPLUS(J) + F(ARCB)
         IF (NXTQUEUE(J).EQ.0) THEN
         IF (SURPLUS(J).GT.0) THEN
         NXTQUEUE(PREVNODE)=J
         NXTQUEUE(J)=I
         PREVNODE=J
         END IF
         END IF
```

```
          F(ARCB) = 0
          ARCB = NXTPUSHB(ARCB)
          ELSE
          F(ARCB) = F(ARCB) - SURPI
          SURPLUS(J) = SURPLUS(J) + SURI
          IF (NXTQUEUE(J).EQ.0) THEN
          IF (SURPLUS(J).GT.0) THEN
          NXTQUEUE(PREVNODE)=J
          NXTQUEUE(J)=I
          PREVNODE=J
          END IF
          END IF
          SURPI = 0
          ENDIF
          ELSE
          ARCB = NXTPUSHB(ARCB)
          ENDIF
          GOTO 121
          ENDIF

C NOW WE ENTER A REPEAT...UNTIL SORT OF LOOP UNTIL WI
C HAVE THE SURPLUS REDUCED TO ZERO.

C ******************** PRICE RISE ********************

129       CONTINUE

C FIRST, TRY A (POSSIBLY DEGENERATE) PRICE RISE.

130       IF ((ARCF .EQ. 0) .AND. (ARCB .EQ. 0)) THEN
          PRICE = LARGE
          ARC = FOUT(I)
131       IF (ARC .GT. 0) THEN
          IF (F(ARC) .LT. U(ARC)) THEN
          XP = P(ENDN(ARC)) + 1
          IF (XP .LT. PRICE) THEN
          PRICE = XP
          ARCF = ARC
          NXTPUSHF(ARC)=0
          ELSE
          IF (XP .EQ. PRICE) THEN
          NXTPUSHF(ARC) = ARCF
          ARCF = ARC
          END IF
          ENDIF
          ENDIF
          ARC = NXTOU(ARC)
          GOTO 131
          ENDIF
          ARC = FIN(I)
132       IF (ARC .GT. 0) THEN
          IF (F(ARC) .GT. 0) THEN
          XP = P(STARTN(ARC))+1
          IF (XP .LT. PRICE) THEN
          PRICE = XP
          ARCB = ARC
          ARCF = 0
          NXTPUSHB(ARC) = 0
```

```
                ELSE
                IF (XP .EQ. PRICE) THEN
                NXTPUSHB(ARC) = ARCB
                ARCB = ARC
                END IF
                ENDIF
                ENDIF
                ARC = NXTIN(ARC)
                GOTO 132
                ENDIF


                ENDIF


C ******************** D - PUSHES ********************
C IF THE STEP WAS NOT DEGENERATE, TRY AND DO SOME
C PUSHING. WE DO NOT REUSE THE CODE ABOVE BECAUSE IT IS
C NOT NECESSARY TO CHECK IF THE ARCS USED ARE ADMISSIBLE.

                IF (SURPI .GT. 0) THEN
141             IF (ARCF .GT. 0) THEN
                RESID = U(ARCF) - F(ARCF)
                J = ENDN(ARCF)
                IF (SURPI .GE. RESID) THEN
                F(ARCF) = U(ARCF)
                SURPI = SURPI - RESID
                SURPLUS(J) = SURPLUS(J) + RESID
                IF (NXTQUEUE(J).EQ.0) THEN
                IF (SURPLUS(J).GT.0) THEN
                NXTQUEUE(PREVNODE)=J
                NXTQUEUE(J)=I
                PREVNODE=J
                END IF
                END IF
                ARCF = NXTPUSHF(ARCF)
                IF (SURPI .GT. 0) GOTO 141
                ELSE
                F(ARCF) = F(ARCF) + SURPI
                SURPLUS(J) = SURPLUS(J) + SURPI
                IF (NXTQUEUE(J).EQ.0) THEN
                IF (SURPLUS(J).GT.0) THEN
                NXTQUEUE(PREVNODE)=J
                NXTQUEUE(J)=I
                PREVNODE=J
                END IF
                END IF
                SURPI = 0
                ENDIF
                END IF
142             IF ((SURPI .GT. 0).AND.(ARCB .GT. 0)) THEN
                J = STARTN(ARCB)
                IF (SURPI .GE. F(ARCB)) THEN
                SURPI = SURPI - F(ARCB)
                SURPLUS(J) = SURPLUS(J) + F(ARCB)
                IF (NXTQUEUE(J).EQ.0) THEN
                NXTQUEUE(PREVNODE)=J
                NXTQUEUE(J)=I
                PREVNODE=J
                END IF
```

```
      F(ARCB) = 0
      ARCB = NXTPUSHB(ARCB)
      ELSE
      F(ARCB) = F(ARCB) - SURPI
      SURPLUS(J) = SURPLUS(J) + SURPI
      IF (NXTQUEUE(J).EQ.0) THEN
      NXTQUEUE(PREVNODE)=J
      NXTQUEUE(J)=I
      PREVNODE=J
      END IF
      SURPI = 0
      ENDIF
      GOTO 142
      ENDIF

C WE'VE DONE ALL THE PUSHING WE CAN AT THIS PRICE
C LEVEL. TRY TO DO A (POSSIBLY DEGENERATE) PRICE
C INCREASE.

      GOTO 129
      ENDIF

C THIS IS THE END OF THE UP ITERATION. IF WE GET HERE, THE
C SURPLUS OF I IS 0, AND WE HAVE DONE OUR LAST PRICE RISE.

      SURPLUS(I) = 0
      P(I) = PRICE
      FPUSHF(I) = ARCF
      FPUSHB(I) = ARCB
      ENDIF

C CHECK FOR THE END OF THE QUEUE. THIS STEP IS NOT NECESSARY FOR
C THE ALGORITHM; IT IS INCLUDED FOR COLLECTING STATISTICS ABOUT
C THE ALGORITHM'S BEHAVIOR, E.G. COUNTING THE NUMBER OF CYCLES

      IF (I.EQ.LASTQUEUE) THEN
      LASTQUEUE=PREVNODE
      NCYC=NCYC+1

C PRINT*,'CYCLE # ',NCYC,' # OF UP ITER. =',NITER

      END IF

C CHECK FOR TERMINATION. IF NOT FINISHED
C ADVANCE THE QUEUE AND RETURN TO TAKE ANOTHER NODE.

      NXTNODE=NXTQUEUE(I)
      IF (I.EQ.NXTNODE) THEN
      RETURN
      ELSE
      NXTQUEUE(PREVNODE)=NXTNODE
      NXTQUEUE(I)=0
      I=NXTNODE
      END IF

C PERIODICALLY CHECK FOR TERMINATION; LOOK FOR A SATURATING CUT

      IF (CUTFLAG.NE.1) GOTO 100
```

```
         IF (COUNT.EQ.N) THEN
X        PRINT*,'CHECKING FOR EARLY TERMINATION'
         COUNT=0
         DO 510 NODE=1,N
         MARK(NODE)=.FALSE.
510      CONTINUE
         MARK(SOURCE)=.TRUE.
         NLABEL=1
         LABEL(1)=SINK
         NSCAN=0
550      CONTINUE
         NSCAN=NSCAN+1
         NODE=LABEL(NSCAN)
         MARK(NODE)=.TRUE.
         ARC=FIN(NODE)
580      IF (ARC.GT.0) THEN
         START=STARTN(ARC)

C IF THIS IS AN ARC ALONG WHICH FLOW CAN BE PUSHED TO NODE
C CHECK IF THE OPP. NODE HAS 0 SURPLUS AND IF SO LABEL THE NODE

         IF (START.NE.SINK) THEN
         IF (F(ARC).LT.U(ARC)) THEN
         IF (START.EQ.SOURCE) GOTO 100
         IF (SURPLUS(START).GT.0) GOTO 100
         IF (.NOT.MARK(START)) THEN
         NLABEL=NLABEL+1
         LABEL(NLABEL)=START
         MARK(START)=.TRUE.
         END IF
         END IF
         END IF
         ARC=NXTIN(ARC)
         GOTO 580
         END IF
         ARC=FOUT(NODE)
585      IF (ARC.GT.0) THEN
         END=ENDN(ARC)

C IF THIS IS AN ARC ALONG WHICH FLOW CAN BE PUSHED TO NODE
C CHECK IF THE OPP. NODE HAS 0 SURPLUS AND IF SO LABEL THE NODE

         IF (END.NE.SINK) THEN
         IF (F(ARC).GT.0) THEN
         IF (END.EQ.SOURCE) GOTO 100
         IF (SURPLUS(END).GT.0) GOTO 100
         IF (.NOT.MARK(END)) THEN
         NLABEL=NLABEL+1
         LABEL(NLABEL)=END
         MARK(END)=.TRUE.
         END IF
         END IF
         END IF
         ARC=NXTOU(ARC)
         GOTO 585
         END IF
         IF (NLABEL.GT.NSCAN) THEN
         GOTO 550
```

```
               ELSE
               PRINT*,'SATURATED CUT FOUND'
               RETURN
               END IF
               ELSE
               COUNT=COUNT+1
               GO TO 100
               END IF

               END
```

A.7 ϵ-RELAXATION CODES

A.7.1 ϵ-RELAX

This code implements the ϵ-relaxation method with ϵ-scaling for the minimum cost flow problem (cf. Section 4.5).

```
C ** SAMPLE CALLING PROGRAM FOR E-RELAX **
C THIS PROGRAM WILL READ A PROBLEM FILE IN STANDARD FORMAT
C AND SOLVE IT USING E-RELAX.
C THIS IS AN E-SCALED VERSION THAT USES A CYCLIC QUEUE
C *************************************************

               PARAMETER (MAXNODES=8000, MAXARCS=25000)
               IMPLICIT INTEGER (A-Z)
               COMMON /SCALARS/ N,NA,LARGE,FACTOR,EPS,
               &THRESHSURPLUS,SFACTOR
               COMMON /STATS/ NCYC,NITER,TOTALITER
               COMMON /BLK1/ STARTN
               COMMON /BLK2/ ENDN
               COMMON /UBOUND/ U
               COMMON /FLOW/ F
               COMMON /PRICES/ P
               COMMON /BLK3/ SURPLUS
               COMMON /BLK4/ FIN
               COMMON /BLK5/ FOUT
               COMMON /BLK6/ NXTIN
               COMMON /BLK7/ NXTOU
               COMMON /BLK11/ FPUSHF
               COMMON /BLK12/ NXTPUSHF
               COMMON /BLK13/ FPUSHB
               COMMON /BLK14/ NXTPUSHB
               COMMON /COST/ COST
               COMMON /QUEUE/ NXTQUEUE
               INTEGER NXTQUEUE(MAXNODES)
               INTEGER STARTN(MAXARCS)
               INTEGER ENDN(MAXARCS)
               INTEGER U(MAXARCS)
               INTEGER F(MAXARCS)
               INTEGER SURPLUS(MAXNODES)
```

```
          INTEGER FIN(MAXNODES)
          INTEGER FOUT(MAXNODES)
          INTEGER NXTIN(MAXARCS)
          INTEGER NXTOU(MAXARCS)
          INTEGER P(MAXNODES)
          INTEGER FPUSHF(MAXNODES)
          INTEGER NXTPUSHF(MAXARCS)
          INTEGER FPUSHB(MAXNODES)
          INTEGER NXTPUSHB(MAXARCS)
          INTEGER COST(MAXARCS)
          REAL*8 TCOST,TT,TIMER
          PRINT*,'E-RELAXATION METHOD FOR MIN COST FLOW'
          PRINT*,'*********************************'
          PRINT *,'READING PROBLEM DATA'
          OPEN(13,FILE='FOR013.DAT',STATUS='OLD')
          REWIND(13)

C READ NUMBER OF NODES AND ARCS

          READ(13,1010) N,NA

C READ START, END, COST, AND CAPACITY OF EACH ARC
C AND GENERATE MAX COST VALUE

          MAXCOST=0
          DO 5 I=1,NA
          READ(13,1020) STARTN(I),ENDN(I),COST(I),U(I)
          COST(I)=COST(I)*(N+1)
          IF (ABS(COST(I)).GT.MAXCOST) MAXCOST=ABS(COST(I))
5         CONTINUE

C READ SUPPLY OF EACH NODE

          DO 8 I=1,N
          READ(13,1000) SURPLUS(I)
8         CONTINUE
          ENDFILE(13)
          REWIND(13)
          PRINT*,'END OF READING'
1000      FORMAT(1I8)
1010      FORMAT(2I8)
1020      FORMAT(4I8)
          LARGE=1000000000

C INITIALIZE PRICES & PUSH LISTS

          DO 10 NODE=1,N
          FPUSHF(NODE)=0
          FPUSHB(NODE)=0
          P(NODE)=-LARGE
10        CONTINUE

C IN THE FOLLOWING STATEMENTS, THE E-SCALING PARAMETERS ARE SET.
C THE FOLLOWING RANGES ARE RECOMMENDED:
C STARTING EPSILON: BETWEEN MAXCOST/20 TO MAXCOST/2
C SCALING FACTOR: BETWEEN FOUR AND TEN

25        CONTINUE
```

```
        PRINT*,'ENTER STARTING EPSILON'
        PRINT*,'SHOULD BE BETWEEN 1 & ',MAXCOST
        READ*,EPS
        IF (EPS.LT.1) GO TO 25
        PRINT*,'ENTER SCALING FACTOR'
30      CONTINUE
        READ*,FACTOR
        IF ((EPS.GT.1).AND.(FACTOR.LE.1)) THEN
        PRINT*,'ENTER SCALING FACTOR; SHOULD BE GREATER THAN 1'
        GO TO 30
        END IF
        MAXSURPLUS=-LARGE
        DO 920 NODE=1,N
        IF (SURPLUS(NODE).GT.MAXSURPLUS) THEN
        MAXSURPLUS=SURPLUS(NODE)
        END IF
920     CONTINUE

C SET THE PARAMETER SSCALE TO 1 TO ALLOW SURPLUS SCALING
C A HEURISTIC SCHEME IS USED TO SET THE SFACTOR AND
C THRESHSURPLUS PARAMETERS THAT CONTROL SURPLUS SCALING

        SSCALE=1
        IF (SSCALE.EQ.1) THEN
        SFACTOR=2+INT(FACTOR*MAXSURPLUS/MAXCOST)
        IF (SFACTOR.LT.4) SFACTOR=4
        THRESHSURPLUS=INT(MAXSURPLUS/SFACTOR)
        IF (EPS.EQ.1) THRESHSURPLUS=0
        ELSE
        THRESHSURPLUS=0
        END IF
        PRINT*,'INITIALIZING DATA STRUCTURES'
        CALL INIDAT
        PRINT *,'********************************'
        PRINT *,'CALLING E-RELAX (+ SURPLUS NODES ITERATED ONLY)'
        TIMER = LONG(362)
        CALL EPS_RELAX
        TT =(LONG(362) - TIMER)/60
        PRINT*, 'TOTAL TIME = ',TT, ' secs.'
        TCOST=0
        DO 330 I=1,NA
330     TCOST=TCOST+F(I)*COST(I)/(N+1)
        WRITE(9,1100) TCOST
1100    FORMAT(' ','OPTIMAL COST =',F14.2)
        PRINT *,'********************************'
        PRINT *,'# OF ITERATIONS = ',TOTALITER
        PRINT *,'# OF S. N. PRICE RISES = ',NITER
        PRINT *,'********************************'

C CHECK CORRECTNESS OF THE ANSWER

        IF (EPS.NE.1) THEN
        PRINT*,'* CAUTION * THE FINAL EPSILON IS EQUAL TO ',EPS
        END IF
        DO 80 NODE=1,N
        IF (SURPLUS(NODE).NE.0) THEN
        PRINT*,'NONZERO SURPLUS AT NODE ',NODE
        ENDIF
```

```
80      CONTINUE
        DO 90 ARC=1,NA
        IF (F(ARC).GT.0) THEN
        IF (P(STARTN(ARC))-P(ENDN(ARC)).LT.-EPS+COST(ARC)) THEN
        PRINT*,'E-CS VIOLATED AT ARC ',ARC
        ENDIF
        ENDIF
        IF (F(ARC).LT.U(ARC)) THEN
        IF (P(STARTN(ARC))-P(ENDN(ARC)).GT.EPS+COST(ARC)) THEN
        PRINT*,'E-CS VIOLATED AT ARC ',ARC
        ENDIF
        ENDIF
90      CONTINUE
        PRINT *, ' '
        PRINT *, 'PROGRAM ENDED; PRESS <CR>'
        PAUSE
        STOP
        END


        SUBROUTINE INIDAT
C THIS SUBROUTINE USES THE DATA ARRAYS STARTN AND ENDN
C TO CONSTRUCT AUXILIARY DATA ARRAYS FOUT, NXTOU, FIN, AND
C NXTIN THAT ARE REQUIRED BY E-RELAX. IN THIS SUBROUTINE WE
C ARBITRARILY ORDER THE ARCS LEAVING EACH NODE AND STORE
C THIS INFORMATION IN FOUT AND NXTOU. SIMILARLY, WE ARBITRA-
C RILY ORDER THE ARCS ENTERING EACH NODE AND STORE THIS
C INFORMATION IN FIN AND NXTIN. AT THE COMPLETION OF THE
C CONSTRUCTION, WE HAVE THAT
C FOUT(I) = FIRST ARC LEAVING NODE I.
C NXTOU(J) = NEXT ARC LEAVING THE HEAD NODE OF ARC J.
C FIN(I) = FIRST ARC ENTERING NODE I.
C NXTIN(J) = NEXT ARC ENTERING THE TAIL NODE OF ARC J.

        PARAMETER (MAXNODES=8000, MAXARCS=25000)
        IMPLICIT INTEGER (A-Z)
        COMMON /SCALARS/ N,NA,LARGE,FACTOR,EPS
        COMMON /BLK1/ STARTN
        COMMON /BLK2/ ENDN
        COMMON /BLK4/ FIN
        COMMON /BLK5/ FOUT
        COMMON /BLK6/ NXTIN
        COMMON /BLK7/ NXTOU
        INTEGER STARTN(MAXARCS)
        INTEGER ENDN(MAXARCS)
        INTEGER FIN(MAXNODES)
        INTEGER FOUT(MAXNODES)
        INTEGER NXTIN(MAXARCS)
        INTEGER NXTOU(MAXARCS)
        INTEGER FINALIN(MAXNODES),FINALOU(MAXNODES)
        DO 20 NODE=1,N
        FIN(NODE)=0
        FOUT(NODE)=0
        FINALIN(NODE)=0
        FINALOU(NODE)=0
20      CONTINUE
        DO 30 ARC=1,NA
        START=STARTN(ARC)
        END=ENDN(ARC)
```

```
              IF (FOUT(START).NE.0) THEN
              NXTOU(FINALOU(START))=ARC
              ELSE
              FOUT(START)=ARC
              END IF
              IF (FIN(END).NE.0) THEN
              NXTIN(FINALIN(END))=ARC
              ELSE
              FIN(END)=ARC
              END IF
              FINALOU(START)=ARC
              FINALIN(END)=ARC
              NXTIN(ARC)=0
              NXTOU(ARC)=0
30            CONTINUE
              RETURN
              END


C ************************************************************
C SCALED E-RELAXATION
C THIS VERSION USES A QUEUE TO SELECT NODES.
C NODES JOIN THE QUEUE AT THE BOTTOM.
C ************************************************************

              SUBROUTINE EPS_RELAX
              IMPLICIT NONE
              INTEGER N,NA,LARGE,FACTOR,EPS,ARC,ARCF,ARCB
              INTEGER NCYC,NITER,NODE,PRICE,PRICEINCR
              INTEGER I,J,K,LN,CAPOUT,CAPIN,PREVNODE,LASTQUEUE
              INTEGER SURPI,REJI,NEXT,START,END,PSTART,PEND,MAXPRICE
              INTEGER RESID,DEL,FLOW,NXTNODE,TOTALITER
              INTEGER REFPRICE,PRJ,XP,REFPRJ,PRICEJ,THRESHSURPLUS,SFACTOR
              INTEGER NXTQUEUE(1)
              INTEGER STARTN(1),ENDN(1),U(1),F(1),SURPLUS(1),FIN(1),FOUT(1)
              INTEGER NXTIN(1),NXTOU(1),P(1)
              INTEGER FPUSHF(1),NXTPUSHF(1),FPUSHB(1),NXTPUSHB(1)
              INTEGER COST(1)
              COMMON /SCALARS/ N,NA,LARGE,FACTOR,EPS,
              &THRESHSURPLUS,SFACTOR
              COMMON /STATS/ NCYC,NITER,TOTALITER
              COMMON /BLK1/ STARTN
              COMMON /BLK2/ ENDN
              COMMON /UBOUND/ U
              COMMON /FLOW/ F
              COMMON /PRICES/ P
              COMMON /BLK3/ SURPLUS
              COMMON /BLK4/ FIN
              COMMON /BLK5/ FOUT
              COMMON /BLK6/ NXTIN
              COMMON /BLK7/ NXTOU
              COMMON /BLK11/ FPUSHF
              COMMON /BLK12/ NXTPUSHF
              COMMON /BLK13/ FPUSHB
              COMMON /BLK14/ NXTPUSHB
              COMMON /COST/ COST
              COMMON /QUEUE/ NXTQUEUE

C INITIALIZE COUNT OF NUMBER OF UP ITERATIONS PERFORMED
```

```
        NITER = 0
        TOTALITER=0
        NCYC=0
        MAXPRICE =LARGE

C REDUCE ARC CAPACITIES

        DO 40 NODE=1,N
        CAPOUT=0
        ARC=FOUT(NODE)
41      IF (ARC.GT.0) THEN
        CAPOUT=MIN(LARGE,CAPOUT+U(ARC))
        ARC=NXTOU(ARC)
        GO TO 41
        END IF
        CAPOUT=MIN(LARGE,CAPOUT-SURPLUS(NODE))
        IF (CAPOUT.LT.0) GOTO 400
        CAPIN=0
        ARC=FIN(NODE)
43      IF (ARC.GT.0) THEN
        IF (U(ARC) .GT. CAPOUT) THEN
        U(ARC)=CAPOUT
        ENDIF
        CAPIN=MIN(LARGE,CAPIN+U(ARC))
        ARC=NXTIN(ARC)
        GO TO 43
        END IF
        CAPIN=MIN(LARGE,CAPIN+SURPLUS(NODE))
        IF (CAPIN.LT.0) GOTO 400
        ARC=FOUT(NODE)
45      IF (ARC.GT.0) THEN
        IF (U(ARC) .GT. CAPIN) THEN
        U(ARC)=CAPIN
        ENDIF
        ARC=NXTOU(ARC)
        GO TO 45
        END IF
40      CONTINUE

C SET ARC FLOWS TO SATISFY E-CS

        DO 49 ARC=1,NA
        START=STARTN(ARC)
        END=ENDN(ARC)
        PSTART=P(START)
        PEND=P(END)
        IF (PSTART.GE.PEND+COST(ARC)+EPS) THEN
        SURPLUS(START)=SURPLUS(START)-U(ARC)
        SURPLUS(END)=SURPLUS(END)+U(ARC)
        F(ARC)=U(ARC)
        ELSE
        F(ARC)=0
        END IF
49      CONTINUE

C *********** START OF A NEW SCALING PHASE ***********
```

```
60      CONTINUE

C ***** QUEUE INITIALIZATION *****

        DO 82 NODE=1,N-1
        NXTQUEUE(NODE)=NODE+1
82      CONTINUE
        NXTQUEUE(N)=1
        I=1
        PREVNODE=N
        LASTQUEUE=N

C ************ START A NEW CYCLE OF UP ITERATIONS ************

100     CONTINUE

C TAKE UP NEXT NODE (NODE I) FOR ITERATION

        SURPI=SURPLUS(I)
        IF (SURPI.GT.THRESHSURPLUS) THEN

C ARCF & ARCB ARE THE CURRENT VALUES OF THE
C STARTING ARCS OF THE PUSH LISTS OF I

        TOTALITER=TOTALITER+1
        ARCF = FPUSHF(I)
        ARCB = FPUSHB(I)
        PRICE = P(I)
115     IF ((ARCF .GT. 0) .OR. (ARCB .GT. 0)) THEN

C START BY TRYING TO PUSH AWAY FLOW ON ARCS THAT WERE
C ADMISSIBLE AT THE END OF THE LAST ITERATION (IF ANY)
C AT THIS NODE. WE MUST CHECK THAT THEY ARE STILL
C ADMISSIBLE.

120     IF ((SURPI .GT. 0) .AND. (ARCF .GT. 0)) THEN
        J = ENDN(ARCF)
        IF (PRICE-P(J)-COST(ARCF).EQ.EPS) THEN
        RESID = U(ARCF) - F(ARCF)
        IF (RESID.GT.0) THEN
        IF (SURPI .GE. RESID) THEN
        F(ARCF) = U(ARCF)
        SURPI = SURPI - RESID
        SURPLUS(J) = SURPLUS(J) + RESID
        ARCF = NXTPUSHF(ARCF)
        ELSE
        F(ARCF) = F(ARCF) + SURPI
        SURPLUS(J) = SURPLUS(J) + SURPI
        SURPI = 0
        ENDIF
        IF (SURPLUS(J).GT.THRESHSURPLUS) THEN
        IF (NXTQUEUE(J).EQ.0) THEN
        NXTQUEUE(PREVNODE)=J
        NXTQUEUE(J)=I
        PREVNODE=J
        END IF
        END IF
        ELSE
```

```
                     ARCF = NXTPUSHF(ARCF)
                     ENDIF
                     ELSE
                     ARCF = NXTPUSHF(ARCF)
                     ENDIF
                     GOTO 120
                     ENDIF

          121    IF ((SURPI .GT. 0) .AND. (ARCB .GT. 0)) THEN
                     J = STARTN(ARCB)
                     IF (PRICE-P(J)+COST(ARCB).EQ.EPS) THEN
                     RESID=F(ARCB)
                     IF (RESID.GT.0) THEN
                     IF (SURPI .GE. RESID) THEN
                     SURPI = SURPI - RESID
                     SURPLUS(J) = SURPLUS(J) + RESID
                     F(ARCB) = 0
                     ARCB = NXTPUSHB(ARCB)
                     ELSE
                     F(ARCB) = F(ARCB) - SURPI
                     SURPLUS(J) = SURPLUS(J) + SURPI
                     SURPI = 0
                     ENDIF
                     IF (SURPLUS(J).GT.THRESHSURPLUS) THEN
                     IF (NXTQUEUE(J).EQ.0) THEN
                     NXTQUEUE(PREVNODE)=J
                     NXTQUEUE(J)=I
                     PREVNODE=J
                     END IF
                     END IF
                     ELSE
                     ARCB = NXTPUSHB(ARCB)
                     ENDIF
                     ELSE
                     ARCB = NXTPUSHB(ARCB)
                     ENDIF
                     GOTO 121
                     ENDIF
                     ENDIF

C ***** END OF D-PUSHES; CHECK IF PRICE RISE IS NEEDED *****

                     IF ((ARCF .EQ. 0) .AND. (ARCB .EQ. 0)) THEN

C *****************DO A PRICE RISE ********************

                     REFPRICE=PRICE
                     PRICE = LARGE
                     NITER=NITER+1
                     ARC = FOUT(I)
          111    IF (ARC .GT. 0) THEN
                     IF (F(ARC) .LT. U(ARC)) THEN
                     XP = P(ENDN(ARC))+COST(ARC)
                     IF (XP.LT.PRICE) THEN
                     PRICE = XP
                     ARCF = ARC
                     NXTPUSHF(ARC)=0
                     ELSE
```

```
        IF (XP.EQ.PRICE) THEN
        NXTPUSHF(ARC) = ARCF
        ARCF = ARC
        END IF
        ENDIF
        ENDIF
        ARC = NXTOU(ARC)
        GOTO 111
        ENDIF
        ARC = FIN(I)
112     IF (ARC .GT. 0) THEN
        IF (F(ARC) .GT. 0) THEN
        XP = P(STARTN(ARC))-COST(ARC)
        IF (XP.LT.PRICE) THEN
        PRICE = XP
        ARCB = ARC
        ARCF=0
        NXTPUSHB(ARC)=0
        ELSE
        IF (XP.EQ.PRICE) THEN
        NXTPUSHB(ARC) = ARCB
        ARCB = ARC
        END IF
        ENDIF
        ENDIF
        ARC = NXTIN(ARC)
        GOTO 112
        ENDIF

C SET PRICE OF NODE I

        PRICE=PRICE+EPS
        P(I) = PRICE
        FPUSHF(I) = ARCF
        FPUSHB(I) = ARCB

X       PRICEINCR=PRICE-REFPRICE
X       IF (PRICEINCR.LE.0) THEN
X       PRINT*,'NONPOSITIVE PRICE INCREMENT=',PRICEINCR
X       PAUSE
X       STOP
X       ENDIF

C END OF PRICE RISE; IF THERE IS STILL A LOT OF SURPLUS,
C TRY AND DO SOME PUSHING.

        IF (SURPI.GT.THRESHSURPLUS) GOTO 115
        ELSE

C IF NO PRICE RISE TOOK PLACE RESET THE START OF THE PUSH LISTS

        FPUSHF(I) = ARCF
        FPUSHB(I) = ARCB
        ENDIF

C DO THE FINAL BOOKKEEPING OF THE ITERATION
```

```
          SURPLUS(I) = SURPI

C IF THE PRICE IS TOO HIGH, THEN SOMETHING IS WRONG

X         IF (PRICE.GT.MAXPRICE) THEN
X         GO TO 400
X         ENDIF
            ENDIF

C ********** END OF UP ITERATION STARTING AT NODE I *********
C CHECK FOR THE END OF THE QUEUE. THIS STEP IS NOT NECESSARY FOR
C THE ALGORITHM; IT IS INCLUDED FOR COLLECTING STATISTICS ABOUT
C THE ALGORITHM'S BEHAVIOR, E.G. COUNTING THE NUMBER OF CYCLES

X         IF (I.EQ.LASTQUEUE) THEN
X         LASTQUEUE=PREVNODE
X         NCYC=NCYC+1
X         PRINT*,'CYCLE # ',NCYC,' # OF PRICE RISES ',NITER
X         END IF

C CHECK FOR TERMINATION OF SCALING PHASE. IF SCALING PHASE IS
C NOT FINISHED, ADVANCE THE QUEUE AND RETURN TO TAKE
C ANOTHER NODE.

          NXTNODE=NXTQUEUE(I)
          IF (I.NE.NXTNODE) THEN
          NXTQUEUE(I)=0
          NXTQUEUE(PREVNODE)=NXTNODE
          I=NXTNODE
          GO TO 100
          END IF

C ************* END OF SUBPROBLEM (SCALING PHASE) *************

X         PRINT*,'END OF SCALING PHASE'

C DO A DIAGNOSTIC CHECK

X         LN=0
X         DO 500 NODE=1,N
X         IF (SURPLUS(NODE).NE.0) THEN
X         LN=LN+1
X         ENDIF
500       CONTINUE
X         PRINT*,'NONZERO SURPLUS AT ',LN,' NODES '
X         DO 600 ARC=1,NA
X         IF (F(ARC).GT.0) THEN
X         IF (P(STARTN(ARC))-P(ENDN(ARC)).LT.-EPS+COST(ARC)) THEN
X          PRINT*,'E-CS VIOLATED AT ARC ',ARC
X         ENDIF
X         ENDIF
X         IF (F(ARC).LT.U(ARC)) THEN
X         IF (P(STARTN(ARC))-P(ENDN(ARC)).GT.EPS+COST(ARC)) THEN
X         PRINT*,'E-CS VIOLATED AT ARC ',ARC
X         ENDIF
X         ENDIF
600       CONTINUE
X         PRINT*,'END OF CHECK OF OLD PHASE'
```

```
C ****** IF EPSILON IS 1 TERMINATE; ELSE REDUCE EPSILON******

        IF (EPS.EQ.1) THEN
        RETURN
        ELSE
        EPS=INT(EPS/FACTOR)
        IF (EPS.LT.1) EPS=1
        END IF
        THRESHSURPLUS=INT(THRESHSURPLUS/SFACTOR)
        IF (EPS.EQ.1) THRESHSURPLUS=0

C RESET THE FLOWS & THE PUSH LISTS; FIND THE MINIMAL PRICE

        XP=LARGE
        DO 800 NODE=1,N
        FPUSHF(NODE)=0
        FPUSHB(NODE)=0
        IF (P(NODE).LT.XP) XP=P(NODE)
800     CONTINUE

C REDUCE ALL PRICES TO REDUCE DANGER OF OVERFLOW

        DEL=XP+INT(LARGE/2)
        DO 810 NODE=1,N
        P(NODE)=P(NODE)-DEL
810     CONTINUE
X       PRINT*,'MODIFYING ARC FLOWS TO SATISFY E-CS'
        DO 900 ARC=1,NA
        START=STARTN(ARC)
        END=ENDN(ARC)
        PSTART=P(START)
        PEND=P(END)
        IF (PSTART.GT.PEND+EPS+COST(ARC)) THEN
        RESID=U(ARC)-F(ARC)
        IF (RESID.GT.0) THEN
        SURPLUS(START)=SURPLUS(START)-RESID
        SURPLUS(END)=SURPLUS(END)+RESID
        F(ARC)=U(ARC)
        END IF
        ELSE
        IF (PSTART.LT.PEND-EPS+COST(ARC)) THEN
        FLOW=F(ARC)
        IF (FLOW.GT.0) THEN
        SURPLUS(START)=SURPLUS(START)+FLOW
        SURPLUS(END)=SURPLUS(END)-FLOW
        F(ARC)=0
        END IF
        END IF
        END IF
900     CONTINUE

C RETURN FOR ANOTHER PHASE

X       PRINT*,'CHECKING E-CS BEFORE STARTING NEW PHASE'
X       DO 700 ARC=1,NA
X       IF (F(ARC).GT.0) THEN
X       IF (P(STARTN(ARC))-P(ENDN(ARC)).LT.-EPS+COST(ARC)) THEN
```

```
X        PRINT*,'E-CS VIOLATED AT ARC ',ARC
X        ENDIF
X        ENDIF
X        IF (F(ARC).LT.U(ARC)) THEN
X        IF (P(STARTN(ARC))-P(ENDN(ARC)).GT.EPS+COST(ARC)) THEN
X        PRINT*,'E-CS VIOLATED AT ARC ',ARC
X        ENDIF
X        ENDIF
700      CONTINUE
         GO TO 60

400      PRINT*,'PROBLEM IS INFEASIBLE'
         PAUSE
         STOP

         END
```

A.7.2 ϵ-RELAX-N

This code is the same as ϵ-RELAX but allows relaxation iterations starting from nodes with negative as well as positive surplus. The code is available from the author.

REFERENCES

[AMO88] Ahuja, R. K., Mehlhorn, K., Orlin, J. B., and Tarjan, R. E., 1988. "Faster Algorithms for the Shortest Path Problem," Tech. Report No. 193, Operations Research Center, M.I.T., Cambridge, MA, (also in J. ACM, Vol. 37, 1990, pp. 213-223).

[AMO89] Ahuja, R. K., Magnanti, T. L., and Orlin, J. B., 1989. "Network Flows," Sloan W. P. No. 2059-88, M.I.T., Cambridge, MA, (also in Handbooks in Operations Research and Management Science, Vol. 1, Optimization, G. L. Nemhauser, A. H. G. Rinnooy-Kan, and M. J. Todd (eds.), North-Holland, Amsterdam, 1989, pp. 211-369).

[AaM76] Aashtiani, H. A., and Magnanti, T. L., 1976. "Implementing Primal-Dual Network Flow Algorithms," Working Paper OR-055-76, Operations Research Center, M.I.T., Cambridge, MA.

[AhO86] Ahuja, R. K., and Orlin, J. B., 1986. "A Fast and Simple Algorithm for the Maximum Flow Problem," Working paper, M.I.T., Cambridge, MA, (also in Operations Research, Vol. 37, 1989, pp. 748-759).

[Akg86] Akgul, M., 1986. "Shortest Paths and the Simplex Method," Tech. Report, Department of Computer Sciences and Operations Research Program, North Carolina State Univ., Raleigh, N.C.

[BBG77] Bradley, G. H., Brown, G. G., and Graves, G. W., 1977. "Design and Implementation of Large-Scale Primal Transshipment Problems," Management Science, Vol. 24, pp. 1-38.

[BCT91] Bertsekas, D. P., Castañon, D. A., and Tsaknakis, H., 1991. "Reverse Auction and the Solution of Inequality Constrained Assignment Problems," Unpublished Report.

[BGK77] Barr, R., Glover, F., and Klingman, D., 1977. "The Alternating Basis Algorithm for Assignment Problems," Math. Programming, Vol. 13, pp. 1-13.

[BGK78] Barr, R., Glover, F., and Klingman, D., 1978. "Generalized Alternating Path Algorithm for Transportation Problems," Euro. J. of Operations Research, Vol. 2, pp. 137-144.

[BGK79] Barr, R., Glover, F., and Klingman, D., 1979. "Enhancement of Spanning Tree Labeling Procedures for Network Optimization," INFOR, Vol. 17, pp. 16-34.

[BHT87] Bertsekas, D. P., Hossein, P., and Tseng, P., 1987. "Relaxation Methods for Network Flow Problems with Convex Arc Costs," SIAM J. on Control and Optimization, Vol. 25, pp. 1219-1243.

[BJS90] Bazaraa, M. S., Jarvis, J. J., and Sherali, H. D., 1990. Linear Programming and Network Flows (2nd edition), Wiley, N. Y.

[BMP89] Balas, E., Miller, D., Pekny, J., and Toth, P., 1989. "A Parallel Shortest Path Algorithm for the Assignment Problem," Management Science Report MSRR 552, Carnegie Mellon Univ., Pittsburgh, PA.

[BaF88] Bar-Shalom, Y., and Fortman, T. E., 1988. Tracking and Data Association, Academic Press, N. Y.

[BaJ78] Bazaraa, M. S., and Jarvis, J. J., 1978. Linear Programming and Network Flows, Wiley, N. Y.

[Bal85] Balinski, M. L., 1985. "Signature Methods for the Assignment Problem," Operations Research, Vol. 33, pp. 527-537.

[Bal86] Balinski, M. L., 1986. "A Competitive (Dual) Simplex Method for the Assignment Problem," Math. Programming, Vol. 34, pp. 125-141.

[BeC89a] Bertsekas, D. P., and Castañon, D. A., 1989. "The Auction Algorithm for Transportation Problems," Annals of Operations Research, Vol. 20, pp. 67-96.

[BeC89b] Bertsekas, D. P., and Castañon, D. A., 1989. "The Auction Algorithm for the Minimum Cost Network Flow Problem," Laboratory for Information and Decision Systems Report LIDS-P-1925, M.I.T., Cambridge, MA.

[BeC89c] Bertsekas, D. P., and Castañon, D. A., 1989. "Parallel Synchronous and Asynchronous Implementations of the Auction Algorithm," Alphatech Report, Burlington, MA, to appear in Parallel Computing.

[BeC90a] Bertsekas, D. P., and Castañon, D. A., 1990. "Parallel Asynchronous

Hungarian Methods for the Assignment Problem," Report LIDS-P-1997, M.I.T., Cambridge, MA.

[BeC90b] Bertsekas, D. P., and Castañon, D. A., 1990. "Parallel Asynchronous Primal-Dual Methods for the Minimum Cost Flow Problem," Report LIDS-P-1998, M.I.T., Cambridge, MA.

[BeE87a] Bertsekas, D. P., and El Baz, D., 1987. "Distributed Asynchronous Relaxation Methods for Convex Network Flow Problems," SIAM J. on Control and Optimization, Vol. 25, pp. 74-85.

[BeE87b] Bertsekas, D. P., and Eckstein, J., 1987. "Distributed Asynchronous Relaxation Methods for Linear Network Flow Problems," Proc. of IFAC '87, Munich, Germany.

[BeE88] Bertsekas, D. P., and Eckstein, J., 1988. "Dual Coordinate Step Methods for Linear Network Flow Problems," Math. Programming, Series B, Vol. 42, pp. 203-243.

[BeG62] Berge, C., and Ghouila-Houri, A., 1962. Programming, Games, and Transportation Networks, Wiley, N. Y.

[BeG87] Bertsekas, D. P., and Gallager, R. G., 1987. Data Networks, Prentice-Hall, Englewood Cliffs, N. J.

[BeM73] Bertsekas, D. P., and Mitter, S. K., 1973. "Descent Numerical Methods for Optimization Problems with Nondifferentiable Cost Functions," SIAM Journal on Control, Vol. 11, pp. 637-652.

[BeT85] Bertsekas, D. P., and Tseng, P., 1985. "Relaxation Methods for Minimum Cost Ordinary and Generalized Network Flow Problems," Lab. for Information and Decision Systems Report P-1462, M.I.T., Cambridge, MA.; also Operations Research, Vol. 36, 1988, pp. 93-114.

[BeT88] Bertsekas, D. P., and Tseng, P., 1988. "RELAX: A Computer Code for Minimum Cost Network Flow Problems," Annals of Operations Research, Vol. 13, pp. 127-190.

[BeT89] Bertsekas, D. P., and Tsitsiklis, J. N., 1989. Parallel and Distributed Computation: Numerical Methods, Prentice-Hall, Englewood Cliffs, N. J.

[BeT90] Bertsekas, D. P., and Tseng, P., 1990. "RELAXT-III: A New and Improved Version of the RELAX Code," Lab. for Information and Decision Systems Report P-1990, M.I.T., Cambridge, MA.

[BeT91] Bertsekas, D. P., and Tsaknakis, H., 1991. Unpublished Work.

[Bel57] Bellman, R., 1957. Dynamic Programming, Princeton Univ. Press, Princeton, N. J.

[Ber79] Bertsekas, D. P., 1979. "A Distributed Algorithm for the Assignment Problem," Lab. for Information and Decision Systems Working Paper, M.I.T.,

Cambridge, MA.

[Ber81] Bertsekas, D. P., 1981. "A New Algorithm for the Assignment Problem," Math. Programming, Vol. 21, pp. 152-171.

[Ber82a] Bertsekas, D. P., 1982. Constrained Optimization and Lagrange Multiplier Methods, Academic Press, N. Y.

[Ber82b] Bertsekas, D. P., 1982. "A Unified Framework for Minimum Cost Network Flow Problems," Laboratory for Information and Decision Systems Report LIDS-P-1245-A, M.I.T., Cambridge, MA; also in Math. Programming, Vol. 32, 1985, pp. 125-145.

[Ber85] Bertsekas, D. P., 1985. "A Distributed Asynchronous Relaxation Algorithm for the Assignment Problem," Proc. 24th IEEE Conference on Decision and Control, Ft Lauderdale, Fla., pp. 1703-1704.

[Ber86a] Bertsekas, D. P., 1986. "Distributed Asynchronous Relaxation Methods for Linear Network Flow Problems," Lab. for Information and Decision Systems Report P-1606, M.I.T., Cambridge, MA.

[Ber86b] Bertsekas, D. P., 1986. "Distributed Relaxation Methods for Linear Network Flow Problems," Proceedings of 25th IEEE Conference on Decision and Control, Athens, Greece, pp. 2101-2106.

[Ber87] Bertsekas, D. P., 1987. Dynamic Programming: Deterministic and Stochastic Models, Prentice-Hall, Englewood Cliffs, N. J.

[Ber88] Bertsekas, D. P., 1988. "The Auction Algorithm: A Distributed Relaxation Method for the Assignment Problem," Annals of Operations Research, Vol. 14, pp. 105-123.

[Ber90] Bertsekas, D. P., 1990. "An Auction Algorithm for Shortest Paths," Lab. for Information and Decision Systems Report P-2000, M.I.T., Cambridge, MA., SIAM J. on Optimization, to appear.

[BlJ85] Bland, R. G., and Jensen, D. L., 1985. "On the Computational Behavior of a Polynomial- Time Network Flow Algorithm," Tech. Report 661, School of Operations Research and Industrial Engineering, Cornell University.

[Bla86] Blackman, S. S., 1986. Multi-Target Tracking with Radar Applications, Artech House, Dehdam, MA.

[BuG61] Busacker, R. G., and Gowen, P. J., 1961. "A Procedure for Determining a Family of Minimal-Cost Network Flow Patterns," O.R.O. Technical Report No. 15, Operational Research Office, John Hopkins University, Baltimore, MD.

[BuS65] Busacker, R. G., and Saaty, T. L., 1965. Finite Graphs and Networks: An Introduction with Applications, McGraw-Hill, N. Y.

[CMT88] Carpaneto, G., Martello, S., and Toth, P., 1988. "Algorithms and

Codes for the Assignment Problem," Annals of Operations Research, Vol. 13, pp. 193-223.

[CaS86] Carraresi, P., and Sodini, C., 1986. "An Efficient Algorithm for the Bipartite Matching Problem," Eur. J. Operations Research, Vol. 23, pp. 86-93.

[Cas91] Castañon, D. A., 1991. Private Communication.

[ChZ90] Chajakis, E. D., and Zenios, S. A., 1990. "Synchronous and Asynchronous Implementations of Relaxation Algorithms for Nonlinear Network Optimization," Report 89-10-07, Decision Sciences Dept., The Wharton School, University of Pennsylvania, Phila., Pa.

[Che77] Cherkasky, R. V., 1977. "Algorithm for Construction of Maximum Flow in Networks with Complexity of $O(V^2\sqrt{E})$ Operations," Mathematical Methods of Solution of Economical Problems, Vol. 7, pp. 112-125.

[Chr75] Christofides, N., 1975. Graph Theory: An Algorithmic Approach, Academic Press, N. Y.

[Chv83] Chvatal, V., 1983. Linear Programming, W. H. Freeman and Co., N. Y.

[Cun76] Cunningham, W. H., 1976. "A Network Simplex Method," Math. Programming, Vol. 4, pp. 105-116.

[Cun79] Cunningham, W. H., 1979. "Theoretical Properties of the Network Simplex Method," Math. of Operations Research, Vol. 11, pp. 196-208.

[DGK79] Dial, R., Glover, F., Karney, D., and Klingman, D., 1979. "A Computational Analysis of Alternative Algorithms and Labeling Techniques for Finding Shortest Path Trees," Networks, Vol. 9, pp. 215-248.

[DaF56] Dantzig, G. B., and Fulkerson, D. R., 1956. "On the Max-Flow Min-Cut Theorem of Networks," in H. W. Kuhn and A. W. Tucker (ed.), Linear Inequalities and Related Systems, Annals of Mathematics Study 38, Princeton University Press, pp. 215-221.

[Dan51] Dantzig, G. B., 1951. "Application of the Simplex Method to a Transportation Problem," in T. C. Koopmans (ed.), Activity Analysis of Production and Allocation, Wiley, pp. 359-373.

[Dan60] Dantzig, G. B., 1960. "On the Shortest Route Problem Through a Network," Management Science, Vol. 6, pp. 187-190.

[Dan63] Dantzig, G. B., 1963. Linear Programming and Extensions, Princeton Univ. Press, Princeton, N. J.

[Dan67] Dantzig, G. B., 1967. "All Shortest Routes in a Graph," in P. Rosenthier (ed.), Theory of Graphs, Gordan and Breach, N. Y., pp. 92-92.

[DeF79] Denardo, E. V., and Fox, B. L., 1979. "Shortest-Route Methods: 1. Reaching, Pruning and Buckets," Operations Research, Vol. 27, pp. 161-186.

[DeP84] Deo, N., and Pang, C., 1984. "Shortest Path Algorithms: Taxonomy and Annotation," Networks, Vol. 14, pp. 275-323.

[Der85] Derigs, U., 1985. "The Shortest Augmenting Path Method for Solving Assignment Problems – Motivation and Computational Experience," Annals of Operations Research, Vol. 4, pp. 57-102.

[Dia69] Dial, R. B., 1969. "Algorithm 360: Shortest Path Forest with Topological Ordering," Commun. ACM, Vol. 12, pp. 632-633.

[Dij59] Dijkstra, E., 1959. "A Note on Two Problems in Connexion with Graphs," Numerische Mathematik, Vol. 1, pp. 269-271.

[Din70] Dinic, E. A., 1970. "Algorithm for Solution of a Problem of Maximum Flow in Networks with Power Estimation," Soviet Math. Doklady, Vol. 11, pp. 1277-1280.

[Dre69] Dreyfus, S. E., 1969. "An Appraisal of Some Shortest-Path Algorithms," Operations Research, Vol. 17, pp. 395-412.

[EFS56] Elias, P., Feinstein, A., and Shannon, C. E., 1956. "Note on Maximum Flow Through a Network," IRE Trans. Infor. Theory, Vol. IT-2, pp. 117-119.

[EdK72] Edmonds, J., and Karp, R. M., 1972. "Theoretical Improvements in Algorithmic Efficiency for Network Flow Problems," Journal of the ACM, Vol. 19, pp. 248-264.

[Ege31] Egervary, J., 1931. "Matrixok Kombinatoricus Tulajonsagairol," Mat. Es Fiz. Lapok, Vol. 38, pp. 16-28.

[ElB89] El Baz, D., 1989. "A Computational Experience with Distributed Asynchronous Iterative Methods for Convex Network Flow Problems," Proc. of the 28th IEEE Conference on Decision and Control, Tampa, Fl, pp. 590-591.

[Eng82] Engquist, M., 1982. "A Successive Shortest Path Algorithm for the Assignment Problem," INFOR, Vol. 20, pp. 370-384.

[FNP81] Florian, M. S., Nguyen, S., and Pallottino, S., 1981. "A Dual Simplex Algorithm for Finding All Shortest Paths," Networks, Vol. 11, pp. 367-378.

[Flo62] Floyd, R. W., 1962. "Algorithm 97: Shortest Path," Comm. ACM, Vol. 5, pp. 345.

[FoF56a] Ford, L. R., Jr., and Fulkerson, D. R., 1956. "Solving the Transportation Problem," Management Science, Vol. 3, pp. 24-32.

[FoF56b] Ford, L. R., Jr., and Fulkerson, D. R., 1956. "Maximal Flow Through a Network," Can. Journal of Math., Vol. 8, pp. 339-404.

[FoF57] Ford, L. R., Jr., and Fulkerson, D. R., 1957. "A Primal-Dual Algorithm for the Capacitated Hitchcock Problem," Naval Res. Logist. Quart., Vol. 4, pp. 47-54.

[FoF62] Ford, L. R., Jr., and Fulkerson, D. R., 1962. Flows in Networks, Princeton Univ. Press, Princeton, N. J.

[For56] Ford, L. R., Jr., 1956. "Network Flow Theory," Report P-923, The Rand Corporation, Santa Monica, Cal.

[FrF70] Frank, H., and Frisch, I. T., 1970. Communication, Transmission, and Transportation Networks, Addison-Wesley, Reading, MA.

[FrT84] Fredman, M. L., and Tarjan, R. E., 1984. "Fibonacci Heaps and their Uses in Improved Network Optimization Algorithms," Proc. 25th Annual Symp. on Found. of Comp. Sci., pp. 338-346.

[FuD55] Fulkerson, D. R., and Dantzig, G. B., 1955. "Computation of Maximum Flow in Networks," Naval Res. Log. Quart., Vol. 2, pp. 277-283.

[GGK83] Gibby, D., Glover, F., Klingman, D., and Mead, M., 1983. "A Comparison of Pivot Selection Rules for Primal Simplex Based Network Codes," Operations Research Letters, Vol. 2, pp. 199-202.

[GGK86a] Glover, F., Glover, R., and Klingman, D., 1986. "The Threshold Shortest Path Algorithm," Networks, Vol. 14, No. 1.

[GGK86b] Glover, F., Glover, R., and Klingman, D., 1986. "Threshold Assignment Algorithm, Math. Programming Study, Vol. 26, pp. 12-37.

[GHK86] Goldfarb, D., Hao, J., and Kai, S., 1986. "Efficient Shortest Path Simplex Algorithms," Research Report, Dept. of OR and IE, Columbia University, New York, N. Y., (also in Operations Research, Vol. 38, 1990, pp. 624-628).

[GHK87] Goldfarb, D., Hao, J., and Kai, S., 1987. "Anti-Stalling Pivot Rules for the Network Simplex Algorithm," Research Report, Dept. of OR and IE, Columbia University, New York, N. Y.

[GKK74a] Glover, F., Karney, D., and Klingman, D., 1974. "Implementation and Computational Comparisons of Primal, Dual, and Primal-Dual Computer Codes for Minimum Cost Network Flow Problem," Networks, Vol. 4, pp. 191-212.

[GKK74b] Glover, F., Karney, D., Klingman, D., and Napier, A., 1974. "A Computation Study on Start Procedures, Basis Change Criteria, and Solution Algorithms for Transportation Problems," Management Science, Vol. 20, pp. 793-819.

[GKM84] Glover, F., Klingman, D., Mote, J., and Whitman, D., 1984. "A Primal Simplex Variant for the Maximum Flow Problem," Naval Res. Logist.

Quart., Vol. 31, pp. 41-61.

[GKP85a] Glover, F., Klingman, D., and Phillips, N., 1985. "A New Polynomially Bounded Shortest Path Algorithm," Operations Research, Vol. 33, pp. 65-73.

[GKP85b] Glover, F., Klingman, D., Phillips, N., and Schneider, R. F., 1985. "New Polynomial Shortest Path Algorithms and Their Computational Attributes," Management Science, Vol. 31, pp. 1106-1128.

[GPR82] Gallo, G. S., Pallotino, S., Ruggen, C., and Starchi, G., 1982. "Shortest Paths: A Bibliography," Sofmat Document 81-P1-4-SOFMAT-27, Rome, Italy.

[GSS77] Gavish, B., Schweitzer, P., and Shlifer, E., 1977. "The Zero Pivot Phenomenon in Transportation Problems and Its Computational Implications," Math. Programming, Vol. 12, pp. 226-240.

[GaN80] Galil, Z., and Naamad, A., 1980. "$O(VE \log^2 V)$ Algorithm for the Maximum Flow Problem," J. of Comput. Sys. Sci., Vol. 21, pp. 203-217.

[GaP86] Gallo, G. S., and Pallotino, S., 1986. "Shortest Path Methods: A Unified Approach," Math. Programming Study, Vol. 26, pp. 38-64.

[GaP88] Gallo, G. S., and Pallotino, S., 1988. "Shortest Path Algorithms," Annals of Operations Research, Vol. 7, pp. 3-79.

[Gal57] Gale, D., 1957. "A Theorem of Flows in Networks," Pacific J. Math., Vol. 7, pp. 1073-1082.

[Gal80] Galil, Z., 1980. "$O(V^{5/3}E^{2/3})$ Algorithm for the Maximum Flow Problem," Acta Informatica, Vol. 14, pp. 221-242.

[GoH88] Goldfarb, D., and Hao, J., 1988. "A Primal Simplex Algorithm that Solves the Maximum Flow Problem in At Most nm Pivots and $O(n^2m)$ Time," Technical Report, Dept. of IE and OR, Columbia University, New York.

[GoM77] Golden, B., and Magnanti, T. L., 1977. "Deterministic Network Optimization: A Bibliography," Networks, Vol. 7, pp. 149-183.

[GoM84] Gondran, M., and Minoux, M., 1984. Graphs and Algorithms, Wiley, N. Y.

[GoR77] Goldfarb, D., and Reid, J. K., 1977. "A Practicable Steepest Edge Simplex Algorithm," Math. Programming, Vol. 12, pp. 361-371.

[GoT86] Goldberg, A. V., and Tarjan, R. E., 1986. "A New Approach to the Maximum Flow Problem," Proc. 18th ACM STOC, pp. 136-146.

[GoT90] Goldberg, A. V., and Tarjan, R. E., 1990. "Solving Minimum Cost Flow Problems by Successive Approximation," Math. of Operations Research, Vol. 15, pp. 430-466.

[Gol85a] Goldfarb, D., 1985. "Efficient Dual Simplex Algorithms for the Assignment Problem," Math. Programming, Vol. 33, pp. 187-203.

[Gol85b] Goldberg, A. V., 1985. "A New Max-Flow Algorithm," Tech. Mem. MIT/LCS/TM-291, Laboratory for Computer Science, M.I.T., Cambridge, MA.

[Gol87] Goldberg, A. V., 1987. "Efficient Graph Algorithms for Sequential and Parallel Computers," Tech. Report TR-374, Laboratory for Computer Science, M.I.T., Cambridge, MA.

[HKS89] Helgason, R. V., Kennington, J. L., and Stewart, B. D., 1989. "Computational Comparison of Sequential and Parallel Algorithms for the One-To-One Shortest-Path Problem," Tech. Report 89-CSE-32, Dept. of Computer Science and Engineering, Southern Methodist Univ., Dallas, TX.

[Hal56] Hall, M., Jr., 1956. "An Algorithm for Distinct Representatives," Amer. Math. Monthly, Vol. 51, pp. 716-717.

[HeK77] Helgason, R. V., and Kennington, J. L., 1977. "An Efficient Procedure for Implementing a Dual-Simplex Network Flow Algorithm," AIIE Trans., Vol. 9, pp. 63-68.

[HoK56] Hoffman, A. J., and Kuhn, H. W., 1956. "Systems of Distinct Representatives and Linear Programming," Amer. Math. Monthly, Vol. 63, pp. 455-460.

[Hof60] Hoffman, A. J., 1960. "Some Recent Applications of the Theory of Linear Inequalities to Extremal Combinatorial Analysis," Proc. Sym. Appl. Math., Vol. 10, pp. 113-128.

[Hu69] Hu, T. C., 1969. Integer Programming and Network Flows, Addison-Wesley, Reading, MA.

[Hun83] Hung, M., 1983. "A Polynomial Simplex Method for the Assignment Problem," Operations Research, Vol. 31, pp. 595-600.

[Iri69] Iri, M., 1969. Network Flows, Transportation, and Scheduling, Academic Press, N. Y.

[JeB80] Jensen, P. A., and Barnes, J. W., 1980. Network Flow Programming, Wiley, N. Y.

[Jew62] Jewell, W. S., 1982. "Optimal Flow Through Networks with Gains," Operations Research, Vol. 10, pp. 476-499.

[JoV86] Jonker, R., and Volgenant, A., 1986. "Improving the Hungarian Assignment Algorithm," Operations Research Letters, Vol. 5, pp. 171-175.

[JoV87] Jonker, R., and Volgenant, A., 1987. "A Shortest Augmenting Path Algorithm for Dense and Sparse Linear Assignment Problems," Computing, Vol. 38, pp. 325-340.

[Joh66] Johnson, E. L., 1966. "Networks and Basic Solutions," Operations Research, Vol. 14, pp. 619-624.

[Joh77] Johnson, D. B., 1977. "Efficient Algorithms for Shortest Paths in Sparse Networks," J. ACM, Vol. 24, pp. 1-13.

[KKZ89] Kempa, D., Kennington, J., and Zaki, H., 1989. "Performance Characteristics of the Jacobi and Gauss-Seidel Versions of the Auction Algorithm on the Alliant FX/8," Report OR-89-008, Dept. of Mech. and Ind. Eng., Univ. of Illinois, Urbana, Ill.

[KNS74] Klingman, D., Napier, A., and Stutz, J., 1974. "NETGEN - A Program for Generating Large Scale (Un)Capacitated Assignment, Transportation, and Minimum Cost Flow Network Problems," Management Science, Vol. 20, pp. 814-822.

[Kar74] Karzanov, A. V., 1974. "Determining the Maximal Flow in a Network with the Method of Preflows," Soviet Math Dokl., Vol. 15, pp. 1277-1280.

[KeH80] Kennington, J., and Helgason, R., 1980. Algorithms for Network Programming, Wiley, N. Y.

[Ker81] Kershenbaum, A., 1981. "A Note on Finding Shortest Path Trees," Networks, Vol. 11, pp. 399-400.

[KlM72] Klee, V., and Minty, G. J., 1972. "How Good is the Simplex Algorithm?," in Inequalities III, O. Shisha (ed.), Academic Press, N. Y, pp. 159-175.

[Kle67] Klein, M., 1967. "A Primal Method for Minimal Cost Flow with Applications to the Assignment and Transportation Problems," Management Science, Vol. 14, pp. 205-220.

[Kon31] Konig, D., 1931. "Graphok es Matrixok," Mat. Es Fiz. Lapok, Vol. 38, pp. 116-119.

[Kuh55] Kuhn, H. W., 1955. "The Hungarian Method for the Assignment Problem," Naval Research Logistics Quarterly, Vol. 2, pp. 83-97.

[Law76] Lawler, E., 1976. Combinatorial Optimization: Networks and Matroids, Holt, Reinhart, and Winston, N. Y.

[Lem74] Lemarechal, C., 1974. "An Algorithm for Minimizing Convex Functions," in Information Processing '74, J. L. Rosenfeld (ed.), North Holland Publ. Co., Amsterdam, pp. 552-556.

[Lue69] Luenberger, D. G., 1969. Optimization by Vector Space Methods, Wiley, N. Y.

[Lue84] Luenberger, D. G., 1984. Linear and Nonlinear Programming, Addison-Wesley, Reading, MA.

[MKM78] Malhotra, V. M., Kumar, M. P., and Maheshwari, S. N., 1978. "An $O(|V|^3)$ Algorithm for Finding Maximum Flows in Networks," Inform. Process. Lett., Vol. 7, pp. 277-278.

[McG83] McGinnis, L. F., 1983. "Implementation and Testing of a Primal-Dual Algorithm for the Assignment Problem," Operations Research, Vol. 31, pp. 277-291.

[MeD58] Mendelssohn, N. S., and Dulmage, A. L., 1958. "Some Generalizations of Distinct Representatives," Canad. J. Math., Vol. 10, pp. 230-241.

[Min57] Minty, G. J., 1957. "A Comment on the Shortest Route Problem," Operations Research, Vol. 5, p. 724.

[Min60] Minty, G. J., 1960. "Monotone Networks," Proc. Roy. Soc. London, A, Vol. 257, pp. 194-212.

[Min78] Minieka, E., 1978. Optimization Algorithms for Networks and Graphs, Marcel Dekker, N. Y.

[Mul78a] Mulvey, J., 1978. "Pivot Strategies for Primal-Simplex Network Codes," J. ACM, Vol. 25, pp. 266-270.

[Mul78b] Mulvey, J., 1978. "Testing a Large-Scale Network Optimization Program," Math. Programming, Vol. 15, pp. 291-314.

[Mur76] Murty, K. G., 1976. Linear and Combinatorial Programming, Wiley, N. Y.

[Nic66] Nicholson, T., 1966. "Finding the Shortest Route Between Two Points in a Network", The Computer Journal, Vol. 9, pp. 275-280.

[OrR70] Ortega, J. M., and Rheinboldt, W. C., 1970. Iterative Solution of Nonlinear Equations in Several Variables, Academic Press, N. Y.

[PaS82] Papadimitriou, C. H., and Steiglitz, K., 1982. Combinatorial Optimization: Algorithms and Complexity, Prentice-Hall, Englewood Cliffs, N. J.

[Pal84] Pallotino, S., 1984. "Shortest Path Methods: Complexity, Interrelations and New Propositions," Networks, Vol. 14, pp. 257-267.

[Pap74] Pape, U., 1974. "Implementation and Efficiency of Moore - Algorithms for the Shortest Path Problem," Math. Programming, Vol. 7, pp. 212-222.

[PhZ88] Phillips, C., and Zenios, S. A., 1988. "Experiences with Large Scale Network Optimization on the Connection Machine," Report 88-11-05, Dept. of Decision Sciences, The Wharton School, Univ. of Pennsylvania, Phil., Penn.

[Pol91] Polymenakos, L., 1991. "Analysis of Parallel Asynchronous Schemes for the Auction Shortest Path Algorithm," MS Thesis, EECS Dept., M.I.T., Cambridge, MA.

[Roc70] Rockafellar, R. T., 1970. Convex Analysis, Princeton Univ. Press, Princeton, N. J.

[Roc84] Rockafellar, R. T., 1984. Network Flows and Monotropic Programming, Wiley-Interscience, N. Y.

[Rud76] Rudin, W., 1976. Real Analysis, Mc Graw Hill, N. Y.

[Sch90] Schwartz, B. L., 1990. "A Computational Analysis of the Auction Algorithm," Unpublished Manuscript.

[ShW81] Shier, D. R., and Witzgall, C., 1981. "Properties of Labeling Methods for Determining Shortest Path Trees," J. Res. Natl. Bureau of Standards, Vol. 86, p. 317.

[SrT73] Srinivasan, V., and Thompson, G. L., 1973. "Benefit-Cost Analysis of Coding Techniques for Primal Transportation Algorithm," J. ACM, Vol. 20, pp. 194-213.

[TBT90] Tseng, P., Bertsekas, D. P., and Tsitsiklis, J. N., 1990. "Partially Asynchronous Parallel Algorithms for Network Flow and Other Problems," SIAM J. Control and Optimization, Vol. 28, pp. 678-710.

[Tab73] Tabourier, Y., 1973. "All Shortest Distances in a Graph: An Improvement to Dantzig's Inductive Algorithm," Disc. Math., Vol. 4, pp. 83-87.

[TsB87a] Tseng, P., and Bertsekas, D. P., 1987. "Relaxation Methods for Linear Programs," Math. of Operations Research, Vol. 12, pp. 569-596.

[TsB87b] Tseng, P., and Bertsekas, D. P., 1987. "Relaxation Methods for Monotropic Programs," Laboratory for Information and Decision Systems Report P-1697, M.I.T., Cambridge, MA.; also Math. Programming, Vol. 46, 1990, pp. 127-151.

[Tse86] Tseng, P., 1986. "Relaxation Methods for Monotropic Programming Problems," PhD Thesis, Dept. of Electrical Engineering and Operations Research Center, M.I.T., Cambridge, MA.

[VoR82] Von Randow, R., 1982. Integer Programming and Related Areas: A Classified Bibliography 1978-1981, Lecture Notes in Economics and Mathematical Systems, Vol. 197, Springer-Verlag, N. Y.

[VoR85] Von Randow, R., 1985. Integer Programming and Related Areas: A Classified Bibliography 1982-1984, Lecture Notes in Economics and Mathematical Systems, Vol. 243, Springer-Verlag, N. Y.

[War62] Warshall, S., 1962. "A Theorem on Boolean Matrices," J. ACM, Vol. 9, pp. 11-12.

[WeZ90] Wein, J., and Zenios, S. A., 1990. "Massively Parallel Auction Algorithms for the Assignment Problem," Proc. of 3rd Symposium on the Frontiers of Massively Parallel Computation, Md.

[WhH60] Whitting, P. D., and Hillier, J. A., 1960. "A Method for Finding the Shortest Route Through a Road Network," Operations Research Quart., Vol. 11, pp. 37-40.

[Wol75] Wolfe, P., 1975. "A Method of Conjugate Subgradients for Minimizing Nondifferentiable Functions," Math. Programming Study, Vol. 3, pp. 145-173.

[Zad73a] Zadeh, N., 1973. "A Bad Network Problem for the Simplex Method and Other Minimum Cost Flow Algorithms," Math. Programming, Vol. 5, pp. 255-266.

[Zad73b] Zadeh, N., 1973. "More Pathological Examples for Network Flow Problems," Math. Programming, Vol. 5, pp. 217-224.

[Zad79] Zadeh, N., 1979. "Near Equivalence of Network Flow Algorithms," Technical Report No. 26, Dept. of Operations Research, Stanford University, CA.

[Zou76] Zoutendijk, G., 1976. Mathematical Programming Methods, North-Holland, Amsterdam.

[Zak90] Zaki, H., 1990. "A Comparison of Two Algorithms for the Assignment Problem," Report ORL 90-002, Dept. of Mechanical and Industrial Engineering, Univ. of Illinois, Urbana, Ill.

Index

The MIT Press, with Peter Denning as general consulting editor, publishes computer science books in the following series:

ACL-MIT Press Series in Natural Language Processing
Aravind K. Joshi, Mark Liberman, and Karen Sparck Jones, editors

ACM Doctoral Disseration Award and Distinguished Dissertation Series

Artificial Intelligence
Patrick Winston, founding editor
J. Michael Brady, Daniel G. Bobrow, and Randall Davis, editors

Charles Babbage Institute Reprint Series for the History of Computing
Martin Campbell-Kelly, editor

Computer Systems
Herb Schwetman, editor

Explorations with Logo
E. Paul Goldenberg, editor

Foundations of Computing
Michael Garey and Albert Meyer, editors

History of Computing
I. Bernard Cohen and William Aspray, editors

Logic Programming
Ehud Shapiro, editor; Fernando Pereira, Koichi Furukawa, Jean-Louis Lassez, and David H. D. Warren, associate editors

The MIT Press Electrical Engineering and Computer Science Series

Research Monographs in Parallel and Distributed Processing
Christopher Jesshope and David Klappholz, editors

Scientific and Engineering Computation
Janusz Kowalik, editor

Technical Communication and Information Systems
Ed Barrett, editor